W9-AUY-597

THE JEWS IN AMERICA

A Treasury of Art and Literature

THE JEWS IN AMERICA

A TREASURY OF ART AND LITERATURE

Edited by Abraham J. Karp

Design by Philip Grushkin
Editorial production by Diane Lawrence
Photo research by Cynthia Deubel Horowitz
Printed in China
ISBN 0-88363-960-2

CONTENTS

Acknowledgments

"Life," Justice Oliver Wendell Holmes observed, "is painting a picture, not doing a sum." It is a pointillist portrait of "The Jews in America" that we attempt, through joining together works of the plastic arts—portraits, folk art, architecture, ritual artifacts—all that may be subsumed under "Judaica," with works of literature in its widest meaning—documents, letters, articles in newspapers and journals, short stories, excerpts of novels, reminiscences, poems, addresses, exhortation, and plea. We seek neither completeness nor facile coherence, hoping rather that what has been assembled will please the eye, inform the mind, touch the heart, bring a smile to the face—and here and there a chuckle as well.

Many have had a hand in fashioning this portrait, and to them, the editor is pleased to express his abiding gratitude: Hugh Lauter Levin who conceived the contours of the "Treasury of Art and Literature" series; Ellin Silberblatt, who with great devotion, energy, and skill, organized and accomplished every facet of this production; Diane Lawrence, for making the text more telling, the selections more coherent; designer Philip Grushkin for his handsome and classic design of the book; Dr. Grace Cohen Grossman; Dr. David Geffen and Cantor Ramon Gilbert, for valuable and valued suggestions; and to the great depositories of Jewish cultural treasures, The Jewish Museum; the Skirball Museum; the Yeshiva University Museum, and the Library of the Jewish Theological Seminary of America for gathering and now sharing the treasures of Jewish artistic and literary creativity.

Let this volume celebrate a half century of cooperative endeavors with Deborah, whose dedication to Judaism is all embracing; whose knowledge of Jewish culture is wide and thorough; whose expertise in her chosen academic discipline ranges from Beowulf to the contemporary American Jewish literary scene, and who lovingly shared these gifts and passions with her husband,

THE EDITOR.

INTRODUCTION

In the letter to the king and queen of Spain which opens his *Journal of the First Voyage*, Christopher Columbus writes ". . . having expelled the Jews from your dominions, Your Highnesses, in the same month ordered me to proceed to the same region of India." Four centuries later, poet Emma Lazarus, whose sonnet, "The New Colossus," is inscribed on the base of the Statue of Liberty in New York Harbor, makes this juxtaposition—of the exile of the greatest Jewish community in the Middle Ages and the discovery of America, the home of the leading Jewish community in the modern age—the theme of her prose poem "The Exodus: August 3, 1492."

> The Spanish noon is a blaze of azure fire, and
> the dusty pilgrims crawl like an endless serpent
> along treeless plains and bleached high roads,
> through rock-split ravines and castellated
> towns . . .
> Whither shall they turn? for the West hath cast
> them out and the East refuseth to receive.
> O bird of air, whisper to the despairing exiles,
> that to-day, to-day, from the many-masted,
> gayly-bannered port of Palos, sails the world-
> unveiling Genoese, to unlock the golden gates of
> sunset and bequeath a Continent to Freedom.

Echoes of perceived intersecting of destinies of an ancient people and a new nation resonate in the common history of both. In the nineteenth century, Herman Melville wrote, "We Americans are a peculiar, chosen people, the Israel of our times; we bear the ark of liberties of the world"; and the Hebrew poet Gerson Rosenzweig, in a preface to his translation of the patriotic hymn "America," asserted: "The youngest nation is heir of the oldest, and all that was best in the Jewish nation is now in the possession of the American nation to be developed and cultivated for all humanity." In the twentieth century, Woodrow Wilson proclaimed, "America lives in the heart of every man everywhere who wishes to find a region where he will be free to work out his destiny as he chooses." As if in response, Yiddish poet I. J. Schwartz wrote in his epic poem "Kentucky":

> From a great distance comes a Jew, with pack on
> shoulders, stick in hand.
> Into a new and free and spreading land.

The earliest description of Jewish life on the North American continent is in a letter from Johannes Megapolensis, a predicant of the Dutch Reform Church in New Amsterdam to his superiors in the mother city, Amsterdam. "Some Jews arrived here last summer," he wrote in March 1655. "Later more came . . . they were healthy but poor . . . they report that more will come, and build here their synagogue." These few words foretell the central components of the American Jewish historical experience—immigration and integration—seeking and finding a haven, settling down and making a living, and turning haven into home through institutions founded to help retain a distinct identity and a distinctive way of life. (These dual enterprises also inform the contour and contents of this volume.)

Among those who arrived first was Jacob Barsimson of Amsterdam, and those who came later were the four men, six women, and thirteen children who came in September from Recife, Brazil, having been forced to leave the city when it was recaptured by the Portuguese from the Dutch. For three decades Jews had lived and thrived in Dutch Brazil; now they had to take up the wanderer's staff again. Most returned to Amsterdam, but some chose to remain in the New World. Among these were the twenty-three who, at the end of September 1654, were greeted by Barsimson (as Louis Zara describes in the excerpt from his novel, *Blessed Is the Land*).

The immigration of Jews to America in the seventeenth and eighteenth centuries was part of the general movement of the center of the Occidental world from the Mediterranean to the Atlantic. The discoveries of the sixteenth century turned the attention of nations and men to the promise of the Americas. Tales and evidence of the great wealth of the new continents began to fill the dreams of the daring and raise the hopes of the hungry. We can read here the tale from the New World found in Thomas Thorowgood's *Jewes in America* (London, 1650). According to the account of Antonio de Montezinos (Aaron Levi), returning to Amsterdam from Brazil, he claimed to have met Indian tribes descended from the ancient Israelites—the legendary Ten Lost Tribes exiled by the Assyrians in the eighth century, B.C.E.

The twenty-three refugees from Brazil had no legal right to settle. Indeed, Governor Peter Stuyvesant and his council ordered them to depart. The Jews won the right to remain, to engage in trade, to own property, to keep watch and ward, and to gain citizenship, only after petition in the colony and with help from affluent Jews in Holland. The successful petition that Amsterdam Jews put before the board of the Dutch West India Company, owner of the New Amsterdam colony, is extant and published here in translation.

A synagogue was built in 1730, but that was under British rule, the colony having been taken and renamed New York in 1664. We even have before us a description of the synagogue and congregation of worshippers in 1740, by a Maryland doctor on a tour of the colonies.

Old World prejudices were transplanted to the New, but there were factors here that mitigated anti-Jewish sentiments. Land was plentiful in colonial America; people were not. The general well-being of the new settlement was enhanced by increased population, so despite imported and inherited bigotry, the at-first unwanted newcomer, having proved his usefulness, was grudgingly accepted. And having established his worth to the community, he was welcomed, respected, and esteemed as was the case with Moses Michael Hays in Boston which we document. Even Jews in Europe knew this, as the letter from German Jews to "The President of the Continental Congress," published in the June 1783 issue of the Leipzig and Berlin periodical, *Deutches Museum*, indicates.

Some German Jews came to America in the latter part of the eighteenth century, among them Hyman and Rebecca Samuel of Hamburg. In a most instructive early Jewish immigrant letter, Rebecca writes to her parents extolling America as a wonderful land, a land in which they have succeeded financially. But in their town of Petersburg, Virginia, they languish spiritually, so they are moving to the large and blessed Jewish community of Charleston, South Carolina.

We shall also learn what the Jews of Philadelphia were busy with, while the Declaration of Independence was being composed there, and what Haym Solomon, American Jewry's premier patriot, reported to the Continental Congress. An aspect of Jewish adventure on the frontier makes for an exciting and informing story set down by novelist Howard Fast. Jonas Phillips, who arrived in 1740, now settled in Philadelphia, wrote to the Constitutional Convention meeting there in the summer of 1787 on a matter of Jewish concern. We shall also have the opportunity to read the letter of newly elected President George Washington sent in 1790 to the Jewish Congregation of Newport, Rhode Island, a warm, friendly, uplifting letter. Similar letters were received by the Jews of Philadelphia, New York, Charleston, and Richmond as a group, and by the Jewish community of Savannah. All this, when the Jews in all the United States numbered no more than 1,300 in a nation of almost 4 million.

Although the greatest influx of Jews was to the United States, the Jewish immigrant experience in Canada has not been neglected throughout this anthology. The strange case of a Jewish girl disguised as a boy who arrived in Québec in 1738, a fur trader captured by Indians, and agricultural settlements like those in the United States are part of the Canadian Jewish experience presented here.

In the first two decades of the nineteenth century, the Jewish population of the United States increased from less than two thousand to just under three thousand. In the next three decades, when the general population multiplied less than threefold, the Jewish population soared to some 50,000—a seventeenfold increase! (We will be surprised to learn from Hannah Adam's survey of Jewish life in the United States in 1811 that the largest Jewish community in the United States at that time was *not* New York.)

This phenomenal growth took place despite the fact that the American Jewish community was adversely affected by intermarriage and assimilation. As in most immigrant societies, men outnumbered women. A Jew wishing to marry within his faith often had to return to his native country to seek a mate or import a bride. For many of the younger generation, the solution was to marry a Gentile. In the free and open society of America, the children of such marriages generally entered the majority Protestant community, and therefore the rate of attrition among the native-born generation of Jews was high. So disturbed was Simeon Abrahams that he published a letter in *The Occident* urging "a desperate remedy" for this "desperate disease." In 1820 Penina Moise of Charleston, South Carolina, the first in a long line of Jewish women poets in America, wrote a poem urging "persecuted foreigners," especially fellow Jews, to come to the home of the free. An increasing number needed little urging. In 1837 Germany's leading Jewish newspaper reported: "They are emigrating indeed . . . young men who completed their apprenticeship . . . who meet all requirements . . . yet cannot obtain letters of protection and domicile . . . what else should they do but seek a new fatherland?" Two years later: "From certain places in which there are 30–40 Jewish families, 15–20 persons are leaving . . . young, hard-working people."

In 1820 the Jews of America were mainly a native-born community; by 1850 the community had become largely German-born and German-speaking. The most prominent—and most colorful—Jew during the first half of the nineteenth century was Mordecai Manuel Noah, a fourth-generation American Jew, a newspaper editor, playwright, diplomat, judge, political practitioner, and Jewish leader and spokesman. We meet him in this volume in two of his most fascinating roles, as founder of a projected Jewish state in America and as America's first advocate for Zionism.

In the years from 1840 to 1850 the Jewish population of the United States increased from 15,000 to 50,000. In the next decade, it tripled. This tenfold increase in twenty years was due both to worsening economic and political conditions in post-Napoleonic Europe and a rapidly expanding America which opened doors to needed population. The Jews, mainly from southern Germany, were part of a German wave of immigration which settled the Midwest.

In 1860 Cincinnati's German-Jewish journal *Die Deborah* reported: "Many of the beggarly-poor immigrants are now at the head of business concerns . . . The signs of their enterprises blaze in all the big commercial cities of the Union, New York, Philadelphia, Cincinnati, St. Louis, New Orleans . . ."

By the middle of the century the American Jewish community stretched from New York to San Francisco; more than one hundred congregations and an even larger number of charitable, social, and cultural organizations served its needs. One could travel clear across the continent and find a place to worship, a charitable society to extend a helping hand, a fraternal order to offer fellowship. We shall be able to reexperience religious activity across the continent in the late 1850s in a transplanted East European synagogue prayer hall and study room in New York; with a group of Cincinnati Jewish merchants proposing a pact to observe the sabbath by refraining from business; and on the furthest frontier, in the hamlet of San Diego, a Yom Kippur service which turns into a true "Western," with a fifty-mile ride on horseback, a deputy sheriff, a posse, and a courtroom drama.

The growing self-awareness of mid-nineteenth-century America had its Jewish expression in the desire to establish an American Judaism. Its chief exponents were Isaac Leeser and Isaac Mayer Wise.

Leeser, a German immigrant who became the minister of several Sephardic congregations in America, was a traditionalist and expressed his "Americanism" by introducing the English sermon and inspiring the first Sunday School. He had faith that America would be hospitable to a traditionally religious and highly cultured Jewish community, if only the Jews willed it and matched will with enterprise and accomplishment. He set out to establish the institutions which would fashion such a community.

Isaac Mayer Wise, an enormously energetic and optimistic newcomer from Bohemia, believed that Judaism would in time become the religion of enlightened modern man. But first it had to be modernized and democratized, or better still, "Americanized." He thus became the exponent of a moderate pragmatic Reform Judaism, based on the pressures and practicalities of modern, democratic living. Thus, for example, the prayer book which he prepared and vigorously promoted was a modified traditional order of services with Hebrew text and facing German or English translations. Modernity ordered the elimination of hopes for the restoration of sacrifices. References to a Messiah and return to a homeland were eliminated, for America was Zion and "Washington our Jerusalem." Appropriately, it was titled *Minhag America (The American Rite).*

Overriding any individual differences and preferences was the conviction that American Jewry needed unity, and American Judaism, some kind of central authority. Reform and Traditionalist elements were brought together at a conference convened in Cleveland in 1855. Unity demanded compromise. Leeser's compromise consisted of attending a conference planned and dominated by Reform Jews; Wise's in accepting the Talmud as the authoritative interpretation of the Bible.

The conference did not lead to unity. It strengthened division and led to subdivision. Leeser and Wise dissolved their "partnership" with recriminations which grew progressively more acrimonious as the years went on. The Reform group of the East, led by Rabbi David Einhorn of Baltimore, attacked the conference and dissociated itself from the Reform movement of Wise, rejecting it as puerile and retrograde, and accusing its chief proponent of opportunism. The rift between the moderate, practical Reform of the West and the radical, ideological Reform of the East divided the movement for three decades. Whatever chance Leeser had of giving leadership to or exerting influence on the Eastern European Orthodox immigrant, he lost by consorting with the enemy, Reform.

What both Leeser and Wise failed to appreciate is the powerful influence of the majority religious establishment on the structure of the religions of the minorities. In a Catholic country, monolithic in its faith, disciplined by a central authority, a uniform Judaism would be acceptable and desirable. But in a vast land, riven by regionalism, with the majority faith splintered by literally hundreds of divisions, and subdivisions, congregational in its organization, a doctrinally unified Judaism would be neither desirable or acceptable.

We shall be meeting, but too briefly, Leeser as a defender of the faith, warding off with courage and vigor, missionary activity at the doors of his synagogue; and Wise as expander of the faith, investing his influence and person in a campaign towards full religious enfranchisement of women. This enterprise was accomplished after almost a full century of endeavor with the ordination of a woman as a rabbi. And we may note that this took place more than a century after "An American Jewess" had written the most advanced and most effective textbook for the religious training of children.

On the great issue of the day in mid-century America, slavery, American Jewry was as divided as the rest of the nation. Jewish traditions and values played a role, but regionalism was more powerful still. There were rabbis who were outspoken abolitionists, and those who were the defenders of the status quo, and those who chose neutrality, like Wise and Leeser. We read the powerful plea of the Reverend Samuel M. Isaacs of New York and the response of the Shreveport, Louisiana, Jewish community. More universal was the respect and affection for Abraham Lincoln whose great humanity is demonstrated in a touching vignette. Widespread, too, was the response to a plea to the "Israelites of the United States" by a congregation devastated by the Civil War and Reconstruction.

In 1878 Dr. Gustav Gottheil, rabbi of America's most prestigious congregation, Temple Emanu-El of New York, attempted to explain to the readers of *The North American Review*, the immigration experience—the uprooting, the journey, the resettlement—always a difficult, often an embittering experience. Written at a time when immigration from Western Europe was waning and the mass migration from Eastern Europe was beginning, it may serve both as an appreciation of the former, and an introduction to the latter.

> When, thirty or forty years ago, the current of Hebrew immigration set in strongly, what encouragement did it find? Suspicion and contempt met [the Jew] at every step . . . On this free soil he was often obliged to perform the rites of his religion behind locked doors. It was not until personal contact had proved him to be a man

> that he could safely avow himself a Jew . . . He was thrown upon his own resources in every respect, and in sickness and death, which he faced often enough in traveling over the prairies, or camping in the swamps, or venturing into the neighborhood of pioneer settlers . . . He had, however, been nerved and equipped for the battle . . . He had not been spoiled by the world . . . Hard work and self-denial were his wont. His family affections, deep, holy, permanent, were his guardian angels . . . The father who sought here relief . . . from oppressive rule kept the remembrance of wife and children constantly in mind. The prospect of being reunited with them was the vision of his hope . . . The young man who came here in search of a better future knew of no higher ambition than to become the benefactor of his kindred. The more he learned to love his new home, the more intense grew his yearning for his loved ones to share his happiness.

Few events had greater influence on the course of American Jewish history than the assassination of Alexander II, "Czar of all the Russias," in March 1881. The government and the populace, seeking a scapegoat, turned upon the Jews, touching off pogroms in more than a hundred communities. These were followed by restrictive laws against the Jews aimed at eliminating them from economic and civic life. Physical persecution, political oppression, and economic disabilities set in motion a wave of immigration which brought more than two and one-half million Jews from Eastern Europe to America in the next half century.

The Jews of the Russian Empire and Galicia were generally the first of their region to undertake large-scale migration westward. The endeavor was, therefore, fraught with all the anxieties and difficulties which beset any pioneering effort.

The first to leave were almost always the young, depleting the community of its most productive element and weakening its physical security, for in that hostile environment the presence of the young and strong tended to discourage persecution and pogroms. The trauma of leaving was greatest for the first to depart. On the way to America, Benjamin L. Gordon remembered his thoughts as he wandered about the streets of Hamburg waiting for the *Bohemia* to sail.

> I knew I was going to the Land of the Free, but I also was cognizant of the fact that no one expected or awaited me there. I did not have the slightest idea as to how I was going to make a living; I had no trade and was physically unfit for hard manual labor. Then, too, the fact that I was leaving the continent where my ancestors had lived for so many centuries weighed heavily on my mind.

For Jewish emigrants, the journey was eased by agencies set up in Europe and America to aid them. In the twentieth century, they were emboldened to undertake the journey by the reports that those who preceded them had already established those cultural, religious, and social institutions which their life demanded. The religious heard of synagogues, rabbis, schools. The Freethinkers read of an atmosphere free of societal constraints and of governmental surveillance. So the East European migration to America, which began with thousands in the 1880s, grew to hundreds of thousands in the latter years of the nineteenth century and millions in the first decades of the twentieth.

In 1925 more than forty percent of America's Jews lived in the greater New York area and more than eighty percent were concentrated in six states: New York, Pennsylvania, Illinois, Massachusetts, New Jersey, and Ohio. Such concentration made possible the rapid establishment of Jewish institutions, the proliferation of organizations, and some degree of political presence, if not power; but it also subjected the immigrant Jew to urban slum conditions, to the uncertainty and oppressiveness of sweatshop labor and to the tensions which mark congested urban living. Above all other immigrant groups, the Jews came to stay. Others may have come to test the New World, or "make their fortune" and return home; for the Jews who came, America was to be both haven and home. More than other groups, they came as family units. Often, the father came first to earn money to bring the rest of the family. Joining father in America is a recurring theme in immigrant literature. For the young Mary Antin, as we shall see, it was a wondrous, joyful reunion; for the teenage Ephraim Lisitzky, it was fraught with disillusion and remorse.

With the beginning of mass emigration in Eastern Europe, the Jews of Western Europe formed a network of organizations to help the migration to America. A tripartite division of responsibility was arranged. The journey westward across Europe became the responsibility of the German Jews; the London Manor House Committee was to get the immigrants to their destination, America. On arrival, their settlement and integration were the responsibility of American Jewry.

Ultimately, the Russian Jewish immigrants themselves took the leadership in organizing aid for the new arrivals. One of the first organizations offering direct aid to the arriving immigrant was the Association of Jewish Immigrants of Philadelphia. The nature of its activities is described in the president's report offered at its third annual meeting in 1886.

> We have assisted immigrants to reach other points to which they were destined, and have provided them with food on their route. We have lodged and fed those who remained in the city until their friends were found . . . We have hunted up lost baggage, rescued some from the thieves who frequent the wharves, and redeemed it when held for unpaid freight.

One of the chief problems was the concentration of the immigrant population in the port cities of the eastern seaboard, particularly in New York. This presented a twofold evil: It was a hindrance in the social integration of the resident population, and it worked unusual hardships, economic, social, and moral, on the immigrants. Unventilated sweatshops and dank tenements brought the incidence of tuberculosis to epidemic proportions. The concentration of the immigrant population in self-contained communities prevented a more rapid rate of acculturation and integration, driving an ever-widening gap between the immigrants and their rapidly Americanizing children. Attempts to place immigrants in agricultural colonies were well-meaning but ineffective due to their lack of practical farming experience. More effective was the dispersal of new arrivals to host communities outside the large urban centers, and some forty thousand were thus relocated, mainly in the Midwest, in the first five years of the new century.

The structured, religiously ordered life which Jews had experienced in the European *shtetl* (Jewish town) was replaced by the socially fluid, economically pressured, and religiously lax life of the American urban center. The change brought disorientation and social disintegration as well. Life was difficult in Europe, but it had a degree of security and status which gave the individual a sense of personal worth. Each man had his recognized role in the family, his place in the community, his seat in the synagogue. In America he was depersonalized, dehumanized—bereft of extended family, devoid of status.

The Jew in Russia dreamed of the Golden Land. The folk poet, Elyakum Zunser, sang of this land. He believed his songs and came to America. Here he again sang of the Golden Land:

> I came to the land, saw it and lo!
> Tears and suffering and tales of woe . . .

The New World bard, Morris Rosenfeld, sang of the plight of a candle seller on the lower East Side, of sweatshop workers made slaves to the machines, and a father's dirge, "I Have A Little Son," whom "I never see, for I go to work when he's still asleep, and come home so late, that he's asleep again."

Yet immigrant Jews proved equal to the dehumanizing challenge of America. They persisted in the faith that this was but a temporary situation, that work and will would make an easier life in better surroundings, that their children's lot would be better still.

In the *shtetl* culture which had shaped the Old World Jew, learning was the vehicle for social mobility, desirable marriage partners, community status, influence. The same obtained in the immigrant ghetto, with some variations. *Heder* (a one-room religious school) learning gave way to public-school education; the *yeshiva bochur* (a student of advanced religious studies) of Europe became the college student in America.

Immigrant Jews kept dawn-to-dark hours in their grocery or candy stores, or coughed out their lungs in sweatshops, to afford the schooling for their sons that would free them from store counter and shop bench. Their children took to public school and college with a passion; these institutions were the means to improve economic opportunity and social status.

For the immigrant generation, a rich and varied cultural life was available. The religious could attend a wide variety of synagogues featuring "star" cantors; the "enlightened" had their lectures in popular culture and meetings of a bewildering variety of socialist and anarchist groups. Most popular of all was the Yiddish theater, which offered escape and provided social activity. It gave the ghetto heroes and heroines to adore and idolize; their romantic exploits provided delectable gossip. Historical musical dramas were popular because they not only offered entertainment but also lifted the immigrant out of everyday fears and frustrations. *Shulamit* reminded him of Jewish sovereignty, and *Bar Kochba* recalled Jewish victories. Contemporary melodrama brought the release that free-flowing tears often provide. And what better topic for discussion and arguments than the quality of the writing and the success of the acting? And a Yiddish press flourished. As early as 1898, Abraham Cahan could boast:

> The five million Jews living under the Czar had not a single Yiddish daily paper even when the government allowed such publication, while their fellow countrymen who have taken up abode in America publish six dailies . . . not to mention the countless Yiddish weeklies and monthlies, and the pamphlets and books which today make New York the largest Yiddish book market in the world . . .

Restrictive immigration laws in 1921 and 1924 brought to an end the era of mass immigration. The first quarter of the twentieth century was the time the immigrants were settling down, economically, socially, and culturally. It was a time when the Jews as a group were becoming aware of political realities, being wooed as a reading of the "Plea for the Jewish Vote" indicates, and being used, as their personal experiences suggested. Culturally, the Yiddish theater was a powerful institution of significant social import. We offer both a historical review and a contemporary descriptive report.

From the *Bintel Brief (A Sheaf of Letters)* column we learn some of the concerns and problems of immigrant life. The noted Yiddish writer, Sholem Aleichem, describes with sharp stinging humor the American way of life and death, and in a poem of gentler humor but serious import, he is united with Mark Twain in an affectionate dialogue. We read how his early life was remembered by a legendary teacher of philosophy, who was singularly instrumental in making the campus of New York's City College arguably the most intellectually exciting in the nation. An upstate New York peddler is affectionately remembered by his son. A young immigrant boy begins a life of fear and anxiety, and a clothing manufacturer grown old and rich reviews a life filled with economic triumphs but bereft of satisfying accomplishment and meaning. A stunning autobiographical short story of a young woman of fierce will and stubborn optimism hungering to rise high, high above the common immigrant dreams, is deeply moving. The section concludes with a fond farewell to the mother of Jewish immigrant neighborhoods, New York's lower East Side; memories of Boston synagogues, and a humorous look at the pitfalls of teaching (and learning) English. A fascinating time peopled by heroes of the common life.

In the section dealing with the life of the spirit, two future justices of the United States Supreme Court, Louis D. Brandeis and Felix Frankfurter, urge young educated Jews to accept the call of noblesse oblige and call upon all to support the cause of Zionist endeavor.

The most innovative American Jewish theologian, Mordecai M. Kaplan, tells of a personal spiritual crisis which brought about a radical reorientation of his view of God and the traditions of Judaism. The most influential American Jewish theologian, Abraham Joshua Heschel, intimates how we might view the world with a radical amazement which can light up one's life.

Novelist Chaim Potok describes advanced Talmud study and introduces the world of worldly Orthodoxy and ultra-Orthodoxy. Orthodox novelist Herman Wouk describes the sabbath in his home and the dimension it adds to his life. Yiddish writer Joseph Opatoshu, playwright Neil Simon, and, most powerfully, Nobel Laureate Elie Wiesel afford us oblique glimpses of aspects of the Holocaust.

George Burns recalls Jews in popular culture, three brothers who made America laugh and a cantor's son who sang with a tear in his voice. Sammy Levenson reminds us that the violin was the Jewish mother's vehicle of choice to lift her son to fame and fortune. Cynthia Ozick describes the death knell of Yiddish in a brilliant piece of writing. The Yiddish literary lion, Nobel Laureate Isaac Bashevis Singer, writes about his son and exposes his own deepest anxieties.

Three Jewish novelists have dominated the American literary scene: Bernard Malamud, Canadian-born Saul Bellow, and Philip Roth. Each has placed works on the best-seller lists and received most prestigious awards—Bellow, the Nobel Prize in Literature in 1976. We offer excerpts of particular personal appropriateness from their finest works.

Leonard Bernstein, the finest flowering of an American musical talent, discourses on his Jewish identity shaping his person and influencing his work. David Amram describes how a commission to write music for the synagogue brought him back to his roots.

The rabbis Finkelstein, father Simon and son Louis, tell of their love for America, and of their yearning for the values and way of life of Slobodka, the ancestral home in Russian Lithuania. Novelist Nessa Rapoport sounds the clarion for "Jewish Cultural Confidence."

We conclude as we began, with text and commentary.

Observation: "The great advantage of the Americans is, that they arrived at a state of democracy without having to endure a democratic revolution; and that they are born equal, instead of becoming so."

ALEXIS DE TOCQUEVILLE,
Democracy in America, 1835

Comment: The Jewish experience in America suggests that democracy is an ongoing revolution, equality, a never-ending becoming.

Observation: "Perhaps one of the greatest contributions of Judaism to the United States will be to help other Americans understand how the United States can be a truly pluralistic society in which the pluralism is maintained in a way that is enriching rather than impoverishing, a society of dual commitments which need not be in conflict but can be complementary . . . From the long experience of Judaism, Americans of other faiths can learn how this may be done with both grace and integrity."

WINTHROP S. HUDSON,
Religion in America, 1973

Comment: The serious person accepts a compliment as a mandate.

The Eve of the Festival of Freedom, 5754
New York, 1994

IN THE NEW WORLD

Thomas Thorowgood

Legend of the Lost Tribes in the New World

In 1650 a small volume, Jewes in America *or* Probabilities that the Americans are of that Race *by Thomas Thorowgood, appeared in London. The author asserts that "the rites, fashions, ceremonies, and opinions of the Americans are in many things agreeable to the customs of the Jews." As proof that Native Americans are indeed the descendants of the Lost Tribes of Israel exiled by the Assyrians in 722 B.C.E., he offers "The Relation of Master Antonie Montezinos, translated out of the French Copie sent by Manasseh Ben Israel." Here is an edited, modernized version of that account.*

On August 18, 1644, there arrived in Amsterdam, from South America, one Antonio de Montezinos. To the Jewish community, by whom he was called Aaron Levi, he brought a tale of a discovered lost tribe of Jews in the New World, unfolding his tale in a deposition before the leaders of the community.

Two and a half years earlier, while caught in a blizzard during a journey across the Cordillera mountains, the Indian porters exclaimed that they deserved the punishment of nature, even as their cruel Spanish masters, because of the way they had mistreated "a holy people, the best in the world." Later, the leader of the Indians, one Francisco, confided to Montezinos that deserved retribution would be meted out to the cruel, tyrannical, inhuman Spaniards by the "hidden" holy people whom the Indians had mentioned.

While imprisoned by the Inquisition on the charge of Judaizing, Montezinos had ample time to ponder this tale. Emotion suggested that the hidden people might be the Ten Lost Tribes, and he vowed that if the God of Israel would set him free, he would seek out this remnant of His people.

Once released, Montezinos sought out his Indian friend, confessed that he was a Jew of the tribe of Levi, and persuaded him to take him to the "holy people." After a week's journey, they reached a wide river. Francisco signaled, and a boat carrying three men and a woman arrived. After some talk, they greeted Montezinos with a brotherly embrace, and with a recital in Hebrew of the *Shema,* "Hear, O Israel, the Lord our God, the Lord is One." They disclosed that they were of the tribe of Reuben; the tribe of Joseph lived nearby on an island. They were anxious to rejoin their brother Jews, invited settlement among them, and asked for instructors who would teach them the art of writing. The time was near, they claimed, when they would go out to defeat their enemies. But traveler and guide were not permitted to cross the river.

Aernaut Naghtagael, engraver. *Isaac Aboab da Fonseca, Rabbi of Amsterdam.* 1686. The Jewish Theological Seminary of America, New York. Print collection. *Isaac Aboab da Fonseca was the rabbi of the Jewish community of Recife (Pernambuco), Brazil, at the time Antonio de Montezinos was there. Born in Portugal of a Marrano family, educated in Amsterdam, he served in Brazil from 1641 to 1654, the first rabbi in the New World when three leaders of that community petitioned the Dutch West India Company on behalf of their co-religionists in New Amsterdam.*

Francisco then told Montezinos that the tribes of Israel, brought to this continent by God, had been mistreated by the Indians, but could not be destroyed. Finally peace was declared when the wise man of the Indians declared that this holy people was destined to rule the world. The Indians then established relations with them, visiting them at six-year intervals or in time of great emergency.

The journey over, Montezinos was introduced by Francisco to three other hereditary chiefs of the Indians. They assured him that the day was nearing when the Indians would rise up, defeat and destroy their hated Spanish overlords, and bring the tribes of Israel out of exile and bondage.

Request of the Jewish Merchants of Amsterdam in Behalf of the Jews in New Netherland A Complaint Against Peter Stuyvesant

In early September, 1654, twenty-three Jewish refugees, fleeing the wrath of the Portuguese who had retaken Brazil from the Dutch, reached New Amsterdam, a colony established by the Dutch West India Company on the shores where the Hudson River meets the Atlantic Ocean. Governor Peter Stuyvesant asked permission from the company "to require them in a friendly manner to depart." The intercession of leading members of the Amsterdam Jewish community helped avert the "evil decree."

To the Honorable Lords Directors of the West India Company, Chamber of the City of Amsterdam:

With due reverence, the merchants of the Portuguese Nation of this city state that, on the representation of the petitioners, your Honors, on the 15th of February, in the year 1655, consented and permitted the Portuguese Jews to navigate and trade near and in New Netherland, and to live and reside there, as is shown in the requests and apostilles here annexed.

In the same sense the Honorable High Mightinesses, in December of 1645, ordered and commanded the High Government in Brazil to recognize the Jewish

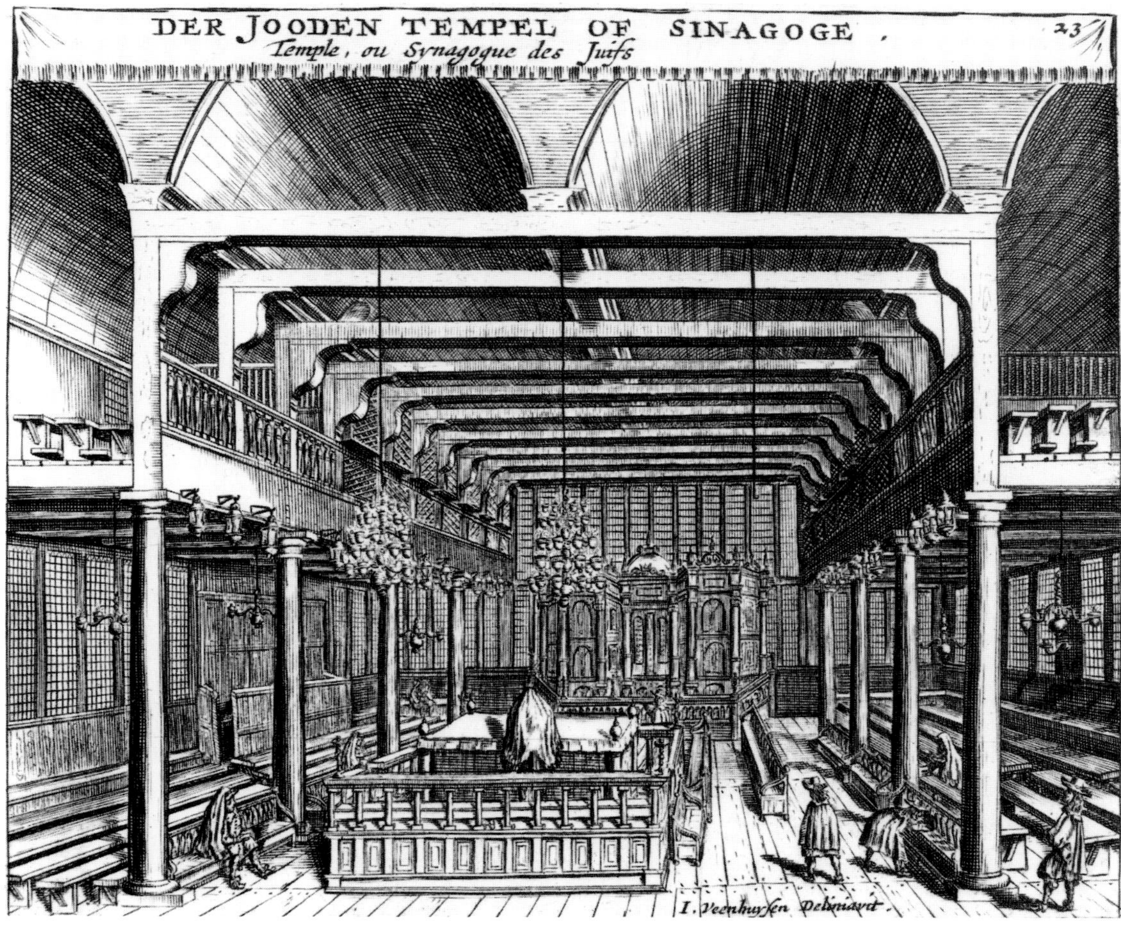

I. VEENHUISER, ENGRAVER. *Interior of the Amsterdam Portuguese Synagogue.* The Jewish Theological Seminary of America, New York. Print collection.

Nation and to let it enjoy the same rights and protection in its business dealings and actions as the natives of this country.

How much more reason that the same rights should be extended in New Netherland and in all other places under the jurisdiction of the Company when we consider the great desolation suffered by this Nation and the loyalty shown by it everywhere to the state of the Company!

However, it appears that Mr. Stuyvesant, the general over there, does not permit the Jewish Nation to enjoy in quietness the exercise of its religion, at its own expense, as it may in all the places of the Company, and at present in this country. Nor does he permit them to buy and sell real estate, to employ Christians if there is no other possibility, to trade and traffic in all places of the Company, just as the Christians are permitted by the Company to trade and transport in their own ships, just like all other natives of this country, provided they support their own poor and pay their contributions together with all the other natives.

And thus Mr. Stuyvesant does not follow, in this matter, the instructions of this Chamber in accordance with the orders of Her High Mightiness. Therefore, the petitioners request your Honors kindly to order the aforesaid Stuyvesant to grant to the Portuguese Jews everything that has been agreed upon and to recognize and admit them like all other natives, and kindly to take such measures so that the Lord General will act according to your consent and orders.

Louis Zara

From *Blessed Is the Land*

"The Landing in New Amsterdam"

Except for official company documents and court records, the only description of the arrival of Jews in New Amsterdam is a few phrases in a letter from a preacher in the Dutch Reform Church in the colony. He urges his superiors in Amsterdam to use their good offices to prevent permission to remain for the newly arrived immigrant Jews, whom he describes as "mendicants" who would become a burden on the community. He also fears that more would arrive and "build here their synagogue." We turn to the informed imagination of author Louis Zara to experience a brief moment in their arrival and welcome. The selection is taken from his novel published in 1954, three hundred years after the Jews landed in New Amsterdam.

We had reached New Amsterdam with its thousand inhabitants. No palace like Fribourg, no twin towers, no bridges, but a welcome, tranquil sight nonetheless. Recife was so far away! I looked up: tiled roofs and gables, weathercocks, smoke curling from the chimneypots. These were solid homes, fresh and clean. The odors of good living tantalized me; we were so famished.

I don't know what we were waiting for; after seventy terrible days, we were on Dutch soil again. Soldiers were watching from the ramparts of the fort. Somewhere, a *doedalsak*, sadly played, was skirling out a drinking song. We gawked at the settlers. They stared at us silently.

View of New Amsterdam. 1650–1653. Museum of the City of New York. The J. Clarence Davies Collection. *Permission for Jews to settle in New Amsterdam was granted in 1655.*

Sarah Pietersen, pulling Rebecca da Silva after her, addressed an older woman who wore a lace cap with a gray satin stomacher above her black petticoat. "Mevrouw—"

My eyes fell upon a huge, barrel-chested man, with an unkempt beard and a hooked nose. He was scratching in his doublet. The red face looked strangely familiar.

But I spied a stocky burgher stooping to pat a mastiff. A man who can afford to feed a dog that big and who wears a fine gold ring must have means!

"Mynheer, we have just arrived from Brazil. I have a strong back and a willing heart. What work can you give me to earn a bed?"

"We have enough workers." He straightened up, and spat through teeth that were nubbins of yellow maize. "Enough, enough!"

"Don't make a spectacle of yourself so soon!" da Silva rasped. "We are strangers here."

"Better a spectacle than a pauper!" I retorted. "We are not strangers. We need lodgings and food. Do you know a better way than to ask for work?"

D'Acosta and Gomez also spoke up.

"Brazil!" someone muttered. "Recife! Is it still war with the Portuguese?"

A French sailor shouted that we were "survivors!" A murmur ran through the crowd. Everyone began to talk.

A baker, Hendrik Jansen, his hands and his breeches still dusted with flour, clapped his hands on d'Acosta's shoulders, and agreed to take him for a week. Hendrik Kip, the tailor, hired that grumbler da Silva. Isaac de Forest, a brewer, pinched Abraham Israel's arm and thighs, and took him. Maximilian van Geele, a merchant from Amsterdam, engaged Solomon Pietersen.

Hellegonda Joris, an enormous woman with a little head and apple cheeks, introduced herself to Sarah as the midwife. She gently caressed Rivke Nunez's trembling hands and murmured: "Kindje, kindje!"

A hard finger prodded my shoulder.

It was the red-faced Esau. Except for his forehead, his temples, eyes and nose, his whole face was shaggy. The rosy lips shaped words silently. He rubbed the tip of his nose, and squinted at me.

"Heh, you have just arrived?" The head jerked toward the *St. Charles*. "On that ship?" I thought his mouth wanted to break into a smile.

I said quickly. "Mynheer, our legs are still shaky from the months at sea. We sailed on a fine Dutchman, were captured by a filthy Spaniard, and were rescued by the good Frenchman. I am a willing worker, Mynheer———"

He blinked. "From Brazil?"

"From Brazil. We came from Recife which the Portuguese have taken. I———"

He was fumbling for something. "Heh, not—not Jews?"

I glared. Another Jew-baiter? With shoulders like a bull. "Mynheer, we are Jews."

A broad grin split the red face and revealed strong teeth. The brow creased, and the cheeks puffed up like peaches. "Heh!" He thrust out his hand. "Then—*Sholem aleichem!* brother!" He glowed. "Heh, then, *Sholem aleichem!*"

I gaped. Were we not the first Jews to set foot in New Amsterdam? "You are a Jew?" I mumbled. "Mynheer———"

Again the big teeth sparkled. (He does not guffaw, he neighs.) "Mynheer!" he snorted. "Heh, what then? Two months ago, I arrived from Amsterdam on *De Pereboom*. Do I really look so much the Dutchman?" Like most Jews, he was not displeased to be taken for a Goy.

I seized that friendly palm, which was as hard as horn, and shouted back, "Then, *Aleichem sholem, aleichem sholem!*"

"Heh! Yes, yes, *Aleichem sholem!*"

I pumped his hand. 'Listen to this, d'Acosta!" I called. "Hear him, Pietersen, Israel, Burgos! A Jew from Amsterdam! Hear now: *'Sholem aleichem, aleichem sholem!'* Well, well, God is good!"

We clustered around him. *"Sholem aleichem, aleichem sholem!* Peace unto you, unto you let there be peace!" We wrung his hand, and we squeezed his arms. "From Amsterdam! A Jew!" We stood off and looked at his wind-burned face and his barrel-chest, and chortled and clucked: *"Aleichem sholem, sholem aleichem!"* (I should not be surprised to learn that when Columbus first reached the Indies he was greeted by a Jew with *Sholem aleichem!* and was invited to a Minyan to be the tenth man for prayer!)

He bobbed and he grinned, and he cried, "Heh, *Sholem aleichem!*" and his whinnying laugh rang out over the wharf.

D'Acosta, who had already squeezed the horny palm three times, whispered, "Ashur, he *is* a Jew?"

I startled New Amsterdam with my bellow. "A Jew? Who else would cry *'Sholem aleichem'?"* Had our hospitable, pipe-smoking Dutchman not been watching, I would have tripped a Simchas Torah dance there on the dock.

"And what is your name, Jew?" I asked. Among ourselves when we say "Jew," it is different.

"Heh, Jacob Barsimson is the name." He twinkled. I wish he would not say "Heh!" every time he opens his mouth. "A good, circumcised Jew! As soon as the authorities have cleared you, we'll go over and drink a *L'chaim!*"

Well, we introduced him to our women and they cried *"Sholem aleichem!"* and put their hands into his big paw, and smiled. He stared at Nina Rivera like a cat at a saucer of cream. If the man beneath the bushy beard looks presentable and is unmarried, I shall find him a bride before his hair grows long again. If he is a Jew, he should not be parading on the dock like an unkempt bear.

"Is there a tavern?"

He roared. "Tavern, heh! There's the Frenchman's tavern on the Marckveldt, Pieter Kock's tavern near the market landing, Sergeant Litschko's tavern where the Long Islanders go———"

By noon, we had drunk *L'chaim*—to Life!—in good Dutch ale. As I drained the tankard, I stuck out my elbow to steady my arm against the next rise of a deck that was no longer swimming beneath me. Barsimson procured us a meal of fresh bread, eggs, butter—such butter!—dried fish, boiled maize, and ripe apples.

He had been in the Colony a whole month. A special mission had brought him over on *De Pereboom* on 22 August. He was to report to our Amsterdam Elders on the possibilities for migration for other Jews. He knew the settlement; we went up and down the narrow streets, and knocked on doors. Sturdy houses with glass windows, wash drying in the sun, and flaxen-haired children playing in the courtyards! By two o'clock he had found us lodgings for twelve in private residences and in barns, storehouses, and cattle-sheds.

"The women have suffered," I hinted. "They need good beds. The weather is fair. We men could be comfortable on the bowling-green, and trouble no one."

He frowned. "These Dutchmen are the same as in Amsterdam, good souls but stubborn. Their Director-General Stuyvesant is a despot! Last year, the West India Company granted the Colony the right to govern itself. Do you think he will permit it? He is sovereign here. Levy, they will let no one sleep on the green. Would they let a grain of sand fall in their kitchens? And the nightwatch will not let you show a leg after curfew!"

"Gam zeh l'tovo!" I returned. "Then find us beds indoors!" I confided a little more about the catastrophe on the *San Diego.*

He paled. "A thousand curses on the Spaniards!" And he leaped into action like a runaway horse.

Before the red sun had sunk to the western cliffs, we had quarters for everyone. The midwife, good soul, arranged for the women to be lodged in the Stadthuis which, until last May, had been the City Tavern and contained an ample number of rooms and beds.

Barsimson blustered, "Did you think I would let fellow-Jews sleep on the bare grounds?" He threw his long arms about me. "Heh, *Sholem aleichem!"* He gave out with that neighing laugh, and we marched off for another *L'chaim!*

Dr. Alexander Hamilton

From *Hamilton's Itinerarium*

A Visit to Shearith Israel Synagogue

Congregation Shearith Israel, New York, dedicated its synagogue on Mill Street, lower Manhattan, the first structure designed and built to be a synagogue in continental North America, on the seventh day of Passover, 1730. Fourteen years later, Dr. Alexander Hamilton of Annapolis, Maryland, attended services there on the second day of Rosh Hashanah. In a diary he kept on a tour of the American colonies in the summer of 1744, Dr. Hamilton describes the synagogue, the worship service, and the congregation—the earliest description extant of an American synagogue and a congregation of Jews at prayer.

View of the Junction of Pearl and Chatham Streets, New York. 1861. The New York Historical Society. *This area is the site of the first Jews Burying Ground in New York City, maintained to the present day.*

I went in the morning with Mr. Hog to the Jews' sinagogue where was an assembly of about 50 of the seed of Abraham chanting and singing their doleful hymns, (they had 4 great wax candles lighted, as large as a man's arm, round the sanctuary where was contained the ark of the covenant and Aaron's rod), dressed in robes of white silk. Before the rabbi, who was elevated above the rest, in a kind of desk, stood the seven golden candlesticks transformed into silver gilt. They were all slip shod. The men wore their hats in the synagogue and had a veil of some white stuff which they sometimes threw over their heads in their devotion; the women, of whom some were very pritty, stood up in a gallery like a hen coop. They sometimes paused or rested a little from singing and talked about business. My ears were so filled with their lugubrious songs that I could not get the sound out of my head all day . . .

Samuel J. May

From *The Life of Samuel J. May*

The Hays Family of Boston

Moses Michael Hays, his wife Rachel, their son and five daughters; his sister Reyna, the widow of the Reverend Isaac Touro of Newport, Rhode Island, and her sons Abraham and Judah (later to become the first of America's great Jewish philanthropists) were the only Jewish residents of Boston at the end of the eighteenth century and beginning of the nineteenth. Arriving in Boston at the outbreak of the Revolutionary War, he soon became a man of wealth and promi-

nence, serving at one time as Grand Master of the Masonic Grand Lodge of Massachusetts. The Reverend Mr. May, who as a child often visited the Hays home, recalls: "I witnessed their religious exercises, their fastings and prayers . . . and Sabbaths at their table." This account of the Hays family appeared in Samuel May's memoirs (1874).

If the children of my day were taught among other foolish things, to dread, if not despise, Jews, a very different lesson was impressed upon my young heart. There was but one family of the despised children of the house of Israel resident in Boston, the family of Moses Michael Hays; a man much respected, not only on account of his large wealth, but for his many personal virtues and the high culture and great excellence of his wife, his son Judah, and his daughters especially Catherine and Slowey. His home far down on Hanover Street, then one of the fashionable streets of the town, was the abode of hospitality, and his family moved in what were the first circles of society. He and his truly good wife were hospitable, not only to the rich alone, but also to the poor. Many indigent families were fed pretty regularly from his table. These would come especially after his frequent dinner parties, and were sure to be made welcome, not to the crumbs only, but to ampler portions of the food that might be left.

Always, on Saturday, he expected a number of friends to dine with him. A full-length table was always spread and loaded with the luxuries of the season, and he

New York, March 27 1767.

TEN POUNDS Reward

WHEREAS the Houſe of Mrs. REBECCA HAYS, of this City, was, laſt ThurſdayNight robbed of the following Pieces of Plate & Money, viz

1 Two Quart Silver Tankard, marked I. H. R.
1 Large Silver Punch Bowl, with two Handles.
3 Silver Porringers, marked M. M K.
1 Silver Sugar Caſtor, marked M. M. K
2 Pair of Round Silver Salts, with Feet, marked I, H. R.——And one odd ditto, marked in the ſame Manner.
1 Small Silver Salver, without any Mark.
6 Table Spoons, marked B, H. Maker's Name *Myers.*
1 Pair of Diamond Rings, with Drops.
1 Silver Coffee-Pot, no Mark, Maker's Name I.-P, And a Silver Tea Pot.
1 £ 6 10 Jerſey Bill, 35 Dollars, 25 Quarter Dollars, 12 Pieces of Engliſh Money, and three Pocket Pieces.

'Tis poſſible more of the Plate is marked, than what is mentioned above. Whoever takes up and ſecures any Perſon or Perſons concerned in the above Robbery, ſo that they may be brought to Juſtice, ſhall have the above Reward, paid by me MOSES M HAYS.

Advertisement for Reward of Stolen Goods by Moses Michael Hays. March 27, 1767. *The goods were taken from his widowed mother, a resident of New York. The six tablespoons were made by her son-in-law, the noted colonial silversmith, Myer Myers.*

loved to sit surrounded by a few regular visitors and others especially invited. My father was a favorite guest. He was regarded by Mr. Hays and his whole family as a particular friend, their chosen counsellor in times of perplexity, and their comforter in the days of their affliction. My father seldom failed to dine at Mr. Hays on Saturday, and often took me with him; for he was sure I should meet refined company there.

Benjamin G. Sack

From *History of the Jews in Canada*

The Mystery of Esther Brandeau

It may be said that Jewish presence in Canada began in 1759, when New France, in which only Catholics were permitted to settle, fell to the British. There is evidence that individual Jews did arrive before that date, none more intriguing than a young Jew who arrived in 1738 as Jacques La Fargue, but who was soon identified to be Esther Brandeau. She told a fantastic tale to the Marine Commissioner of Québec on September 15, 1738.

Mention of Jews in Canada as such is made for the first time in connection with two separate incidents. The first has an almost picaresque quality . . .

Disguised as a boy and under the assumed name of "Jacques La Fargue," a Jewish girl arrived at Quebec in September, 1738, on the ship *Saint Michel*. This passenger had attracted considerable attention until the remarkable discovery was made that the comely, spirited youth whose manners were so refined was in fact no "Jacques" but "Esther"—Esther Brandeau. The Intendant ordered her arrest but, due to lack of suitable quarters, she was held under surveillance at the Quebec hospital. The problem of what to do with her so baffled the Minister of Colonies and the Intendant that the King himself was compelled to intervene and settle the question of defraying the cost of her return passage to France.

The incident is fully detailed in the archives. In his first report to the Minister outlining the case of Esther Brandeau, Hocquart, the Intendant writes: "Since her arrival in Quebec she has maintained a great reserve, and seems to be desirous of being converted to Catholicism, but fears lest her relatives should come here and discover her."

The Intendant was greatly embarrassed by her presence. She could not be kept long in the hospital and a more convenient place for her had to be found. In addition,the girl's story was fantastic as revealed in the declaration made by her before the Marine Commissioner of Quebec on September 15, 1738, part of which is given below:

> This day, before the undersigned, Commissaire de la marine, chargé à Québec de la police des gens de mer, appeared Esther Brandeau, aged about twenty years, who embarked at La Rochelle as a passenger, dressed in boy's clothes, under the name of Jacques La Fargue, on the vessel *St. Michel*, Sieur de Salaberry commander, and declared her name to be Esther Brandeau, daughter of David Brandeau, a Jew, trader, of St. Esprit, diocese of Daxe, near Bayonne, and that she is of Jewish religion; that five years ago her father and mother placed her on a Dutch vessel, Captain Geoffroy,

> in order to send her to Amsterdam, to one of her aunts and to her brother; that the vessel having been lost on the bar of Bayonne, in the moon of April or May, 1733, she was happily brought safe to shore with one of the crew; that she was received by Catherine Churiau, a widow living at Biaris; that two weeks thereafter she started, dressed as a man, for Bordeaux, where she shipped as a boy, under the name of Pierre Alansiette, on a vessel commanded by Captain Bernard destined for Nantes, that she returned on the same vessel to Bordeaux, and there shipped again in the same capacity on a Spanish vessel, Captain Antonio, for Nantes, that on reaching Nantes, she deserted and went to Rennes, where she took service as a boy at the house of one Augustin, a tailor, and so on and so on.

Upon being asked why she had concealed her sex for five years, she replied that "after she had been rescued from shipwreck and had arrived at Bayonne, she had entered the house of Catherine Churiau, as above stated, whereupon the latter made her eat pork and other meats the use whereof is forbidden among the Jews, and that she thereupon resolved not to return to her father and mother in order that she might enjoy the same liberty as the Christians."

A record of the case was drafted and forwarded to the Minister in France who, in his reply to the Intendant, confessed that he had grave doubts concerning the girl's story. "I do not know," he wrote, "if we can completely believe the declaration of Esther Brandeau who, disguised as a boy, last year embarked for Canada on the ship *St. Michel*, and who claims that she is a Jewess. However that may be, I approve her admission into the Quebec hospital and shall be pleased to hear that she has been converted. Apart from this, your behaviour toward her should be governed by her conduct in the colony and also by the information about her which Sieur de Pelissier, Ordinator of Bayonne, will forward to you."

Many attempts were made to persuade the girl to abandon her religion, an act which she steadfastly refused to consider. All the eloquence of her would-be reformers was of no avail and it was finally decided to deport her to France. In a letter to the Minister, the Intendant complained that nothing could be done with the Jewess: "Her conduct has not been wholly bad, but she is so frivolous that at different times she has been both obedient and obstinate with regard to the instruction the priests desired to give her. I have no other alternative than to send her back. Sieur Lafergue, captain of the ship *Le Comte de Matignon*, will see to it."

Later, the question of payment for her return passage compelled Louis XV himself to intervene. After the case had been brought to his attention, he declared that he himself, that is, the State, would indemnify the owner of the ship which by that time had returned the Jewess to France. Failing her adoption of the Catholic faith, as was desired, it was considered of vital importance to deal with her in the strictest manner. The possibility of her remaining in New France could no longer be tolerated. It was necessary to deport her.

The deportation of the obstinate girl, in whose behalf couriers kept travelling between France and the North American colony, was carried out on the express orders of the King. By this time her deportation had become an "affaire officielle" and conferences and audiences had taken place between the King and the Minister of Colonies. In a letter dated January 25, 1740, written to the admiral of the French fleet, the King among other things divulges that after "my cousin, Sieur Hocquart, Intendant of Canada, upon my orders had sent the Jewish girl, Esther Brandeau, back to France on the ship *Le Comte de Matignon* of La Rochelle, the owner of the ship, Sieur La Pointe, applied to me for reimbursement of the passage money . . ." and, as can be seen from a subsequent passage, the King granted this request.

Sheldon and Judy Godfrey

From *Search Out the Land*

Captured by the Indians

His own affidavit, presented to a military court in Detroit on August 9, 1763, and the account heard by a missionary, the Reverend John Heckenelder, are representative of the many "captured by the Indians" tales told and retold in the British American colonies. The hero of this tale was a Jew, Chapman Abraham, a trader on the Niagara frontier.

Chapman Abraham, coming up the Detroit River from Lake Erie in early May, 1763, about a month before the massacre at Michilmackinac, learned of his own mortality. The diary of John Porteous, one of the Detroit merchants, gave only a terse note: "Friday 13th May. Had account this morning that Chapman Abrams and a Dutch trader named Barkman, with five Batteaux and horses were taken at the lower settlement by the Hurons there, the enemy got seventeen Barrels of Powder besides all the other merchandise . . ." The "Diary of the Siege of Detroit" made by Major Robert Rogers three months later, gave scarcely more detail saying that on 13 May, 1763 "Mr. Chapman a trader from Niagara was taken Prisoner by the Waindotes, with five Battoes loaded with goods."

From 9 May, Fort Detroit, the fur-trading post between Lake Erie and the Upper Great Lakes, had been under siege by hundreds of Indian warriors led by Chief Pontiac, still loyal to the French regime. The 120 British soldiers and English traders inside the fort watched helplessly as the "English" unlucky enough to be outside the fort, including Sir Robert Davers, Captain Robertson and at least a dozen more, were killed and scalped. On Wednesday, May 11, five or six hundred Indians attacked the fort but withdrew with three men killed and more than a dozen wounded. From that point on, Pontiac's men waited, hoping to starve out the defenders of the fort.

Chapman Abraham, a forty-year-old trader, had been in the area for at least a year, having come from Holland to New York by 1756 after a stay in Plymouth, England. He was proudly Jewish and was so known on the frontier. His own account of the incident was set out in his affidavit on 9 August, 1763, presented to the military court at Detroit under Major Henry Gladwin:

> Mr. Chapman Abraham being sworn informs the Court, that in coming up Detroit River, having put on shore at the place of Monsieur St. Lewis, he [St. Lewis] acquainted this Deponant [Abraham] that the Fort was besieged by the Indians & Capt. Robertson, Sir Robert Daviss and a great many more English were killed, & that they intended to kill all the English that would come up Detroit River. This Deponant immediately told his men to go back with him; but the before mentioned soldiers told his men if they returned that all would be killed, as the Indians were round the whole Lake and at Niagara, upon which they absolutely refused to return with him. In consequence of which this Deponant put all his goods in said St. Lewis's house, who told him he could do his best to save them from the Indians; Then this Deponant asked him where he should go to hide himself to save his life. He and Madam Esperame (who was present) answered him he

Gomez House. American Jewish Historical Society, Waltham, Massachusetts. *To expand their trade with the Indians, Luis Moses Gomez (c. 1660–1740) and his five sons built a stone trading post in 1717 on land a few miles north of Newburgh, New York, which (later enlarged) still stands. Descendants have given leadership to New York's Shearith Israel Congregation for almost three centuries.*

> should go to her home and hide himself in her cellar; where he continued about ten minutes and then was told by said Madam Esperame to go out of the house; which he obeyed and in going out she perceived his watch chain & told him to give it to her that she was certain the Indians would kill him; upon which this Deponant told her he would make her a present of it, if she would let him stay in the cellar to save him from the Indians. She answered he should stay no longer in the House; upon which he endeavored to gain the woods; she followed him, demanding the watch a second time, which I again refused. By this time the Indians discovered him, took him prisoner and carried him to St. Lewis's house, where he found some of his goods were put in his canoe.

At this point the story is picked up by the missionary, Reverend John Heckenelder, who wrote that he had first heard it from the inhabitants of Detroit, the facts being "afterwards confirmed to me by Mr. Chapman himself":

> About the commencement of the Indian War in 1763, a trading Jew, named Chapman who was going up the Detroit River with a batteau-load of goods he had brought from Albany, was taken by some of the Indians of the Chippeway nation and destined to be put to death. A Frenchman impelled by motives of friendship and humanity, found means to steal the prisoner, and kept him so concealed for some time, that although the most diligent search was made, the place of his confinement could not be discovered. At last, however, the unfortunate man was betrayed by some false friend, and again fell into the power of the Indians who took him across the river to be burned and tortured. Tied to the stake and the fire burning by his side, his thirst from the great heat became intolerable and he begged that some drink might be given to him. It is a custom of the Indians, previous to a prisoner being put to death, to give him what they call his last meal; a bowl of pottage or broth was therefore brought to him for that purpose. Eager to quench his thirst, he put the bowl immediately to his lips, and the liquor being very hot, he was dreadfully scalded. Being a man of very quick tem-

> per, the moment he felt his mouth burned, he threw the bowl and its contents full in the face of the man who handed it to him. "He is mad! He is mad!" resounded from all quarters. The bystanders considered his conduct as an act of insanity, and immediately untied the cords with which he was bound, and let him go where he pleased.

Abraham may have been free, but like Ezekiel Solomons he had lost all his inventory of trade goods and furs. His affidavit before Major Gladwin named a number of French Canadian residents of the fort who he had seen wearing or trading goods he recognized as his, to others. But he was able to recover nothing.

Howard Fast

From "Where Are Your Guns?"

As one of the most popular historical novelists, Howard Fast has produced works drawn from his dual identity as an American and a Jew. In this powerful vignette Fast depicts the clash between Jewish values and prejudice set against the backdrop of colonial America.

In the land of the goyim, my father traded with the Indians. We traded for beaver, and my father's word was as good as his bond, and we never carried a weapon except for our knives. From the lakes in the north to the canebrake in the south and as far west as the great river—there we traded and we never carried a weapon, never a musket or a rifle or a pistol, for these are weapons of death; and if you deal with death, what else can you expect in return? Is it not said in the Book, "Thou shalt not hate thy brother in thy heart"? And is it not also said, "I will also give thee for a light to the Gentiles"?

Among the Mingoes, we dwelt and traded, and among the Delawares, too, and among the Wyandottes and the Shawnees and the Eries and the Miamis and the Kickapoos, and even among the Menomini, where only the French have been, and never did we carry a weapon. "Men do not kill for the sake of killing," my father answered once to a hunter who could not understand why we didn't walk in fear of the red savage. "My people walked in fear for too long," my father said. "I don't fear what is different."

The hunter was one who slew his meat and ate it, even as the red men do, but our law is different. We kept the Law. Would you understand if I told you how we suffered to keep the Law? The Law says that when a beast is slain, it must be with the hand of a holy man, so that the lifeblood will run out as an offering to God rather than as a wanton slaughter of one of His creatures—with God's will and God's blessing.

Long, long ago, when I was only nine, my father said, "The high holy days are coming, and we have not sat down with our own people since your mother's death three years ago," speaking in the old tongue, which he taught me so carefully, being a man of learning. "I would have you pray for your mother's soul, and I would be with my own people for a little while, there is such a hunger in me." So we saddled our horses and made the long journey eastward to Philadelphia, where were a handful of our own people. Not that they welcomed us so well, we were two such wild buckskin-

Early View of Fort Pitt, Pennsylvania. 1759–1761. Drawing. Courtesy of the Carnegie Library of Pittsburgh. *Fort Pitt, located along the Allegheny River in Pennsylvania, was the location of the imprisonment and execution of the fictitious hero of Howard Fast's story.*

folk, my father's great black beard falling to his waist; but we prayed with them and we ate meat with them . . .

I speak of this because I must make you understand my father, the man who traded with the Indians, so you will not judge me too harshly. I am not my father. My father fared forth to a wild land from far-off Poland, and of Poland I know no more than a dream and a legend, nor do I care. With his own hands he buried his wife in the wilderness, and he was mother and father to me, even though he left me with the Indians when I was small, and I lived in their lodges and learned their tongue. I am not like my father. He had a dream, which was to trade with the Indians until there was enough money to buy freedom, peace, security—all those things which, so it goes, only money can buy for a Jew; and because he had that dream, he never knew any comfort and the taste of meat was a strange thing to him. A stream of beaver skins went back to the Company on the donkeys and the flatboats that were owned by the Company, and all of it went to a place called London, and in this place there was a thing called an *account.*

Those were names and words and without meaning to me. I cared nothing of the beaver skins and nothing of the account, but if my father said that these things were of such importance, then indeed they were, even as the Law was. I knew other things; I knew the talk of the Shawnees and Algonquin talk, and I could make palaver with the men of the Six Nations too, if need be. I knew Yankee talk, the talk of those long-boned hunters of the East, and I knew the French talk and the high-pitched nasal talk of the British, who claimed to own the land, but knew nothing of it and stayed huddled in their outposts and stockades. I spoke the old language of the Book and I knew the Law, and I could catch trout with my bare hands and steal the eggs from under the nesting bird never disturbing it. I knew the step and the stride of nineteen moccasins, and where the wild parsnip grows and the wild turnip too, and with only a knife I could live the year round in the dark woods, where never the sky is seen. By heart in the old Hebrew, I knew the Song of Songs, which is Solomon's, and I knew forty psalms. And from the time I was thirteen, I prayed twice a day.

I also knew what it is to be a Jew.

But not like my father, whom you would have remembered, had you seen him come into Fort Pitt on that day. My father was six feet and two inches tall; fifteen stone he scaled, and never an ounce of fat, but hard as rock, with a black beard that fell to his waist. All through the woods, in those times, which are the old times now, the half-forgotten times, were Jews who traded with the Indians and went where no other white man had ever trod, but there was no one like my father, you may believe me. No one so tall or so wide or so heavy—or so sweet of speech and gentle of mien, yet I remember so well a cart and horse mired belly-deep, and my father heaved the horse out and the cart too. Or the time a year before at the company post of Elizabeth, where two Delawares were crazed with drink; they would have been slain, for what is better sport for a redcoat than to slay a drunken Indian? But my father lifted them from the ground like puppies and shook them until the drink went out of them, and instead of going to their deaths they went home to their lodges and were grateful . . .

That was my father, who bound the phylacteries on his head faithfully every morning, and kept the Law, and did justice to all who knew him. That was my father, who came into Fort Pitt with me on this day. We drove seven donkeys and they carried eleven hundred skins, and for a month I had listened to my father plan how now we would go to New York and demand an accounting from the Company, and there we would live with our own people and roam the woods no more. He was filled with it. A mile from the fort, we had stopped to drink water at the outhouse and mill of MacIntyre, and my father told him.

"No more this way, Angus," my father said, "but eastward and the boy will wear woven cloth on his back."

"Ye been a woodsy man these twenty year," MacIntyre said somberly.

"I'll be woodsy no more. And young Reuben here will make a company of his own, the good Lord willing."

"Heed the new commandant. He has no love for Jews, or for Scots either. I am glad to see you safe, because there is war with the Mingoes."

My father laughed because we had bought two hundred skins from the Mingoes, and there was no war talk in their cities. But when we came to the fort, there was a new guard at the gate. The doors were closed, and the men on the walls wore yellow facings and shakos I had not seen before. It was a new regiment for the woods.

"Who goes there?" a sergeant called.

"Two traders with skins."

"And where are your guns?"

"We bear no guns," my father said. "We are Jews who trade with the Indians."

Then the doors opened, and we entered with our donkeys, but there was never a smile or a nod. I looked at my father and he looked at me, but there was nothing to make out of his face; and when we looked around us, we saw that these were new men. Their cloth clothes were still fresh with the East, and they stared at us as if we were creatures; were we not Jews, they would have stared at us too, but there was that in their eyes that was singular for Jews . . .

"Who are you and what are your names?"

"We are Jews who trade with the Indians," my father said. "My name is David, and this is my son, Reuben. Twelve years I have been in and out of this place, even when it was Duquesne, and I am known in the forest country."

"I don't know you," the young man said, as if we were dirt and less than dirt.

"Then I be sorry," my father said. "Stevenson knows me, for I have always traded with him and paid my loanings. Benson knows me, for he shod my beasts, and Bryan knows me, for he boxed my goods. I am not a stranger here."

"You are a Jew and damned insolent," the young man replied. "As for the scum of this place, they know the dregs of the woods. Where are your arms?"

"We bear no arms but our knives."

"And how did you come through the Mingoes? There is war with the Mingoes."

A mass of soldiers were around us now, and now I could see Benson and some of the others, but keeping off. I am not like my father. I would have made a story then, but it was not in him to speak anything but the truth. He was going to New York, but I knew of a sudden that he would be lonely and forsaken in such a place. The green woods was his home, and it was not in him to speak anything but the truth.

"There is no war with the Mingoes," he said slowly. "I traded two hundred skins with the Mingoes, and I lay in their lodges this fortnight past. There is no war with the Mingoes."

The young officer said, "You're a damned liar, a filthy Jew, and a spy as well."

My father's face was sad and hard and woeful. I moved, but he moved quicker, and he struck the officer a blow that would have felled an ox. Then we fought a little, but there were too many of them.

They put us in a cell and they gave us no food and no water. We were bleeding and bruised, but it was not hard to go without food. It was hard for my father to go without his phylacteries, but after the second day I didn't care. They came every few hours and asked us to tell what we knew of the Mingoes, but what we knew was of no interest to them.

The colonel came finally. It is so different now that you cannot know what a colonel was in those days in a place like Fort Pitt. He was an English gentleman and he was God too, and he prodded us with his stick.

"How old are you?" he asked me.

"I am fifteen," I croaked.

"You are large for fifteen," he lisped, holding a lace handkerchief over his nose. "The Yankees come large, but I should not think it would be so with a Jew. I shall hang your father tomorrow, but if you will tell me what you know of the Mingoes, you may go free and take your seven beasts with the skins."

"I know nothing of the Mingoes."

"And how do you travel in the woods without guns? I am very curious."

"That you could never know," my father said, almost sadly.

Even these days you will hear things said of Jews; it is that way; but once my father found a robin with a broken wing, and made splints for the wing and a sling, so that we could carry the bird with us, and he nursed it until it flew away. So I will remember until I die how the British drums rolled as they hanged my father, who traded with the Indians in the land of the goyim, and whose word was as good as his bond. And then they gave me thirty lashes until I bled like a pig, and drove me from the fort to die in the forest.

A Jew dies hard, they say. I crawled a mile to Angus MacIntyre's mill, and he washed my back and cared for me until I returned to my senses and could walk again.

"Weep for your father," he said, "for you are only a laddie, and he was much of a man."

"I weep no more and pray no more. My father is dead, and I am not like him."

"You will be like him, lad."

"I will never be like him, Angus, but I will make my word like my bond. I give you my word I will bring you forty beaver skins if you give me a musket and powder and shot."

A long time the old Scot looked at me, measuring me and weighing me. "Go to the land of the Yankees, lad," he said, "and wear woolen clothes on your back."

"The Yankees stood by while my father was hanged. When that redcoat filth drove the Mingoes from the fort, the Yankees stood by. When two Mingoes came back for the little they left behind and were slain at the gate, the Yankees said nothing."

"How many of them were there?" the Scot said quietly. "They are a strange folk, dirty, and bragging and mean and sometimes, in a most curious way, a little noble. Will they be silent forever?"

"Will you give me the gun?"

"You are one of them," the Scot said.

"When they are no longer silent—I will be one of them. When they strike, I will strike with them."

"And your father traded in the woods with never more than a knife. For the Company. Are you for the Company?"

"I am against any man in a uniform."

"I will give you the gun, lad," the Scot said sadly, "and you will slay your meat and eat it."

"And other things."

"Then put no price on it, for what you seek has no price but a man's blood. You are one of them."

He gave me the gun, and I left him and walked eastward.

Haym Solomon

A Patriot Petitions the Continental Congress

The papers of the Continental Congress, which was in existence from 1774 to 1788, contain this Memorial from the best-known American Jew of that period, Haym Solomon. In this petition he asks for assistance and reminds the Congress of his service to the country and support of the revolutionary cause. For a good part of the nineteenth century his descendants petitioned Congress for monies owed him by the national government. These demands were deemed justifiable, but no reimbursement was ever made.

To the Honorable the Continental Congress:

The Memorial of Haym Solomon late of the City of New York, Merchant. Humbly Sheweth,

That your Memorialist was some time before the Entry of the British Troops at the said City of New York and soon after taken up as a Spy and by General Robertson committed to the Provost—That by the Interposition of Lieut. General Heister (who wanted him on account of his knowledge in the French, Polish Russian Italian &c Languages) he was given over to the Hessian Commander who appointed him in the Commissary Way as purveyor chiefly for the Officers—That being at New York he has been of great Service to the French and American prisoners and has assisted them with Money and helped them off to make their Escape—That this and his close connexions with such of the Hessian Officers as were inclined to resign and with Monsieur Samuel Demezes has rendered him at last so obnoxious to the British Head Quarters that he was already pursued by the Guards and on Tuesday the 11th inst. he made his happy Escape from thence—This Monsieur Demezes is now most barbarously treated at the Provost's and is seemingly in danger of his Life. And the Memorialist begs leave to cause him to be remembered to Congress for an Exchange.

COLORPLATE 1

ARTIST UNKNOWN. *Jacob Franks.* c. 1740. Oil on canvas. 45 x 35 in. Gift of Captain N. Taylor Phillips to the American Jewish Historical Society, Waltham, Massachusetts. *One of the wealthiest merchants in New York City, Franks served as* parnas *(president) of Congregation Shearith Israel when its first synagogue was consecrated on April 8, 1730.*

COLORPLATE 2

ATTRIBUTED TO GERARDOS DUYCKINK (1695–1746) OR PETER VANDERLYN (1687–1778). *Portrait of Mrs. Moses Levy (Grace Mears).* c. 1720–1728. Oil on canvas. 44 1/4 x 35 7/8 in. The Museum of the City of New York. Bequest of Alphonse H. Kursheed. *London-born Grace Mears, the second wife of Moses Levy, bore him eight children whom she raised along with the five children from his previous marriage.*

COLORPLATE 3

ATTRIBUTED TO GERARDOS DUYCKINK (1695–1746) OR PETER VANDERLYN (1687–1778). *Portrait of Moses Levy.* c. 1720–1728. Oil on canvas. 42 1/2 x 33 1/2 in. The Museum of the City of New York. Bequest of Alphonse H. Kursheed. *Levy was born in Germany in 1665, went to London and then to New York where he became a leader of its small Jewish community. The ship in the background symbolizes his immigrant beginnings and the international trade in which he was engaged.*

COLORPLATE 4

GILBERT STUART. *Sarah Rivera Lopez and Son Joshua.* c. 1775. Oil on canvas. 26 x 21 1/2 in. The Detroit Institute of Fine Arts. *Newport's leading Jewish citizen, Portuguese-born Aaron Lopez, was a shipping magnate wealthy enough to commission Gilbert Stuart to paint his wife and son. Stuart's portraits of George Washington are probably the best-known in America.*

COLORPLATE 5 *(left)*

ARTIST UNKNOWN. *Philip Russel.* 1774. Oil on board. 3 x 2 1/2 in. Collection of Mrs. Harry A. Mayer. *Russel was the son of Reverend Mordecai Russel and the only Jew known to have served with George Washington at Valley Forge. As a surgeon's mate, he gave "assiduous and faithful attention to the sick and wounded," a commendation attributed to George Washington.*

COLORPLATE 6 *(below, left)*

ATTRIBUTED TO THOMAS SULLY. *Rachel Gratz.* c. 1815. Oil on canvas. Collection, Congregation Mikveh Israel, Philadelphia. *Rachel, younger sister of Rebecca, married New York-born Solomon Moses, who became a successful Philadelphia merchant and a leader of Congregation Mikveh Israel.*

COLORPLATE 7 *(below)*

THOMAS SULLY. *Rebecca Gratz.* 1858. Oil on canvas. 20 x 16 in. American Jewish Historical Society, Waltham, Massachusetts. Gift of Louis Bamberger. *Educator and philanthropist, Rebecca Gratz founded the first Hebrew Sunday School in the United States. She is said to have been the model for the character Rebecca in Sir Walter Scott's novel* Ivanhoe.

COLORPLATE 8

THOMAS SULLY. *Michael Gratz.* c. 1805. Pastel. 22 1/2 x 19 in. American Jewish Historical Society, Waltham, Massachusetts. Anonymous gift. *Michael Gratz, a German immigrant, was a leading merchant and a founder of the Jewish community in Philadelphia and the father of Rebecca and Rachel Gratz.*

COLORPLATE 9

ARTIST UNKNOWN. *Uriah Phillips Levy.* c. 1815. Oil on canvas. 32 1/2 x 27 in. American Jewish Historical Society, Waltham, Massachusetts. Bequest of Mrs. Amelia Levy Mayhoff. *Levy was an officer in the United States Navy who fought in the War of 1812. He campaigned vigorously for the abolition of flogging as a punishment in the Navy.*

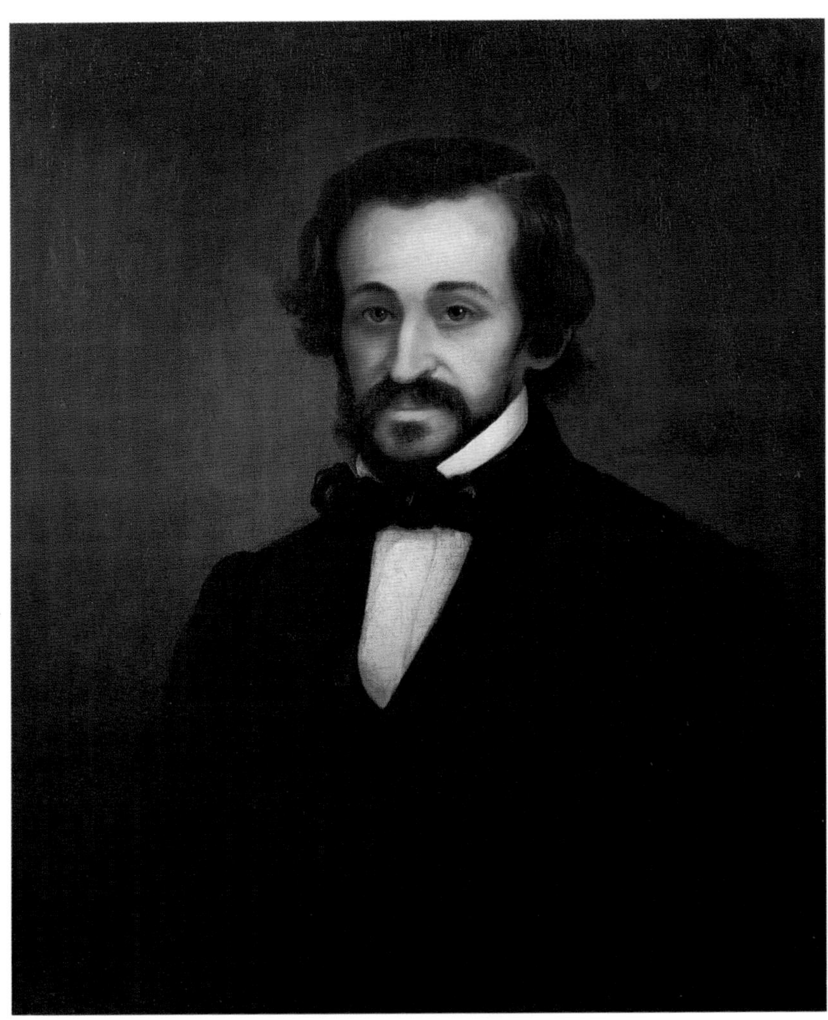

COLORPLATE 10

S. N. CARVALHO. *David Hays Solis.* c. 1850. Oil on canvas. 41 1/2 x 36 in. The National Museum of American Jewish History, Philadelphia. Gift of D. Hays Solis-Cohen and Helen Spiegel Sax.

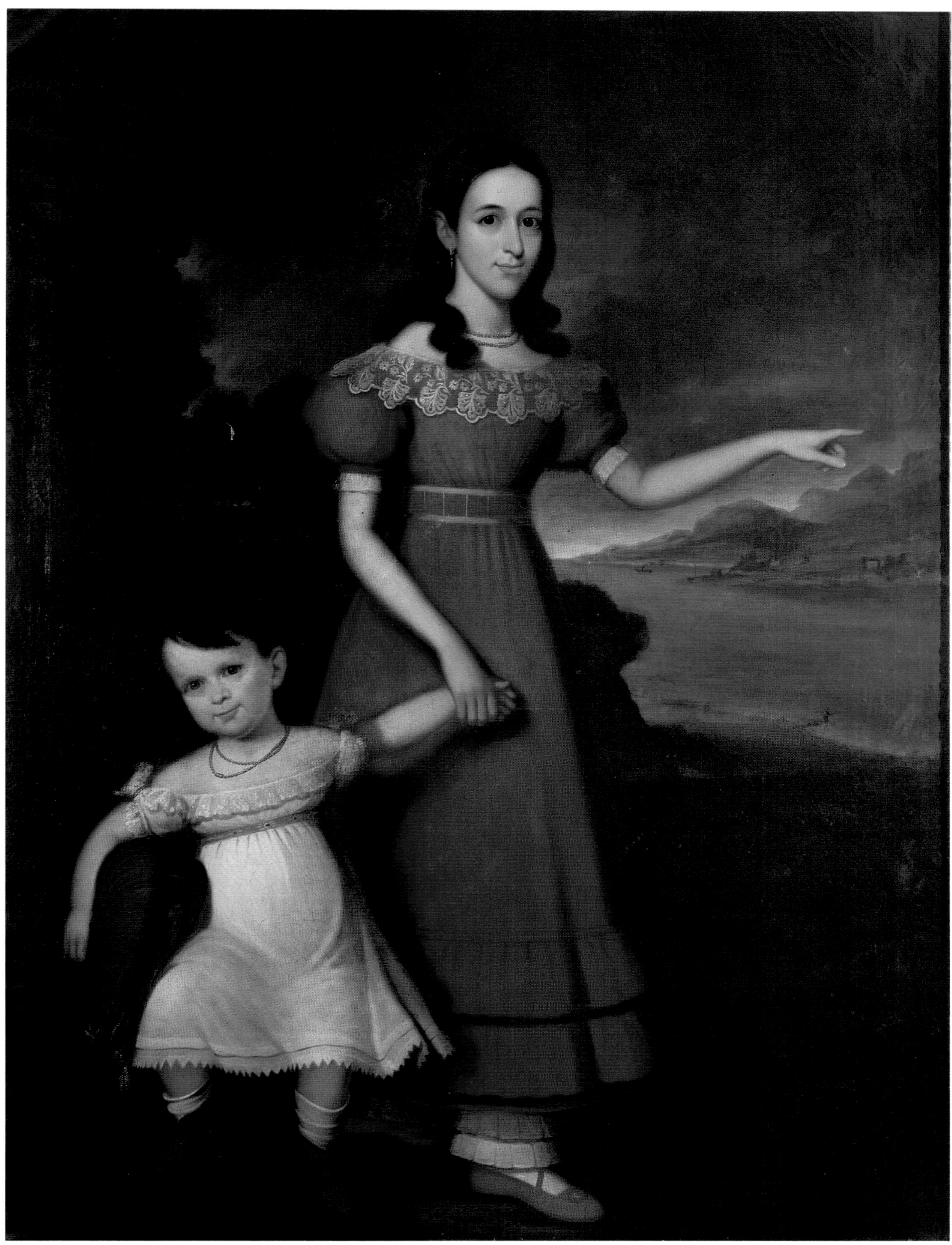

COLORPLATE 11

ARTIST UNKNOWN. *Adolphus Simeon Solomons and Mary Jane Solomons.* 1828. Oil on canvas. 54 x 44 in. American Jewish Historical Society, Waltham, Massachusetts. *Adolphus and Mary Jane were the children of John and Julia Levy Solomons. Adolphus later became a founder of New York's Mount Sinai Hospital, the American Red Cross, and the Jewish Theological Seminary of America.*

COLORPLATE 12

HENRY MOSLER. *Portrait of a Rabbi*. Cincinnati, Ohio. c. 1866. Oil on canvas. 41 1/2 x 31 1/2 in. Hebrew Union College Skirball Museum, Los Angeles.

Haym Salomon,

Authoriſed Broker to the Office of Finance,

&c. &c.

Has now to diſpoſe of, at his OFFICE *in Front-ſtreet, (where he tranſacts, in the moſt extenſive manner, every branch of buſineſs relative to his profeſſion)*

BANK STOCK.

THE *various ſorts of Certificates, Notes, &c. iſſued by the public,--Bills of Exchange upon France, Spain, Holland, England, Denmark, Hamburgh, &c. and the principal Weſt India Iſlands,--and can draw Bills upon moſt of the principal places on this Continent.*

He receives every ſpecies of Merchandiſe to ſell upon commiſſion; for which purpoſe he has provided proper ſtores---and procures freight for veſſels. --Any perſons reſiding in this or any of the United States, who will ſend their orders to his office, may depend on having their buſineſs tranſacted with as much fidelity, as if they were themſelves preſent.

He flatters himſelf his aſſiduity, punctuality, and extenſive connexions in his buſineſs as a Broker, are well eſtabliſhed in ſeveral parts of Europe, and the United States in particular.

All thoſe who ſhall pleaſe to favour him with their buſineſs may depend upon his utmoſt exertions for their intereſt, and part of the money advanced, if deſired.

He has alſo for SALE,

The Square bounded by Cheſnut, Walnut, Seventh and Eighth-ſtreets---A Lot upon the eaſt ſide of Seventh ſtreet, between Market and Arch ſtreets---The Slate Houſe (as it is called) and Lot, at the corner of Norris's Alley, in Second ſtreet, nearly oppoſite to the City Tavern---Three Houſes in Norris's Alley, adjoining the Slate Houſe lot--Two contiguous Lots at Kenſington, one of them being part of the Batchelor's Halllot---The Houſe on the north ſide of Cheſnut ſtreet, between Fourth and Fifth ſtreets, lately occupied by his Excellency the Preſident---The elegant Houſe and Lot in the ſame ſtreet in which the French Ambaſſador lives---One in Arch ſtreet---Two in Second ſtreet, one of them near the corner of Cheſnut ſtreet, in a good ſtand for buſineſs---One in Market ſtreet, an excellent ſtand.--A houſe in Market-ſtreet, and a lot in the ſame ſtreet--A three ſtory houſe and lot in Cheſnut-ſtreet---And two three ſtory houſes on the weſt ſide of Moravian alley. 9--

Haym Solomon, "Authorized Broker to the (U.S.) Office of Finance," Advertises Bank Stock, Financial Services, and Real Estate in Philadelphia's Independent Gazetteer, *February 28, 1784.*

Your Memorialist has upon this Event most irrecoverably lost all his Effects and Credits to the amount of Five or six thousand Pounds Sterling and left his distressed Wife and a Child of a Month old at New York waiting that they may soon have an Opportunity to come out from thence with empty hands.

In these Circumstances he most humbly prayeth to grant him any Employ in the way of his Business whereby he may be enabled to support himself and family—And Your Memorialist as in duty bound &c &c

Haym Solomon

Philadel. August 25th 1778.

Hiring a Religious Factotum—1776

On June 18, 1776, a contract was signed by Michael Gratz on behalf of the Jewish Society of Philadelphia and Abraham Levy and his son Ezekiel, engaging the latter to join his father in serving as shohet, *Torah reader, and Hebrew teacher of that city's as yet unnamed congregation. Momentous events were taking place in the city at that time. Eleven days earlier, a resolution had been introduced to the Continental Congress meeting there that the colonies declare themselves as "free and independent." Thomas Jefferson was drafting the Declaration to be adopted two weeks later. Even as the colonies were laboring to secure their future, the Jews of Philadelphia were doing the same, engaging the personnel that would secure theirs through observance, worship, and education. It is of interest to note that the house at the corner of Seventh and Market Streets, in which Jefferson inscribed the Declaration, would later serve as the place of business of the sons of Michael Gratz.*

Articles of Agreement made between Michael Gratz of the City of Philadelphia, for and in behalf of the Jewish Society held here, of the one part, and Abraham Levy and his son Ezekiel Levy of this province, of the other part.

Whereas, the said Michael Gratz for himself and the rest of the society hath engaged the said Ezekiel Levy to act in the capacity of a Jewish killer [ritual slaughterer], reader in the synagogue, and to teach six children the art of reading the Hebrew tongue for one year, for which offices he, the said Ezekiel Levy, is to receive an annual salary of £30, paid him quarterly by the acting *gaboy* [treasurer], for the time being with board and lodging,

And the said Ezekiel Levy doth hereby bind himself for and in consideration of £30 to act for the society in the capacities of killer [slaughterer], reader, etc., for the continuation of one year, to commence from the day of the date hereof; and that the said Ezekiel Levy cannot discharge himself after the expiration of the year, without giving one quarter's notice of his intention to the society,

For the true performance of which we, the said Abraham Levy and Ezekiel Levy, have signed our hands to these presents to observe the same in all its due forms, under the penal sum of thirty pounds Pennsylvania currency, for the use of the said society. Given this day, Philadelphia, the 18th June, 1776.

Abraham Levy
Ezekiel Levy

Omer Calendar. Wood and parchment. 1818. Congregation Mikveh Israel, Philadelphia. Courtesy of the National Museum of America Jewish History, Philadelphia. *Traditionally, the scroll inside is turned to count the 49 days between Passover and Shavuot, linking the celebration of the exodus out of Egypt to the holiday celebrating the giving of the Ten Commandments.*

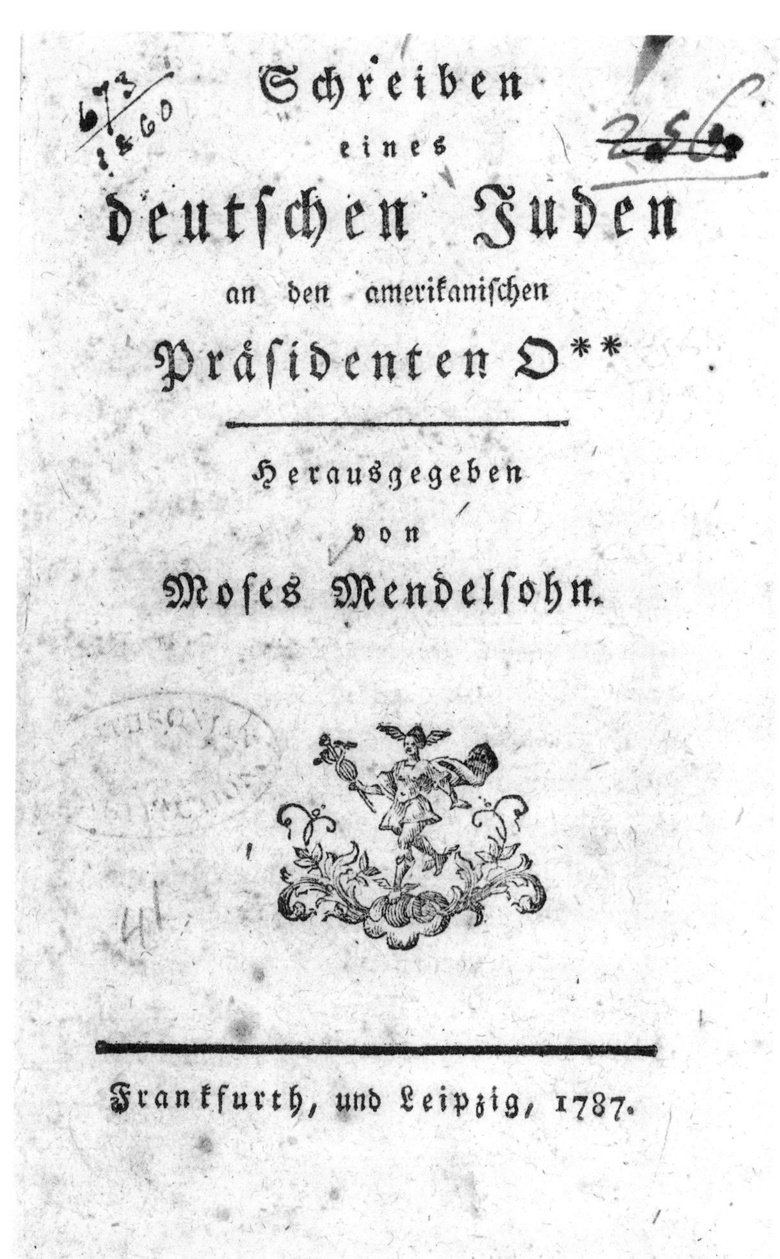
Schreiben
eines
deutschen Juden
an den amerikanischen
Präsidenten O**

Herausgegeben
von
Moses Mendelsohn.

Frankfurth, und Leipzig, 1787.

Title Page of a Letter from a German Jew to the American President. 1787. Frankfurt and Leipzig, Germany. Library of Congress, Rare Book and Special Collections Division.

Memorial from German Jews to the Continental Congress

How did European Jews conceive of the United States of America, the newest of nations? An article in the June 1783, issue of the Deutches Museum, *Leipzig and Berlin, reflects the perception of America as a vast dominion hungry for settlers and cultivation and a benign society tolerant to Jews. The author suggests that America welcome the hardworking German Jews, who in appreciation would make most loyal citizens.*

Many of us have learned with much satisfaction, from the peace made by the mighty American States with England, that wide tracts of land had been ceded to them which are as yet almost uninhabited. More than a century may elapse before the inhabitants of the thirteen united provinces will so increase as to populate and cultivate even the land which is already possessed by these provinces, in such a degree as a duchy in our country is populated and cultivated. Your religion cannot prohibit you from leaving these deserts to us for cultivation; besides, you have been for a long time tolerating Jews near you. Whether policy might forbid you that, I do not know. At all events you have the legislative power in your hands, and we ask no more than to be permitted to become subjects of these thirteen provinces, and would gladly contribute two-fold taxes for their benefit if we can only obtain permission to establish colonies at our own cost and to engage in agriculture, commerce, arts and sciences. Do we not believe in the same God as the Quakers do? Can our admission become more dangerous and precarious than that of the Quakers? Supposing that two thousand families of us would settle in a desert of America and convert it into a fertile land, will the old inhabitants of the provinces suffer by it? Let the conditions be stated to us, gracious President, under which you will admit us; we will then consider whether we can accept and keep them.

You would be astonished, most mighty President, at the perseverance of a German Jew, if you could witness it. The great, nay, perhaps the greatest part of them, spend almost their whole life on the highway in the pursuit of retail business, and the trader consumes for his own person nothing but a herring and a penny loaf; the nearest brook or well has to supply his drink. All that he earns besides he conscientiously lays aside in order to bring it home on Friday to supply food and clothing for wife and children. During these one and a half days when he enjoys somewhat better food and rests in the bosom of his family he forgets the wretched life which he is compelled to take up again on the next Sunday. And would you believe it, this wretch, who has to strain all his wits to convert a capital of fifty florins nearly as many times during the year, if he wants to live by it with his family, is nevertheless not infrequently envied by many Jews? . . . Granted that a Jew has at last become possessor of a capital that would suffice to support a family, still he will not be able to marry the woman he loves. Most of the time and in most of the German provinces he is obliged to acquire protection money for a sum which reduces his property to a half or one-third. But love overcomes this difficulty too. He strains his energies anew, again completes his capital and then seeks for permission to marry. If he obtains it, the experience just described is repeated, for he has to pay dearly for this permission, and the expenses of a wedding are not less among Jews than among Christians.

Here and there something has been done for us, but this may be likened to the taking off of two pounds from one who carries a burden of two tons.

Jonas Phillips
The Right of Jews to Hold Public Office

The Jew in Germany pleaded for tolerance. The American Jew looked beyond toleration. Over thirty years of residence in America emboldened Jonas Phillips, an immigrant from Germany and a merchant patriot of New York and Philadelphia, to demand that rights promised by the Declaration of Independence be guaranteed by the Constitution. He asks this "for myself, my children [of whom he had twenty-one] and posterity . . . and all the Israelites through the 13 United States of America." Three weeks before this letter was written, that clause of the Consti-

tution providing that no religious test shall ever be required as a qualification to any office or public trust under the United States had been unanimously adopted.

To His Excellency the president and the Honorable Members of the Convention assembled

Sires

With leave and submission I address myself To those in whom there is wisdom understanding and knowledge, they are the honourable personages appointed and Made overseers of a part of the terrestrial globe of the Earth, Namely the 13 united states of america in Convention Assembled, the Lord preserve them amen—

I the subscriber being one of the people called Jews of the City of Philadelphia, a people scattered & dispersed among all nations do behold with Concern that among the laws in the Constitution of Pennsylvania, there is a Clause Sect 10 to viz—I do believe in one God the Creatur and

Attributed to Charles Willson Peale. *Jonas Phillips.* Mid 18th century. Oil on canvas. 29 1/2 x24 1/2 in. American Jewish Historical Society, Waltham, Massachusetts. Bequest of Isaac Graff, Esq. *Jonas Phillips (1735–1803) of Philadelphia was a merchant, president of Congregation Mikveh Israel, and a Master Mason.*

governor of the universe the Rewarder of the good & the punisher of the wicked—and I do acknowledge the Scriptures of the old & New testiment to be given by divine inspiration—to swear & believe that the new testiment was given by divine inspiration is absolutely against the Religious principle of a Jew, and is against his Conscience to take any such oath—By the above law a Jew is deprived of holding any publick office or place of Government which is a Contridictory to the bill of Right Sect 2 viz

That all men have a natural & unalienable Right to worship almighty God according to the dictates of their own Conscience and understanding & that no man ought or of Right can be Compelled to attend any Religious Worship or Creed or support any place of worship or Maintain any minister contrary to or against his own free will and Consent, nor can any man who acknowledges the being of a God be Justly deprived or abridged of any Civil Right as a Citizen on account of his Religious sentiments or peculiar mode of Religious Worship, and that no authority can or ought to be vested in or assumed by any power whatever that shall in any case interfere or in any manner Controul the Right of Conscience in the free Exercise of Religious Worship.—

It is well known among all the Citizens of the 13 united states that the Jews have been true and faithfull whigs, & during the late Contest with England they have been foremost in aiding and assisting the states with their lifes & fortunes, they have supported the cause, have bravely fought and bled for liberty which they can not Enjoy.—

Therefore if the honourable Convention shall in their Wisdom think fit and alter the said oath & leave out the words to viz—and I do acknowledge the scripture of the new testiment to be given by divine inspiration, then the Israelites will think themself happy to live under a government where all Religious societys are on an Equal footing—I solicit this favour for myself my children & posterity, & for the benefit of all the Israelites through the 13 united states of America.

My prayers is unto the Lord. May the people of this states Rise up as a great & young lion, May they prevail against their Enemies, may the degrees of honour of his Excellency the president of the Convention George Washington, be Exhalted & Raise up. May Everyone speak of his glorious Exploits.

May God prolong his days among us in this land of Liberty—May he lead the armies against his Enemys as he has done hereuntofore. May God Extend peace unto the united states—May they get up to the highest Prosperitys—May God Extend peace to them & their seed after them so long as the sun & moon Endureth—and May the almight God of our father Abraham Isaac & Jacob indue this Noble Assembly with wisdom Judgment a unanimity in their Counsells & may they have the satisfaction to see that their present toil & labour for the wellfair of the united states may be approved of Through all the world & perticular by the united states of america, is the ardent prayer of Sires

Your Most devoted obed. Servant
Jonas Phillips
Philadelphia 24th Ellul 5547 or Sepr 7th 1787.

George Washington

Letter to the Hebrew Congregation of Newport, Rhode Island

On August 17, 1790, newly elected President George Washington honored Newport, Rhode Island, with a visit. The following morning, prior to his departure, deputations called upon the president to present to him expressions of affection and devotion. Moses Seixas, Warden of Kahal Kadosh Yeshuat Israel, the Hebrew congregation of Newport, presented him a letter stating that the "government erected by the majesty of the people" is "a government which to bigotry gives no sanction to persecution no assistance . . ." Mr. Seixas must have been enormously gratified that President Washington adopted this description (with but the slightest change) in his reply to the congregation.

Gentlemen:—While I received with much satisfaction your address replete with expressions of esteem, I rejoice in the opportunity of assuring you that I shall always retain grateful remembrance of the cordial welcome I experienced on my visit to Newport from all classes of citizens.

Gravestone of Rebecca Polock. c. 1764. Old Jewish Burial Ground of Touro Synagogue, Newport, Rhode Island. Photograph courtesy of Touro Synagogue, Newport. *The land for this burial ground was purchased in 1677, second oldest Jewish cemetery in the United States. New York's Jews established a cemetery shortly after their arrival in 1645.*

The reflection on the days of difficulty and danger which are past is rendered the more sweet from a consciousness that they are succeeded by days of uncommon prosperity and security.

If we have wisdom to make the best use of the advantages with which we are now favored, we cannot fail, under the just administration of a good government, to become a great and happy people.

The citizens of the United States of America have a right to applaud themselves for having given to mankind examples of an enlarged and liberal policy—a policy worthy of imitation. All possess alike liberty of conscience and immunities of citizenship.

It is now no more that toleration is spoken of as if it were the indulgence of one class of people that another enjoyed the exercise of their inherent natural rights, for, happily, the Government of the United States, which gives to bigotry no factions, to persecution no assistance, requires only that they who live under its protection should demean themselves as good citizens in giving it on all occasions their effectual support.

It would be inconsistent with the frankness of my character not to avow that I am pleased with your favorable opinion of my administration and fervent wishes for my felicity.

May the children of the stock of Abraham who dwell in this land continue to merit and enjoy the good will of the other inhabitants—while every one shall sit in safety under his own vine and fig tree and there shall be none to make him afraid.

May the father of all mercies scatter light, and not darkness, upon our paths, and make us all in our several vocations useful here, and in His own due time and way everlastingly happy.

G. WASHINGTON

REBECCA SAMUEL

Letter to Her Parents in Hamburg, Germany

Written in 1790, this may well be the quintessential American Jewish immigrant letter, touching, as it does, so many of the components which make up the immigrant experience: tearing up roots and the attempt to restrike them in new, strange, and often hostile soil; the heavy burden of worries remaining with those left behind; and for the Jewish grandparents—will our grandchildren whom we will never see know our names? Rebecca Samuel writes to reassure her parents of the "wonderful country" they have found, a land of peace and security; and so that their grandchildren will be cultured and loyal Jews, they are relocating to "a blessed community of three hundred Jews," Charleston, South Carolina.

Dear Parents:

I hope my letter will ease your mind. You can now be reassured and send me one of the family to Charleston, South Carolina. This is the place to which, with God's help, we will go after Passover. The whole reason why we are leaving this place is because of [lack of] *Yehudishkeit*.

Congregation Beth Elohim, Charleston, South Carolina. American Jewish Historical Society, Waltham, Massachusetts. *The exterior of this 1795 synagogue was destroyed by fire in 1838. When the synagogue was built, Charleston was the largest Jewish community in the United States.*

Dear parents, I know quite well you will not want me to bring up my children like Gentiles. Here they cannot become anything else. Jewishness is pushed aside here. There are here [in Petersburg] ten or twelve Jews, and they are not worthy of being called Jews. We have a shohet here who goes to market and buys terefah [nonkosher] meat and then brings it home. On Rosh Ha-Shanah and on Yom Kippur the people worshipped here without one sefer torah, and not one of them wore the tallit or the *arba kanfot*, except Hyman and my Sammy's godfather. The latter is an old man of sixty, a man from Holland. He has been in America for thirty years already; for twenty years he was in Charleston, and he has been living here for four years. He does not want to remain here any longer and will go with us to Charleston. In that place there is a blessed community of three hundred Jews.

You can believe me that I crave to see a synagogue to which I can go. The way we live now is no life at all. We do not know what the Sabbath and the holidays are. On the Sabbath all the Jewish shops are open; and they do business on that day as they do throughout the whole week. But ours we do not allow to open. With us there is still some Sabbath. You must believe me that in our house we all live as Jews as much as we can.

As for the Gentiles [?], we have nothing to complain about. For the sake of a livelihood we do not have to leave here. Nor do we have to leave because of debts. I believe ever since Hyman has grown up that he has not had it so good. You cannot know what a wonderful country this is for the common man. One can live here peacefully. Hyman made a clock that goes very accurately, just like the one in the Buchenstrasse in Hamburg. Now you can imagine what honors Hyman has been getting here. In all Virginia there is no clock [like this one], and Virginia is the greatest province in the whole of America, and America is the largest section of the world. Now you know what sort of a country this is. It is not too long since Virginia was discovered. It is a young country. And it is amazing to see the business they do in this little Petersburg. At times as many as a thousand hogsheads of tobacco arrive at one time and each hogshead contains 1,000 and sometimes 1,200 pounds of tobacco. The tobacco is shipped from here to the whole world.

When Judah [my brother?] comes here, he can become a watchmaker and a goldsmith, if he so desires. Here it is not like Germany where a watchmaker is not permitted to sell silverware. [The contrary is true in this country.] They do not know otherwise here. They expect a watchmaker to be a silversmith here. Hyman has more to do in making silverware than with watchmaking. He has a journeyman, a silversmith, a very good artisan, and he, Hyman, takes care of the watches. This work is well paid here, but in Charleston, it pays even better.

All the people who hear that we are leaving give us their blessings. They say that it is sinful that such blessed children should be brought up here in Petersburg. My children cannot learn anything here, nothing Jewish, nothing of general culture. My Schoene, God bless her, is already three years old. I think it is time that she should learn something, and she has a good head to learn. I have taught her the bedtime prayers and grace after meals in just two lessons. I believe that no one among the Jews here can do as well as she. And my Sammy [born in 1790], God bless him, is already beginning to talk.

I could write more. However, I do not have any more paper.

I remain, your devoted daughter and servant,
Rebecca, the wife of Hayyim, the son of Samuel the Levite

JEWS AS AMERICANS

Benjamin Nones
A Broadside on Being a Jew, a Republican, and Poor

French-born Benjamin Nones arrived from Bordeaux in 1777. Two years later, serving in the Revolutionary War, he was cited for "bravery and courage." After the war, as a leader of Philadelphia Jewry and of the Democrat-Republicans, his bravery and courage were put to test. A scurrilous, anonymous letter in the Federalist journal, the Gazette of the United States, *attacked him as a Jew, a Republican, and a pauper. To these accusations he pleaded "guilty" in a broadside distributed in Philadelphia and reprinted in the Republican newspaper, the* Aurora, *on August 13, 1800.*

I hope, if you take the liberty of inserting calumnies against individuals, for the amusement of your readers, you will have so much regard to justice, as to permit the injured through the same channel that conveyed the slander, to appeal to the public in self defence. I expect of you therefore, to insert this reply to your ironical reporter of the proceedings at the meeting of the republican citizens of Philadelphia, contained in your gazette of the fifth instant; so far as I am concerned in that statement. I am no enemy Mr. Wayne to wit; nor do I think the political parties have much right to complain, if they enable the public to laugh at each others expence, provided it be managed with the same degree of ingenuity, and some attention to truth and candour. But your reporter of the proceedings at that meeting is as destitute of truth and candour, as he is of ingenuity, and I think, I can shew, that the want of prudence of this Mr.

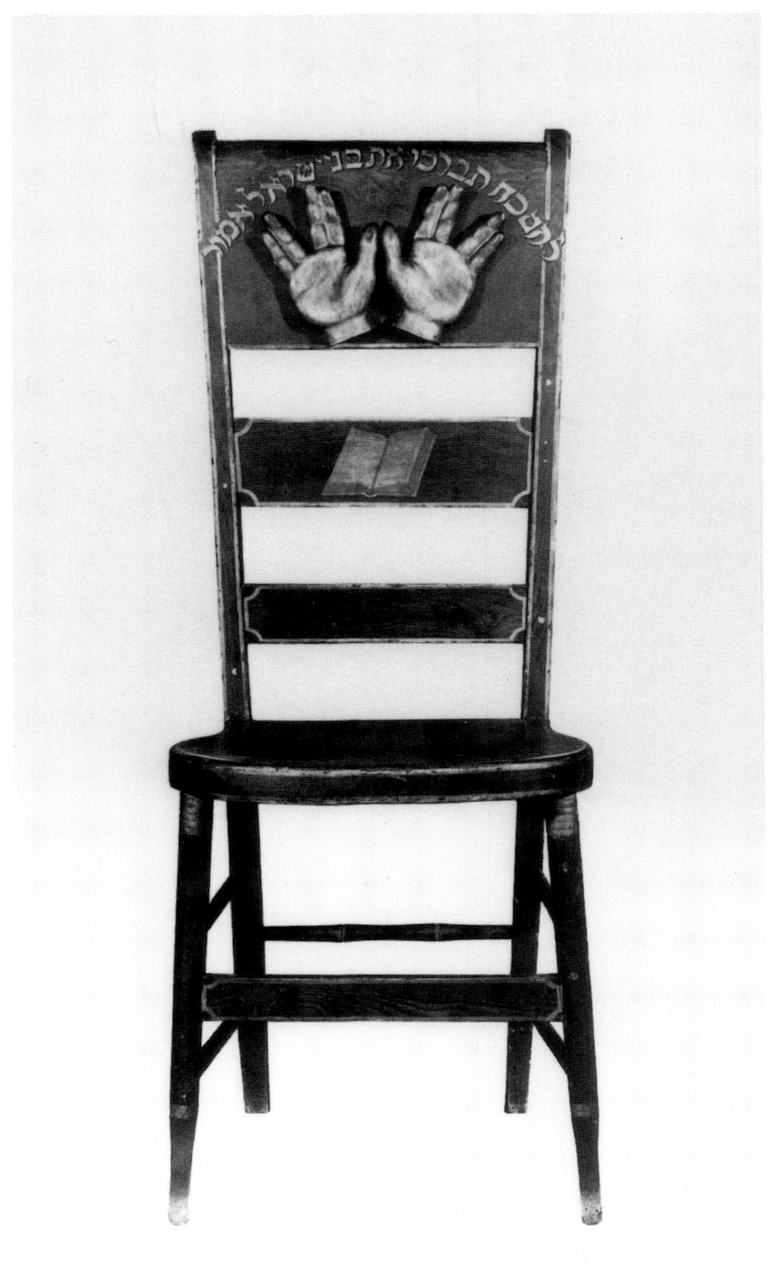

Ceremonial Chair. Walnut, painted, stained, and gilded. 52 1/2 x 19 1/2 x 18 in. Congregation Mikveh Israel, Philadelphia. Photograph courtesy of the National Museum of American Jewish History, Philadelphia. *Presented October 12th, 1816 by Moses Lopez, a new congregant, to Congregation Mikveh Israel, Philadelphia, this chair held the ewer and basin for the ritual washing of hands by the priests prior to their blessing of the congregation.*

Marplot, in his slander upon me, is equally glaring with his want of wit, his want of veracity, his want of decency, and his want of humanity.

I am accused of being a *Jew*, of being a *Republican*, and of being *Poor*.

I *am a Jew*. I glory in belonging to that persuasion, which even its opponents, whether Christian, or Mahomedan, allow to be of divine origin—of that persuasion on which christianity itself was originally founded, and must ultimately rest—which has preserved its faith secure and undefiled, for near three thousand years, whose votaries have never murdered each other in religious wars, or cherished the theological hatred so general, so unextinguishable among those who revile them. A persuasion, whose patient followers have endured for ages the pious cruelties of Pagans, and of Christians, and persevered in the unoffending practice of their rites and ceremonies, amidst poverties and privations; amidst pains, penalties, confiscations, banishments, tortures and deaths, beyond the example of any other sect, which the page of history has hitherto recorded.

To be of such a persuasion, is to me no disgrace; though I well understand the inhuman language of bigotted contempt, in which your reporter by attempting to make me ridiculous, as a Jew, has made himself detestable, whatever religious persuasion may be dishonored by his adherence.

But I am a Jew. I am so; and so were Abraham, and Isaac, and Moses and the prophets, and so too were Christ and his apostles; and I feel no disgrace in ranking with such society, however, it may be subject to the illiberal buffoonery of such men as your correspondents.

I am a *Republican!* Thank God I have not been so heedless and so ignorant of what has passed, and is now passing in the political world. I have not been so proud or so prejudiced as to renounce the cause for which I have *fought*, as an American, throughout the whole of the revolutionary war, in the militia of Charleston, and in Polafkey's [Pulaski's] legion, I fought in almost every action which took place in Carolina, and in the disastrous affair of Savannah, shared the hardships of that sanguinary day, and for three and twenty years I felt no disposition to change my political any more than my religious principles. And which in spite of the witling scribblers of aristocracy, I shall hold sacred until death, as not to feel the ardour of republicanism. Your correspondent, Mr. Wayne, cannot have known what it is to serve his country from principle in time of danger and difficulties, at the expence of his health and his peace, of his pocket and his person, as I have done; or he would not be as he is, a pert reviler of those who have so done. As I do not suspect you Mr. Wayne of being the author of the attack on me, I shall not enquire what share you or your relations had in establishing the liberties of your country. On religious grounds I am a republican. Kingly government was first conceded to the foolish complaints of the Jewish people as a punishment and a curse; and so it was to them until their dispersion, and so it has been to every nation who have been as foolishly tempted to submit to it. Great-Britain has a king, and her enemies need not wish her the sword, the pestilence, and the famine.

In the history of the Jews, are contained the earliest warnings against kingly government, as any one may know who has read the fable of Abimelick, or the exhortations of Samuel. But I do not recommend them to your reporter, Mr. Wayne; to him the language of truth and soberness would be unintelligible.

I am a Jew, and if for no other reason, for that reason am I a republican. Among the pious priesthood of church establishments, we are compassionately ranked with Turks, Infidels and Heretics. In the *monarchies* of Europe we are hunted from society, stigmatized as unworthy of common civility, thrust out as it were from the converse of men; objects of mockery and insult to froward children, the butts of vulgar wit and low buffoonery, such as your correspondent, Mr. Wayne, is not ashamed to set us an example of. Among the nations of Europe we are inhabitants every where; but citizens no where *unless in republics*. Here, in France, and in the Batavian republic alone, we are treated as men and as brethern. In republics we have *rights*, in monarchies we live but to experience *wrongs*. And why? because we and our forefathers have *not* sacrificed our principles to our interest, or earned an exemption from pain and poverty, by the dereliction of our religious duties, no wonder we are objects of derision to those, who have *no* principles, moral or religious, to guide their conduct.

How then can a Jew but be a Republican? in America particularly. Unfeeling and ungrateful would he be if he were callous to the glorious and benevolent cause of the difference between his situation in this land of freedom and among the proud and privileged law-givers of Europe.

But I am *poor;* I am so, my family also is large, but soberly and decently brought up. They have not been taught to revile a christian because his religion is not *so old* as theirs. They have not been taught to mock even at the errors of good intention, and conscientious belief. I trust they will always leave this to men as unlike themselves, as I hope I am to your scurrilous correspondent.

I know that to purse proud aristocracy poverty is a crime, but it may sometimes be accompanied with honesty even in a Jew: I was bankrupt some years ago; I obtained my certificate and was discharged from my debts. Having been more successful afterwards, I called my creditors together, and eight years afterwards, unsolicited, I discharged all my old debts. I offered interest which was refused by my creditors, and they gave me from under their hands without any solicitations of mine, as a testimonial of the fact, (to use their own language) "as a tribute due to my honor and honesty." This testimonial was signed by Messrs. J. Ball, W. Wister, George Meade, J. Philips, C. G. Paleske, J. Bispham, J. Cohen, Robert Smith, J. H. Leuffer, A. Kuhn, John Stille, S. Pleasants, M. Woodhouse, Thomas Harrison, M. Boraef, E. Laskey, and Thomas Allibone, &c.

I was discharged by the insolvent act; true, because having the amount of my debts owing to me from the French republic, the differences between France and America have prevented the recovery of what was due to me, in time to discharge what was due to my creditors. Hitherto it has been the fault of the political situation of the two countries that my creditors are not paid. When peace shall enable me to receive what I am entitled to, it will be my fault if they are not fully paid.

This is a long defence Mr. Wayne, but you have called it forth, and therefore, I hope you at least will not object to it. The public will now judge who is the proper object of ridicule and contempt, your facetious reporter, or

Your humble servant,
BENJAMIN NONES.
PHILADELPHIA, August 11, 1800.

HANNAH ADAMS
From *The History of the Jews*
The Jews of the United States of America

Hannah Adams, the first professional woman writer in America, published a two-volume History of the Jews *(1812), the first protracted history of the Jews in America. Adams solicited*

information from leading Jews about life in their respective communities, and these firsthand descriptions provide fascinating insights into the secular and religious life of Jews in the United States at that time.

There are about fifty families of Jews in New York, which, with a number of unmarried men, make from seventy to eighty subscribing members to the congregation

Rabbi Maximilian J. Michelbacher. c. 1850. The Cook Collection/The Valentine Museum, Richmond, Virginia. *The Rev. M.J. Michelbacher was the rabbi of Richmond, Virginia's Beth Ahabab Congregation in the Civil War era and an outspoken proponent of the Confederate cause.*

Sherith Israel, which is incorporated by an act of the legislature of the state, empowering all religious societies to hold their property by charter, under the direction of trustees chosen annually by the communicants of the society, according to certain rules prescribed in the act.

The trustees have the management of all the temporalities, as is customary in other societies. They have one synagogue established conformably to the customs and forms of prayer used among the Portuguese Jews in Europe. Their publick service is altogether in the Hebrew language, excepting in particular cases provided for in the constitution of the society. There were some Jewish families in the city when it was owned by the Dutch; but the documents which are among the archives of the congregation, do not extend farther back than about one hundred and fifty years.

Some of the Jews who settled in New York were of Portuguese, others of German extraction, besides Hollanders. There are also the descendants of those who arrived after New York became an English colony. The Jews had the right of soil under the Dutch government, and the English never attempted to deprive them of it; on the contrary, they granted letters patent to several Jewish families in the time of Queen Anne, who had arrived in London from France among the Huguenots, to settle in North America.

In Philadelphia there may be about thirty families of Jews. They have two synagogues, one for those who observe the Portuguese customs and forms of prayer, and the other for those who adhere to the German rules, customs, &c.; neither of them are incorporated. There may be about from eighty to one hundred men, in the whole state of Pennsylvania, who all occasionally attend the synagogues in Philadelphia.

There is in Charleston (South Carolina) a large society incorporated (with their laws). They have an elegant synagogue established on the Portuguese customs, &c. They also have different institutions with appropriate funds for benevolent and charitable purposes likewise incorporated.

* * *

The first emigration of the Jews to Charleston took place long before the revolution. The spirit of commerce can never be extinct in them; and their wealth increased with their numbers, which were augmented from time to time, both by marriages, and acquisitions from Europe. The present number of Jews may be estimated at about a thousand. Charleston alone contains about six or seven hundred individuals.

The present number of Hebrews in the city are chiefly Carolinians, the descendants of German, English, and Portuguese emigrants, who, from the civil and religious tyranny of Europe, sought an asylum in the western world. While the contest for freedom and independence was carried on, the majority distinguished themselves as brave soldiers and gallant defenders of the cause of a country which protected them. This spirit still actuates them; and as it is but natural that a people, who for ages have groaned under the impolitic barbarity and blind fanaticism of Europe, should inhale the breath of freedom with delight, the Hebrews in this city pay their hearty homage to the laws, which guarantee their rights, and consolidate them into the mass of a free people . . .

The Jews in Charleston enjoy equal literary advantages with the other members of the community. Most of the parents being rich, the prejudice is here despised, which confines the important object of education to the tenets of religion; and the Hebrews can boast of several men of talents and learning among them. Those Jewish children who are intended for professions, receive a handsome classical education. There is now in the city an academy, where the French, Italian, Latin, and Greek languages are taught, together with other branches of learning. The Rev. Cavalho, mentioned above, also teaches the Hebrew and Spanish languages.

The dress and habits of the Jews in Charleston do not distinguish them from the other citizens. Open and hospitable, as Carolinians generally are, they unite, with considerable industry and knowledge of commercial affairs, rather too much of that love of ease and pleasure, which climate, as well as national character, tends to nourish. Individuals, however, among those in this country, for their enterprize and judgment, have been entrusted with municipal offices; and one has held a seat with honour to himself and his constituents among the representatives of the state.

The institutions which the Jews have established in Charleston, are chiefly religious and charitable. They have built an elegant synagogue; and what strongly exhibits the liberality of the city is, that the Roman Catholick church is directly opposite to it. They have also societies for the relief of strangers, for attending the sick, and for administering the rites of humanity, and burial to the dying and the dead. The most modern institution is a society for the relief of orphans. The capital is already considerable, and it is yearly increasing. The children receive every advantage which is necessary to enable them to be well informed and honourable citizens of their country.

In Richmond (Virginia) there are about thirty Jewish families, who are now building a synagogue; but they are not as yet incorporated. The number of unmarried men is unknown, though there may be about an hundred scattered throughout the state, who are and will become members of the congregation. At Savannah in Georgia there are but few Jewish families, who assemble at times, and commune with each other in publick prayers. The United States is, perhaps, the only place where the Jews have not suffered persecution, but have, on the contrary, been encouraged and indulged in every right of citizens.

The Jews in all the United States, except Massachusetts, are eligible to offices of trust and honour; and some of them in the southern states are in office. They are generally commercial men, and a number of them considerable merchants.

Penina Moise

"To Persecuted Foreigners"

Born in Charleston, South Carolina in 1797, Penina Moise lived all eighty-three years of her life in that cultured, cosmopolitan city. Self-taught, she became a widely published author of poems and sketches. Hers was a deep love for her God and her people. Of the 210 religious poems in Hymns Written for the Use of Hebrew Congregations *(1856), fully 180 are signed "P.M." Her one book of poems,* Fancy's Sketch Book, *contains this poetic invitation written in 1820.*

Fly from the soil whose desolating creed,
Outraging faith, makes human victims bleed.
Welcome! where every Muse has reared a shrine,
The aspect of wild Freedom to refine.

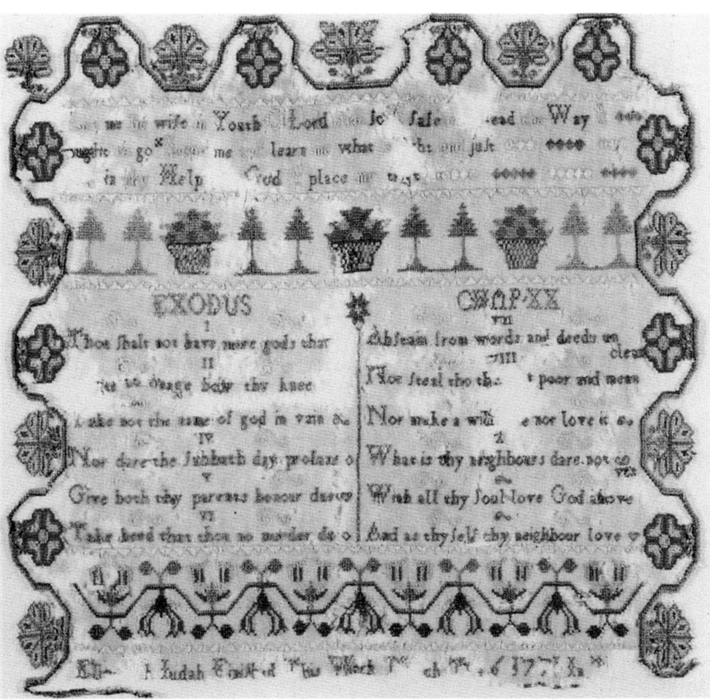

COLORPLATE 13

Sampler. Québec. 1771. Gershon and Rebecca Fenster Museum of Jewish Art, Tulsa. *This sampler was made by Elizabeth Judah when she was eight years old. It depicts the Ten Commandments.*

COLORPLATE 14

Sampler. United States. 1813. Cotton embroidery on linen, signed SGM. 19 3/4 x 17 1/8 in. National Museum of American Jewish History, Philadelphia. Gift of Mr. and Mrs. Lawrence Blumenthal. Conservation, gift of Mrs. Louis Foster. *This work is distinctive as one of the earliest known American-made samplers to incorporate Hebrew characters.*

COLORPLATE 15

Quilt. Frederick County, Maryland. 1846. Cotton. 93 x 93 in. Collection of Joanna S. Rose, New York. *This quilt was made as a wedding gift for a Jewish bride. In one square, slightly lower than center, is a yellow* huppah *and under it a table with a pair of candlesticks with candles. Between them is the* Kiddush *cup. The pineapple symbolizes hospitality and is a motif commonly seen in colonial American art and architecture.*

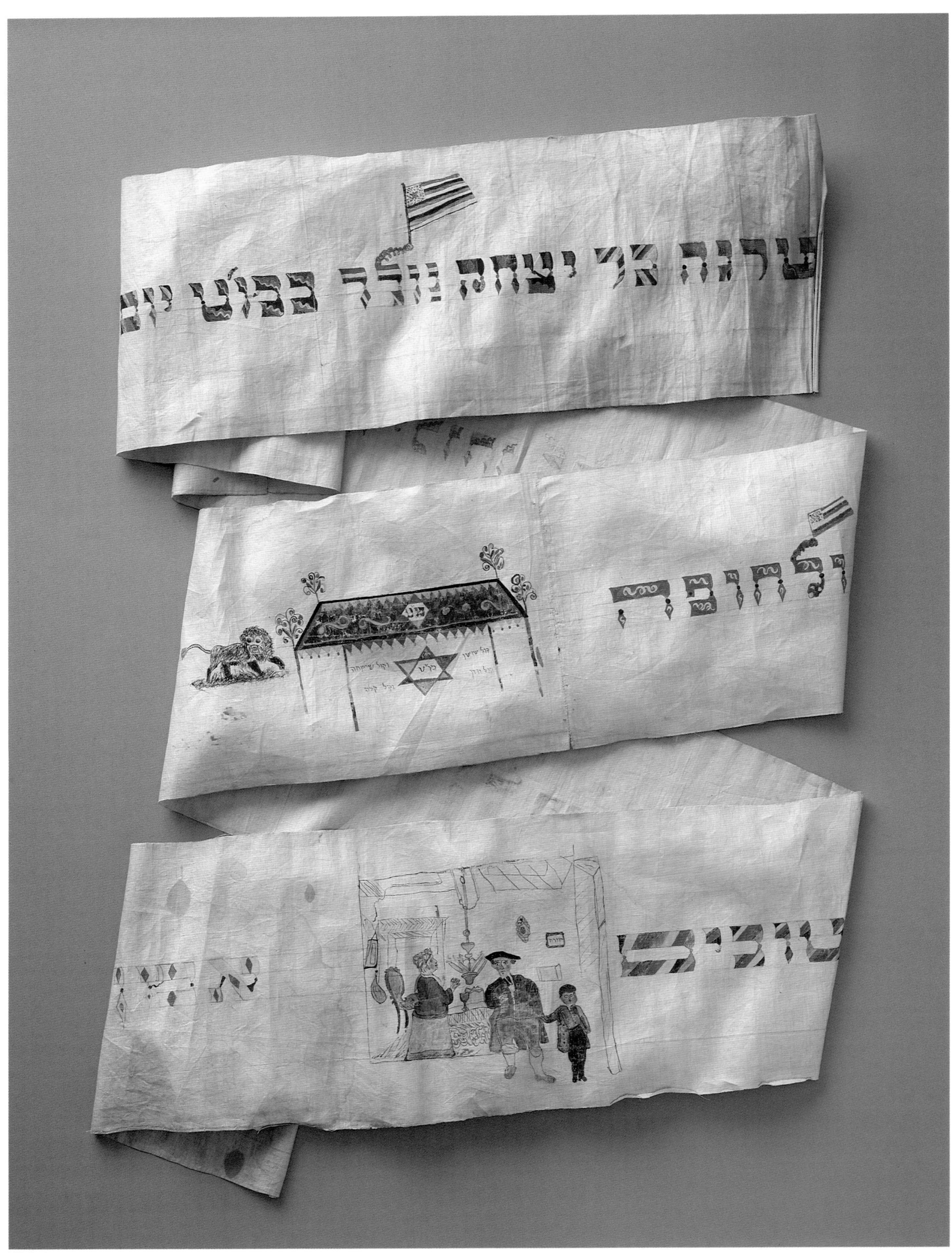

COLORPLATE 16

Torah Binder (Wimpel) of Felix Half. Athens, Ohio. 1869. Undyed linen, polychrome pigments. 8 1/2 x 44 in. Courtesy of Nancy Frank. *A* wimpel *is used to tie the two sides of a Torah scroll together. Made of the swaddling clothes used at a circumcision,* wimpels *were embroidered or painted with the child's name, date of birth, and a prayer that his life be marked by Torah study, marriage, and good deeds.*

COLORPLATE 17

Torah Binder (Wimpel). Trinidad, Colorado. 1889. Undyed linen, polychrome pigments. 9 1/2 x 141 in. Hebrew Union College Skirball Museum, Los Angeles. Gift of Gilbert Sanders.

COLORPLATE 18

Torah Binder (Wimpel). 1929. Undyed cotton, polychrome pigments. 8 1/2 x 122 1/2 in. Private collection. *Symbols typical of life in the United States were used to decorate this Torah binder. Torah binders were donated to the synagogue the first time the child was taken there.*

COLORPLATE 19

Torah Binder (Wimpel). New York. 1869. Undyed linen, painted. 8 1/2 x 140 in. The Jewish Museum, New York. Gift of Colonel George Feigel through Augusta and Harry Berger.

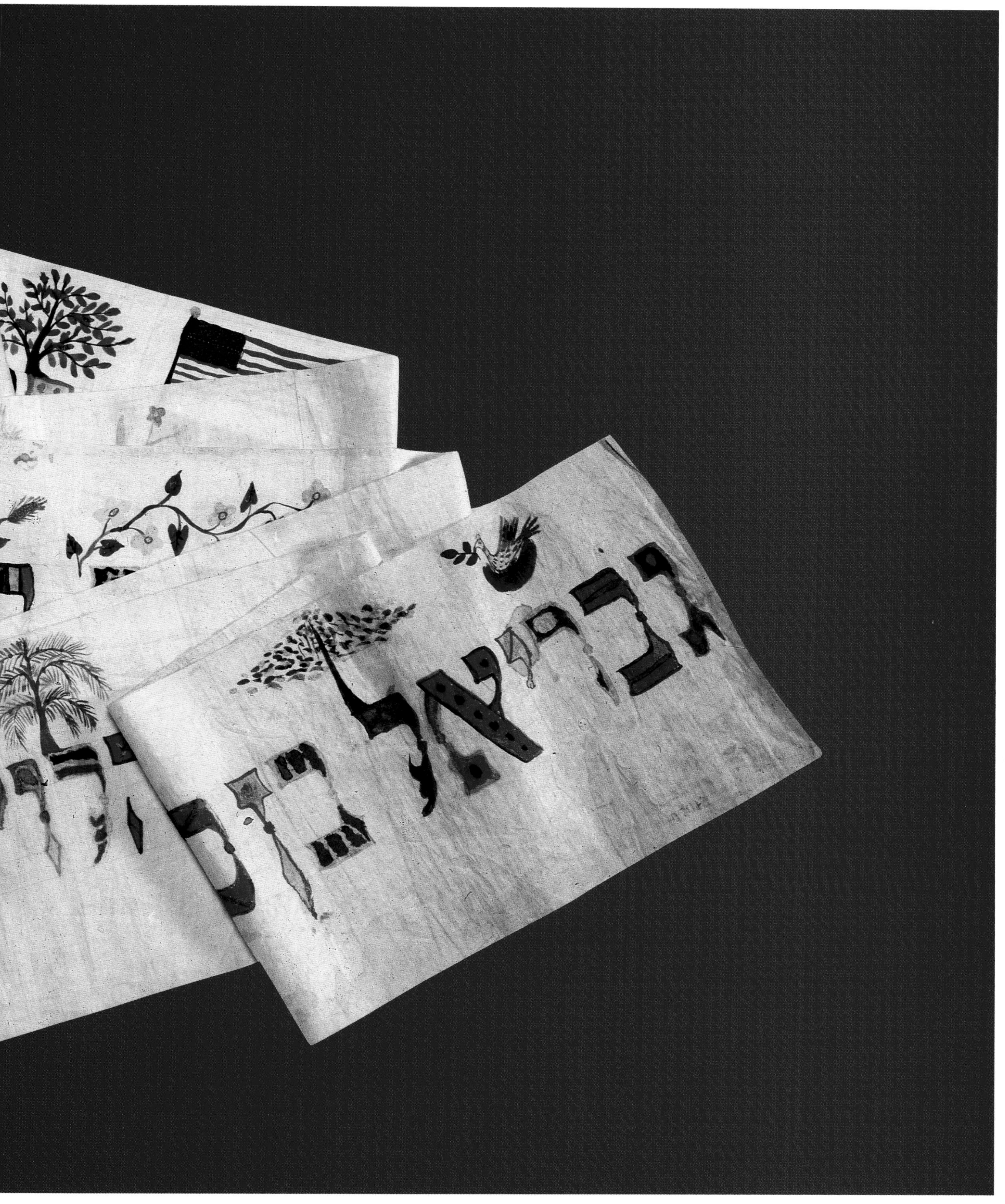

COLORPLATE 20

Assorted Tfillin Bags. Turn of the century. Collection of Abraham and Deborah Karp. *These bags were found in* genizot, *storage spaces for holy objects no longer usable, awaiting burial in consecrated ground.*

COLORPLATE 21

Assorted Tfillin Bags. Turn of the century. Collection of Abraham and Deborah Karp.

COLORPLATE 22

Challah Cover. 1852. Green brocade silk, metallic embroidery, red velvet appliqué; border decorated with looped braid. 20 x 19 in. Judah L. Magnes Museum, Berkeley, California. Purchasd in 1977. *This challah cover has as its central motif a golden eagle, wings outstretched over a red velvet drape with thirteen stars. There are two Hebrew inscriptions: "Gedalia the Son of Simion Halev, called Ullman" above the eagle and "See that the Lord has given you the Sabbath (1852)" inside the red drape.* "E Pluribus Unum" *appears under the eagle.*

COLORPLATE 23

MYER MYERS. *Torah Finials (Rimmonim).* Designed in 1772. Embossed and chased silver, partial gilt with cast ornaments. Congregation Mikveh Israel, Philadelphia. *The Hebrew word* rimmonim *(pomegranates) refers to the decorative form of the finials, and by analogy, to the seeds of learning of the Torah, numerous as the seeds of a pomegranate. Myers, a prominent colonial silversmith, fashioned* rimmonim *for the three earliest Jewish congregations in the United States: Shearith Israel, New York; Yeshuat Israel, Newport; and Mikveh Israel, Philadelphia.*

COLORPLATE 24

Torah Breastplate. Cincinnati, Ohio. 1889. Silver, cast, chased. 10 1/2 x 6 1/4 in. Hebrew Union College Skirball Museum, Los Angeles. *This Torah shield was presented to Isaac Mayer Wise on the occasion of his eightieth birthday by his students.*

COLORPLATE 25 *(opposite)*

POSEN. *Schiff Torah Shield (Tas).* 1890. Gilded silver, embossed and chased; castings, enameling, lapis, semiprecious stones, niello. 15 3/4 x 11 3/8 in. Courtesy of Congregation Emanu-El of the City of New York. Gift of Jacob H. and Therese Schiff, 1890. (From *A Temple Treasury: The Judaica Collection of Congregation Emanu-El of the City of New York* by Cissy Grossman).

כתר תורה
אנכי ה
לא יהיה
לא תשא
זכור את
כבד את
לא תרצח
לא תנאף
לא תגנב
לא תענה
לא תחמד

COLORPLATE 26

Bloomingdale Torah Crowns. New York. 1891. Gilded brass, cutout work, appliqué, colored stones. Heights: 12 in., 21 in., 20 1/2 in. Courtesy of Congregation Emanu-El of the City of New York. Gift of Lyman G. Bloomingdale in memory of his brother, Samuel. (From *A Temple Treasury: The Judaica Collection of Congregation Emanu-El of the City of New York* by Cissy Grossman).

COLORPLATE 27

BERNARD BERNSTEIN. *Torah Crown.* 1963. Silver, partially gold-plated; velvet. Height: 10 in.; diameter: 10 in. Courtesy of Bernard Bernstein. *The inscription on the base reads: "And this is the law which Moses set before the children of Israel" (Deuteronomy 4:44) and on the crown-shaped finial "Render honor unto the Law." The images represent the twelve tribes of Israel. The cone-shaped inner section with radiating ribs and finial suggests the shape of the "tent of meeting" in the wilderness.*

COLORPLATE 28

NISSIM HIZME. *Liberty Bell Rimmonim.* 1963. Sterling silver. Courtesy of Congregation Shearith Israel, New York. *These were commissioned by the Shearith Israel League in 1963 and presented on his seventieth birthday to Edgar J. Nathan, Jr. who was then president of the congregation and a descendant of the founders. The Hebrew inscription is taken from Leviticus 25:9: "Proclaim Liberty throughout the Land unto all the inhabitants thereof" which also appears on the Liberty Bell in Philadelphia.*

COLORPLATE 29 *(opposite)*

MASTER E.R. OR F.R. *Rimmonim.* c. 1800. British Colonies, probably North America or the West Indies. Silver, cast, cut out; partially gilt, engraved, and punched; gold bells. 18 x 6 in. The Jewish Museum, New York. Gift of Jacobo Furman in memory of his wife Asea.

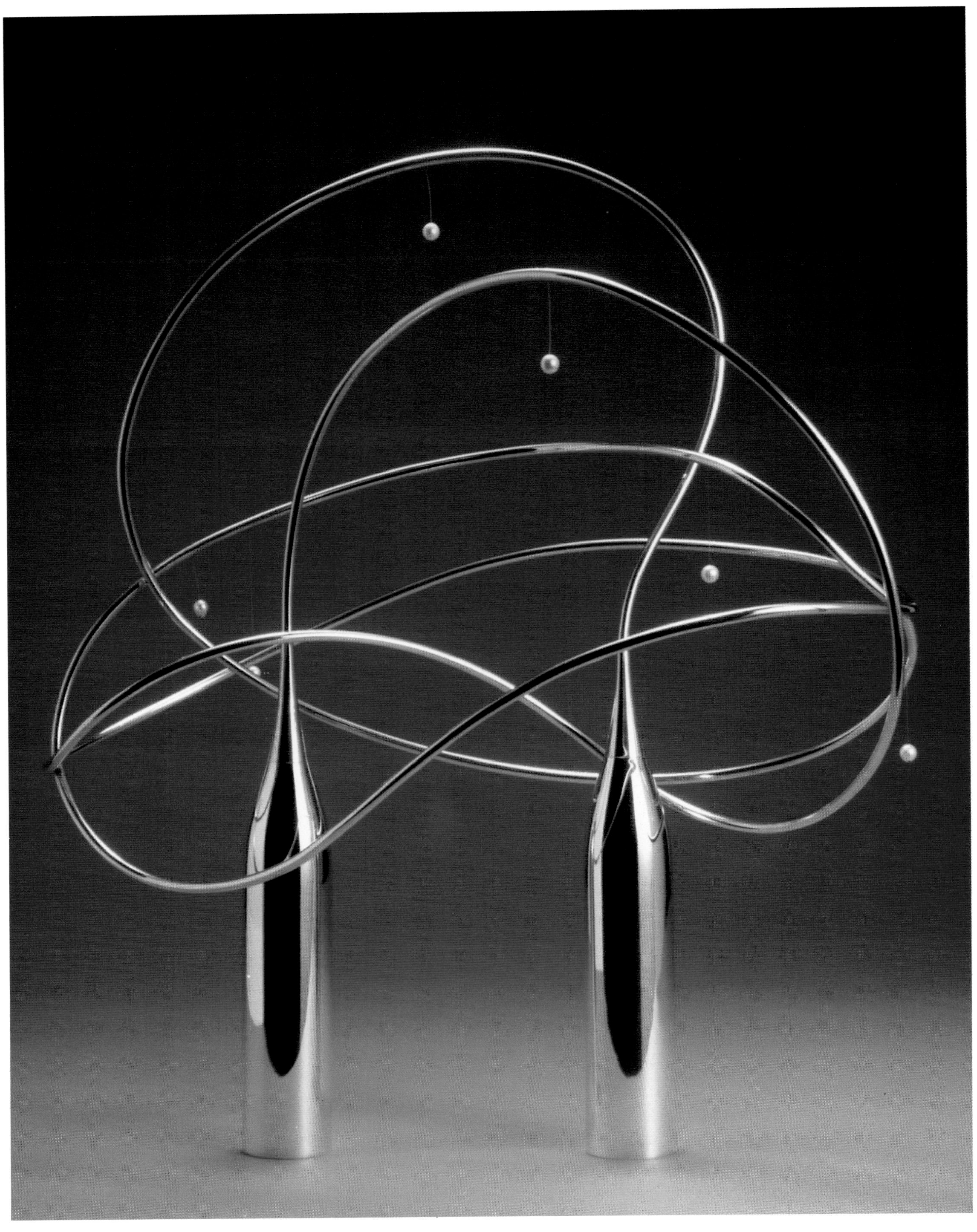

COLORPLATE 30

MOSHE ZABARI. *Torah Crown*. New York. 1969. Silver, raised and forged, pearls. 13 1/2 x 15 in. The Jewish Museum, New York. Gift of the Albert A. List Family.

Solomon N. Carvalho. *Interior of Congregation Beth Elohim, Charleston, South Carolina.* c. 1838. Drawing. American Jewish Historical Society, Waltham, Massachusetts. *The hymnal used in this synagogue was largely the work of the American Jewish woman poet, Penina Moise.*

Upon *our* Chieftain's brow no crown appears;
No gems are mingled with his silver hairs,
Enough that Laurels bloom amid its snows,
Enriched with these, the sage all else foregoes.

If thou art one of that oppressed race,
Whose pilgrimage from Palestine we trace,
Brave the Atlantic—Hope's broad anchor weigh,
A Western Sun will gild your future day.

Zeal is not blind in this our temp'rate soil;
She has no scourge to make the soul recoil.
Her darkness vanished when our stars did flash;
Her red arm grasped by Reason dropt the lash.

Our Union, Liberty and Peace imparts,
Stampt on our standards, graven on our hearts,
The first, from crush'd Ambition's ruin rose,
The last, on Victory's field spontaneous grows.

Rise, then, elastic from Oppression's tread,
Come and repose on Plenty's flowery bed.
Oh! not as Strangers shall your welcome be,
Come to the homes and bosoms of the free!

Israel Zangwill

"Noah's Ark"

In 1825 Mordecai Manuel Noah conceived the idea of founding a Jewish state on Grand Island in the Niagara River near Buffalo, New York. This state was to be part of the federal union. He outlined the concept in a proclamation published in newspapers throughout America and Europe. Israel Zangwill, the Anglo-Jewish novelist, lectured extensively in Europe and America. In this fictional piece he describes the reaction of European Jews to Noah's proposed project.

There seemed an unwonted stir in the "Judengasse" when Peloni returned to it. Was there another riot threatening? he thought, as he passed along the narrow street of three-storied frame houses, most of them gabled, and all marked by peculiar signs and figures—the Bear or the Lion or the Garlic or the Red Shield (*Rothschild*)!

Outside the synagogue loitered a crowd, and as he drew near he perceived that there was a long Proclamation in a couple of folio sheets nailed on the door. It was doubtless this which was being discussed by the little groups he had already noted. About the synagogue door the throng was so thick that he could not get near enough to read it himself. But fortunately some one was engaged in reading it aloud for the benefit of those on the outskirts.

" 'Wherefore I, Mordecai Manuel Noah, Citizen of the United States of America, late Consul of said States to the City and Kingdom of Tunis, High Sheriff of New York, Counsellor-at-Law, and by the Grace of God Governor and Judge of Israel, have issued this my proclamation.' "

A derisive laugh from a dwarfish figure in the crowd interrupted the reading. "Father Noah come to life again!" It was the *possemacher*, or wedding-jester, who was not sparing of his wit, even when not professionally engaged.

"A foreigner—an American!" sneered a more serious voice. "Who made him ruler in Israel?"

"That's what the wicked Israelite asked Moses!" cried Peloni, curiously excited.

"*Nun, nun!* Go on!" cried others.

" 'Announcing to the Jews throughout the world, that an asylum is prepared and hereby offered to them, where they can enjoy that Peace, Comfort, and Happiness which have been denied them through the intolerance and misgovernment of former ages. An asylum in a free and powerful country, where ample protection is secured to their persons, their property, and religious rights; an asylum in a country remarkable for its vast resources, the richness of its soil, and the salubrity of its climate; where industry is encouraged, education promoted, and good faith rewarded. "A land of Milk and Honey," where Israel may repose in Peace, under his "Vine and Fig tree," and where our People may so familiarize themselves with the science of government and the lights of learning and civilization, as may qualify them for that great and final Restoration to their ancient heritage, which the times so powerfully indicate.' "

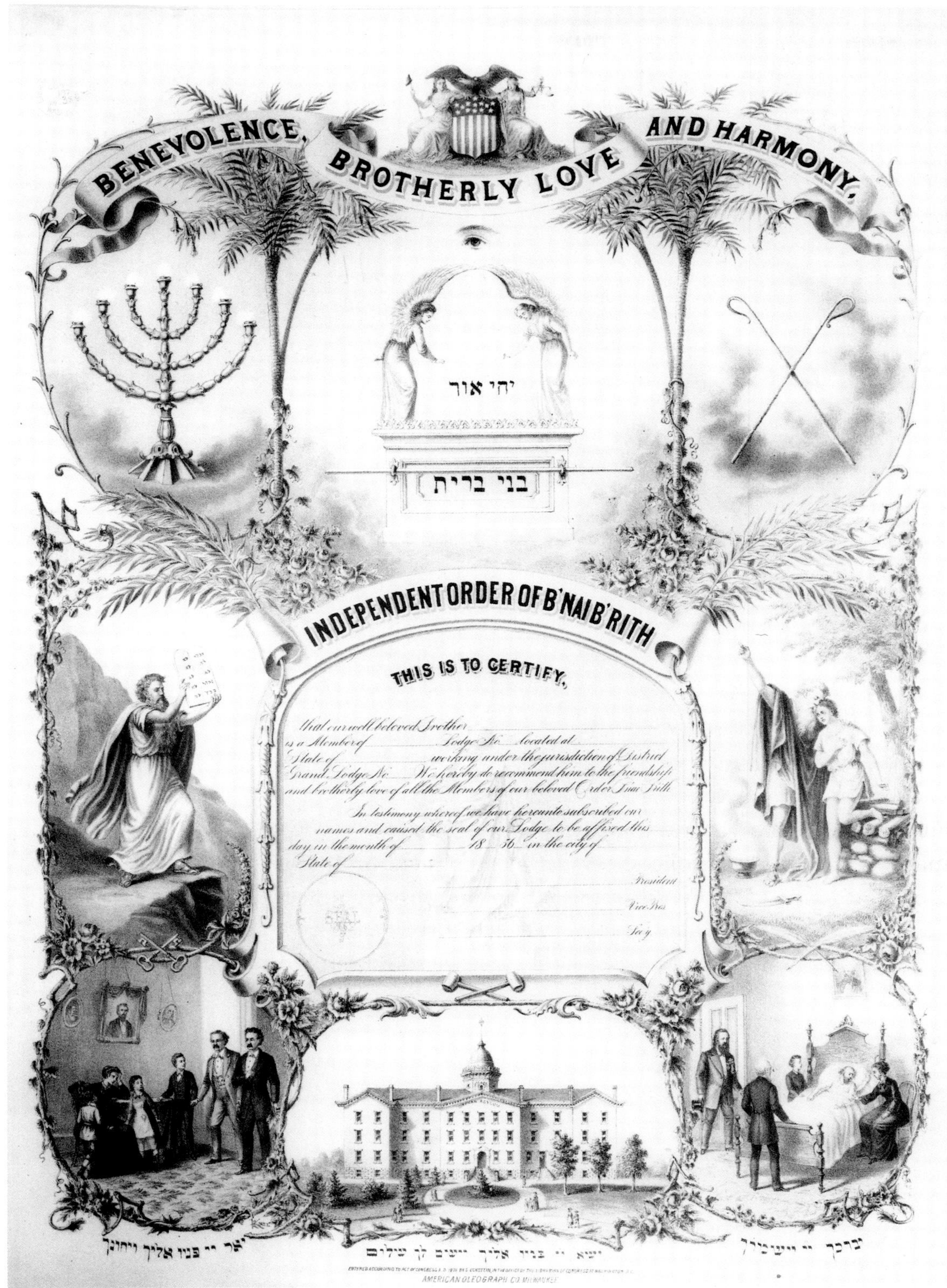

Independent Order of B'nai B'rith Certificate. Milwaukee. 1876. Library of Congress. *The fraternal order of B'nai B'rith, founded in 1843, was the first in the United States and exists to the present day.*

The crowd had grown attentive. Peloni's face was pale as death. What was this great thing, fallen so unexpectedly from the impassive heaven his hopelessness had challenged?

But the *possemacher* captured the moment. "Father Noah's drunk again!"

A great laugh shook the crowd. But Peloni dug his nails into his palms. "Read on! Read on!" he cried hoarsely.

" 'The Place of Refuge is in the State of New York, the largest in the American Union, and the spot to which I invite my beloved People from the whole world is called Grand Island.' "

Peloni drew a deep breath. His face had now changed to the other extreme and was flushed with excitement.

"Noah's Ark!" shot the *possemacher* dryly, and had his audience swaying hysterically.

"For God's sake, bretheren!" cried Peloni. "This is no joke. Have you forgotten already that here we are only animals?"

"And they went in two by two," said the *possemacher*, "the clean beasts, and the unclean beasts!"

"Hush, hush, let us hear!" from some of the crowd.

" 'Here I am resolved to lay the foundation of a State, named Ararat.' "

"Ah! what did I say?" the exultant *possemacher* shrieked at Peloni.

"Ha! ha! ha!" laughed the crowd. "Noah's Ark resting on Ararat!" The dullest saw that.

Peloni was taken aback for a moment.

"But why should not the place of Israel's Ark of Refuge be named Ararat?" he asked of his neighbors.

"If only his name wasn't Noah!" they answered.

"That makes it even more appropriate," he murmured.

But "Noah's Ark" was the nickname that kills. Though the reader continued, it was only to an audience exhilarated by a sense of Arabian Nights fantasy. But the elaborate description of the grandeurs of this Grand Island, and the eloquent passages about the Century of Right, and the ancient Oracles, restored Peloni's enthusiasm to fever heat.

"It is too long," said the reader, wearying at last.

Peloni rushed forward and took up the task. The first sentence exalted him still further.

" 'In God's name I revive, renew, and re-establish the government of the Jewish Nation, under the auspices and protection of the Constitution and the Laws of the United States, confirming and perpetuating all our Rights and Privileges, our Name, our Rank, and our Power among the nations of the Earth, as they existed and were recognized under the government of the Judges of Israel.' " Peloni's voice shook with fervor. As he began the next sentence, " 'It is my will,' " he stretched out his hand with an involuntary regal gesture. The spirit of Noah was entering into him, and he felt him, and he felt almost as if it was he who was re-creating the Jewish nation—"'It is my will that a Census of the Jews throughout the world be taken, that those who are well treated and wish to remain in their respective countries shall aid those who wish to go; that those who are in military service shall until further orders remain true and loyal to their rulers.

" 'I command' "—Peloni read the words with expansive magnificence, his poet's soul vibrating to that other royal dreamer's across the great Atlantic—" 'that a strict Neutrality be maintained in the pending war betwixt Greece and Turkey.

" 'I abolish forever'"—Peloni's hand swept the air—" 'Polygamy among the Jews.' "

"But where have we polygamy?" interrupted the *possemacher.*

" 'As it is still practiced in Africa and Asia,' " read on Peloni severely.

"I'm off at once for Africa and Asia!" cried the marriage-jester, pretending to run. "Good business for me there."

"You'll find better business in America," said Peloni scathingly. "For do not all our Austrian young men fly thither to marry, seeing that at home only the eldest son may found a family? A pretty fatherland indeed to be a citizen of—a step-fatherland. Listen, on the contrary, to the noble tolerance of the Jew. 'Christians are freely invited.' "

"Ah! Do you know who'll go?" broke in a narrow-faced zealot. "The missionaries."

Peloni continued hastily: " 'Ararat is open, too, to the Karaites and the Samaritans. The Black Jews of India and Africa shall be welcome; our brethren in Cochin-China and the sect on the coast of Malabar; all are welcome.' "

"Ha! ha! ha!" laughed a burly Jew. "So we're to live with the blacks. Enough of this joke!"

But Peloni went on solemnly: " 'A Capitation-tax on every Jew of Three Silver Shekels per annum———' "

"Ah, now we have got to it!" and a great roar broke from the crowd. "Not a bad *geschaft*, eh?" and they winked. "He is no fool, this Noah."

Peloni's blood boiled. "Do you believe everybody is like yourselves?" he cried. "Listen!"

" 'I do appoint the first day of next Adar for a Thanksgiving Day to the God of Israel, for His divine protection and the fulfilment of His promises to the House of Israel. I recommend Peace and Union among ourselves, Charity and Good-Will to all, Toleration and Liberality toward our Brethren of all Religions———' "

"Didn't I say a missionary in disguise?" murmured the zealot.

Peloni ended, with tremulous emotion: " 'I humbly entreat to be remembered in your prayers, and earnestly do I enjoin you to "keep the charge of the Holy God," to walk in His ways, to keep His Statutes and His commandments and His judgments and Testimonies, as written in the Laws of Moses; "that thou mayest prosper in all thou doest and whithersoever thou turnest thyself."

" 'Given under our hand and seal in the State of New York, on the 2nd of Ab 5586 in the Fiftieth Year of American Independence.' "

Peloni's efforts to organize a company of pilgrims to the New Jerusalem brought him only heart-ache. The very rabbi who had good-naturedly consented to circulate the fantastic foreigner's invitation, tapped his forehead significantly: "A visionary! of good intentions, doubtless, but still—a visionary. Besides, according to our dogmas, God alone knows the epoch of the Israelitish restoration; He alone will make it known to the whole universe, by signs entirely unequivocal; and every attempt on our part to reassemble with any political, national design, is forbidden as an act of high treason against the Divine Majesty. Mr. Noah has doubtless forgotten that the Israelities, faithful to the principles of their belief, are too much attached to the countries where they dwell, and devoted to the governments under which they enjoy liberty and protection, not to treat as a mere jest the chimerical consulate of a pseudo-restorer."

"Noah's a madman, and you're an infant," Peloni's friends told him.

"Since the destruction of the Temple," he quoted in retort, "the gift of prophecy has been confined to children and fools."

"You are giving up a decent livelihood," they warned him. "You are throwing it into the Atlantic."

" 'Cast thy bread upon the waters and it shall return to thee after many days.' "

"But in the meantime?"

" 'Man doth not live by bread alone.' "

"As you please. But don't ask *us* to throw up our comfortable home here."

"Comfortable home!" and Peloni grew almost apoplectic as he reminded them of their miseries.

"Persecution?" They shrugged their shoulders. "It comes only now and again, like a snow-storm, and we crawl through it."

"That's just it—the lack of manliness—the poisoned atmosphere!"

"Bah! The *goyim* refuse us equal right because they know we're their superiors. Let us not jump from the frying-pan into the fire."

So Peloni sailed for New York alone.

Mordecai M. Noah

From *Discourse on the Restoration of the Jews* "Liberty and Independence of the Jewish Nation"

Newspaper editor, playwright, politician, U.S. consul to Tunis, sheriff and port inspector of New York City, justice of the court of general sessions, and ardent advocate, Mordecai Manuel Noah was the most visible, colorful, and prominent American Jew in the first half of the nineteenth century. History will remember him best as America's first Zionist. On October 28, 1844, Noah proposed the founding of a Jewish nation before a gathering of leading New York citizens. The address aroused so much interest that it was repeated on December 2 and soon after was published as a pamphlet by Harper & Brothers.

I have long desired, my friends and countrymen, for an opportunity to appear before you in behalf of a venerable people, whose history, whose sufferings, and whose extraordinary destiny have, for a period of 4000 years, filled the world with awe and astonishment: a people at once the most favoured and the most neglected, the most beloved, and yet the most persecuted; a people under whose salutary laws all the civilized nations of the earth now repose; a people whose origin may date from the cradle of creation, and who are likely to be preserved to the last moment of recorded time . . .

Political events in Syria, Egypt, Turkey, and Russia, indicate the approach of great and important revolutions, which may facilitate the return of the Jews to Jerusalem, and the organization of a powerful government in Judea, and lead to that millennium which we all look for, all hope for, all pray for.

Where, I ask, can we commence this great work of regeneration with a better prospect of success than in a free country and liberal government? Where can we plead the cause of independence for the children of Israel with greater confidence than in the cradle of American liberty? Where ask for toleration and kindness for the seed of Abraham, if we find it not among the descendants of the Pilgrims? Here we can unfurl the standard, and seventeen millions of people will say, "God is with you; we are with you: in his name, and in the name of civil and religious liberty, go forth and repossess the land of your fathers. We have advocated the independence of the South American republics, we have given a home to our red brethren beyond the Mississippi, we have combated for the independence of Greece, we have restored the African to his native land. If these nations were entitled to our sympathies, how much more powerful and irrepressible are the claims of that beloved people, before whom the Almighty walked like a cloud by day and a pillar of fire by night; who spoke to them words of comfort and salvation, of promise, of hope, of consolation, and protection; who swore they should be *his* people, and he would be their God; who, for their special protection and final restoration, dispersed them among the nations of the earth, without confounding them with any!"

Within the last twenty-five years great revolutions have occurred in the East, affecting in a peculiar manner the future destiny of the followers of Mohammed, and distinctly marking the gradual advancement of the Christian power . . .

Russia has assailed the wandering hordes of the Caucasses. England has had various contests with the native princes of India, and has waged war with China. France has carried its victorious arms through the north of Africa. Russia, with a steady

J.R. SMITH. *Mordecai Manual Noah.* 1819. *This piece was the frontispiece of* Travels in England, France, Spain, and the Barbary States in the Years 1813–14 and 15.

glance and firm step, approaches Turkey in Europe, and when her railroads are completed to the Black Sea, will nearly embrace all Europe . . . England must possess Egypt, as affording the only secure route to her possessions in India through the Red Sea; then Palestine, thus placed between the Russian possessions and Egypt, reverts to its legitimate proprietors, and for the safety of the surrounding nations, a powerful, wealthy, independent, and enterprising people are placed there by and with the consent of the Christian powers, and with their aid and agency the land of Israel passes once more into the possession of the descendants of Abraham. The ports of the Mediterranean will be again opened to the busy hum of commerce; the fields will again bear the fruitful harvest, and Christian and Jew will together, on Mount Zion, raise their voices in praise of Him whose covenant with Abraham was to endure forever, and in whose seed all the nations of the earth are to be blessed. This is our destiny. Every attempt to colonize the Jews in other countries has failed: their eye has steadily rested on their own beloved Jerusalem, and they have said, "The time will come, the promise will be fulfilled."

The Jews are in a most favourable position to repossess themselves of the promised land, and organize a free and liberal government; they are at this time zealously and strenuously engaged in advancing the cause of education. In Poland, Moldavia, Wallachia, on the Rhine and Danube, and wherever the liberality of the governments have not interposed obstacles, they are practical farmers. Agriculture was once their only natural employment; the land is now desolate, according to the prediction of the prophets, but it is full of hope and promise. The soil is rich, loamy, and everywhere indicates fruitfulness, and the magnificent cedars of Lebanon, show the strength of the soil on the highest elevations; the climate is mild and salubrious, and double crops in the low lands may be annually anticipated. Everything is produced in the greatest variety. Wheat, barley, rye, corn, oats, and the cotton plant in great abundance. The sugar cane is cultivated with success; tobacco grows plentifully on the mountains; indigo is produced in abundance on the banks of the Jordan; olives and olive oil are everywhere found; the mulberry almost grows wild, out of which the most beautiful silk is made; grapes of the largest kind flourish everywhere . . . The several ports in the Mediterranean which formerly carried on a most valuable commerce can be advantageously reoccupied. Manufactures of wool, cotton, and silk could furnish all the Levant and the islands of the Mediterranean with useful fabrics. In a circumference within twenty days' travel of the Holy City, two millions of Jews reside.

The whole sect are therefore in a position, as far as intelligence, education, industry, undivided enterprise, variety of pursuits, science, a love of the arts, political economy, and wealth could desire, to adopt the initiatory steps for the organization of a free government in Syria, by, and with the consent, and under the protection of the Christian powers. I propose, therefore, for all the Christian societies who take an interest in the fate of Israel, to assist in their restoration by aiding to colonize the Jews in Judea; the progress may be slow, but the result will be certain . . .

The first step is to solicit from the Sultan of Turkey permission for the Jews to purchase and hold land; to build houses, and to follow any occupation they may desire, without molestation and in perfect security.

What a glorious privilege is reserved for the free people of the United States: the only country which has given civil and religious rights to the Jews equal with all other sects; the only country which has not persecuted them, selected and pointedly distinguished in prophecy as *the* nation which, at a proper time, shall present to the Lord his chosen and trodden-down people, and pave the way for their restoration to Zion. But will they go, I am asked, when the day of redemption arrives? All will go who feel the oppressor's yoke. *We* may repose where we are free and happy, but those who, bowed to the earth by oppression, would gladly exchange a condition of vassalage for the hope of freedom: that hope the Jews never can surrender; they cannot stand up against the prediction of our prophets, against the promises of God; they cease to be a nation, a people, a sect, when they do so . . .

We must not stop to ask whether the Jews will consent to occupy the land of Israel as freemen. Restoration is not for us alone, but for millions unborn. There is no fanaticism in it; it is easy, tranquil, natural, and gradual. Let the people go: point out the path for them in safety, and they will go, not all, but sufficient to constitute the elements of a powerful government; and those who are happy here may cast their eyes towards the sun as it rises, and know that it rises on a free and happy people beyond the mountains of Judea, and feel doubly happy in the conviction that God has redeemed all his promises to Jacob . . . I should think that the very idea, the hope, the prospect, and, above all, the certainty of restoring Israel to his own and promised land, would arouse the whole civilized world to a cordial and happy cooperation.

Let me therefore impress upon your minds the important fact, that the liberty and independence of the Jewish nation may grow out of a single effort which this country may make in their behalf. That effort is to procure for them a permission to purchase and hold land in security and peace; their titles and possessions confirmed; their fields and flocks undisturbed. They want only PROTECTION, and the work is accomplished.

ISAAC LEESER

To the American Tract Society: A Warning

In 1829 German-born Isaac Leeser was elected to the pulpit of Philadelphia's pioneer congregation, Mikveh Israel. During the following four decades he laid the foundation for American Jewish religious, cultural, and communal life, as founder and editor of the first important Jewish journal, The Occident, *translator of the Bible and prayerbook into English, author of ten volumes of essays on Judaism, inspirer and organizer of educational and social institutions and organizations. He was a courageous and effective defender of the faith and leading spokesman for traditional Judaism. Here is his polite but forceful warning, published in the* United States Gazette *in 1836, to missionaries who had come to the synagogue passing out literature to persuade Jews to convert to Christianity.*

To the American Tract Society, & to whomsoever else it may concern, the Reader of the Jewish Congregation of Philadelphia sends greeting—

An agent of your honorable body, or a volunteer in your cause, his precise character not being known to us, visited our place of worship on last Sabbath, the 30th January, and after the conclusion of the service, he posted himself at the entrance, and as the congregation was leaving the Synagogue, he handed copies of a tract, of a controversial nature, and contravening the tenets which we profess, to ladies, gentlemen and even children; and you will, no doubt, be happy to learn that, it is believed, with but one exception, no one refused the proffered gift. You will observe from this fact, that Jews have no unwillingness to receive or even read your books; and are by no means disinclined to examine your doctrines and system of faith. No doubt this announcement will be very gratifying to your piety, and it is believed that you will think it an earnest of further success. But at the same time I think it my duty to warn you against a repetition of a similar kindness; for as we are naturally jealous of our religious rights, being unwilling to allow any one to interfere in our conscientious scruples, and totally averse to listening to doctrines which we believe erroneous, another visit of your agent, or one distributing controversial tracts, emanating from your or any other body, may be received rather unkindly; and much as we might deprecate any violence or disturbance, we cannot answer for the forbearance of the zealous ones amongst us, who might perhaps be induced in their honest indignation, to eject an impertinent intermeddler, mildly if they can, forcibly if they must. Every visitor is welcome at our Synagogues, no less here than in every other town, but we expect from strangers the

Eminent American Clergymen. From *The American Phrenological Journal*, April 1868 issue. *A portrait of Isaac Leeser is seen, second from the top, right side. Benjamin Szold, father of Henrietta Szold, the founder of Hadassah, is seen on the bottom left.*

same politeness which we extend to others; no sect would allow us to present ourselves at the doors of their meeting places, and distribute papers contradicting their doctrines and tenets; and though our numbers be but small, we must insist that we too have rights, as well as every other class of citizens, which we can suffer on no account to be violated.

We seek not controversy—but if we are compelled by any species of intermeddling to defend our rights and the religion which we love, there will be found among us, men enough with sufficient courage, with sufficient faith, and with sufficient intelligence, to defend what we deem to be right and true. But as we are the minority, we seek not to disturb others, and only fanatical, but always hitherto unavailing efforts at conversion, will rouse in us a spirit of honest, but determined resistance.

The above has not been written by order of, or in concert with the members of the congregation; but since I have been elected their minister, I think it incumbent on me to give this warning, to present the so much desired feelings of amity which Jews cherish towards the Christians of this country, and which I fain would hope the latter feel towards the few of the persecuted house of Israel, whose lot has been cast among them.

86 Walnut Street, January 31, 1836.

The editors generally would confer a favor by giving the above an insertion in their respective papers, if their columns are not too much occupied.

Simeon Abrahams

Intermarrying with Gentiles

Intermarriage was a persistent problem throughout the three and a half centuries of the American Jewish historical experience. It rose when Jews were few and highly integrated; it abated when Jews lived in large self-sufficient communities in sharply defined ethnic enclaves. Suggested strategies to deal with the problem were widely diverse and often divisive. In 1845 when the entire Jewish population of the United States was less than 20,000, intermarrying with Gentiles was viewed with great concern by Simeon Abrahams in a letter to the editor of The Occident.

Mr. Editor:

I perceive by the last number of your valuable periodical, that you have not been unmindful of the importance of the above subject, which concerns a practice, which, unless something be done and that in the most decisive manner, and with the most unflinching firmness, will shortly undermine and destroy the harmony and well-being of our religious society in this country. It is a subject, above all others, demanding at this time our consideration, from the large number of persons who have contracted marriage with those not of our faith; a subject which presses itself upon the attention of every well-wisher of his religion, and which concerns the very existence of the Israelites as a separate nation. In this country, where, by its peculiar form of government, and the liberality of its laws, there are no legal disabilities for the maintenance of any opinion, the Jew, like every other citizen, is untrammelled in his religious and civil rights; it is therefore a natural consequence that he should mingle and associate with persons of different religious beliefs in social and friendly intercourse and business pursuits. But it is a great misfortune, and one which ought speedily to be remedied by the great body of Jews in the United States, that many of our people, and generally those who could support a wife of their own persuasion comfortably, and often in affluence, become intermingled with the gentiles by marriage; and it so happens, that after so marrying, they are allowed to remain in good standing in the various congregations and societies to which they formerly belonged, as if they had committed no wrong, nor done any thing against the common welfare of Jewish society, much less been guilty of an act which, above all others, is most certain to destroy them and their associates from being a nation on the earth with distinct laws and origin. It has farther to be remarked, that the offspring of such marriages are generally introduced into the community of Jews, without their having become regular proselytes; they are unfortu-

Ketubbah. New York. 1899. Ink and watercolor on paper, with printing and calligraphy. 25 1/2 x 20 in. The Jewish Museum, New York. Gift of Dr. Harry G. Friedman.
The groom was Reuven, son of Eliezer; the bride, Rivka, daughter of Hayim. The inscribed blessing reads "Good fortune and much blessing, wealth, joy, and accomplishment, length of days, and happiness."

nately not looked upon by many as strangers to our faith, which they actually are; and thus the landmarks of our religion are broken down by the intermarriage of such children with those who are truly of the house of Israel, destroying thus those well-established lines of ancestry, and those religious and national distinctions, which have kept us a peculiar people during so long a period, amidst all the troubles, oppressions, and persecutions, which we had to encounter.

In fact the time has now arrived, when it is actually necessary, in self-defence, to commence doing something towards remedying this growing evil; for every congregation has ample power within itself of discarding all its members who marry gentiles, and unless something of the kind be shortly done, it will be difficult, in but a few years hence, to know who among us are actually entitled, according to our laws, to be regarded as Jews. How ridiculous it is to see a man who has married a gentile wife, and has for her sake given up every thing which his religion demands of him, mount the reading-desk on our most solemn days, and participate in the religious services of the day; or to see a woman who openly says that she has married a gentile, boldly entering the place of worship, and placing herself in the front ranks among the true daughters of Israel, as though she had not violated the duties of her religion. It is a great fault in the trustees of congregations, that they do nothing to prevent these things; and that they in a manner encourage them, by selling seats in their places of worship to persons of this class, thus setting a baleful example for their own sons and daughters. To countenance acts like these is not the way to put a stop to them; not to punish by setting on them a mark of public disapprobation, is to encourage them; and surely we do not set a good example to the rising generation, whom, we pretend, we are striving to rear by all means at our disposal to become proper representatives of Judaism, whilst we do nothing to prevent this increasing bane of our nation, since we allow a person who has in a measure voluntarily abandoned his religion, to remain a member of our societies and congregations. Among us the object of punishment is not so much the disgrace of the guilty as the deterring of the yet innocent from the committal of wrongs; and I therefore hold it requisite, in order to infuse a wholesome fear in the minds of the young, not to permit any of those who have married out of the congregation, be they men or women, to have any part or share with us in the religious rites or services of our ancient and holy religion; they have voluntarily withdrawn themselves from us, there let them remain, it is an act of their own, done without any necessity, and our very existence as Jews demands of us, as such, that they should not be permitted to re-enter, or to have extended to them, any of the rites or privileges of our religion; they should not be permitted to purchase or hire a seat in the Synagogues; the men should not be allowed to be called to the reading of the law, nor to be reckoned to make Minyan, nor in any way to be countenanced or regarded as Jews. Besides this, in case of their death no especial notice should be taken of them, they having made their selections of companions for life, let their gentile relatives take care of their dead bodies, and inter them in any manner they may deem proper.

This may be considered severe punishment, but desperate diseases require desperate remedies. To put this much needed reform into practice is, however, not without its many difficulties; for many of the above persons have fathers, and brothers, and other relatives, among the rulers or managers of our congregations and religious societies, and this cause, if no other, offers great obstacles to carrying out effectually and fully the great principles I have just presented. But however unpleasant it may be for a person to be compelled to refuse another those offices or services, which he would under any other circumstances willingly render, stern necessity requires that this class of offenders should no longer be permitted to be associated with us in the conducting of our religious affairs; for if not prohibited from interfering in our societies, and this intermarrying with gentiles be permitted without any show of opposition on our part, by allowing the transgressors to retain their former rights in congregations and societies, the name of Jew, in this country especially, will, I fear, soon be a matter of history, but not of reality. Yours, &c.

Simeon Abrahams
New York, January 24th, 5605

An American Jewess
From *"The Teachers' and Parents' Assistant"*

These lessons on how to teach young children the concept of God are part of a small book subtitled "Conveying to Uninformed Minds the First Ideas of God and His Attributes (1845)." The book is comprised of thirteen lessons, two of which are presented here. It is not a catechism, the traditional textbook for teaching the tenets of religion—questions read and answers memorized—but a surprisingly modern example of teaching by leading children to think for themselves.

LESSON I

The First Idea Of God

Do you know who God is?

Probably no answer from the child, but a downcast or confused look. After a pause proceed to the next question.

Do you know who made the bright warm sun, and the lovely moon and the shining stars?

The teacher, after giving the child time to think upon this, may, if no answer be made, answer for him:

God.

Can you tell me how we know that God made these things?

Let the child think, but expect no answer. Continue to question:

Could they have made themselves? Could any *man* have made them?

The child will unhesitatingly answer "No," to both these questions.

Then you see that some being, more powerful than the most powerful man, must have made them, and that Great Being is GOD.

Can you mention to me some other things that could not have made themselves, and that no *man* could have made?

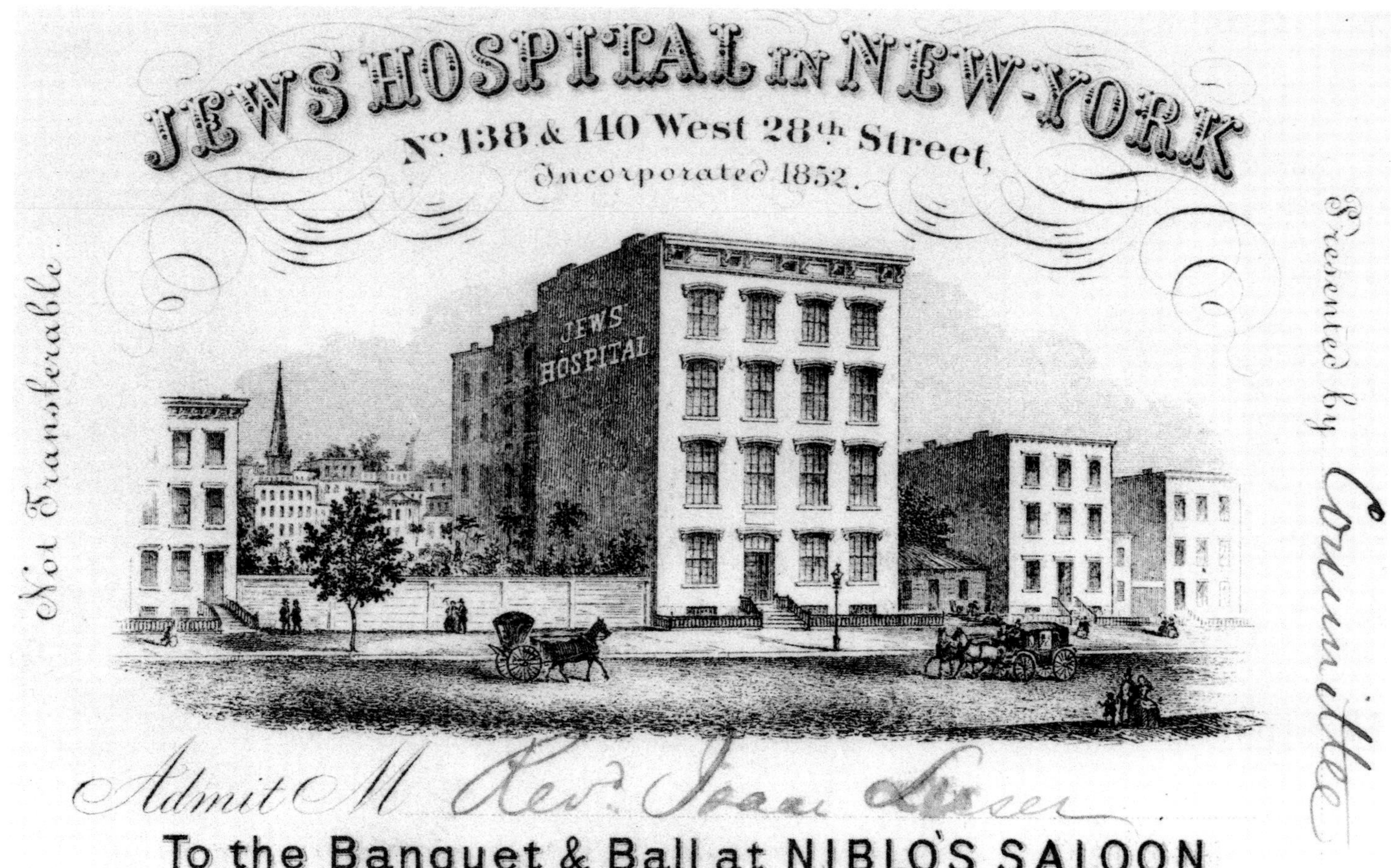

JEWS HOSPITAL IN NEW-YORK
No. 138 & 140 West 28th Street,
Incorporated 1852.
JEWS HOSPITAL
Not Transferable.
Presented by Committee
Admit Mr Rev. Isaac Leeser
To the Banquet & Ball at NIBLO'S SALOON,
Thursday 28 October 1858.

Jews Hospital Charity Ball Invitation. 1858. American Jewish Historical Society, Waltham, Massachusetts. *The hospital, incorporated in 1852, was the first Jewish hospital in America. It exists today as Mount Sinai Hospital, one of New York's leading nonsectarian health institutions.*

Assist the child here, after having given him time to reflect, by reminding him of some of the various familiar objects of creation; as the trees, the flowers, different animals, &c.

You know that all the things we have just mentioned, live upon the earth. Now did the earth make itself? Could any *man* have made it?

The child will of course answer correctly.

Who then must have made the earth?

God.

You have now found out that God made the sun, moon and stars, the earth, and all the things and animals that live and grow upon it. Now can you answer my first question, and tell me who God is?

The child will not now require much assistance to answer:

God is the Maker of all that is in the heavens, of the earth and of every thing that belongs to the earth.

LESSON II

Of God As The Creator

What did God make all that we see in the skies, the earth, and all that we see on the earth, out of?

Let the teacher answer, after giving the child time to think:

God is so great and so powerful that He made all these wonderful things out of nothing. No child and no man can think how great He is.

There is a word which means to make something where before there was nothing.

This word is "to create." Now tell me the meaning of "to create."

After the child has answered as well as he can, let the teacher say:

It means, to make something, where before there was nothing. God *created* all his works, because He made them at first out of nothing. What is God called because He made all things out of nothing?

Let the child think for a moment, and then let the teacher answer for him:

He is called the Creator.

Now tell me the meaning of Creator.

After the child has given such a definition as he is capable of, let the teacher say:

Creator means one who has made something, where before there was nothing. Who is the only Being who can make something out of nothing?

The child will readily answer,

God.

God then, you see, is the Creator.

Abraham J. Asch

The Occident (1855)

Beth Hammidrash, the House of Study

During the 1850s, the Jewish population of the United States increased threefold, from 50,000 to 150,000. Immigrants from central Europe enlarged the Jewish presence in the Midwest and established Jewish communities in the Far West. East European Jewish immigrants began to establish a visible presence in the eastern seaboard cities. The decade also saw the establishment of institutions and organizations to serve the spiritual needs of the new and enlarged communities. In 1852 the first congregation of Jews from eastern Europe, the Beth Hammidrash, was established in New York. Rabbi Asch describes the virtues of this house of study.

For several years past there has existed a congregation in our sister city, the object of which was, as we understood, the promotion of Talmudical knowledge and meetings for prayer. The late Sampson Simson left to it by his will the sum of two thousand dollars; and we have been requested to lay before our readers the following synopsis of its objects, sent us in Hebrew by the Rabbi, Abraham Joseph [Asch]. We can only give the translation this month, perhaps the original hereafter. [Isaac Leeser] Ed. Occ.

The following is an account of the founding of the Beth Hammidrash, and the views of its originators, whom our God may remember for good.

This institution, which is at present situated in New York, is like a lily in the country of America—pleasant as the dawn, and trusting for support from the Friend of all good.

1. It is one that awakens the heart of every man of Israel, saying, "Rouse thee from thy sleep, get thee ready, and return to the God ere thy light be quenched . . ."

2. It has drawn to itself these five years, from the day of its founding till the present, morning and evening, every man in whom the spirit of the Almighty is active, to pray in the assembly of the faithful.

3. It is open all the day for . . . every one whose mind may spur him on to quench his thirst in the study of the law.

Preparation and Baking of Matzahs. 1877. *This scene appeared in* Frank Leslie's Popular Monthly.

COLORPLATE 31

ARTIST UNKNOWN. *Banner of the Fraternal Organization (Kesher shel Barzel).* Last third of the 19th century. Oil on canvas window-shade. 60 x 36 in. Buccleuch Mansion Museum, Jersey Blue Chapter D.A.R., New Brunswick, New Jersey. On loan to the Jewish Historical Society of Central Jersey, New Brunswick. *The Kesher shel Barzel was an American Jewish fraternal organization that existed from 1860 until 1903.*

COLORPLATE 32

Tablets of the Law. Philadelphia. 1918. Wood, carved and painted. 48 x 20 x 8 in. Courtesy of the National Museum of American Jewish History, Philadelphia. *This was originally from Shaarei Eli Synagogue in South Philadelphia, one of the largest synagogues started by new immigrants in 1917. By 1981, however, the neighborhood's Jewish population had dwindled, and this synagogue was scheduled for demolition. The National Museum of American Jewish History established legal title to the ark and religious furnishings in 1984 and raised funds to preserve and restore these historic objects.*

COLORPLATE 33 *(opposite)*

ABRAHAM SCHULKIN. *Ark.* Sioux City, Iowa. 1899. Carved pine, stained, gold-colored bronze paint. 120 x 96 x 30 in. The Jewish Museum, New York. Gift of the Jewish Federation of Sioux City, Iowa.

זה מעשה ידי
אברהם שולקין
אנכי ה
לא יהיה
לא תשא
שמור את
לא תרצח
לא תנאף
לא תגנב
לא תענה
זה האק׳ נדבה הה׳ שימקע
בתר דוד דייווידסאן

COLORPLATE 34 *(top)*

MARCUS CHARLES ILLIONS. *Ark Lions.* New York. Early 20th century. Wood, carved and painted. 20 x 53 x 3 3/4 in. Hebrew Union College Skirball Museum, Los Angeles. Purchased with Project Americana Acquisition Funds provided by Gerald M. and Carolyn Z. Bronstein, Lee and Irving Kalsman, and Peach and Mark Levy.

COLORPLATE 35 *(bottom)*

Ark Lions. Early 20th century. Wood. Height of each: 29 in.; diameter: 3 in.; width: 21 1/2 in. Collection of Abraham and Deborah Karp. *The lions were carved for Congregation Linas Hazedek, Kansas City, Missouri.*

COLORPLATE 36

Ark Lions. c. 1900. Height of each: 17 1/2 in.; diameter: 11 in.; width: 7 in. Collection of Abraham and Deborah Karp.

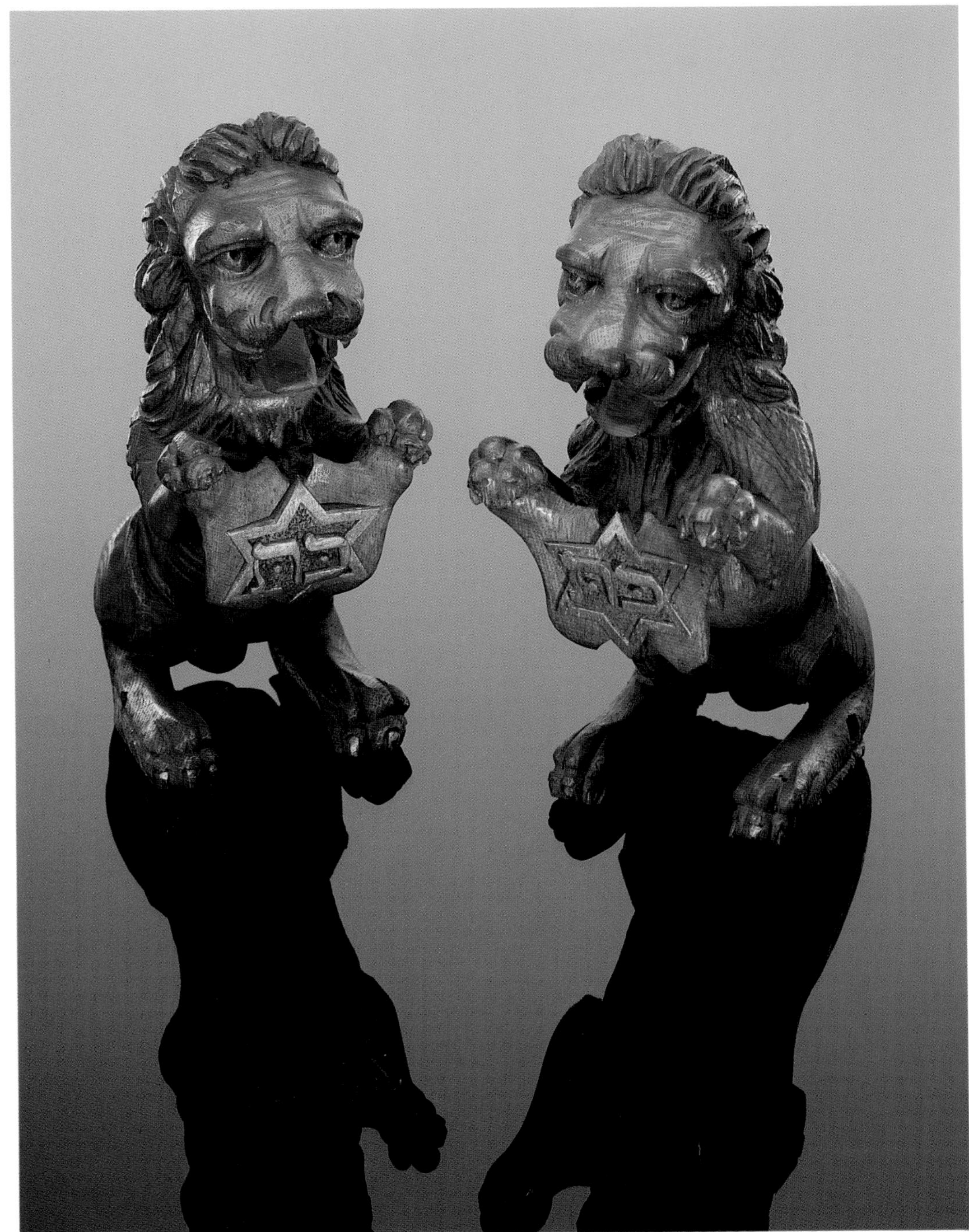

COLORPLATE 37

Hands of Priestly Blessing. Philadelphia. 1918. Wood, carved and painted. Height: 20 in.; width: 42 in.; diameter: 7 1/2 in. Originally from the Shaarei Eli Synagogue, Philadelphia. Courtesy of the National Museum of American Jewish History, Philadelphia. *The carved hands are in the position held during the priestly blessing.*

COLORPLATE 39

JEANETTE KUVIN OREN AND N. AMANDA FORD. *Torah Mantles. Seven Days of Creation.* 1993. Painted silks, lamés, synthetics; appliquéd and quilted. Gift from the artists to Congregation Beth El, Bethesda, Maryland. *These mantles depict, from lower left to upper right, the six days of creation and the sabbath.*

COLORPLATE 38 *(opposite)*

ADOLPH GOTTLIEB. *Torah Curtain.* Millburn, New Jersey. 1950–1951. Velvet, appliqué, embroidered with metallic thread. Upper section: 80 1/2 x 112 3/4 in. Lower section: 80 1/2 x 121 3/4 in. The Jewish Museum, New York. On extended loan by Congregation B'nai Israel, Millburn, New Jersey. *During the postwar boom in synagogue construction, sweeping redefinition of synagogue design began. Based on a modernistic aesthetic, it rejected historical references. In this curtain, Gottlieb abstracts such basic elements of religious belief as the Tablets of the Law, the twelve tribes, the temple, and the Ark of the Covenant. He also includes stylizations of objects developed for synagogue use (Torah mantles and Torah shields) and emblems which have become synonymous with Judaism (the Lion of Judah and the Star of David).*

COLORPLATE 40

CHAVA WOLPERT RICHARD. *High Holidays Machzor (Prayerbook) Cover.* 1980. 24K gold cloisonné enamel on fine silver plaques, bound in leather. Open book: 8 3/4 x 12 3/4 in. Private collection. *The Hebrew inscriptions read: on the front left side, "God Is King, Was King, and Will Be King For Ever and Ever"; on the back right side: "Who maketh the barren woman to dwell in her house as a joyful mother of children, Hallelujah" (Psalms 113:9); on the spine of the book: "Machzor for Rosh Hashanah and Yom Kippur."*

4. There are found therein at this day students of the law, many of whom know how to decide for the people correctly in matters of religious duty.

5. There is daily a portion of law expounded publicly, from its founding until now, every evening, when the people rest from their daily task, to teach them the law, that they may know the God of their fathers, and the deeds which they should do in his service, and to warn them that they may not be caught in the snare of transgression.

6. Besides this, there are persons who study the law for themselves, either in pairs or singly.

7. The house is full to overflowing, on Sabbaths and festivals, in the evening and morning, to pray in common before they put food or drink into their mouths.

8. It is well calculated to excite the heart of every Israelite who enters into this house to pray, to incite him to make ready his heart to appear before his Maker with the fire of religious fervor and devotion.

9. It is filled with all sorts of holy books, several sets of Babylonian and Jerusalem Talmuds, the Turim, Rambam, Rif, Shulchan Aruch, rabbinical opinions, Bibles, commentaries, books of devotion and instruction, Midrashim, Kabbalah, and it has many Sepharim in the Hechal, so that every one who seeks may obtain pleasant instruction for his soul.

10. It is the only institution in the land, that is otherwise a waste, as regards religious knowledge . . .

The Beth Hammidrash calls aloud on all, that whoever longs for eternal life, who desires to cause his soul to escape from perdition, should flee to it; for there is the refuge which will rescue him, to make even his path, that he may believe in God, his law and his commandments; so that after his death he may inherit his portion among the association of those who listen to the voice of our Father, the Lord . . .

Resolution Regarding Sabbath Observance in Cincinnati

In 1859, Jewish merchants in America's "Queen City," Cincinnati, proposed a resolution to close all Jewish businesses for Sabbath observance.

Whereas the observation of the Sabbath is a fundamental doctrine of our religion; and

Whereas a strict observation of the Sabbath is only then practicable among merchants, if business is entirely suspended on that day, and all unite on it as a day of rest; and furthermore,

Whereas the merchants of Cincinnati professing the creed of Israel, now occupy such a position in business that they are capable of effecting this purpose—therefore be it

Resolved, That this meeting recommends to all business men of this city, professing the Jewish creed, to keep their places of business closed during the Sabbath.

Hebrew Union College, Cincinnati. Courtesy of American Jewish Archives, Cincinnati Campus, Hebrew Union College. *Located at 724 West Sixth Street, this structure was the first home of the Hebrew Union College from 1881 to 1912.*

Resolved, That we will unite our influence to persuade all business men of our creed in this city, to observe the Sabbath by abstaining from all business transactions.

Resolved, That we in signing our names to these Preamble and Resolutions, declare that we pledge our word and honor to each other and to all, to keep our places of business closed during every Sabbath of ours; to transact no business ourselves, nor allow any of our clerks, book keepers, or any other person in our employment to transact business for us on that day on our premises.

Resolved, That a committee of five be appointed whose special duty it shall be to call on every business house of this city, if the members thereof profess our creed, and solicit the consent and signature of all of them to these Preamble and Resolutions.

Resolved, That the members of those firms, who now observe the Sabbath, by keeping closed their places of business, shall also be requested to place their signatures under these Preamble and Resolutions.

Resolved, That the third resolution of this series shall take effect immediately after Twenty-Five wholesale houses, besides those who now keep their places of business closed on Sabbath—shall have given their consent to these Preamble and Resolutions.

Lewis A. Franklin
The San Diego Contempt Case

The author of a letter to the editor of The Gleaner, *a San Francisco Jewish weekly, bristles with righteous indignation. He seeks redress for an outrageous occurrence and asks that it be publicized to shame those responsible. The story he tells is of an incident that took place on Yom Kippur, 1859, in San Diego, California, when a minyan of Jews in America's farthest frontier joined together for worship on this holiest day of the year.*

EDITOR GLEANER:—I know not what feeling mostly actuates me, in recapitulating to you the occurrences which have disgraced civilization in this, our remote little town of San Diego. Were I to say that unmitigated disgust fills my bosom, I would scarcely express myself; as a wrong of the nature I shall here recount to you, knows no parallel in the annals of the civilized world. An offence has been committed against all decency, and I, in common with all my co-religionists, call upon you to give publicity to the matter, so that the perpetrators may be marked with the rebuke of scorn by a free and independent press.

My preface may be out of place; but it is with difficulty that I restrain myself from enlarging, as I am literally boiling over with a strong impulse of resentment; however, I will proceed to a narration of the facts. Know, then, that in this town and county of San Diego, there number some twelve or fourteen Israelites. These scattered few of God's chosen people, agreed to unite in the observance of the sacred festival of the New Year, as well as in the solemnities of the Day of Atonement—a day, by Divine command, observed as a day of fast and prayer—a day devoted to the worship of God—a day set apart for humiliation and expiation of sins. On the eve of that memorable day, a worthy citizen named M. Manasse journeyed fifty miles to be with us, *and complete the number designated and requisite to form a congregation.*

Between the hours of twelve and one o'clock, P.M., the deputy sheriff presented himself at the door of the room set apart by us as a temporary Synagogue, and calling Mr. M., requested him, in the name of the Grand Jury, then in session, to appear and testify in matters and things then under their investigation. This Mr. M. declined to do, pleading as an excuse that he was engaged in his devotions. Ere a quarter of an hour had elapsed, this same minion of the law reappeared, opened the door of our temporary temple, and straightway walked up to Mr. M., with a paper in hand, and said, "Mr. M., I have a subpoena for you." At this juncture I and every other member present protested against the service of any process in a place of worship, resolutely telling the sheriff (*id est* his minion) that Mr. M. neither would nor should attend unless forced, as we were then engaged in divine service—that Mr. M. was indispensable to the requisite number to form our congregation, and that that apartment was for the time being, a Synagogue. Before this official again retired, he stated that he (the under sheriff) was of the opinion that the proceedings he was taking were improper, and that he told the District Attorney that he would prefer losing fifty dollars to making the service, but that he had no alternative. He farther stated that many honorable citizens cried shame at the authorities for this outrage. His last remark, however, was—"he guessed he could get a writ of attachment and *make* him go." Upon this threat Mr. M. suggested the propriety of our locking the door, so as to prevent farther intrusion.

Solomon Yaekel. c. 1882. Photograph. Bancroft Library, University of California, Berkeley, California.

In less than half an hour that same deputy sheriff was heard at the door, demanding entrance, which, not being granted, he burst open the door, walked in, laid hands on Mr. M., and, spite of all remonstrance, insisted on executing his functions. With one voice the whole assembly told this intruder that force alone could convey Mr. M. from our midst. He again left, but speedily returned with a posse, who unceremoniously rushed in. With this body all remonstrance or protest was futile, so Mr. M. consented to accompany them. He was immediately ushered into the presence of that august body of inquisitors, miscalled Grand Jurors; but lo! he refused to be sworn on that day! In their indignation they remanded Mr. M. to the court room of the Court of Sessions, where he was subjected to a severe cross-examination on the scruples he entertained, and, persisting in his refusal to be sworn, the *learned* judge ordered him into the custody of the sheriff until he should relent and testify. The sheriff (*in propria persona*) had no sooner crossed the threshold of the court house door, than he told Mr. M. that he might proceed whither he pleased, he, the sheriff, being answerable for his appearance at sundown. At nightfall, sure enough, Mr. M. appeared before the Grand Jury, and after answering such questions as were then propounded to him, he was set at liberty.

Now, what great crime, think you, had been committed to render necessary the course pursued, in order to obtain testimony? I answer, A *drunken broil*, of which due and formal complaint had already been made, and which a majority of the jurors were opposed to entertaining: in fine, the bill was ignored. Even this is not all to be said in evidence of the persecution of those wrapped in a little brief authority, but whose ignorance was made manifest by A. S. Ensworth, Esq., late member of the Legislature from this county. The Court of Sessions, consisting of D. B. Kurtz, Judge, W. H. Noyes, and A. B. Smith, Associates, and D. B. Hoffman as District Attorney, was convened on the 3d inst., and a panel of twenty-four jurors ordered to be summoned to serve as Grand Jurors. On the 5th inst. that number of citizens, at the command of the sheriff, appeared, were sworn, and retired for deliberation. Two days were they thus engaged. They investigated and deliberated upon all complaints or causes of action; but behold! the Court had to be taught that the law under which they had proceeded, had been repealed, and that therefore their proceedings were informal. The jurymen were then, on the 7th, discharged, and the *enlightened* court ordered a new panel, as by law directed.

The sheriff turned right round, and re-summoned a sufficient number from the discharged jury, among whom were Mr. Marcus Schiller and Mr. Charles Gerson. These two gentlemen prayed the Court to be excused, as the holy day of Solemn Assembly was at hand on the morrow, and they then and there gave the Court to understand, that nothing could induce them *ever to appear in court on that day.* Judge Kurtz, finding that his associates conceded the excuse as valid, had no alternative but to grant them their prayer. You will thus perceive that the Court, and all the jurors, who were at this time in court, were apprized of the religious scruples of every Israelite on the Day of Atonement. Again, neither the first nor second body of Grand Jurors deemed it necessary to send for Mr. M., he residing, as before stated, some fifty miles from town, and it was only when, actuated by religious fervor, he journeyed hither to unite with his brethren, that the Grand Jury resolved upon having him before them. Having once made this resolution, and meeting with the ready and willing assistants of the District Attorney and Judge of the Court, they carried out the persecutions which I have thus lengthily described to you, and which every member of our holy faith who resides here is ready to substantiate.

Although we are but few in number here, we are yet resolved to seek redress for this untoward outrage, and with this object, a full statement of the facts is being forwarded to one of the most able counsel in the State, for him to represent us in any action which he, in his wisdom, thinks he can sustain in the Supreme Court of this State. I could say much more in animadversion, but I leave the matter in your hands as a better defender. I accompany this with a full list of the Jurors, that they may be known, and subscribe myself,

Very truly, yours,
LEWIS A. FRANKLIN

SAMUEL M. ISAACS

From *The Jewish Messenger*

"Stand by the Flag!"

The Jews of the United States reacted to the war between the states like the rest of the population. In Cincinnati, Isaac Mayer Wise wrote in the American Israelite *on April 19, 1851: "Silence must henceforth be our policy, silence on all the questions of the day, until a spirit of*

conciliation shall move the hearts of the millions . . ." while in New York, the Reverend Samuel M. Isaacs, rabbi of Congregation Shaaray Tefila and editor of the weekly The Jewish Messenger, *urged his readers on April 26, 1861 to stand by the flag.*

It is almost a work of supererogation for us to call upon our readers to be loyal to the Union, which protects them. It is needless for us to say anything to induce them to proclaim their devotion to the land in which they live. But we desire our voice, too, to be heard at this time, joining in the hearty and spontaneous shout ascending from the whole American people, to stand by the stars and stripes!

Already we hear of many of our young friends taking up arms in defence of their country, pledging themselves to assist in maintaining inviolate its integrity, and ready to respond, if need be, with their lives, to the call of the constituted authorities, in the cause of law and order.

The time is past for forbearance and temporizing. We are now to *act*, and sure we are that those whom these words may reach will not be backward in realizing the duty that is incumbent upon them—to rally as one man for the *Union* and the *Constitution*. The Union—which binds together, by so many sacred ties, millions of freemen—which extends its hearty invitation to the oppressed of all nations to come and be sheltered beneath its protecting wings—shall it be severed, destroyed, or even impaired? Shall

Colonel Marcus M. Spiegel. c. 1863. From *Our True Marcus, Marcus Spiegel.* Kent State University Press, 1985. Photo collection of Jean P. Soman. *Spiegel came from Germany at the age of 19, operated a general store in Ohio, volunteered to fight to preserve America, and was one of the highest ranking Jews in the Union Army. He fought at the Battle of Vicksburg and was a member of the 120th Ohio Regiment.*

those whom we once called our brethren be permitted to overthrow the fabric reared by the noble patriots of the Revolution, and cemented with their blood?

And the Constitution—guaranteeing to all the free exercise of their religious opinions—extending to all liberty, justice, and equality—the pride of Americans, the admiration of the world—shall that Constitution be subverted, and anarchy usurp the place of a sound, safe, and stable government, deriving its authority from the consent of the American people?

The voice of millions yet unborn cries out, "Forbid it, Heaven!" The voice of the American people declares, in tones not to be misunderstood, "It shall not be!"

Then stand by the flag! What death can be so glorious as that of the patriot, surrendering up life in defence of his country—pouring forth his blood on the battlefield—to live for ever in the hearts of a grateful people? Stand by the flag! Whether native or foreign born, Christian or Israelite, stand by it, and you are doing your duty, and acting well your part on the side of liberty and justice!

We know full well that our young men, who have left their homes to respond to the call of their country, will, on their return, render a good account of themselves. We have no fears for their bravery and patriotism. Our prayers are with them. God speed them on the work which they have volunteered to perform!

And if they fall—if, fighting in defence of that flag, they meet a glorious and honorable death, their last moments will be cheered by the consciousness that they have done their duty, and grateful America will not forget her sons, who have yielded up their spirit in her behalf.

And as for us, who do not accompany them on their noble journey, our duty, too, is plain. We are to pray to Heaven that He may restore them soon again to our midst, after having assisted in vindicating the honor and integrity of the flag they have sworn to defend; and we are to pledge ourselves to assume for them, should they fall in their country's cause, the obligation of supporting those whom their departure leaves unprotected. Such is our duty. Let them, and all of us, renew our solemn oath that whatever may betide, we will be true to the Union and the Constitution, and

STAND BY THE FLAG!

From *The Jewish Messenger* A Rebuttal from Southern Rebels, Shreveport, Louisiana

Jews loyal to the Confederacy responded to the call to stand by the flag with this angry rebuttal. Samuel Isaacs published the letter in The Jewish Messenger *along with an amusing aside on the irony of banning the paper in Shreveport.*

TERRIBLE CENSURE.— We have refrained from publishing the many extraordinary letters we have recently received from the South, though we have carefully laid them by for future reference. But the following "resolutions" are so peculiarly rich, especially considering that we

The Menken Brothers of Cincinnati. Photograph. The American Jewish Archives, Cincinnati. *Shown here in their Civil War uniforms, these brothers were among a small number of Jews who fought in the Civil War.*

have only one subscriber in Shreveport, and he has not paid for two years, that we cannot resist the temptation of putting them in print:

Whereas, we received the JEWISH MESSENGER of the 26th of April, a paper published in New York, in which an appeal has been made to all, whether native or foreign born, Christian or Israelite. An article headed, "Stand by the Flag!" in which the editor makes an appeal to support the stars and stripes, and to rally as one man for the Union and the Constitution. Therefore be it

Resolved, That we, the Hebrew congregation of Shreveport, scorn and repel your advice, although we might be called Southern rebels; still, as law-abiding citizens, we solemnly pledge ourselves to stand by, protect, and honor the flag, with its stars and stripes, the Union and Constitution of the Southern Confederacy with our lives, liberty, and all that is dear to us.

Resolved, That we, the members of said congregation, bind ourselves to discontinue the subscription of the JEWISH MESSENGER, and all Northern papers opposed to our holy cause, and also to use all honorable means in having said paper banished from our beloved country.

Resolved, That while we mistook your paper for a religious one, which ought to be strictly neutral in politics, we shall from this but treat it with scorn, as a black republi-

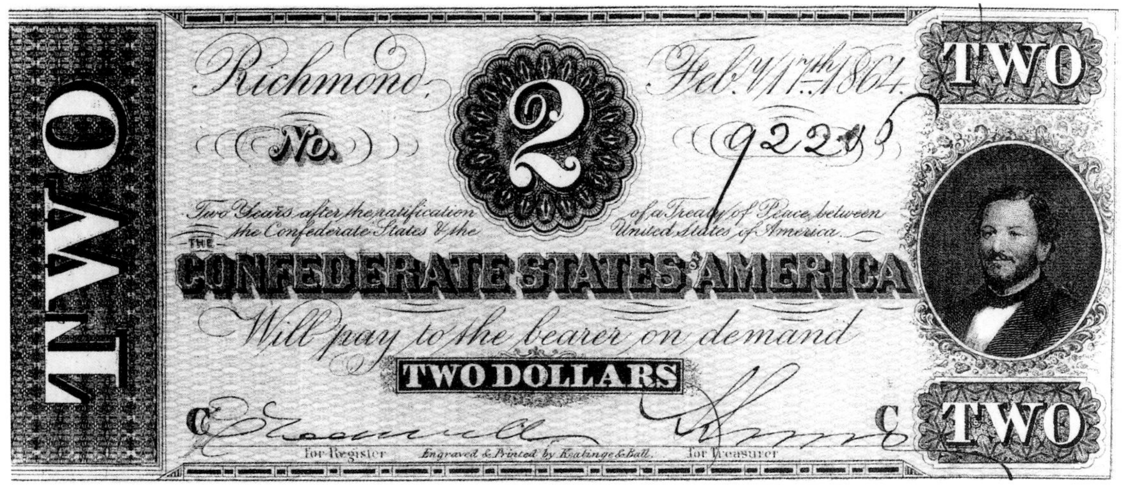

Two-Dollar Confederate Bill. 1864. Collection of Abraham and Deborah Karp. *This bill prominently features the portrait of Judah Philip Benjamin (1811–1884). Benjamin, born in the West Indies and raised in the United States, twice served as senator of Louisiana before the secession. During the Civil War, he served as Attorney General, Secretary of War, and Secretary of State of the Confederate States. At the conclusion of the war, Benjamin left the States for England where he became a prominent member of the English bar.*

can paper, and not worthy of Southern patronage; and that, according to our understanding, church and politics ought never to be mingled, as it has been the ruination of any country captivated by the enticing words of preachers.

Resolved, That we, the members of said congregation, have lost all confidence and regard to the Rev. S. M. Isaacs, editor and proprietor of the JEWISH MESSENGER, and see in him an enemy to our interest and welfare, and believe it to be more unjust for one who preaches the Word of God, and to advise us to act as traitors and renegades to our adopted country, and raise hatred and dissatisfaction in our midst, and assisting to start a bloody civil war amongst us.

Resolved, That we believe, like the Druids of old, the duties of those who preach the Holy Word to be first in the line of battle, and to cheer up those fighting for liberty against their oppressors, in place of those who are proclaiming now, from their pulpits, words to encourage an excited people, and praying for bloody vengeance against us. Brutus, while kissing Caesar, plunged the dagger to his heart.

Resolved, That a copy of these resolutions be sent to the editor of the JEWISH MESSENGER.

Resolved, That papers friendly to the Southern cause are politely requested to publish the foregoing resolutions.

M. Baer, *President*
Ed. Eberstadt, *Secretary, pro tem.*

Isaac Mayer Wise

From *Selected Writings of Isaac M. Wise*

"Woman as Members of Congregations"

Born in Bohemia in 1819, Isaac Mayer Wise came to America in 1846 to embark on a career in the rabbinate. His twin passions were his love for his adopted land and his devotion to the refor-

mation of Jewish religious life and thought. He became the architect of American Reform Judaism, establishing its basic institutions. Here he emphasizes the importance of the full participation of women in Jewish religious life.

(1876)

In the Bible, woman stands very high. At the beginning of Israel's natural life, Miriam appears as a leader so that she could say: "Did God perhaps speak through Moses only, did He not also speak through us?" Rahab saved the spies at Jericho, and Achsah was a heroic woman. During the rude period of the Judges, the Bible mentions five women of exceptional caliber. The mother of Samson, wiser than her husband; Jephtha's daughter, the beloved child, nobler than her father; the inspired patriotic heroine Deborah, the poetess queen of her people; the lovable, idyllic and childlike Ruth, faithful and quietly obedient; and Hannah, the pious mother of the Prophet, who stands in a much higher place than the high-priest. The brief stories of Abigail, the Shunnamite, the wise woman of Tekoah, and the Prophetess Huldah, reveal that woman held a high position during a period of advanced civilization. Queen Esther, the daughters of the Levites who sang in the temple, Susannah and Judith, the wise and pious Queen Salome Alexandra, and the many great women of the Talmud, like Beruriah and Yaltha, all testify to the lofty position woman had in ancient Jewish society.

None of the rabbinical provisions as to law and practice affected the high regard for women; she always remained the queen of the heart and home. But up to 1000 A.C., all Jewish laws and customs adopted in Europe were Oriental in origin. The influence of Oriental society and the Koran gradually excluded woman from public affairs of the community, so that up to our very day she was assigned to a subordinate position in the synagogue. To call a woman to the Thorah, or admit her to public honors equally with men, would have appeared preposterous, and would to-day be considered a desecration by the orthodox synagogue.

In the early days of our activity in America, we admitted females to the choir. Then we confirmed boys and girls together, and we allowed girls to read the Thorah on that occasion. Later on we introduced family pews into the temple.

With the admission of mothers and daughters to a recognized place in public worship, came order and decorum. Abuses that had crept into the synagogue disappeared as soon as woman again took her proper place in the temple. But we cannot stop here; the reform is not complete. You must enfranchise woman in your congregations, she must be a member, must have a voice and a vote in your assemblies. We need women in the congregational meetings to bring heart and piety into them. We must have women in the boards for the sake of the principle. We must have women in the school boards to visit the Sabbath-schools, and to make their influence felt. We must have women in the choir committee, because they understand music better than men. But, all other considerations aside, the principle of justice, and the law of God inherent in every human being, demand that woman be admitted to membership in the congregation, and be given equal rights with man; that her religious feelings be allowed scope for the sacred cause of Israel.

We are ready to appear before any congregation in behalf of any woman wishing to become a member thereof, and to plead her cause. We will debate the question with anyone who will show us in what woman is less entitled to the privileges of the synagogue than man, or where her faith is less important to her salvation than man's is to him. Till then, we maintain that women must become active members of the congregation for their own sake, and for the benefit of Israel's sacred cause.

Louis A. Gratz
Coming to America: Peddling and Military Service

Louis A. Gratz came to America shortly before the outbreak of the Civil War from Inowrazlaw, a Prussian town on the German-Polish border. The letter he wrote to his Uncle Aron and Aunt Emma Kurtzig is a fascinating account of the journey to the New World, rich in human interest of arrival, economic enterprise, social adjustment, illness, and recuperation, and is particularly important for its account of the rise of a recently arrived Jewish immigrant in the ranks of the Union Army. On November 25, 1861, when the letter was written, he was already a first lieutenant in the cavalry on a recruitment assignment in Scranton, Pennsylvania.

Scranton, November 25, 1861

I will start from the moment I came to America, and you will learn from my short biography that America is the only country where one can make his fortune although in a variety of ways. When I came to this country all my property amounted to ten dollars. In addition, I did not understand the English language, and I had neither relatives nor friends. By pure accident I was introduced by a young man to a poor Jewish family of good reputation with whom I lived as a guest paying two and a half dollars a week. Living in this way did not solve my problem; however, I had at least found some people who did not cheat me and who provided me with cheap though poor food.

I wasn't particularly happy, and I felt also very depressed, for I had not learned any trade. I could not expect to become a bookkeeper, even to get a very small position in a business, for who would accept a young man without any other recommendation than his good looks, a young man completely unfamiliar with the language and the customs of this country? In addition, eight weeks on a sailing vessel under every imaginable deprivation had very much weakened my physical and intellectual strength. Although I had the intention of forgetting all my comfortable and easy past after my departure from Europe, and of concentrating my efforts towards the single goal of becoming a rich man — a goal only possible by hard work, toil, and economy — the execution of this plan was harder than I had thought. Everybody whom I asked for advice gave me a discouraging reply. I began to realize, only too clearly, that there is money lying around on the streets of America, but that it is very difficult and hard to pick it up. A young man, who had induced me to emigrate, and who, despite the fact of having more money, promised to work together with me, deserted me after a few days because he had found a position in a shop through the recommendation of one of his relatives. I visited my cousin Louis Basch, but I was coolly received; a question as to how things were at home was his only interest in me.

However, it was necessary for me to do something. My ten dollars was sufficient for four weeks; after that I would be without a penny. During those days I approached one person after another, willing to work for almost nothing, but, unfortunately, people believe that a young man cannot be any good who looks respectable and pretends also to be respectable, but yet is willing to take any small job.

Having spent two and a half dollars for board and lodging during the first week, I was compelled to buy some notions for the remaining seven dollars — fifty cents had been spent for small expenses — and to peddle them. My "splendid" stock in trade consisted of shoelaces, stockings, thimbles, needles and pins. This was to be the cornerstone of my fortune of the future and besides I would have to make enough to eat, drink, and buy clothes, especially shoes.

The first day's attempt at peddling was made in New York. From early in the morning until late in the night I climbed up and down stairs, until finally I made enough to pay for board and lodging for a single day. You can imagine how difficult it was for me to make even that much dealing with notions, for I could barely memorize the English names and prices of my stock, and I could not answer any other question. After having peddled for a week in New York, I had scarcely made enough for my board and lodging. The merchant from whom I bought my articles, seeing how I struggled, advised me to go to the country, and was even willing to loan me merchandise to the value of five dollars. Naturally, I accepted this offer and started at the beginning of the next week.

The first day I did well; I made a little more than I needed for food, although I ate only breakfast and supper, and as cheaply as possible. On the second and third day I also earned the money I needed for my living, but it rained on the fourth. I was compelled to spend the entire day at the inn. When the rain still did not stop the next day, I returned to New York, because it wouldn't cost me so much to live there. There are not as many good roads here as back home. The roads here are of sand and clay and a little rain is sufficient to transform them into mud. It was on a path like this that I had to walk twenty-five English miles with my pack on my back, and sinking into the mud up to my knees.

My dear friends, for the first time in America it was difficult for me to endure these hardships and privations. I finally dragged myself into New York, and the result was a fever and an injured foot which, however, I ignored. I was well aware that my material conditions did not permit me to become sick. So the next day I peddled again in New York. Although I had not eaten during the whole day, I felt too sick in the evening to take any food. In addition, my foot was so badly hurt and swollen that I

C.G. Bush. *The Peddler's Wagon*. c. 1850. Photograph. The Prints and Photographs Division. Library of Congress.

could not walk. I went to bed, and a full eight days passed before the fever disappeared. But the foot! The people with whom I lived did not know, naturally, that I was so poor, otherwise they would not have kept me any longer. My financial situation did not permit me to stay in bed for six weeks. That period, according to my doctor, was absolutely necessary for the recovery of my health. I did not have money enough to pay for my food, and even less to pay for the doctor and his expensive prescriptions. I had to make up my mind to go to a hospital for the poor where medical treatment, medicines, and food were free of charge.

My dear friends! You cannot imagine what I suffered during the six weeks which I had to spend in the hospital among sick people of all kinds and under loathsome conditions. Twice a week the doctors of the hospital operated on my foot, and, in my opinion, made it only worse. I could not understand their reason. Probably the doctors did it in order to find out how a negligible wound could cause so much irritation and swelling. I can only stress that after six weeks I left the hospital on my own initiative, physically and mentally more ill than before I had entered it. From the hospital I returned to the people with whom I had formerly lodged. There a doctor promised to cure me completely within four weeks, and all that for a fee of five dollars. I preferred to spend my last penny for such treatment and even to go into debt rather than to stay longer in the hospital. And so I submitted myself to this treatment by Dr. Berg. To put it briefly, after four weeks I had recovered, but was as poor as a church-mouse. I had to pull in a notch in my belt, for my hosts had reduced the cost of my board, and therefore I had to eat less.

During this time I met a young man whom I had known before in Inowrazlaw and who worked as a clerk in New York. After my complete recovery we agreed to peddle together. I was very happy, since the young man had about fifty dollars, and I was entitled to fifty per cent of our common profit. Eight days later I left New York with my young companion for Carbondale, a city in Pennsylvania. In the meantime I had improved my English somewhat, studying with great zeal until late in the night. Our stock had at least a value of fifty dollars. We had some success working very hard, but then suddenly war broke out in America. You must have learned about this war from your own newspapers, so it is not necessary for me to go into detail.

Business came to a standstill, all public works were stopped, and after the call of the President to defend the country with arms, all the young folks flocked to the colors. Carried away by the general enthusiasm, I became a soldier. I studied English with great zeal until I could talk fairly fluently. Since I had the good will of my superiors, I became a noncommissioned officer in a few weeks. However, the way to a higher position was barred to me, because I had to write and read English perfectly to get such an appointment. I started again, sometimes studying through the better part of the night, and all this without any help, since I did not have enough money to hire a tutor. Now I am able to speak, read, and write English well. In the meantime our enlistment term, fixed for a period of four months, expired. Everybody had believed that this war would last only four months. We had been sworn in for this period only and were discharged on its expiration. However, the war was far from being finished, and therefore the President issued a second proclamation asking for soldiers for a period of three years.

Through the intervention of several high-ranking personalities, who had become interested in me, and possibly also because of the fact that I had shown courage several times during my first enlistment, I was introduced to Secretary of War Cameron and was examined by him. I had used my time profitably to study military tactics whenever I had a moment, and so I became a first lieutenant in the cavalry of the United States. The name of my regiment is the Lochiel Light Cavalry. The name of my colonel is E. C. Williams, and that of my squadron commander is E. G. Savage. I have been given the promise of a captaincy as soon as possible, and therefore I am doing my best to make myself worthy of the commission.

We are now with our regiment in Washington; in a few days we will leave for the theater of war. Formerly a peddler, barely able to make a living, I have now become a respected man in a respected position, one filled by very few Jews.

I have been sent by my general to enlist new recruits and so I am today in Scranton, a city in Pennsylvania only twenty miles away from Carbondale, where I had peddled before. Before this no one paid any attention to me here; now I move in the best and richest circles and am treated with utmost consideration by Jews and Christians.

My dear ones, I beg you with all my heart not to be angry because I have gone to war. The dear Lord can also save me from this as He has saved me from many other perils. And should it be my destiny to lose my life, well I will have sacrificed it for a cause to which I am attached with all my heart, that is: the liberation of the United States. My beloved parents, brothers, sisters, and relatives will be taken care of. Should I fall in battle, use the enclosed address of my bank, where I have deposited my salary; should I survive, well I shall return to Germany and live with you.

Simon Wolf

From *The Presidents I Have Known*

President Lincoln Pardons a Jewish Soldier

For four decades, lawyer, political figure, and community leader Simon Wolf served as unofficial though effective ambassador and lobbyist for the American Jewish community to the government of the United States. As the title of his autobiography published in 1918 implies, the source of his influence was his warm relationship with all the presidents from Lincoln to Wilson. The best-known vignette in that work is his account of his intercession with Lincoln during the Civil War to save the life of a Jewish soldier.

I have on several occasions given the history of the Jewish soldier whom he pardoned at two o'clock in the early morning. While seated in my office prior to going to my home, I received a telegram from a town in New England asking me to wait for a letter that was coming by express. The letter came, and it stated that a young soldier, American born, of Jewish faith, had been condemned to be shot and the execution was to take place the next morning. It was in the crucial days of the war when every soldier was needed at the front and when Edwin M. Stanton, Secretary of War, had threatened to resign unless the President would stop pardoning deserters. It seemed this soldier could not get a furlough. His mother, who was on her death bed, had begged for his return, to lay her hands lovingly on his head and give him a parting blessing. The filial love was superior to his duty to the flag, and he went home, was arrested, tried and condemned to be shot. For a moment I was dazed and uncertain as to the course to be pursued. Night came on apace, and finally I concluded to call on the Hon. Thomas Corwin of Ohio, who was on intimate terms with the President. Mr. Corwin, as ever,

Jewish Union Soldiers with Their Southern Relatives. Albany, Georgia. c. 1867. Courtesy of Dr. Louis Schmier, Valdosta State University, Valdosta, Georgia.

was most gracious, but said, "My dear Mr. Wolf, it is impossible to do anything in this direction. The President has been maligned for being too generous and liberal in this respect." But I begged so hard that finally Corwin sent word over to the White House, inquiring whether an interview could be secured. The word came back, "Later in the night," and it was two o'clock in the morning before we reached the President.

The whole scene is as vividly before me as in those early hours of the morning. The President walked up and down with his hands hanging by his side, his face wore that gravity of expression that has been so often described by his historians and biographers, and yet he greeted us as if we were his boon companions and were indulging in an interchange of anecdotes, of which he was a past master. Corwin told him why we had come. He listened with deep attention, and when Corwin had exhausted the subject the President replied, "Impossible to do anything. I have no influence with this administration," and the twinkle in his eye was indescribable: "Stanton has put his foot down and insists upon one of two things, either that I must quit or he will quit." Corwin turned to me and said, "I told you, my dear friend, that it was hopeless," and was about leaving the room. I said, "Mr. President, you will pardon me for a moment. What would you have done under similar circumstances? If your dying mother had summoned you to her bedside to receive her last message before her soul would be summoned to its Maker, would you have been a deserter to her who gave you birth, rather than deserter in law but not in fact to the flag to which you had sworn allegiance?" He stopped, touched the bell; his secretary, John Hay, who time and again spoke of that occurrence, came in; he ordered a telegram to be sent to stop the execution, and that American citizen of Jewish faith led the forlorn hope with the flag of his country in his hands at the battle of Cold Harbor and was shot to death fighting heroically and patriotically for the country of his birth. When months afterward I told the President what had become of that young soldier, he was visibly moved and with great emotion said, "I thank God for having done what I did." It was an impressive scene, one full of pathos and sublime humanity, and is engraved on the tablets of memory as no other incident of my whole life.

A South Carolina Congregation Appeals to the Israelites of the United States for Aid

The devastation which the Civil War visited upon the South is poignantly reflected in an appeal issued by Congregation Sheayrith Israel in Columbia, South Carolina, to congregations and Israelites of America. For half a century Jews prospered in that city, but now, in 1867, the synagogue has fallen to ruins. The congregation seeks aid to rebuild the synagogue so that they can worship together. But their immediate concern is for the Jewish education of the children. The appeal is written in the expansive formal language of the period.

Israelites and Brethren:

Every attempt to rescue the tottering pillars of our Holy Religion from devastation and ruin; every effort to clear away the smouldering embers heaped upon the ancient relics of Judaism, and lay in its stead a foundation having for its ultimate end the eternal happiness of posterity, must merit the gratitude and deserve the kind cooperation of all who profess to be the lineal descendants of Israel.

Because the Israelite enjoys for himself the satisfactory evidence of the truth of his divine faith, it is not sufficient to exonerate or release him from lasting and binding obligations to his brethren in faith, who are less fortunate than himself. It is therefore

H.C. Norman. *A. Beekman's Dry Goods Store.* c. 1890. Photograph. Collection of Thomas and Joan Gandy.

COLORPLATE 41

MOSES HENRY. *Mizrach.* Cincinnati, Ohio. 1850. Ink on paper. 25 5/8 x 37 1/2 in. Hebrew Union College Skirball Museum, Los Angeles. Gift of Mrs. Jacob Goldsmith. *A* mizrach *(meaning "east") is hung on the eastern wall toward Jerusalem— the orientation for prayer. Profusely illustrated, most also had, as this one does, the Hebrew inscription* "Mizad zeh ruach chayim" *("from this direction the spirit of life") of which* mizrach *is an acronym.*

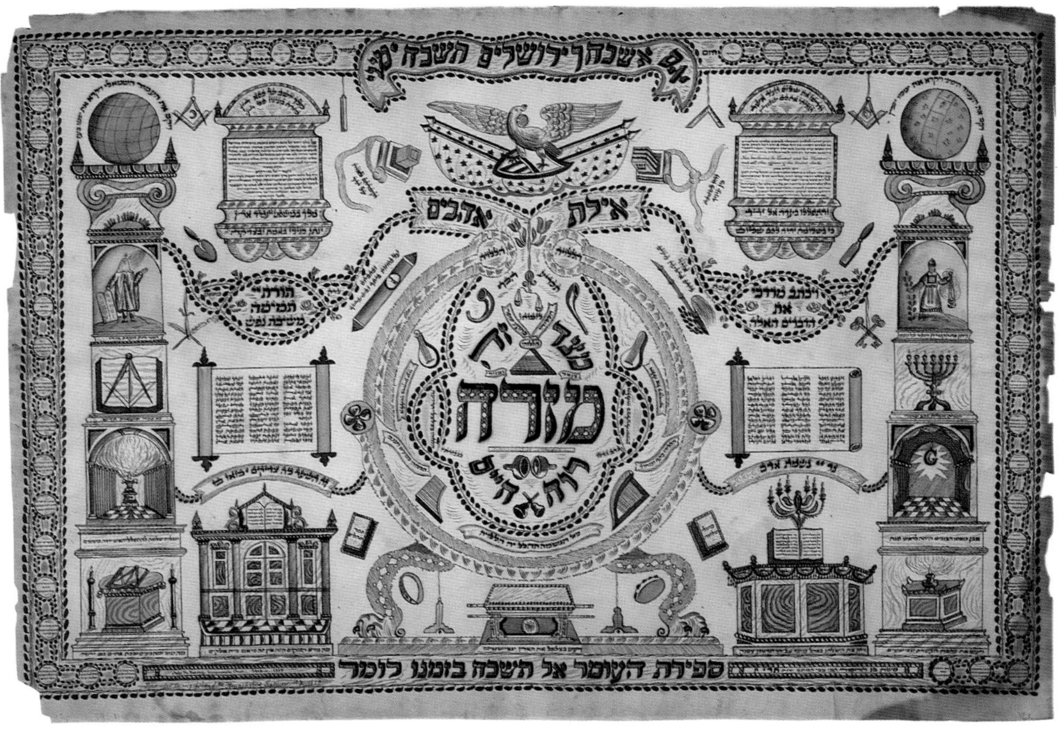

COLORPLATE 42

WOLF KURZMAN. *Mizrach.* 1903. Paper cutout, watercolor. 119 1/8 x 23 1/4 in. The Jewish Museum, New York. Gift of Mrs. Celia Goldstein.

COLORPLATE 43

PHILIP COHEN. *Mizrach.* 1861.
Cut paper and ink. 25 1/4 x 19 3/8 in.
Hebrew Union College Skirball
Museum, Los Angeles.

COLORPLATE 44

Yahrzeit Plaque for Sara Raisa.
1915. Chromolithograph.
15 3/4 x 19 in. Collection of
Peter H. Schweitzer.

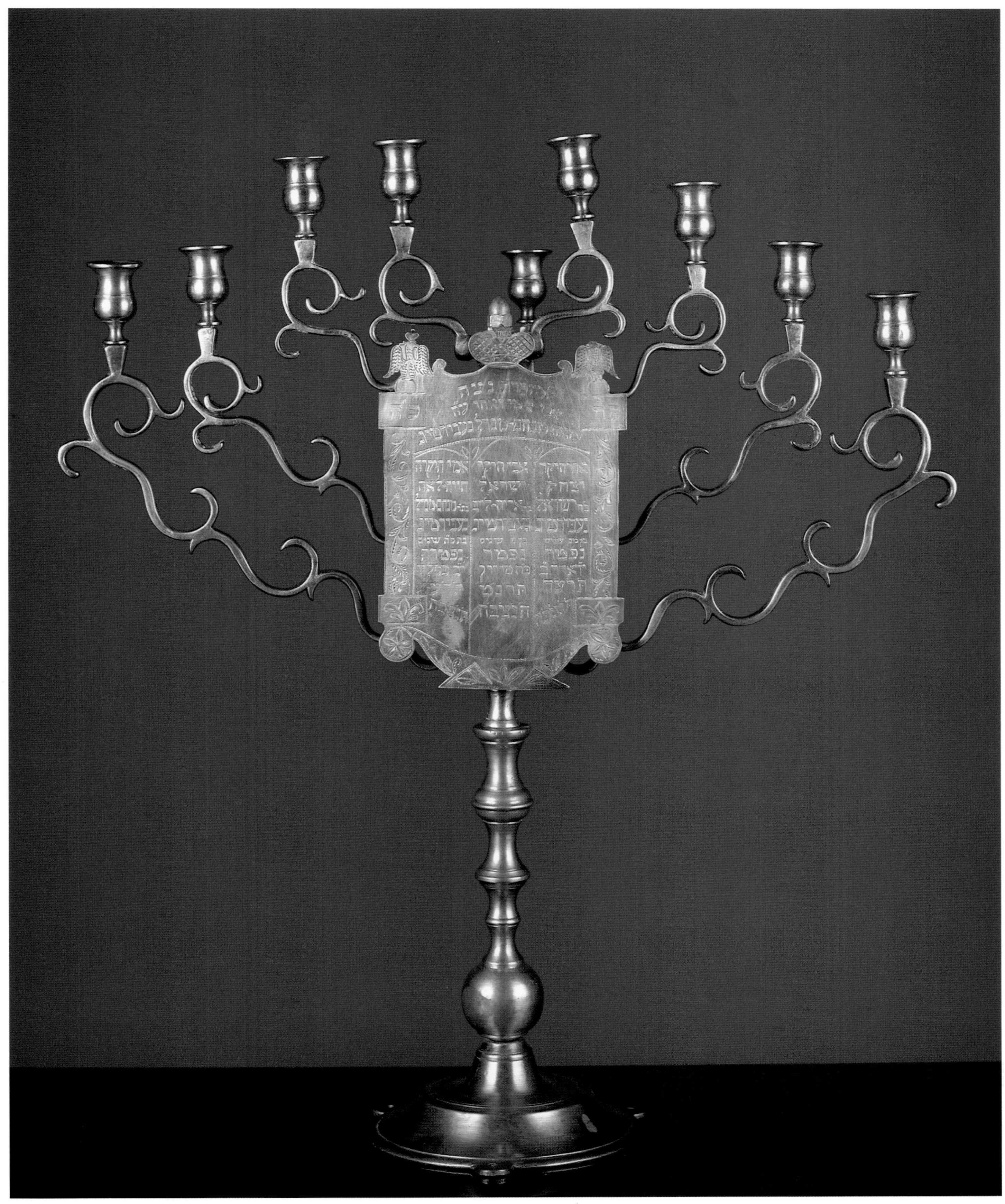

COLORPLATE 45

Silver Hanukkah Menorah. Toronto. 1877. Beth Tzedec Reuben and Helene Dennis Museum, Toronto, Canada. Given to Beth Tzedec Synagogue, Toronto, by Menachem Mendel Gebirtig in memory of his father, mother, and brother.

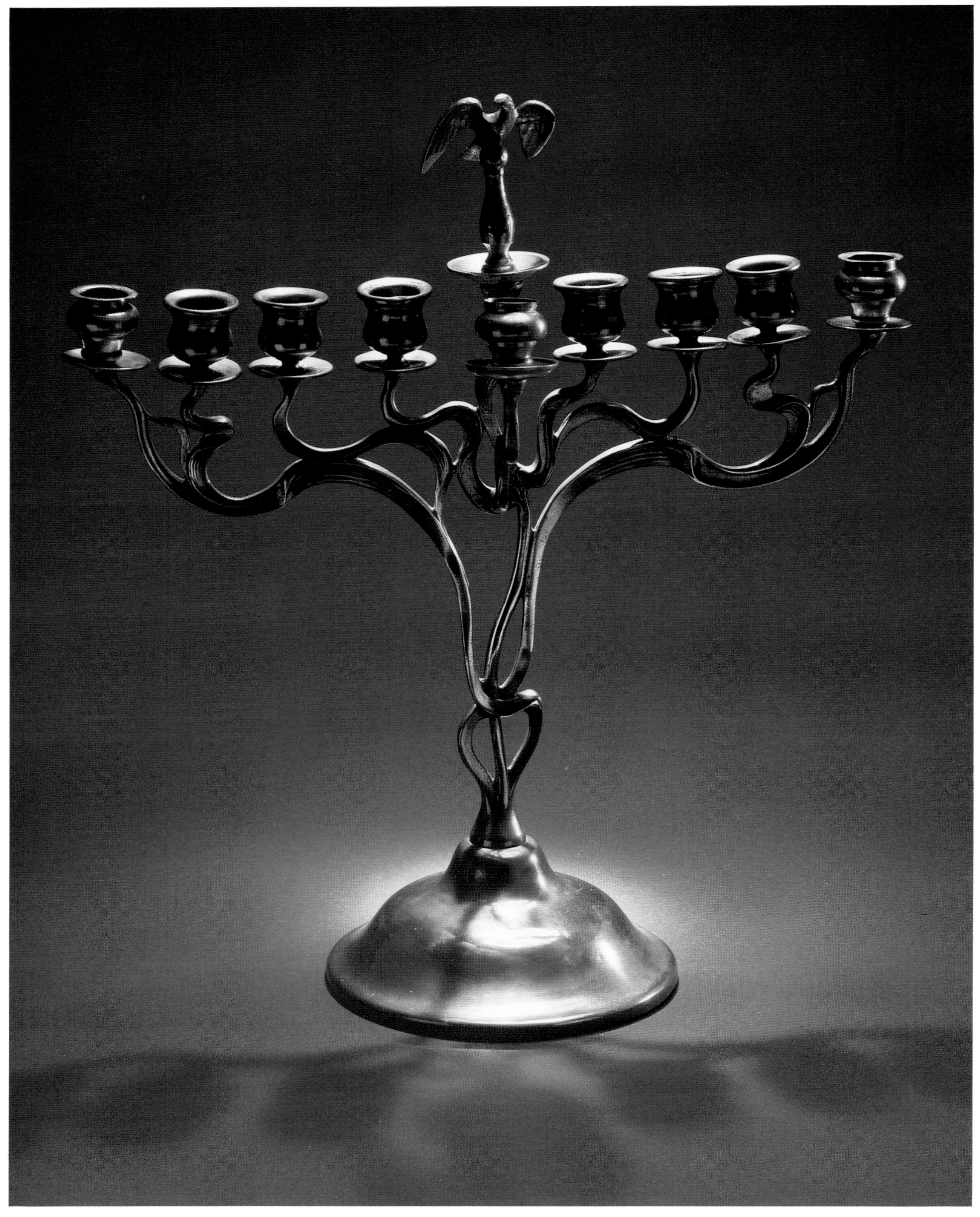

COLORPLATE 46

Hanukkah Menorah with American Eagle. 1900. Tin, cast and brass-plated. 16 x 16 x 6 in. The Jewish Museum, New York. Gift of Dr. Harry G. Friedman in memory of Professor Israel Davidson.

COLORPLATE 47

MANFRED ANSON. *Statue of Liberty Menorah.* 1986. Brass, cast. 23 x 16 1/2 x 7 in. Hebrew Union College Skirball Museum, Los Angeles. Museum purchase with Project Americana Funds provided by Peach and Mark Levy.

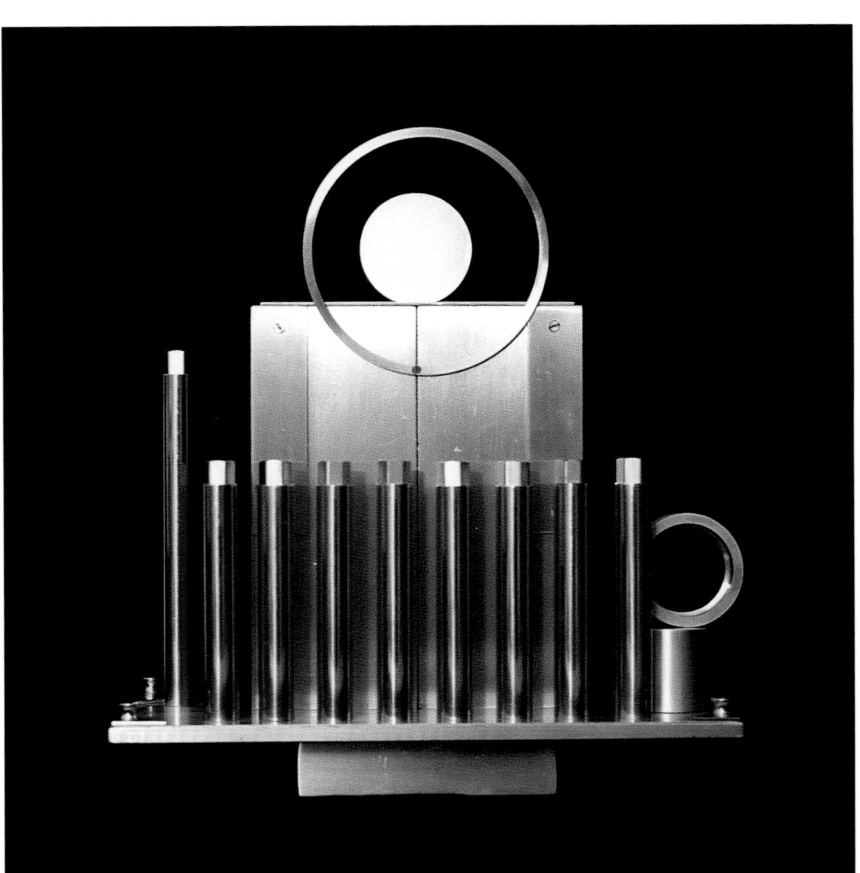

COLORPLATE 48

BRENDA ZALTAS. *Song of Faith Menorah.* 1990. Copper, brass, aluminum. Height: 10 in.; length: 12 in.; depth: 4 in. Private collection.

COLORPLATE 49

ILYA SCHOR. *Mezuzah.* c. 1950. Silver, cast, engraved. 2 3/4 in. The Jewish Museum, New York. Gift of Harold Cohen. *Born in Galicia, Ilya Schor settled in New York in 1941. His jewelry is filled with delicate, intricate design.*

COLORPLATE 50

RESIA SCHOR. *Mezuzah.* 1986. Silver. Height: 8 in.; width: 4 3/4 in.; depth: 1 1/4 in. Collection of the artist.

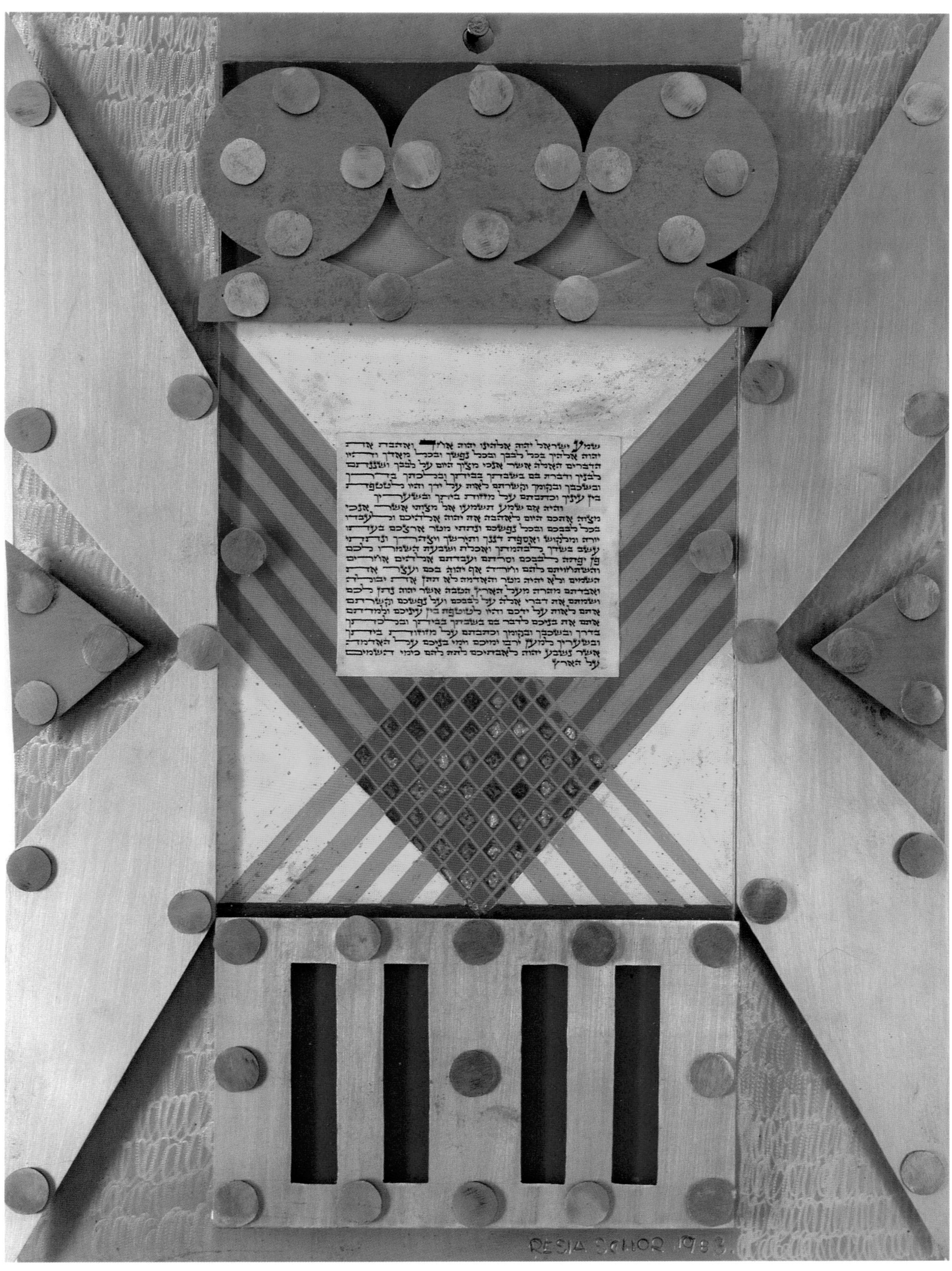

COLORPLATE 51

RESIA SCHOR. *Mezuzah.* 1983. White metal, plexiglass, goauche on paper. 12 x 9 in. Collection of the artist. *Resia Schor, wife of Ilya Schor, created this modern* mezuzah. *On the front is inscribed the* Shema *(Deuteronomy 6:4-9). The three circles on the top of the* mezuzah *represent the Hebrew letter "shin."*

COLORPLATE 52

LORELEI AND ALEX GRUSS. *Tiered Seder Plate: From Slavery to Freedom.* 1990. Ebony, purpleheart, silver. Inlay: padauk, cocobolo, maple, imboya, osage Orange; pink ivory; mahogany; vera wood; mother-of-pearl; abalone; shells; silver; brass; copper; antique ivory; gemstones; gold. 18 x 10 in. Private collection.

COLORPLATE 53

JUDITH GOLDSTEIN. *In The Beginning. A Ceremonial Server for the Round Rosh Hashanah Challah.* 1990. Diameter: 12 in., raised to 3 1/2 in. high. Pewter, ebony, garnet, peridot, black onyx, and Austrian crystal. Collection of the artist. *This plate shows the seven days of creation, the sabbath, and the Ten Commandments.*

COLORPLATE 54

MICHEL SCHWARTZ. *Cup of Elijah.* 1989. Silver and 24K gold. Cup: 9 1/2 x 3 3/4 in. Saucer: 1 x 6 in. Collection of Rabbi Menachem M. Schneerson. *The inscription on this cup contains more than 700 letters meticulously cut by hand.*

important to make this subject of our appeal a matter of serious reflection and consideration. Many of you may be aware that Israelites have been dwelling in Columbia for upwards of half a century—Israelites who have occupied high stations in society, and ornamented the social circle in which they moved. They own a grave-yard, and once owned a place of worship, which has since tumbled to ruins by slow and lingering decay. No effort has been made to raise the crumbling walls, and dedicate them to the service of the Most High.

We have about a hundred Jewish children in this city, who, aside from the faint knowledge that their progenitor Abraham was a Jew, and the condescending declaration that they are not ashamed of their origin, are strangers alike to Judaism and to every thing appertaining to our Holy Religion. These terrible facts stare us in the face in untarnished, solemn and naked truth. And knowing there are responsibilities resting upon us as Israelites; knowing that, sooner or later, we all must pass away, and sink into the profoundest obscurity of night; that a dark and lonely grave will enclose our remains and dissolve us into dust, our paramount duty is manifest. The solemn reflection should be, Is this night to last forever? Is the present visionary life our whole existence? If that which thinks and acts within us, survives the dissolution of our body, what will be our portion then? Such are the solemn reflections which crowd upon our minds, while surveying the dark picture before us. We have done all in our power with our humble and limited means to alleviate in a measure our sad condition; and are endeavoring to brush away the film of indolence and neglect which obscures the best gift from God to man. We have organized a congregation styled SHEAYRITH ISRAEL. We have a *Reader* and *Shochet*, and have prayers every Saturday at a private residence of one of our worthy and esteemed fellow-Israelites who furnishes a room gratis; and as our efforts have been in a measure, crowned with success by our Heavenly Father, it is important that we shall have a regular place of worship, where the old and young, the rich and poor, can assemble and mingle their voices in praise to the Most High.

Brethren of Israel! We, your petitioners, though strangers, perhaps, to some of you, are your own brethren in faith. There was a time when the bright sun of prosperity cast her effulgent and golden rays across our path; there was a time when appeals were made to us, as we now present them to you, and were not made in vain. But, alas! the ruthless march of time and the devastating hand of war have bereft us of all—nay, not of all, not of that trust beyond the grave—not of that hope in a bright futurity, "where the wicked cease from troubling and the weary are at rest." It is to you, fellow-Israelites, that we appeal. We call on you fraternally to assist us as much as in your power; we call on you to assist in rescuing from oblivion the precious relics of our Holy Religion; we appeal to you to lend your aid in raising the tottering pillars of our faith; we appeal to you to assist us in furnishing our young offspring with religious instruction. And where is the Israelite whose heart does not feel, or whose soul does not respond, to the call of a brother?

He who helps to establish more permanently in the minds of the rising generation, the precious truth of our Holy Religion, performs one of the highest duties which that religion inculcates, and if there should result no other benefit to him, the recollection of so just a deed will smooth the pillow of disease and assuage the pangs of dissolving nature.

All donations may be remitted to M. Winstock, Esq., President of the congregation Sheayrith Israel, who is authorized to receive the same, and they will be kindly acknowledged through the medium of the Jewish periodicals, and greatly appreciated by

Yours, very respectfully
M. WINSTOCK, President

THE IMMIGRANT EXPERIENCE

Emma Lazarus

"The New Colossus"

Daughter of a cultured and prestigious Jewish family in New York, the poet Emma Lazarus is indelibly linked to the American soul through her sonnet, "The New Colossus" (1883). In 1903

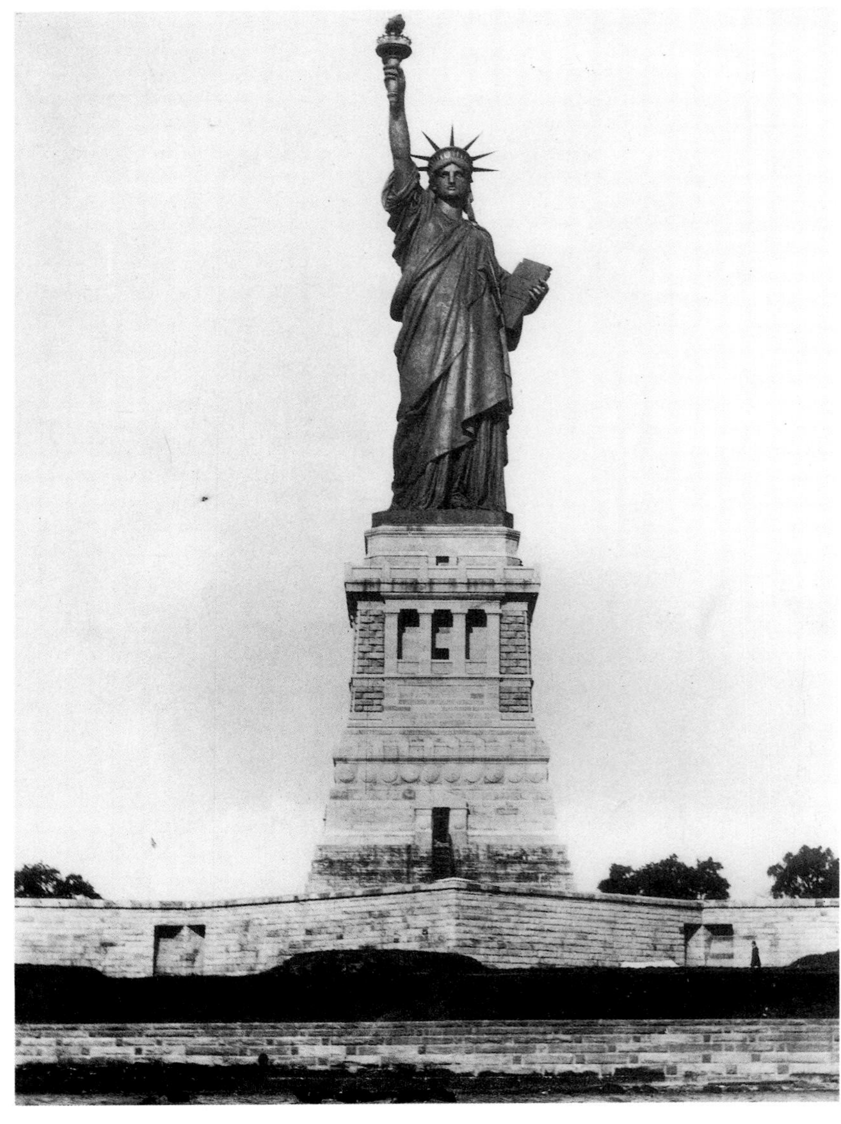

The Statue of Liberty. c. 1890s.
Brown Brothers, Sterling, Pennsylvania.

it was inscribed on the base of the Statue of Liberty and has become part of the vocabulary of America's self-image as a haven for the exiled peoples of the world.

Not like the brazen giant of Greek fame,
With conquering limbs astride from land to land;
Here at our sea-washed, sunset gates shall stand
A mighty woman with a torch, whose flame
Is the imprisoned lightning, and her name
Mother of Exiles. From her beacon-hand
Glows world-wide welcome; her mild eyes command
The air-bridged harbor that twin cities frame.
"Keep, ancient lands, your storied pomp!" cries she
With silent lips. "Give me your tired, your poor,
Your huddled masses yearning to breathe free,
The wretched refuse of your teeming shore.
Send these, the homeless, tempest-tost to me,
I lift my lamp beside the golden door!"

Harry Golden

From *Forgotten Pioneer*

Levi Strauss

How Jewish immigrant ingenuity was wed to an immediate need on the American frontier during the California gold rush of 1849 is described by popular essayist Harry Golden. Levi Strauss had soft tent canvas, made in Nimes, France, called "serge de Nimes." In America this quickly became "de Nimes" and then "denim." Gold rush miners needed strong pants with welded pockets, and the denim pants, known as Levis, came into being, and through them an entire American industrial empire flourishing to the present day.

The denim was not quite taut enough for tenting. In the end, Levi had to part with fifty dollars to purchase a wagon so he could transport his denim, all several rolls of it, through the city streets.

So he was in San Francisco with denim he couldn't sell and a wagon which had cost a good portion of his fast diminishing money and with no way to re-equip himself to make his living.

He started pushing his wagon through the muddy street. It was rough going. The spring thaw had made the street a quagmire. Sometimes Levi had to drop the handles of his wagon and put his shoulder to a wheel to get it over a bad place. Sometimes he

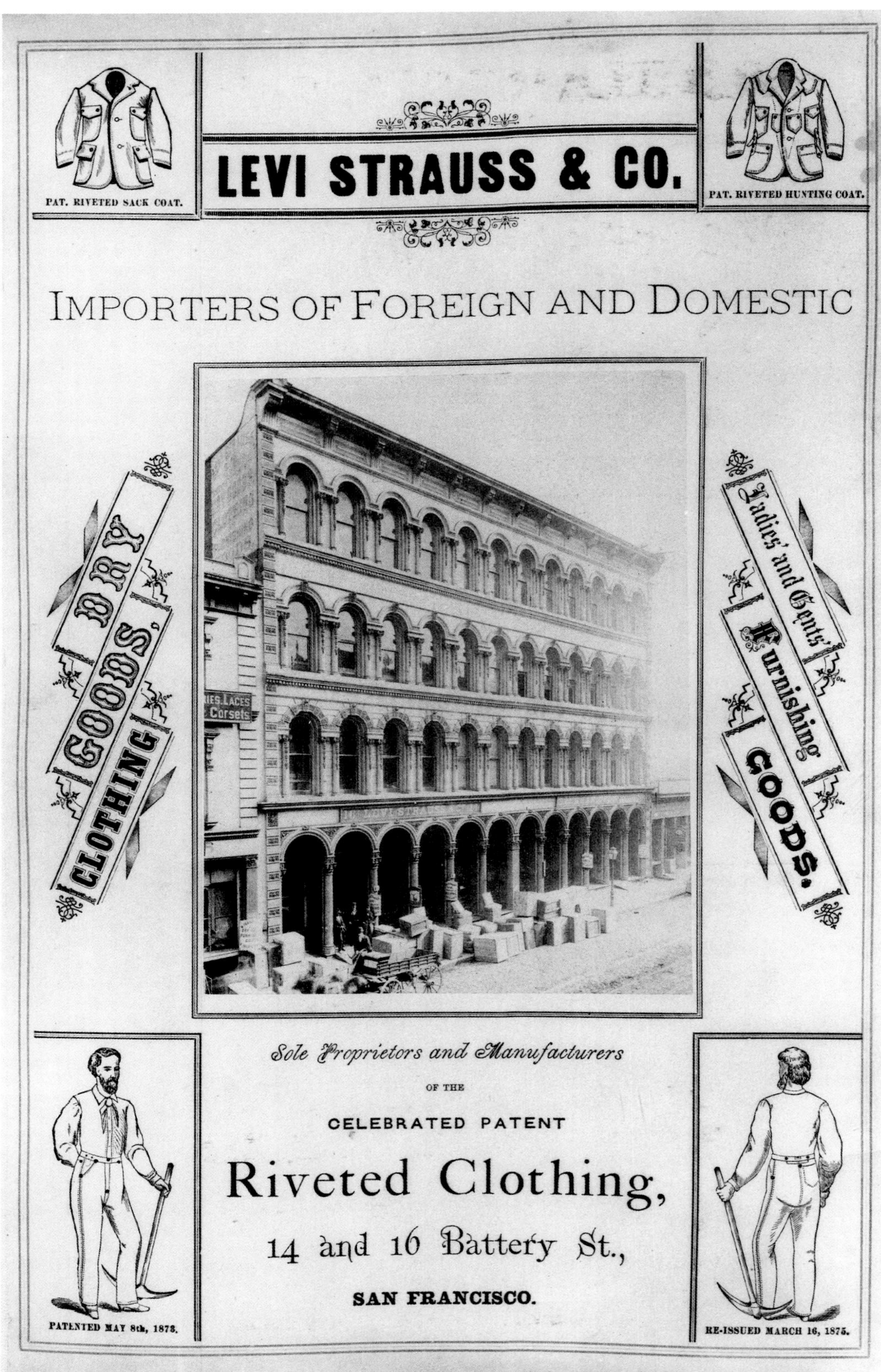

Advertisement, Levi Strauss & Co. c. 1870s. The Bancroft Library, University of California, Berkeley, California. *The company, still under the founding family's contract, is the oldest major clothing manufacturer in the United States.*

had to transport his denim to the wooden sidewalk so he could lift his wagon from where it had bogged down, carry it to a dry spot, and reload his goods. He was trying to reach the trail that started the miners off toward the gold fields and it took him the better part of the day to reach that point.

He hoped to sell some of the denim to the departing forty-niners, but by the time he had positioned himself beside the men selling potatoes and boots and compasses, it was dark. He settled down for the night without food and wrapped himself in the denim to ward off the cold. In the morning he was treated to his first view of the parade of men off to the "diggins." They straggled along, some with mules laden with equipment, some with nothing but a shovel and a pan. There were scores of men banded together and scores starting out singly and alone. They were bearded and old, clean-shaven and young. It was a clear spring day, yet some of them wore heavy mackinaws, probably intending to stay out through the next winter. Some wore simple shirts which would never protect them from freezing weather. One man walked by, his mule laden with equipment, slowly playing a harmonica. Some of them would never come back, leaving their bones to bleach on the California hills; some of them would come back and go out again and spend the best part of themselves searching for riches that would never come; and some would come back and be rich men forever.

None of them this morning stopped at the place of the German immigrant. Few stopped anywhere. Now and then, they halted and inspected the wares laid before them and occasionally bought.

The first man to stop at Levi's wagon in the afternoon was a returning miner. He rode a sway-backed horse and he reined it before Levi's wagon and looked at the denim.

"Whatcha selling there, young fellow?" he asked.

"Tenting," said Levi.

"Don't need no tenting," said the man. "Need pants." He nudged his horse and started off, but Levi stopped him. "I can make you pants. I can make you pants from this that will last you."

"Okay, young fellow," said the man, dismounting. "I'll buy a pair of pants. I'm a sourdough and I need pants up in my diggins."

"What's a sourdough?" asked Levi.

"Why, it's a feller digs or pans for gold. Call us sourdoughs because that's what we eat. Fry ourselves some flour mixed with water."

When the sourdough dismounted, Levi saw readily enough why he needed pants. The pants he wore were out at the seat, and on both knees the patches had come loose.

"Never thought of making pants from tenting," said the sourdough, handling the denim.

"Neither did I," said Levi, "till I saw you."

The sourdough threw his head back and laughed. "Reckon that makes us even," he said.

Levi had no tape measure, but he had some string. He wrapped it around the sourdough's waist, and when he started to measure the inseam the man stopped him, and said, "You make 'em long so I'll have patching material. I'll roll 'em up." Levi followed the man's instructions.

"How much these pants gonna cost me?" asked the sourdough.

Levi did some mental arithmetic and said, "Six dollars."

"Ain't got no six dollars," said the sourdough. "But I got a good pinch of gold dust." He dug into his saddle bags and extracted a small leather pouch identical with the one in which he kept his tobacco that he chewed constantly as though it were food. Levi wondered if he ever got the two pouches mixed up and instead of tobacco stuffed his mouth with gold? The miner extended a good pinch of gold to Levi but the young man shook his head. "We have to go into San Francisco and have the pants cut."

"I need them pants now," said the miner, snatching back his gold and stuffing it into his pouch.

Levi had not been a peddler for nothing. He pointed patiently to San Francisco a mile away and said, just as if he had said it many times before, "We have simply to go into the city and have the pants cut. These are custom-tailored pants as befits a man with gold dust, and you will wear them before nightfall."

Once more Levi struggled with the wagon through the muddy ruts back to the city. The sourdough rode beside him, watching with the casual contempt of the plainsman the incredible struggle of the man of the city. Levi was certain that if the time came when he had to mount a horse he would be frightened of it. Right now he was more concerned with the prospects of finding a tailor than he was with his Herculean labors. He didn't know how much patience the sourdough had.

But he found a tailor and on sudden inspiration, Levi asked him to cut up all the tenting into pants, paying the tailor with the gold dust the miner gave him.

Thus when once again he ventured from the city, he went with a wagon filled with pants, all of which he sold that day. But selling the denim pants was no trick, no fortuitous occurrence. There were no work pants for sale in San Francisco. There were fine clothes, to be sure, and beaver coats and top hats, but there were no proper clothes for the prospectors, clothes that would stand the wear and tear of work at placer mining and mountain digging.

Levi Strauss opened a store on California Street in San Francisco, and proceeded immediately to improve his denim pants. Levi had equipped the pants with pockets, which the sourdough stuffed with nuggets they called "specimens," and which they brought back to the assay office to have examined for gold content. The pockets barely survived one trip, the weight of the "specimens" soon had them torn and flapping. One of these sourdoughs had a blacksmith rivet the back pockets with black iron nails. When Levi heard about it, he was struck with how good an idea it was. He experimented and found that a copper rivet did the trick better. After that, his pants were strengthened with copper rivets at all points of strain. He was selling a strong pair of pants which were like no other pants in the entire world.

It was not unusual in the years that followed for miners, then lumbermen, then cowboys, then farmers to come into this store and ask for a pair of "them pants of Levi's." In this manner did Levi Strauss become part of the West—by lending it his name.

Eventually his pants, which he had sold to a tattered sourdough on a sudden inspiration, became synonymous with the West itself. To this day, who is there who does not know what Levis are? Though Levi outgrew the desire to clothe himself in beaver and wear polished boots, he could have worn such clothes every day had he chosen. He made jeans and made them well. His business flourished and by the time he left this earth he was so much a part of San Francisco that half the front page of the morning newspaper was devoted to his obituary. And one hundred years after Levi Strauss left Germany, the company he founded was back in Europe with a warehouse at Antwerp distributing Levis in the European Common Market.

Levi has become part of our tradition, and though English remained perplexing to him until he died, no one ever could say that the man who made Levis wasn't authentically American.

Mary Antin

From *From Plotsk to Boston*

"The Climax of Our Joy"

First to come was the father. He worked hard, scrimped, and saved up the precious dollars which would enable him to bring his dear ones. In the Old Country, the mother told idyllic sto-

ries of the Golden Land and drew idealized word portraits of her husband. After an arduous journey, the family must endure endless formalities aboard ship before the joyous reunion with the father. Antin, author of a classic of immigrant literature, The Promised Land *(1912), purged her Jewish identity in the melting pot of America.*

Before the ship had fully stopped, the climax of our joy was reached. One of us espied the figure and face we had longed to see for three long years. In a moment five passengers on the "Polynesia" were crying, "Papa," and gesticulating, and laughing, and hugging one another, and going wild altogether. All the rest were roused by our excitement, and came to see our father. He recognized us as soon as we him, and stood apart on the wharf not knowing what to do, I thought.

What followed was slow torture. Like mad things we ran about where there was room, unable to stand still as long as we were on the ship and he on shore. To have crossed the ocean only to come within a few yards of him, unable to get nearer till all the fuss was over, was dreadful enough. But to hear other passengers called who had no reason for hurry, while we were left among the last, was unendurable.

Oh, dear! Why can't we get off the hateful ship? Why can't papa come to us? Why so many ceremonies at the landing?

We said goodbye to our friends as their turn came, wishing we were in their luck. To give us something else to think of, papa succeeded in passing us some fruit; and we wondered to find it anything but a great wonder, for we expected to find everything marvelous in the strange country.

Steerage Deck of the S.S. Pennland of the Red Star Line. 1893. The Museum of the City of New York. The Byron Collection.

Still the ceremonies went on. Each person was asked a hundred or so stupid questions, and all their answers were written down by a very slow man. The baggage had to be examined, the tickets, and a hundred other things done before anyone was allowed to step ashore, all to keep us back as long as possible.

Now imagine yourself parting with all you love, believing it to be a parting for life; breaking up your home, selling the things that years have made dear to you; starting on a journey without the least experience in travelling, in the face of many inconveniences on account of the want of sufficient money; being met with disappointment where it was not to be expected; with rough treatment everywhere, till you are forced to go and make friends for yourself among strangers; being obliged to sell some of your most necessary things to pay bills you did not willingly incur; being mistrusted and searched, then half starved, and lodged in common with a multitude of strangers; suffering the miseries of seasickness, the disturbances and alarms of a stormy sea for sixteen days; and then stand within a few yards of him for whom you did all this, unable to even speak to him easily. How do you feel?

Oh, it's our turn at last! We are questioned, examined, and dismissed! A rush over the planks on one side, over the ground on the other, six wild beings cling to each other, bound by a common bond of tender joy, and the long parting is at an END.

Ephraim E. Lisitzky

From *In the Grip of Crosscurrents*

"In the Dusk My Father's Face. . ."

After an adventurous life in the Northwest and Canada, Ephraim Lisitzky became the principal of a Hebrew School in New Orleans and one of the premier Hebrew poets in America. In this story from his autobiography published in 1959 a young man eagerly anticipates his reunion in America with a father he has not seen in over eight years. But the reality of the reunion is far removed from his fantasies.

During all of my trip to America my imagination kept conjuring up a picture of my encounter with my father. The image of my father's face, which had dimmed in my memory, shone through a haze of eight and a half years as it had registered in it the night before his departure, as I lay at his side holding him in tight desperation. Only now, his melancholy look of compassion had brightened. Anticipation of reunion softened the trials of the journey—stealing across the border, wandering through thick forests in the dark of night, the ship tossed about by storm for three consecutive days.

The picture of our reunion became sharper when, in New York, I boarded the train for Boston. The entire trip I visualized my father at the station, waiting for the train to pull in. When the train arrived and I got off, he would rush over and embrace me. I could see him standing there and hear the clatter of the train wheels bringing his greetings to me: "Welcome, my son!" And my heart responded in joyful tones: "Papa! Papa!"

The train slowed down to enter the station and my heart beat faster, as though to prod the train to hurry. Through the coach window I could see faces and eyes happy, trembling with anticipation. I searched for my father but he wasn't there! I descended from the coach, still looking and my heart scrutinizing every face in the crowd. But my father was nowhere in the crowd! I trudged to my father's home stopping passers-by on the street to show them the crumpled address transcribed in my strange tongue. When I finally got there he was not in—he had gone to work early, as he did every day, for the telegram from New York announcing the time of our arrival in Boston had been misaddressed and had not reached him.

At the entrance to the hall of a house populated with poor tenants, with one of whom my father roomed, I stood tense with anticipation. My eyes scrutinized every passer-by; perhaps father would be there, for his landlord had gone to look for him in the street to tell him of our arrival. The din of the city filled the street. Foot and wagon peddlers shrilly announced their wares. An Italian ground his organ as girls danced on the sidewalk and in the street. Boys skated madly along, holding on to one another's back in a long line that twisted and straightened, broke apart and joined again. In

Back Alley, Jewish Section in Boston. Carpenter Center for the Visual Arts at Harvard University, Cambridge, Massachusetts.

passing they glanced mockingly at me, eyeing my Slutzk garb which branded me as a "greenhorn," and my strange hat—a stiff Homburg acquired in Belgium after I had lost my Slutzk cap en route. They laughed and hurled at me names, which, though uttered in a foreign tongue, were clearly not complimentary.

Many tedious hours I stood and waited, rejecting the pleas of my stepmother and my father's landlady to eat and rest from the journey. I was not going to put off for one moment the anticipated meeting with my father. The hours passed. Standing there, all tensed up, my nerves on edge, the effects of the two weeks at sea overcame me and I swayed and sank to a step near the entrance to the hall. I fell into a kind of exhausted faint which lasted many minutes.

Suddenly, a figure came towards me through a rosy mist. As it approached, the mist lifted and I saw it, radiant and compassionate. I leaped up—it was my father.

In the dusk my father's face loomed up from the street. He walked heavily bent under a sack full of rags and bottles. His face was dark and hard, with an expression of mingled humiliation and forgiveness. I shrank back, offended and silenced.

At midnight, lying on the bedding they had laid out for me in a corner of the kitchen floor in the apartment where my father roomed, I cried in silence over the alienation that screened me from my father.

Israel Kasovich

From *The Days of Our Years*

The Eternal People in the Land of Promise

Am Olam *(The Eternal People), a movement to establish cooperative agricultural colonies in the United States, was founded in 1881 by a group of idealistic Jews in Odessa, Russia. It did succeed in planting colonies in Louisiana, North Dakota, and Oregon, but they were all short-lived. Among those who came to settle on the soil were Israel Kasovich and his family and colleagues. In his autobiography,* The Days of Our Years, *he tells of the adventures of the group on their arrival in New York. By 1890 the movement had dissipated. Kasovich describes how the dream began to fade.*

At last New York hove into sight. The ship drew near to Castle Garden. The members of the Am Olam party were dressed in holiday attire. We were lined up on the deck in expectation of a warm welcome. Thus we stood in a festive frame of mind, and our leaders unfurled our large flag, so that the world might see and know who was coming here. But no sooner had the flag begun to wave triumphantly in the air, displaying conspicuously the large golden words "Am Olam," than a man ran over to us and ordered us to lower the flag. We told him with an air of self-assurance that this was a free country, whereupon he became furious, snatched up the flag and hurled it straight into the sea. We felt as though our faces had been slapped.

We disembarked at Castle Garden. The circular building was jammed with immigrants who had arrived before us. There was no place to sit down, but who cared to sit there, when we felt sure we were being awaited outside?

Currier & Ives. *The Port of New York, Bird's Eye View: Looking South.* 1878. Lithograph. Museum of the City of New York. The Harry T. Peters Collection. *Castle Garden, seen here, served as the place of debarcation for arriving immigrants until 1890 when it was replaced by Ellis Island.*

They took down our names and records. Unlike to-day, they made very little fuss over it in those days, and presently we walked into the small Battery Park just outside Castle Garden, and halted. There was no one there to meet us, and we did not know where to go. Our leaders hurried away to obtain information, and we waited. Tired and weary, the women and the children sat down upon the grass, whereupon a policeman rushed up and ordered them to get off the grass.

A couple of hours later our leaders returned, accompanied by a representative of the Immigrant Aid Committee, and told us to go back to Castle Garden, where we would have to pass the night. As the building was filled with other immigrants, we stayed in the courtyard. Here there were no seats; you either stood or sat upon the cold pavement.

A representative of the aforesaid committee brought us bread and sausages and began to pass them around among us. Many refused to take the victuals, preferring to go out and buy their own food; but they were no longer able to leave the premises, all gates having been locked for the night.

Night fell. Many of the women sat crying softly. The men were despondent. Each asked the other, "What is going on here?" and there was no one to answer. We waited for the morrow. The night happened to be a chilly one, and a cold wind was blowing from the ocean. Our belongings were still in the ship's baggage-room, and we had to sleep on the bare and cold ground. But who slept? We took off our upper garments and wrapped them around the children, who fell asleep on the cold pavement, while their mothers sat on the ground nearby, sighing and groaning and choking with tears.

When it grew light, we presented a sorry spectacle. We all looked exhausted and dismal as though we had just emerged from a long illness, and in addition we were covered with dust. A little later some one brought us again bread and sausages and cold coffee. There was fresh wailing among our womenfolk, who did not want to eat the bread of charity.

A couple of hours later Castle Garden became deserted. The other immigrants, the Gentiles, had no one to wait for, so they went each his way, and meanwhile we were advised to seize the vacant seats in the deserted building.

We spent a couple of days in Castle Garden, sleeping on the bare benches, then a representative of the Immigrant Aid Committee came to take our womenfolk away to houses of shelter on certain islands. Again there was wailing. Our women refused to go alone, but our leaders succeeded in calming them, and finally they went.

We men walked aimlessly around, while our leaders hurried hither and thither and spoke in whispers. Finally, after a couple of days more of uncertainty, we were called together and informed that as regards our becoming farmers, that was now entirely out of the question, and that each of us had better try to find something to do. We divided up the money still remaining in the treasury, and every one felt beaten. We were ashamed of ourselves. To think that we had allowed ourselves to be thus led astray! For who would have gone to America if not to become a tiller of the soil?

Second Annual Report of the Association for Jewish Immigrants of Philadelphia

To facilitate Russian Jewish migration to the United States, a tripartite division of responsibility was arranged. The journey westward across Europe became the responsibility of German Jewry through its Hilfsverein; *The London Manor House Committee was to get the immigrants to America. On arrival, their settlement and immigration were the responsibility of American Jewry, through the Hebrew Emigrant Aid Society. Soon the Russian Jewish immigrant community itself took leadership in organizing aid for new arrivals. One of the first such organizations was the Association for Jewish Immigrants of Philadelphia. Its agent, Moses Klein, offered examples of that aid at their annual meeting, November 7, 1886.*

As a partial illustration of the work accomplished through our agent, Mr. M. Klein, we will cite the following few instances:—

Out of the fifty-three passengers who arrived here on the steamship *British Prince* on March 21, thirty-six left for New York, which place was their original destination. In order to prevent their being returned, as was done on a previous occasion, our agent followed them at midnight, arriving just in time to save them from annoyance. The whole party were taken by him to a respectable restaurant, where they bathed themselves, changed their clothing and held a religious service it being Purim. They then partook of a good breakfast procured by the agent, of which some Christian immigrants also partook. Our agent addressed them in a body, with happy and opportune allusions to the festival, of which that day was the anniversary and gave them wholesome advice as to their future conduct, and the necessity of their becoming good American citizens. Twenty-two of these people obtained immediate employment and the rest were taken charge of by their friends.

Nineteen out of thirty-seven of those who arrived on the 23d of August were advised by some impostors to take their baggage outside of the steamship wharf, where their friends would find them. There they remained in the open street until eleven o'clock at night, where our agent discovered them and removed them with their luggage, back into the station and afterwards to our emigrant house, where they

DAVID COHEN,
The Leading One Price Shoe House,
31 NORTH EIGHTH STREET,
Facing Filbert.

A rural gas-extinguisher/.
S. BERNSTEIN,
WATCHMAKER & JEWELER
1214 N. SECOND ST.
Philadelphia.
FINE SPECTACLES A SPECIALTY.

H. & D. COHEN,
FINE SHOES
No. 123 N. Eighth Street,
(Above Arch St., East Side,) Phila.

Trade Cards for Businesses in Philadelphia. Collection of Peter H. Schweitzer.

remained until rooms and employment were secured. All of these were without a cent of money, and it can readily be imagined the misery that would have been their lot had our society not been in existence.

During a visit to New York our agent went to Castle Garden, accompanied by a friend engaged in charity work, and found one family, consisting of a woman and six children, who were bound for Philadelphia to rejoin the husband and father, but were detained because they had no tickets for this city, and were in danger of being reshipped to Europe. Three hours afterwards the father of the woman, who lived in Fitzwater Street, and the husband, who lived in Lombard Street, were found. The branch office of the foreign company who sold the tickets supposed to be from Europe to Philadelphia was visited, and threatened with exposure and legal proceedings if the family was not at once furnished with transportation to this city. The result was that they arrived here the same night, and were taken to the house that had been procured and furnished for them four weeks previously. Is this not practical, timely and effective charity—a charity no mere outlay of money can effect?

A boy named H. K., eleven years of age, from Kurland, was compelled to remain in our house until his father could be found. He was supposed to be at Lancaster, but was traced to Lykens, Dauphin County, Pennsylvania.

The G. family, consisting of five persons, were supported at our house until their cousin could be discovered. He was called Schatzman, of 500 Widden Street, whereas the correct address was Katzman, 518 Washington Avenue. This confusion in names and numbers occurs frequently.

A Roumanian family were swindled by an expressman out of every cent they possessed. Our agent took them to New York whither they were bound, and had them placed in a respectable family from their own country, and thus relieved our local charity from contributions.

A family of five from the *British Prince,* acting upon the advice of some runners, hired a wagon to take them to some address. After wandering about for a long time, he brought them back to the emigrant station, where being discovered by our agent, they were taken to our house, where they remained until their relations were notified and situations obtained.

Two women with their children arrived on the *British King*, September 13, on their way to join their husbands, supposed to be in this city, viz: Mrs. F. with three children and Mrs. J. with two children. Upon due inquiry the husband of the former was found to be in Chicago, and the latter in New York. They were forwarded to these cities at the expense of our society.

M. G., aged 47 years, a native of Russia, arrived here about seven weeks ago on his way to join a cousin in Wertheimer Colony, Canada, but was persuaded by a countryman to remain here, and the consequence was that in three weeks he had spent all his money. He then applied to us for re-shipment, was taken to the Jefferson Medical College for examination, and found to be physically unable to obtain a livelihood. During the interval prior to his re-shipment he was placed to work in the wood yard, at Seventeenth and Lombard Streets, and earned sufficient to keep him. On November 2d he was re-shipped to Liverpool on the *British King*, furnished by us with bedding, etc., and a letter from the President of this society to the Jewish Immigrant Aid Society at Liverpool, recommending him for further assistance on his return to Russia.

Mrs. R. S. and two children were destined for Cincinnati and forwarded there, but her baggage was missing and was last seen at Liverpool. Upon enquiring by letter, it was discovered, sent here on the *British King*, and then forwarded to Mrs. S. at Cincinnati at a cost of $1.50.

But it is useless to extend these relations further, we have given enough to furnish some idea of the nature of our work.

As an illustration of some of the perils to which unprotected female immigrants are exposed, we will relate two instances:—An attractive young girl, seventeen years of age, was urged by a suspicious-looking man to go under his care to New York. Our agent interposed, and upon examination found she had an uncle residing in Chicago. He took charge of her, procured her food and a railroad ticket, and telegraphed to her uncle to meet her, despite the vexation and chagrin of her would-be betrayer.

A very prepossessing young woman destined for San Francisco was induced to go to a beer saloon to await intelligence from her husband. She fell under the notice of our agent while accompanied by the saloon keeper and another man. Her genteel dress and handsome appearance attracted general attention and there was evidently a concerted effort made to detain her. Our agent enquired of her why she remained at the saloon and where she was to go. She replied that she wished to go to her husband in California, but that all her money was spent and she had acted on the advice of these gentlemen to notify her husband and remain at the saloon until she received money to proceed. He then asked if she wished to go on at once, to which she quickly assented.

The Alliance Agricultural Colony: A Report and a Plea

As early as 1843, Julius Stern, a Jewish immigrant from Germany, expressed the "wish that a considerable number (of Jews) might emigrate to the United States and found a colony in some of the western territories" and the hope that "In such a society, excellent men and worthy women might spring up, who would deserve to be called an ornament to Israel, and an honor to mankind." Beginning in 1880, colonies were founded in the Southwest and South but lack of experience and funding, added to natural calamities, wiped out one after another. Among the earliest was Alliance Colony in southern New Jersey, established under the auspices of the Hebrew Emigrant Aid Society of New York in 1882. Three years later it issued this report.

The soil is not naturally rich, but may be made very productive if properly composed and carefully cultivated. In these circumstances, with lack of experience and an almost total want of supplies, it must not be regarded as a matter of surprise to find that our crops and the results of our skill in management are not what we expected, nor what the founders of the Colony had reason to expect. Still, though very sadly disappointed and in many respects much distressed as to how we are to live, yet we are not disheartened; but hope, with your continual care and encouragement, to be able to accomplish what may be reasonably expected . . .

The area of the Colony is one thousand one hundred and fifty acres. Of this one hundred and fifty acres are the common property of the Colony, intended for burial ground, school buildings, factories, etc. The remaining number of acres is divided into small farms of about fifteen acres. According to the contracts each farmer pays $350 within ten years—for the house and well $150, and $15 per acre for the land. During the first four years only the interest is to be paid; during the six remaining years the full amount is to be paid in equal annual payments.

On each farm there is a two-story house of two rooms, twelve by fourteen feet, and a well. These houses were built by the committee. At present there is not a house in the Colony that has not been enlarged. In some instances one room has been added, in others two rooms. In addition, everyone knows the necessity of a small barn, stable, chicken house and other buildings. Thus it will be seen that with all our want of experience and knowledge of the soil some progress has been made. During the first of the settlement each family, according to the number of men, received eight to twelve dollars a month for nine months and one hundred dollars worth of seed for planting. Each farmer received in addition to the above some furniture, cooking utensils and small farming implements, like axes, saws, grindstones, etc. The second year each received thirty dollars worth of seed.

We have not yet had sufficient time to be getting any real advantage from our farms. Besides, every farmer who has at all succeeded in South Jersey well knows that it takes time to enrich soil, naturally light, in order to get good crops. Then it is a matter of actual fact that the last season in this region was a peculiarly dry and unfruitful year. Even the experienced farmer in many instances did not get a crop large enough to pay for the seed sown . . . It is exceedingly oppressive to us, to know that with all our labor, expenditure of money and loss of time, we are not in circumstances to go on with our farm work as we must in order to live.

While discouraged in one direction, we cannot but feel encouraged in other directions. Our children are attending public school, and thereby enjoying advantages for which we try to feel thankful. Thanks to Mr. M. Heilgrin [Heilprin] and Judge M. S. Isaacs, of New York, we are provided with a teacher of the Hebrew language. Disaster must not be overlooked; five houses have been burned, three only were insured.

At present the Colony consists of forty-nine families—four to six men in a family—total, two hundred and eighty-five. All the Colonists are thrifty, laborious and hard working. Most of the men were traders and merchants in their native home in Russia. The men are healthy and cheerful. This cannot be said of the women. There is more or less of constitutional distress, accompanied with suffering . . . Something, doubtless, may be attributed to exposure. The houses are frail and not substantially

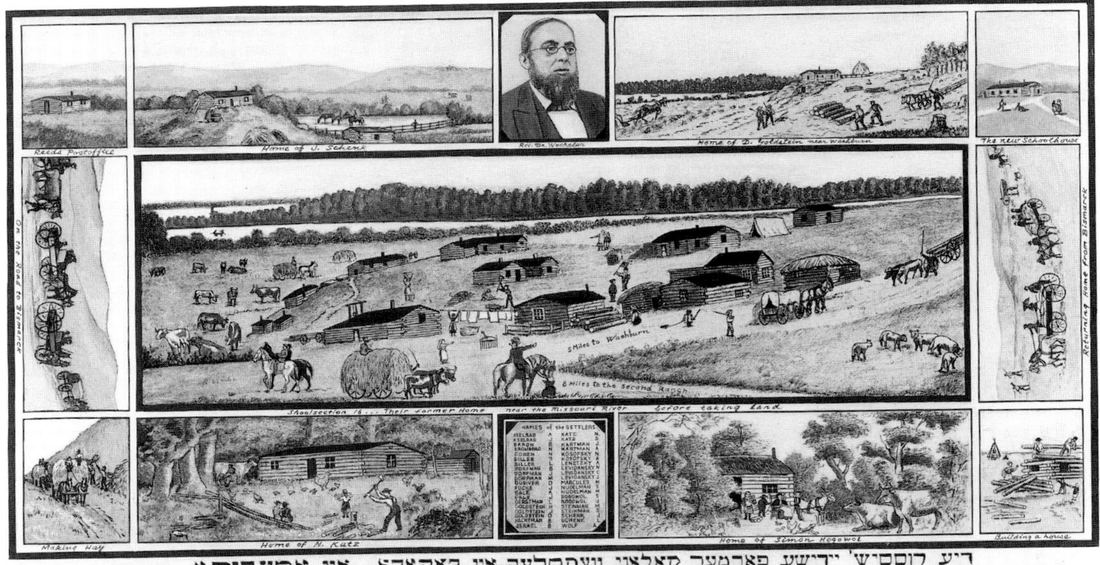
DRAWN FROM NATURE BY S. LEVY
THE RUSSIAN JEWISH FARMER SETTLEMENT WECHSLER
BURLEIGH COUNTY DAKOTA TERRITORY.
COPYRIGHTED BY T. W. INGERSOLL

The Russian Jewish Farmer Settlement, Wechsler. Burleigh County, Dakota Territory. American Jewish Archives, Cincinnati Campus. Hebrew Union College, Jewish Institute of Religion. *This colony was established by 20 familes near the town of Bismarck, North Dakota. Each family had 160 acres of government land.*

built, and, as a consequence, there must be exposure to cold during winter and to heat in summer.

Only two years have gone. We have worked hard, we have worked perseveringly amid many trials and much self-denial. With bad seasons and especially the last season, we have literally nothing on which to lay our plans for the future. True, nominally, we have a home; but a home in a strange land with no money in our purses and no crops, how are we to live?

To avert actual starvation and at the same time enable us, as helpless Colonists, to earn our own living, which we very much prefer to do, two factories were erected; but, as all know, it is not easy to obtain work. One of these buildings was designed to be a sewing establishment; but there was no sewing to do. Consequently the building is now standing idle. The other was intended for a cigar factory. The latter was erected by Mrs. B. Reckendorfer in memory of her late husband, Joseph Reckendorfer. The wages are the lowest possible figure, so that a good man can earn at an average only about one dollar and seventy-five cents a week.

Now, it is not intended to make any reflections upon any one; but the intelligent reader can at once see that, while someone enjoys the large profit connected with the sale of this luxury, we, as humble refugees, are compelled to work at starvation prices. No man can either live himself or farm his land, much less support a family, at $1.75 a week! . . .

With our very limited resources in actual money we have not been able to plant all the fruit trees and vines that ought now to be growing. We have no horses to do our plowing and no plows with which to plow, even if we had the horses, and no money to employ others to do our plowing. It is now time to be making preparations, but being without seed and without ways to earn money, how can we get along? . . .

If plants can be purchased for us, or trees and vines, horses and plows, we propose to plant all we can, as we have done in the past . . . Though disappointed and cast down, we are not in despair; though mistakes have been made, it is never too late to do better . . . Our hope is in the patriotic and benevolent spirit of the citizens of our beloved, adopted country; our reliance is in the perseverance and energy of our own manhood. Others have failed and failed again, and yet in the end have prospered. So may it be—so must it be with us. We wish to remain where we are; we are already warmly attached to our new home.

We know that it is the glory of this blessed Republic to offer a home alike to all;

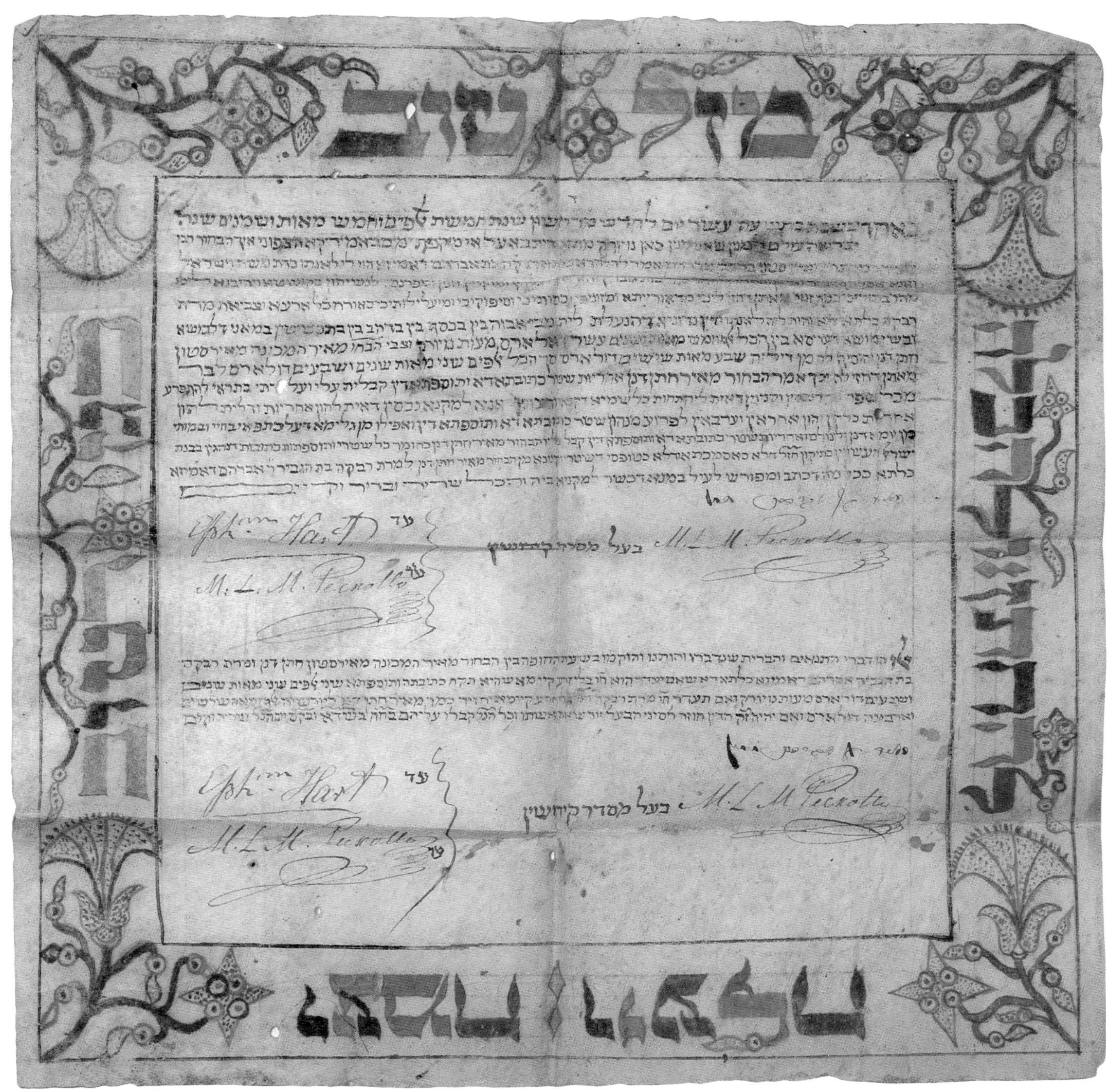

COLORPLATE 55

Ketubbah. New York. 1819. Handmade paper, watercolor, pencil, and ink. 13 7/8 x 14 1/8 in. Hebrew Union College Skirball Museum, Los Angeles. Gift of Mr. and Mrs. William M. Daniel in honor of the seventy-fifth birthday of Mr. Bernard Gordon.

COLORPLATE 56

ZEMAH DAVIDSON. *Ketubbah.* Utica, New York. 1863. Watercolor and ink on paper. 12 13/16 x 9 13/16 in. Courtesy of the Library of the Jewish Theological Seminary of America, New York. *In addition to the texts traditionally calligraphed on a* ketubbah, *this American example includes "L'Mazal Tov"—"good luck"—written in the ovals above the clock faces. The clocks are set at 6:13, a reference to the 613 commandments prescribed in the Torah.*

COLORPLATE 57

ALICE ZLOTNICK. *Ketubbah*. New York. 1987. Oil and gold leaf on parchment. 18 x 26 in. From the collection of Dena and Michael Felsen. *The text is framed by a stylized bridal canopy. On the horizon is Jerusalem, the Holy City.*

COLORPLATE 58

HOWARD FOX. *Ketubbah*. Toronto, Canada. 1987. Ink on paper. The Canadian Museum of Civilization, Québec, Canada. *This* ketubbah *was presented by the artist to his parents on their fortieth wedding anniversary in 1987. Its depictions of Jerusalem, Toronto, and Moscow are symbolic of the coming together of Jews from different lands; Fox's father was born in Toronto and his mother in the Soviet Union.*

and g-d blessed the seventh day, and sanctified it: because in it he rested from all his work which god had created and performed.
הכלה
bride
החתן
groom
עד
witness
עד
witness
הרב
rabbi
הרב
rabbi

the bride and groom then declared before g-d and the community that they have signed their names to this ketubah of their own free will without reservation or restraint, and that they intend to be bound in love by this holy covenant so long as they shall live.

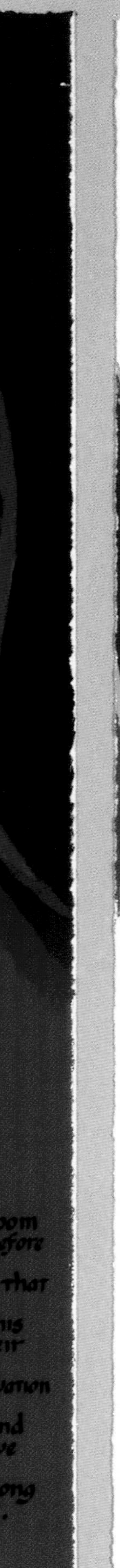

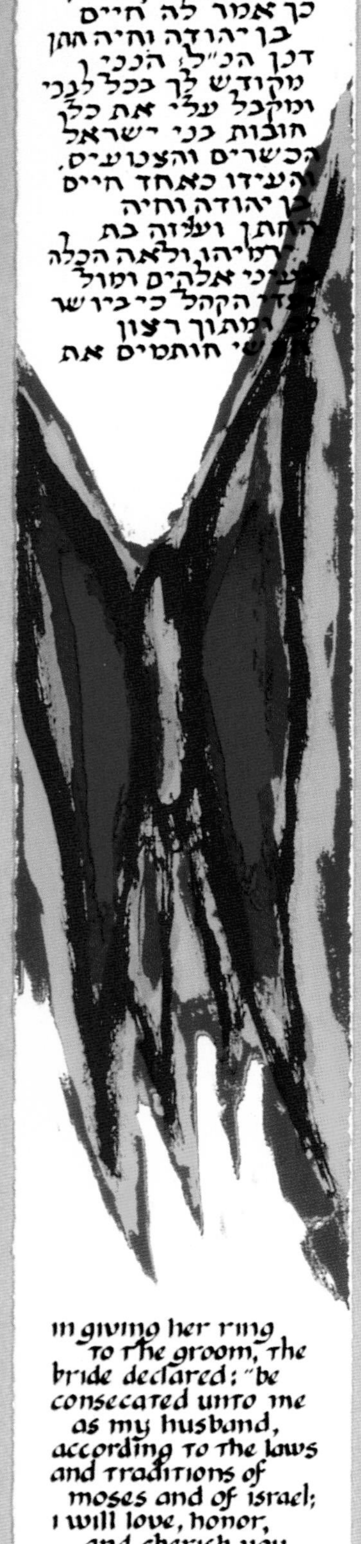

in giving her ring to the groom, the bride declared: "be consecrated unto me as my husband, according to the laws and traditions of moses and of israel; i will love, honor, and cherish you, i will protect and support you, and care for your needs as prescribed by jewish law and tradition."
and the groom ma
the following
declaration to tho
the bride:
"in accepting this
wedding ring i
pledge to you all m
love and devotion,
and take upon
myself the
fulfillment of
all the duties
incumbent upon a
jewish husband."

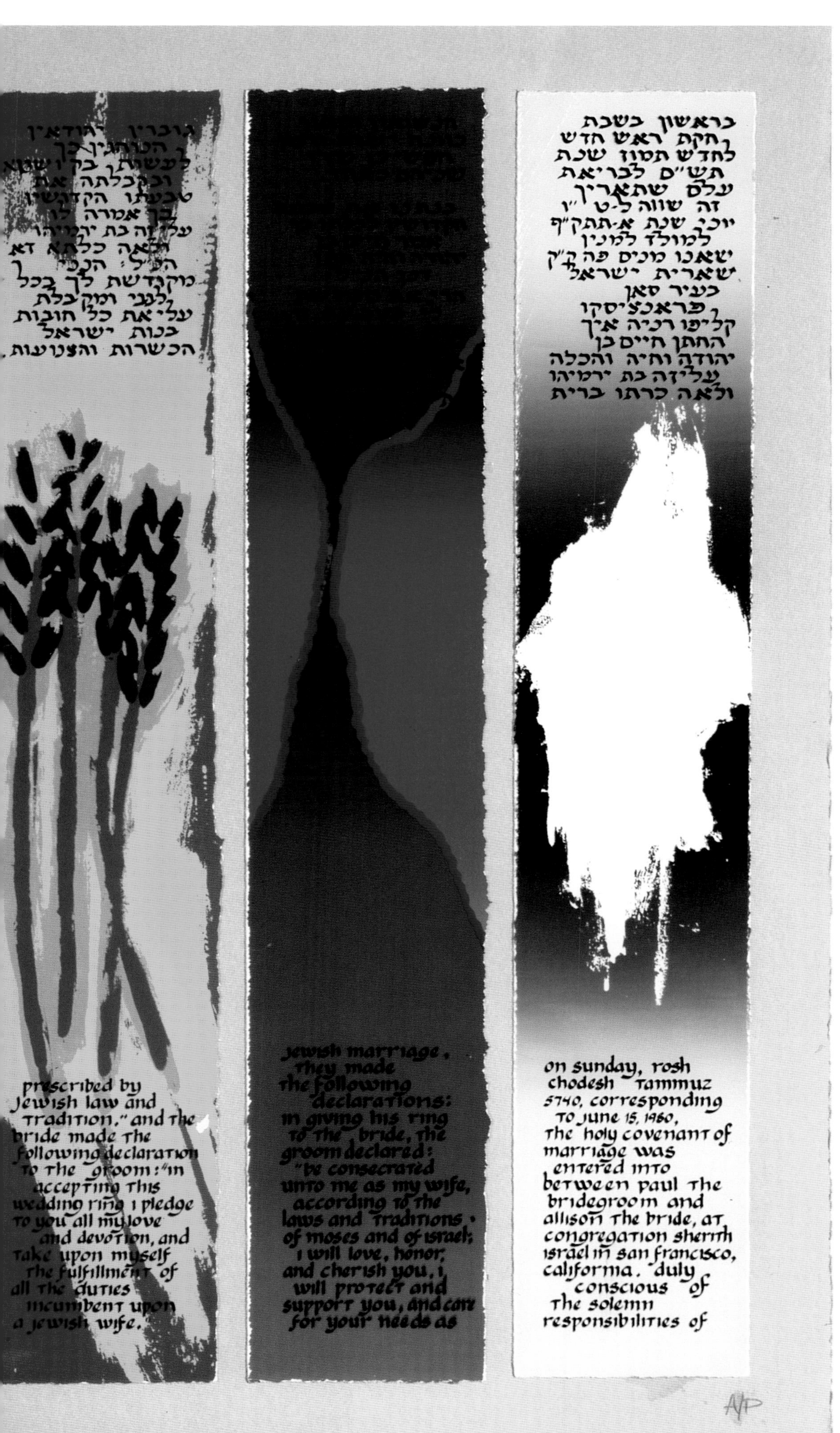
prescribed by
jewish law and
tradition," and the
bride made the
following declaration
to the groom: "in
accepting this
wedding ring i pledge
to you all my love
and devotion, and
take upon myself
the fulfillment of
all the duties
incumbent upon
a jewish wife.
jewish marriage.
they made
the following
declarations:
in giving his ring
to the bride, the
groom declared:
"be consecrated
unto me as my wife,
according to the
laws and traditions
of moses and of israel;
i will love, honor,
and cherish you, i
will protect and
support you, and care
for your needs as
on sunday, rosh
chodesh tammuz
5740, corresponding
to june 15, 1980,
the holy covenant of
marriage was
entered into
between paul the
bridegroom and
allison the bride, at
congregation sherith
israel in san francisco,
california. duly
conscious of
the solemn
responsibilities of

COLORPLATE 59

PERETZ WOLF-PRUSAN. *Ketubbah.* San Francisco. 1980. Paper cutout; colored silkscreen print. 21 1/2 x 29 5/8 in. Hebrew Union College Skirball Museum, Los Angeles. Museum purchase. *The seven panels represent the days of creation, the sabbath, and the seven benedictions chanted at the wedding service.*

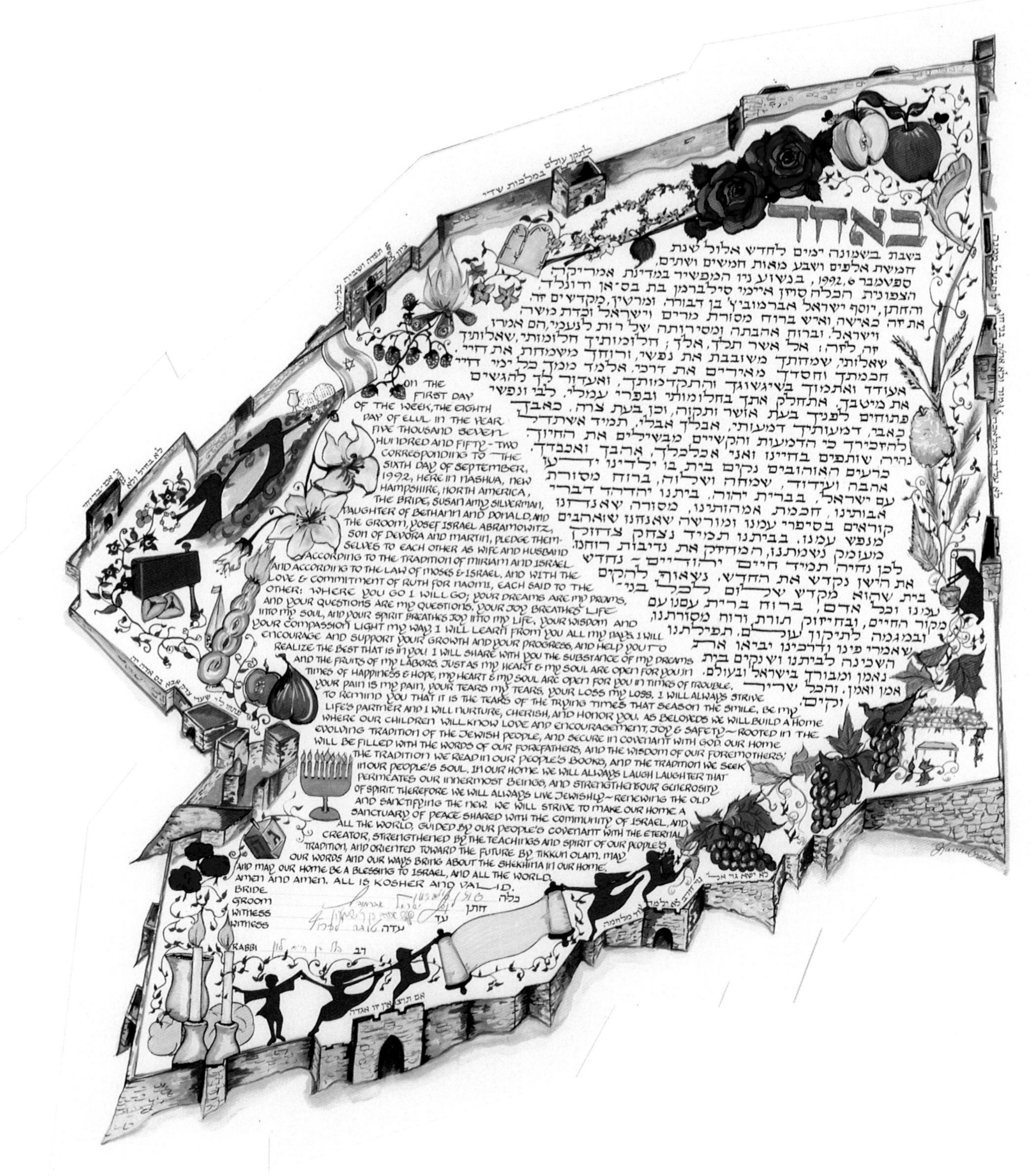

COLORPLATE 60

JEANNETTE KUVIN OREN. *Ketubbah.* 1992. 24 x 24 in. Hebrew and English text; cotton paper, ink, gouache, gold leaf. From the collection of Rabbi Susan Silverman and Yosef I. Abramowitz. *The* ketubbah *text, in Hebrew and English, is surrounded by a painting of an antique map of Jerusalem. Micrographic texts from the Song of Songs and Psalms decorate each of the gates to the city. Within the city walls are symbols from the Jewish year.*

COLORPLATE 61 *(opposite)*

SIMCHA BACK. *"Who Knows One?"* From *The Batkin Haggadah.* 1980. Hand-written and illuminated, astro parch paper; illuminated with gold enamel and watercolors. Courtesy of Stanley Batkin. *"Who Knows One" ("Echad Mi Yodea") is the next to last song in the Passover Haggadah. It is a riddle song taken from a poem by an unknown author and added to the Ashkenazic Haggadah around the fifteenth century.*

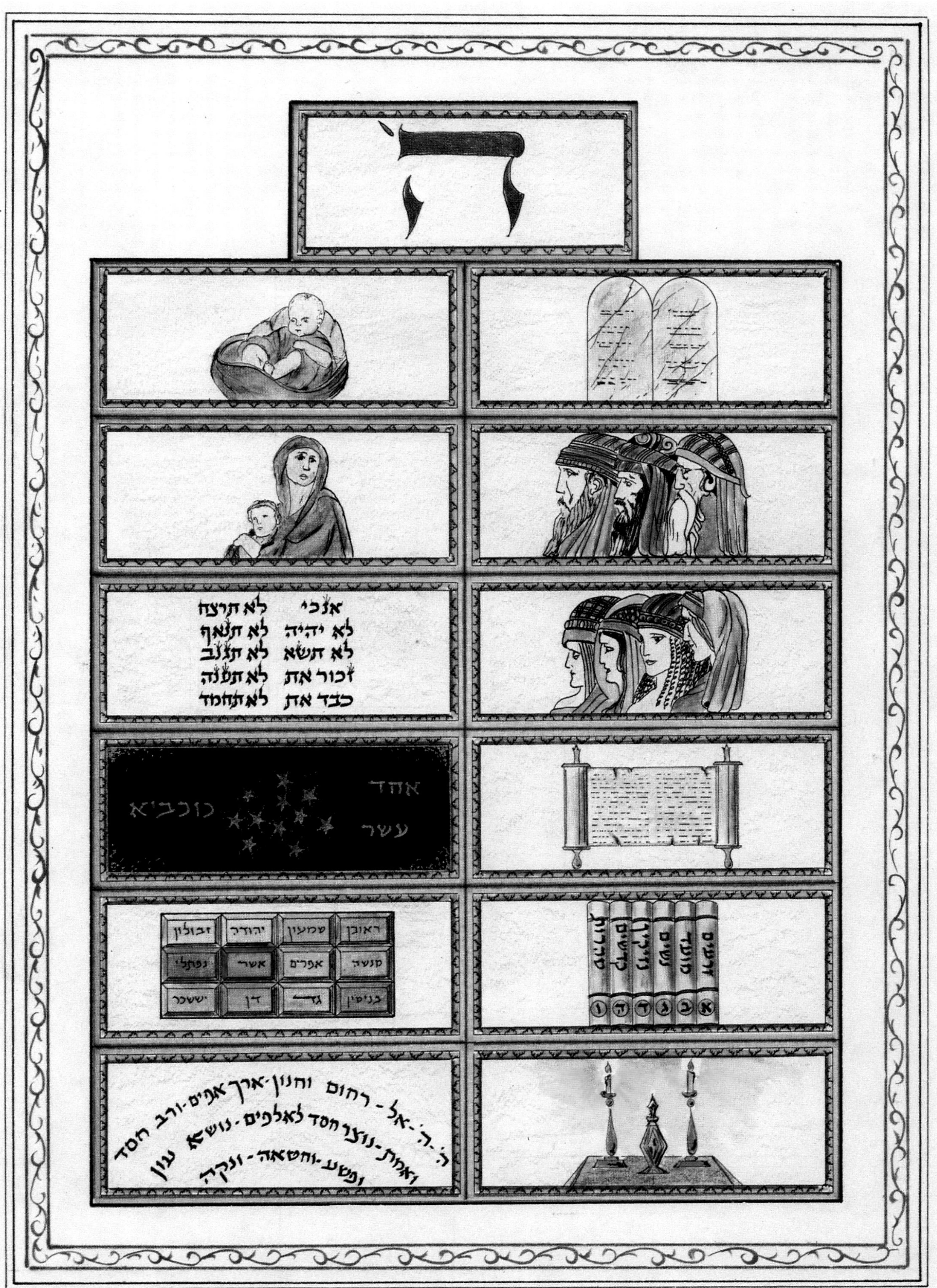

ה
אנכי לא תרצח
לא יהיה לא תנאף
לא תשא לא תגנב
זכור את לא תענה
כבד את לא תחמד
אחד
כוכביא
עשר
זרעים
מועד
נשים
נזיקין
קדשים
טהרות
א ב ג ד ה ו
ראובן שמעון יהודה זבולון
מנשה אפרים אשר נפתלי
בנימין גד דן יששכר
ה׳ ה׳ אל - רחום וחנון ארך אפים ורב חסד
ואמת - נוצר חסד לאלפים - נושא עון
ופשע - וחטאה - ונקה

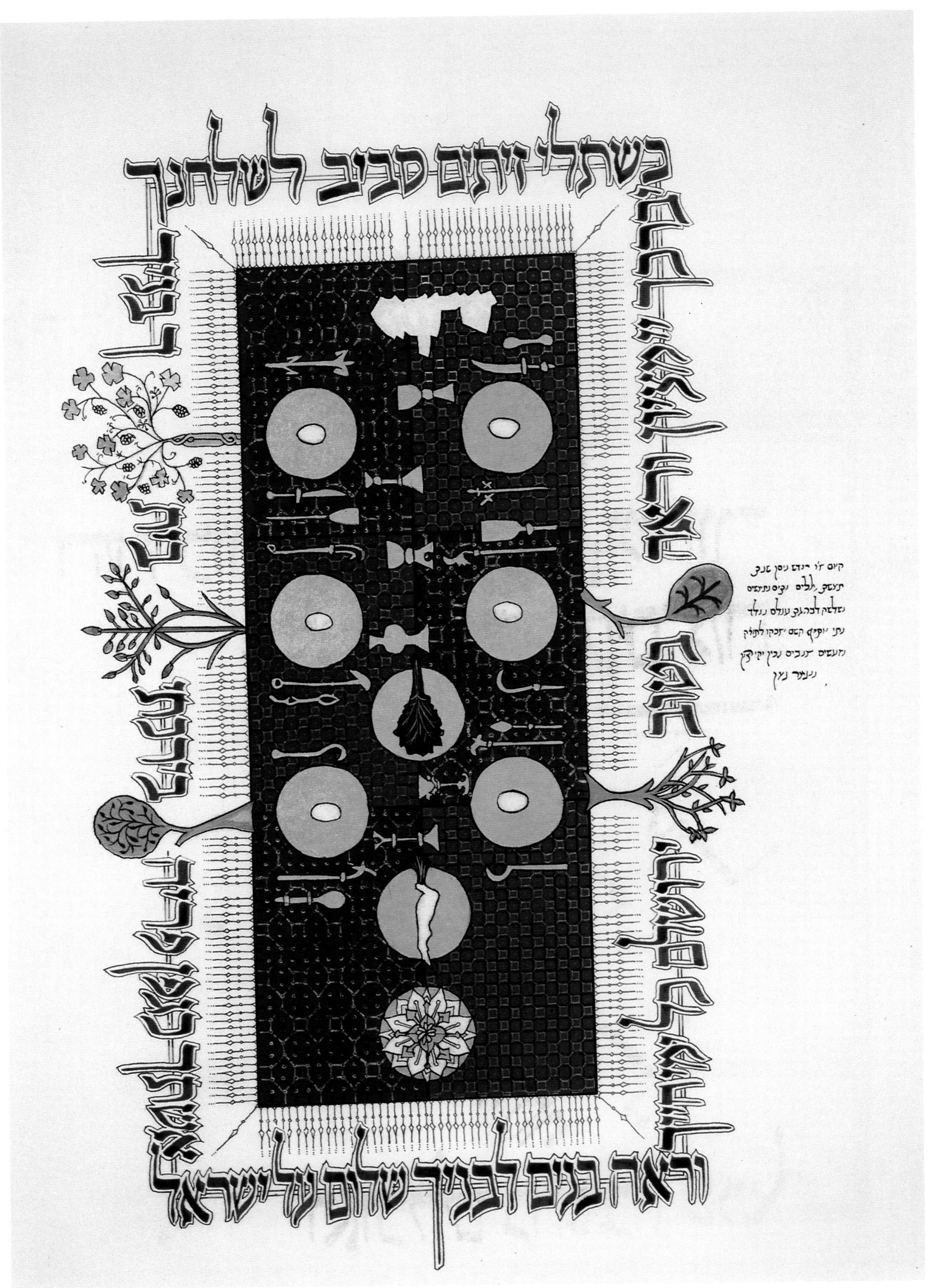

COLORPLATE 62

DAVID MOSS. *The Set Table.* Calligraphy in Chinese and India inks; illuminations in gouaches, acrylics, egg tempera. 19 1/4 x 13 3/8 in. © David Moss, 1994. Permission of Bet Alpha Editions, Rochester, New York. *The table here symbolizes the connection and continuity of the Jewish family, as well as Jewish sanctity.*

Agricultural Colony, Woodbine, New Jersey. 1891. Drawing. Courtesy of Hebrew Union College.

we know, too, that the citizens of this great nation are warm-hearted and sympathetic. No distress ever appeals in vain . . . Only let the distress be real, not pretended. As Colonists, therefore, we respectfully invite any committee to visit us, inquire into our habits of life, our knowledge of labor, our plans for the coming spring, and home-care and domestic order, and see whether we are doing all for ourselves that we can do with our limited means . . .

In closing this Report, we simply leave our case with those who have the struggles and sufferings of our distressed people near to their heart, assured that, when they know our true condition, the help we need will be cheerfully granted. It was so before. When driven from our homes, with the loss of everything, you, as brothers and sisters, gave us all we have; now we come as the adopted citizens of the greatest Republic on earth, and wishing first to offer sincere thanks for all that has been done for us, we can only say, we still need your fostering care, your helping hand and sympathetic heart. Help us in our effort to become independent citizens of our great Brotherly union!

Abraham Cahan

From *The Atlantic Monthly*, July 1898

"The Russian Jew in America"

In the late 1800s powerful social and political forces were urging Congress to severely limit immigration. Countering them were influential Americans marshalling arguments and documentation pointing to the rapid rate of Americanization of the immigrants and their contributions to the well-being of the nation. Among these was this article in the July 1898 issue of The Atlantic Monthly. *Its author, Abraham Cahan, who had arrived from Vilna a dozen years earlier, was already making his contribution to journalism. Later, as editor of the Yiddish daily,* Der Forverts (The Forward) *for almost half a century, he was the most influential leader of the Jewish immigrant community.*

The Jewish population in the United States has grown from a quarter of a million to about one million. Scarcely a large American town but has some Russo-Jewish names in its directory, with an educated Russian-speaking minority forming a colony within a Yiddish-speaking colony, while cities like New York, Chicago, Philadelphia, and Boston have each a Ghetto rivaling in extent of population the largest Jewish cities in Russia, Austria, and Roumania. The number of Jewish residents in Manhattan Borough is estimated at two hundred and fifty thousand, making it the largest centre of Hebrew population in the world. The Russian tongue, which twenty years ago was as little used in this country as Persian, has been added to the list of languages spoken by an appreciable portion of the polyglot immigrant population.

Have the newcomers justified the welcome extended to them? Have they proved a desirable accession to the American nation?

Let Gentile Americans who have made a study of the New York Ghetto answer the question. Here is what Mr. Jacob A. Riis, an accepted authority on "how the other half lives," has to say of Jewish immigrants:—

> They (the Jews) do not rot in their slum, but, rising, pull it up after them . . . As to their poverty, they brought temperate habits and a redeeming love of home. Their strange customs proved the strongest ally of the Gentile health officer in his warfare upon the slum. The death-rate of poverty-stricken Jew-town, despite its crowding, is lower always than that of the homes of the rich . . . . I am a Christian, and hold that in his belief the Jew is sadly in error. So that he may respect mine I insist on fair play for him all round. I am sure that our city has to-day no better and no more loyal citizen than the Jew, be he poor or rich, and none she has less to be ashamed of.

Mr. James B. Reynolds, who, in his capacity of head worker of the university settlement of New York, has for many years been in direct touch with the people of the very heart of the Jewish district, gives the following general description of Hebrew immigrants:—

"My acquaintance has been mainly with the Russian, Polish, and Roumanian Jews. The first quality in them which impresses me is their intellectual avidity. Much has been said about their desire for gain. But while one must recognize among them an almost universal and certainly commendable desire to improve their condition, the proportionate number of those with intellectual aims is larger than that of any other race that I have encountered . . ."

Nothing can be more inspiring to the public-spirited citizen, nothing worthier of the interest of the student of immigration, than the sight of a gray-haired tailor, a patriarch in appearance, coming, after a hard day's work at a sweat-shop, to spell "cat, mat, rat," and to grapple with the difficulties of "th" and "w." Such a spectacle may be seen in scores of the class-rooms in the schools referred to. Hundreds of educated young

Abraham Cahan. Brown Brothers, Sterling, Pennsylvania.

Hebrews earn their living, and often pay their way through college, by giving private lessons in English in the tenement houses of the district,—a type of young men and women peculiar to the Ghetto. The pupils of these private tutors are the same poor overworked sweat-shop "hands" of whom the public hears so much and knows so little. A tenement house kitchen turned, after a scanty supper, into a class-room, with the head of the family and his boarder bent over an English school reader, may perhaps claim attention as one of the curiosities of life in a great city; in the Jewish quarter, however, it is a common spectacle.

Nor does the tailor or peddler who hires these tutors, as a rule, content himself with an elementary knowledge of the language of his new home. I know many Jewish workmen who before they came here knew not a word of Russian, and were ignorant of any book except the Scriptures, or perhaps the Talmud, but whose range of English reading places them on a level with the average college-bred American.

The grammar schools of the Jewish quarter are overcrowded with children of immigrants, who, for progress and deportment, are rated with the very best in the city. At least 500 of 1677 students at the New York City College, where tuition and books are free, are Jewish boys from the East Side. The poor laborer who will pinch himself to keep his child at college, rather than send him to a factory that he may contribute to the family's income, is another type peculiar to the Ghetto.

The innumerable Yiddish publications with which the quarter is flooded are also a potent civilizing and Americanizing agency. The Russian Jews of New York, Philadelphia, and Chicago have within the last fifteen years created a vast periodical literature which furnishes intellectual food not only to themselves, but also to their brethren in Europe. A feverish literary activity unknown among the Jews in Russia, Roumania, and Austria, but which has arisen here among the immigrants from those countries, educates thousands of ignorant tailors and peddlers, lifts their intelligence, facilitates their study of English, and opens to them the doors of the English library. The five million Jews living under the Czar had not a single Yiddish daily paper even when the government allowed such publications, while their fellow countrymen and co-religionists who have taken up their abode in America publish six dailies (five in New York and one in Chicago), not to mention the countless Yiddish weeklies and monthlies, and the pamphlets and books which to-day make New York the largest Yiddish book market in the world. If much that is contained in these publications is rather crude, they are in this respect as good—or as bad—as a certain class of English novels and periodicals from which they partly derive their inspiration. On the other hand, their readers are sure to find in them a good deal of what would be worthy of a more cultivated language. They have among their contributors some of the best Yiddish writers in the world, men of undeniable talent, and these supply the Jewish slums with popular articles on science, on the history and institutions of the adopted country, translations from the best literatures of Europe and America, as well as original sketches, stories, and poems of decided merit. It is sometimes said (usually by those who know the Ghetto at second hand) that this unnatural development of Yiddish journalism threatens to keep the immigrant from an acquaintance with English. Nothing could be further from the truth. The Yiddish periodicals are so many preparatory schools from which the reader is sooner or later promoted to the English newspaper, just as the several Jewish theatres prepare his way to the Broadway playhouse, or as the Yiddish lecture serves him as a stepping-stone to that English-speaking, self-educational society, composed of working-men who have lived a few years in the country, which is another characteristic feature of life in the Ghetto. Truly, the Jews "do not rot in their slum, but, rising, pull it up after them."

Irving Abella

From *A Coat of Many Colours*

"Conquering the Prairies"

By the end of the nineteenth century Canada joined the United States as the destination of choice for the swelling wave of Jewish emigrants from eastern Europe. Leaders of west European Jewry welcomed Canada's indication that it would accept and aid newcomers. It served their purposes to believe that the vast empty spaces of the western provinces of Canada would be a far better place of settlement for transplanted shtetl *dwellers than the overcrowded ghettos of the seaboard cities of the North American continent. But as Irving Abella's simple but compelling account suggests, the hardships experienced on the open frontier were no less daunting than those confronted in the stifling city.*

By the turn of the century the flow of Russian Jewish immigrants had become a flood, and to these were added thousands of others. Lithuanian, Galician and Polish Jews were arriving at Canadian ports in increasing numbers. Romanian Jews were pouring out of their country as the pressure on their communities became more severe, with new restrictions preventing Jews from holding jobs, being educated or even owning land.

To highlight their tribulations—as well as to escape the consequences—in 1899 a large number of Romanian Jews began walking across Europe towards the Atlantic ports. The *fusgeyer*, or wayfarers, became a *cause célèbre* as country after country urged them to go elsewhere. When thousands of Romanian Jews descended on England, British Jewish leaders urged the JCA [Jewish Colonization Association] to resettle

Fur-Trading Post, Alberta, Canada. c. 1888. The American Jewish Archives, Cincinnati. *Albert N. Rose, left, was a successful fur trader in Canada.*

Dave Epstein Store Sign. 1920–1930. Courtesy of the Canadian Museum of Civilization, Québec, Canada. *Dave Epstein was a Russian emigré who arrived in Canada at the age of sixteen. Two years after his arrival, having learned English and Gaelic, he opened his own clothing store in Sydney. Signs such as this were placed around Cape Breton Island advertising his store. They became so popular that people would steal them, putting them up all over the country with the distance to the store indicated. In the 1920s, one such sign was placed on Baffin Island by a member of an arctic expedition indicating 3,800 miles to the store.*

them overseas. Since the United States had introduced a more restrictive immigration policy, Canada seemed to be their only hope.

And Canada seemed initially receptive. A new government under Wilfrid Laurier had been elected in 1896 and an aggressive immigration policy had been launched. The Minister of Interior, Clifford Sifton, was determined to populate the west and to attract as many European agricultural immigrants as he could—but only as long as they were not Jewish. As he told the prime minister, "experience shows . . . [that] Jewish people do not become agriculturalists." Yet Laurier, in a private meeting in London, had assured Herman Landau that Canada would indeed welcome Jewish settlers.

To many European Jewish leaders, Canada with its vast empty plains seemed to be the answer to Europe's "Jewish problem." Where else could the homeless, penurious Jews of Eastern Europe find such an idyllic setting? The climate was much like that they left behind, the land seemed productive, the opportunities appeared endless and most important, the government of Canada gave every sign of welcoming them. Canada was anxious for immigrants; Eastern European Jews were anxious to immigrate. What could have been better?

Such were the thoughts of prominent European Jewish financiers as they desperately sought a home for the hundreds of thousands of Jews pouring out of Russia, Romania, Galicia and Poland, many of whom were victims not only of pogroms but also of poverty and hunger. With the United States closing its gates, only Canada seemed to hold out the promise of a life without hunger, fear and oppression. Led by Israel Zangwill, a number of Jewish financiers from Britain, France and Germany created the Jewish Territorial Organization. Their proposal to the Canadian government in the early years of the twentieth century was to purchase a large area of land in western Canada and to settle it with as many Eastern European Jews as it could accommodate. The organization would cover all the costs of transportation and settlement, and would underwrite the building of a railroad to the settlements, as well as schools, roads and farms.

It would be a multi-million-dollar project, the likes of which the Canadian government had never seen. Here was an opportunity to settle a large expanse of the prairies at minimal cost to the government. It was an intriguing proposition, but it presented one problem: all the immigrants would be Jews. No government official was prepared to recommend approval of the scheme, but how could they say no without offending the Jewish bankers, whose goodwill they wished to retain? In the end they did not say no; they did not say anything. They simply allowed negotiations with the organization to drag on for years until the project died away, the victim of Ottawa's bigotry and inertia.

Meanwhile, immigration officials—particularly Sifton—were aghast at the prime minister's offer to allow Jewish refugees into the country and ordered it rescinded. But before they could countermand it, Canada's chief immigration officer in London, W.R.T. Preston, told JCA authorities that Canada would willingly accept "able-bodied and physically and morally suitable immigrants. . . [so long as they do not] infiltrate into the towns and swell the already overgrown population of Canadian cities". . .

Taking advantage of Laurier and Preston's invitation, the JCA agreed to underwrite all of the transportation and settlement costs of four hundred Romanian refugees. In return, the Canadian government agreed to provide the land to create a colony, but insisted that it must choose both the land and the immigrants. In selecting the former, it could not have acted more irresponsibly. The person assigned to choosing a site was D. H. Macdonald, a local businessman in Fort Qu'Appelle, Saskatchewan. Either dishonest or incompetent—or perhaps both—he selected probably the worst possible location, an area in the Qu'Appelle Valley some forty-five miles northeast of Regina, and twenty-five miles from the closest railway, in a region noted for its poor land and early frosts.

Despite the generous funding provided by the JCA, local officials did not build any shelters for the new immigrants, nor did they provide them with any seed, tools or equipment. Instead the green settlers were taken in hand by Indians from a nearby reservation and taught how to build homes and plough the land. Without this help, the Jewish settlement of Lipton would have been stillborn.

And at the beginning many thought it should have been. The land was unsuitable for wheat, the supervisors and land inspectors could not converse with the immigrants who spoke no English, and both local officials and residents were anti-Semitic and wanted nothing to do with the new settlement.

Over the next few years, though more than half the original settlers left, their place was taken by new recruits from Romania and Russia. And when the JCA realized how destructive was the leadership provided by the government's appointees, it severed the relationship, appointed a new administrator and reorganized the colony on a more productive basis.

By 1904 there were upwards of 375 Jewish settlers and more than 19,500 acres under cultivation. Before long a synagogue was erected, teachers were hired, a cemetery was consecrated and three public schools were built, Herzl, Yeshurun and Tiferes Israel—or Typhus Israel, as it was later known to its numerous non-Jewish students.

Lipton was the last settlement founded by the JCA in Canada. Given the difficult birth and terrible growing pains of Hirsch and Lipton, the JCA thought it more beneficial to support individual farmers rather than entire settlements. And indeed, most Jewish settlers in Canada took up land on their own, without JCA assistance, like other immigrants to this country. Whenever federal officials opened up new land for homesteading, groups of young Jews applied and formed their own communities.

Perhaps the best example of this type of settlement was Sonnenfeld. In 1905, a few graduates of a JCA agricultural school in Galicia arrived in western Canada. Most worked at Hirsch, but within a year three of them, Israel Hoffer, Philip Berger and Majer Feldman, applied for homesteads in an area fifty miles west of Estevan. They first named the colony New Herman, likely for an early settler whose legs had been amputated after an accident, but then chose to honour the director of the JCA, Sigismund Sonnenfeld, by naming it after him.

It is hard to imagine a more forbidding site for a farm settlement. There were no roads and the closest railway stop was in Estevan. The land was rocky, there was little drinking water and the climate was brutal. Yet by 1909, Sonnenfeld was a thriving community of some fifty-five Jews on twenty-five farms. Though there were never more than 150 people in the settlement, Sonnenfeld had a synagogue, two public schools and even a Jewish Farmers' Co-operative Credit Union.

In the first decade of this century, a number of other Jewish settlements came into being. In 1903, a group of Russian immigrants founded a new colony just north of Winnipeg, named Bender Hamlet, in honour of its first settler, Winnipeg land speculator Jacob Bender. This was the only attempt to create in Canada a Jewish settlement modelled on the Eastern European village. Each settler received 160 acres of land, but lived five miles away, in the village. The land was swampy and rocky, and farming was exceedingly difficult, yet up to forty families settled there and did not do badly, especially after the arrival of the railway in 1914. Other Jewish settlements were founded in Camper, Manitoba—also known as New Hirsch—and at Rumsey-Trochu, Alberta and Alsask-Montefiore, Saskatchewan.

Perhaps the most intriguing of these settlements was founded in 1906. A group of about twenty Lithuanian Jews who had migrated to South Africa were attracted by the Canadian government's offer of 160 acres of land to any immigrant willing to settle on the prairies. Without Jewish organizational support, certainly without the support of the JCA, the group headed for northern Saskatchewan, where they set up their homes along the Carrot River.

The Lithuanians, including the Vickar brothers Sam, David and Louis, were soon joined by refugees from the sweatshops of London who arrived brimming with radical ideas. These settlers, including Mike and Dave Usiskin, Alex Springman and others, had been attracted by an advertisement by the Carrot River homesteaders in the London Jewish press. To them, working the land with their own hands was a liberating experience. They were secular Jews, passionate Yiddishists and socialists who insisted on a Jewish name for the colony. They suggested Jew Town and then Israel Villa. But both were rejected by federal authorities as too ethnic. Finally when the creative settlers came up with the euphonious and seemingly meaningless name of Edenbridge, triumphant officials quickly accepted it. But the Jewish farmers had the last laugh. Little did the officials know that Edenbridge stood for "Yidden Bridge," or "Bridge of the Jews," commemorating the narrow steel span over the Carrot River in the middle of the settlement.

Emma Lazarus

"In Exile"

Emma Lazarus felt, as she wrote to Rabbi Gustav Gottheil, "no religious fervor in my soul." But the plight of the Jews in Czarist Russia, and even more so, the needs of the Jewish immigrants arriving in New York touched her deeply, and awakened dormant feelings about her people and her faith. During the last years of her young life, Jews and Judaism ranked highest on her personal and literary agenda. In the early 1880s, shown a letter from a Russian Jewish immigrant settled on the soil in Texas, she responded by writing "In Exile."

"Since that day till now our life is one unbroken paradise. We live a true brotherly life. Every evening after supper we take a seat under the mighty oak and sing our songs."

Extract from a letter of a Russian refugee in Texas.

Twilight is here, soft breezes bow the grass,
    Day's sounds of various toil break slowly off,
The yoke-freed oxen low, the patient ass
    Dips his dry nostril in the cool, deep trough.
Up from the prairie the tanned herdsmen pass
    With frothy pails, guiding with voices rough
Their udder-lightened kine. Fresh smells of earth,
The rich, black furrows of the glebe send forth.

After the Southern day of heavy toil,
    How good to lie, with limbs relaxed, brows bare
To evening's fan, and watch the smoke-wreaths coil
    Up from one's pipe-stem through the rayless air.
So deem these unused tillers of the soil,
    Who stretched beneath the shadowing oak-tree, stare
Peacefully on the star-unfolding skies,
And name their life unbroken paradise.

The hounded stag that has escaped the pack,
    And pants at ease within a thick-leaved dell;
The unimprisoned bird that finds the track
    Through sun-bathed space, to where his fellows dwell;
The martyr, granted respite from the rack,
    The death-doomed victim pardoned from his cell,—
Such only know the joy these exiles gain,—

T. Johnson, engraver. *Emma Lazarus.* 1887. Culver Pictures, Inc. *This portrait appears as the frontispiece of her* Collected Works *(1888) and is based on a photograph by W. Kurz.*

Life's sharpest rapture is surcease of pain.
Strange faces theirs, wherethrough the Orient sun
    Gleams from the eyes and glows athwart the skin.
Grave lines of studious thought and purpose run
    From curl-crowned forehead to dark-bearded chin.
And over all the seal is stamped thereon
    Of anguish branded by a world of sin,
In fire and blood through ages on their name,
Their seal of glory and the Gentiles' shame.

Freedom to love the law that Moses brought,
    To sing the songs of David, and to think
The thoughts Gabirol to Spinoza taught,
    Freedom to dig the common earth, to drink
The universal air—for this they sought
    Refuge o'er wave and continent, to link
Egypt with Texas in their mystic chain,
And truth's perpetual lamp forbid to wane.

Hark! through the quiet evening air, their song
    Floats forth with wild sweet rhythm and glad refrain.
They sing the conquest of the spirit strong,
    The soul that wrests the victory from pain;
The noble joys of manhood that belong
    To comrades and to brothers. In their strain
Rustle of palms and Eastern streams one hears,
And the broad prairie melts in mist of tears.

A Plea for the Jewish Vote "Who Takes Vengeance for Us?"

Late in October, 1899, the streets of the lower East Side of New York were flooded with handbills in Yiddish issued by "Jewish Members of the Republican State Committee," appealing to the Jews of New York to vote for Theodore Roosevelt for governor of New York. The appeal, directed to Jewish pride, asked: Dare a Jew vote against the man who was so instrumental in planning and accomplishing the defeat of Spain—land of the Inquisition and Expulsion—in the Spanish-American War?

Every respectable citizen, every good American and every true Jew, must and will vote for the Republican gubernatorial candidate—*Theodore Roosevelt.*

As citizens who are concerned with the welfare of their city and state, and as Jews, we direct this message to you. We will take for our text the verse in our Psalms: "Oh you murderous Babylonia, may it be done to you, what you have done to us!"

דיא פאקטען איבער

דעם קאנדידאט

בייא

בייראן אנדראוס

פערפאסער פון "איסטערן קאנ-
פליקט", ,,רייף אף לאגא"
,,איינער פון פאלק"
אז אז. אז"וו.

איל'וסטרירט ביי א. דש. קלאפפ

איבערזעצט פון

הרב שמעון בן מה' הרב חיים פרי-

פאבלישד ביי סעם סטאן, שיקאגא

19.4

Presidential Campaign Pamphlet for Teddy Roosevelt. 1904. American Jewish Historical Society, Waltham, Massachusetts. "The Facts About the Candidate *by Byron Andrews. Author of* Eastern Conflict; One of the People, *etc. Illustrated by J. Klapp, translated by Rabbi Simon, Son of Rabbi Hayim Freed, published by Sam Stone, Chicago, 1904."*

Babylonia sinned against the Jewish people. But how small is Babylonia's sins in comparison with the untold crimes which Spain committed against us! Babylonia came as an enemy and took us into exile. Spain did much worse. In Spain our ancestors were good and useful citizens. They made rich Spain's treasury; outfitted the ships which discovered America and gave Spain the power which made her a mighty nation. How did Spain reward them? Spain took away everything her Jews had, and she sent her Jews to the dungeons of the Inquisition and to the fires of the auto da fe. When Jews left Spain they were murdered on the road, as sheep are slaughtered by wolves. Those who remained as disguised Christians were slowly persecuted.

The cruelty and tyranny which Spain set loose, did not remain in its own land. Spain brought it to the new world—Brazil, Mexico, Cuba—Santiago, where Theodore Roosevelt met the Spanish face to face, were long stained by Spain's murderous and bestial methods. And until Theodore Roosevelt charged up San Juan hill, there still rang in our ears the cries and screams of Spain's brutality.

The long felt Jewish desire to see Spain fall was finally fulfilled. The Republican Party through its president gave the word that Spain should move out of the New World and the Republican gubernatorial candidate for New York State *Theodore Roosevelt* was one of the chief instruments of the late war. He worked day and night till he worked out all the plans for our navy, and when Admirals Dewey, Sampson and Schley chased the enemy, Theodore Roosevelt, at his own expense organized a Regiment of Rough Riders and went to the Battle Field to meet the foe.

Under Roosevelt's command there were many Jewish Rough Riders. Roosevelt was like a brother to them. He recommended them to the president for promotions, and sang their praises to the world.

Spain now lies punished and beaten for all her sins. But the *Party* which brought Spain her defeat, and the *man* who fought against her, now stand before the citizens of this State and ask whether they are satisfied with their work.

The decision about President McKinley and the late war with Spain lies now in the hands of the citizens of this State in this present election. Every vote for the

COLONEL OF THE ROUGH RIDERS is approval of McKinley and the war. Every vote for Roosevelt's opponent, who is also McKinley's opponent, is a vote for Spain, for Generals Weiler and Blanco . . .

Can any Jew afford to vote against Theodore Roosevelt and thereby express his disapproval of the war against Spain? Can any Jew thus deny the joy of his nation in the entire world? . . .

Vote for Theodore Roosevelt . . .

Vote to express your approval of Spain's defeat.

Israel Friedlaender

From *Past and Present*

"The Beginnings of a Jewish Renaissance"

Barely four years after his arrival to serve as Professor of Biblical Literature at the Jewish Theological Seminary of America, Israel Friedlaender gave this lecture on December 8, 1907 to the Mikveh Israel Association of Philadelphia on "The Problem of Judaism in America." Taken as "prophecy" or historical projection, his conclusion is an extravagantly optimistic view of the future of an immigrant still overwhelmed by a nation bursting with energy and enthusiasm, host to a Jewish community which had increased those few years by well over a half million. Viewed as a challenge, these words have retained their cogency to the present day. Friedlaender died a martyr's death in 1920 in the Ukraine while on a mission of mercy to the Jewish communities of that war-devastated land.

America presents a happy combination of so manifold and favorable circumstances as have seldom, if ever, been equalled in the history of the Diaspora. It has the numbers which are necessary for the creation of a cultural center. It possesses the economic prosperity indispensable for a successful spiritual development. The freedom enjoyed by the Jews is not the outcome of emancipation, purchased at the cost of national suicide, but the natural product of American civilization. The idea of liberty as evolved by the Anglo-Saxon mind does not merely mean, as it often does in Europe, the privilege of selling new clothes instead of old, but signifies liberty of conscience, the full, untrammelled development of the soul as well as the body. The true American spirit understands and respects the traditions and associations of other nationalities, and on its vast area numerous races live peaceably together, equally devoted to the interests of the land. The influx of Jewish immigrants in the past and present brought and brings to these shores the enormous resources of the Ghetto, and presents American Jewry with a variety of Jewish types which will be of far-reaching significance in its further development. In short, this country has at its disposal all the materials necessary for the upbuilding of a large, powerful center of Judaism, and it only depends on the American Jews whether these potentialities will ever become realities.

But it is to be hoped that the American Jews will not be forgetful of the task—as gigantic as it is honorable—which lies before them. He who feels the pulse of Ameri-

ABRAHAM WALKOWITZ. *The Violinist.* 1895. Oil on canvas. 48 x 34 in. The Jewish Museum, New York.

can-Jewish life can detect, amidst numerous indications to the contrary, the beginnings of a Jewish renaissance, the budding forth of a new spirit. The Jews of America, as represented in their noblest and best, display larger Jewish sympathies, a broader outlook on Jewish life, a deeper understanding of the spiritual interests of Judaism than most of their brethren of the Mosaic persuasion in the lands of assimilation and emancipation. The type of the modern American Jew who is both modern and Jewish, who combines American energy and success with that manliness and self-assertion, which is imbibed with American freedom, is becoming a species, while in other countries the same characteristics are to be met with in but a few exceptional individuals. The American Jews are fully alive to the future of their country as a center of Jewish culture. They build not only hospitals and infirmaries, but also schools and colleges; they welcome not only immigrants, but also libraries; not only tradesmen and laborers, but also scholars and writers. Everywhere we perceive the evidence of a new life. To be sure, we are only at the beginning. Gigantic and complicated tasks confront us in the future. The enormous stores of latent Jewish energy that are formlessly piled up in this country will have to be transformed into living power. The dead capital which we constantly draw from the Ghetto will have to be made into a working capital to produce new values. We first of all have to lay our foundation: to rescue the Jewish education of our future generation from the chaos in which it is now entangled. But we are on the right road. The American Jews will take to heart the lesson afforded by modern Jewish history in Europe. They will not bury Judaism in synagogues and temples, nor imprison it in charitable institutions. They will work and live for a Judaism which will compass all phases of Jewish life and thought; which will not be a faint sickly hothouse plant, but, as it was in the days of old, "a tree of life for those who hold it fast, bestowing happiness on those who cling to it."

Elyakum Zunser

From "For Whom the Golden Land?"

In his native Russia, Elyakum Zunser was the most popular Jewish folk bard. He sang of the sorrows of Jewish life under the Czarist regime, of the exodus to America, and of his love for Zion. He planned to settle on the soil of the ancient homeland, but circumstance confined him to a small print shop on New York's lower East Side. In the New World as in the Old, he continued to sing and publish his songs, and here as there, they became popular ballads. His Yiddish song "For Whom the Golden Land?" was published with music and the author's portrait in 1894, five years after his arrival in America. It sings of anticipation and the reality of golden dreams turned to dross. The translator has attempted to retain the doggerel form of the poem.

While yet a child
Of America, I was told:
"How happy its people,
It's a Land of Gold!"

I came to the land, saw it and Lo!
Tears and suffering and tales of woe.
In its narrow streets, on square and place,
Darkness, poverty, writ on each face
    Stand from morn till night
    Huddled masses, a frightful sight.
One would sacrifice his child for a cent,
Or drive a man from his rooms for rent.
    Here a greenhorn hung'ring for bread
    Falls in the street, starved, dead!
Poverty, misery, darkness, cold—
Everywhere, in this Land of Gold!

Of toil and sweat, and sweat and toil
The worker has no lack
Weary when the season's "busy"
Hungry when it's "slack."
The boss is his worker's keeper
Until a machine can do it cheaper.
What a man is, and what he's been,

Is sacrificed to the machine.
And more and more the streets are filled
With wandering men whom fate has willed
    To be a brother to the horse
    Who pulls the streetcar down the course.
The machine has done its job—
See that broken, crippled mob.
One loses his sight, another his hand
To the machine, in this Golden Land.

* * *

JACOB EPSTEIN. *Elyakum Zunser.* 1902. *This drawing appeared in* The Spirit of the Ghetto *by Hutchins Hapgood.*

Morris Rosenfeld
"The Candle Seller"

Born in Russian Poland in 1862, Morris Rosenfeld left his native land because there was not "any freedom for the Jew." He then left London because he heard that in New York he would need to work only ten hours a day. In New York, as he later reminisced, "I worked in the sweatshop in the daytime, and at night I worked at my poems. I could not help writing them. My heart was full of bitterness. If my poems are sad and plaintive, it is because I expressed my own feelings and because my surroundings were sad." He became the poet laureate of ghetto dwellers. They sang his songs as lullabies, at holiday celebrations, as national hymns, and as defiant cries for social justice. Typical of his poetry is "The Candle Seller."

In Hester Street, hard by a telegraph post,
There sits a poor woman as wan as a ghost.
Her pale face is shrunk, like the face of the dead,
And yet you can tell that her cheeks once were red.
But love, ease and friendship and glory, I ween,
May hardly the cause of their fading have been.
Poor soul, she has wept so, she scarcely can see.
A skeleton infant she holds on her knee.
It tugs at her breast, and it whimpers and sleeps,
But soon at her cry it awakens and weeps—
"Two cents, my good woman, three candles will buy,
As bright as their flame be my star in the sky!"

Tho' few are her wares, and her basket is small,
She earns her own living by these, when at all.
She's there with her baby in wind and in rain,
In frost and in snow-fall, in weakness and pain.
She trades and she trades, through the good times and slack—
No home and no food, and no cloak to her back.
She's kithless and kinless—one friend at the most,
And that one is silent: the telegraph post!
She asks for no alms, the poor Jewess, but still,
Altho' she is wretched, forsaken and ill,
She cries Sabbath candles to those that come nigh,
And all that she pleads is, that people will buy.

To honor the sweet, holy Sabbath, each one
With joy in his heart to the market has gone.
To shops and to pushcarts they hurriedly fare;
But who for the poor, wretched woman will care?
A few of her candles you think they will take?—
They seek the meat patties, the fish and the cake.
She holds forth a hand with the pitiful cry:
"Two cents, my good women, three candles will buy!"
But no one has listened, and no one has heard:

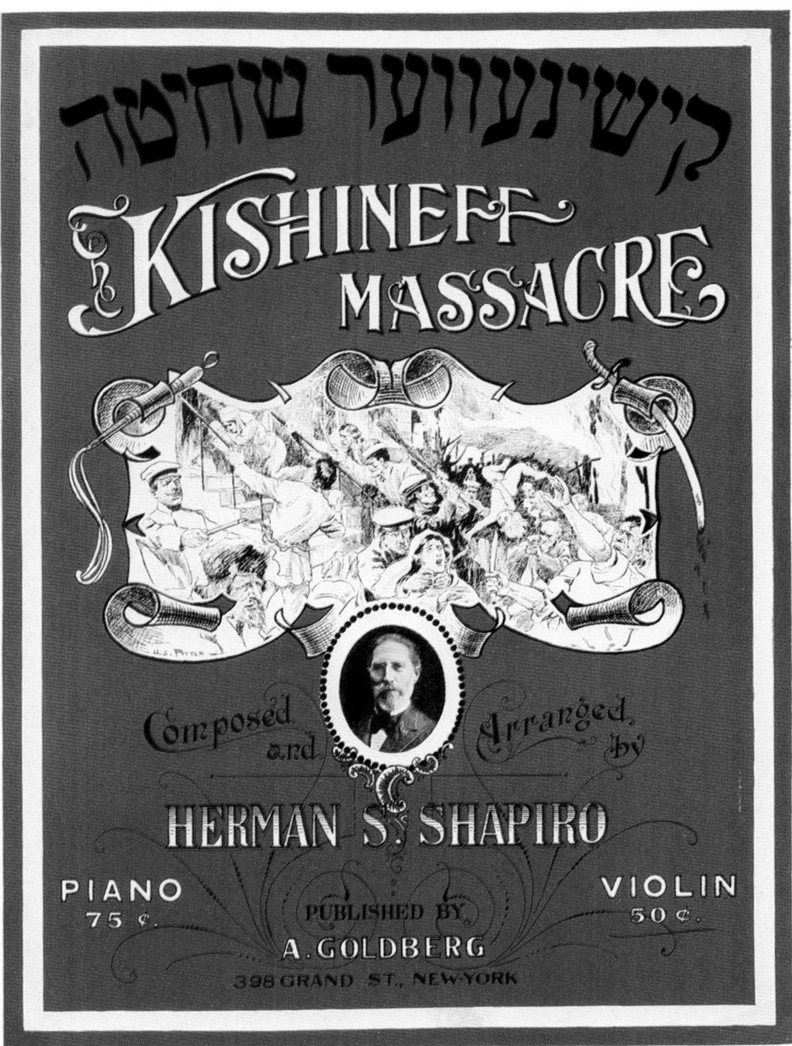

COLORPLATE 63

HERMAN SHAPIRO. *Kishineff Massacre.* 1904. Sheet music cover, published by A. Goldberg, New York. The National Museum of American Jewish History, Philadelphia. *The pogrom in Kishineff in 1903 took the lives of 49 Jews and wounded 500 more. It was met with outraged protest by American Jewry and condemnation by fellow Americans led by President Theodore Roosevelt. Protest meetings were held in 50 cities from Boston to San Francisco.*

COLORPLATE 64

The Green Millionaire. c. 1915. Yiddish theater poster; multicolored engraving of Thomashefsky. 42 x 14 in. American Jewish Historical Society, Waltham, Massachusetts. *Boris Thomashefsky was one of the leading actors of the Yiddish theater.*

COLORPLATE 65

The Rabbi's Family. c. 1921. Yiddish theater poster; multicolored illustration of scene. 41 x 27 in. American Jewish Historical Society, Waltham, Massachusetts. *The Yiddish theater was one of the most popular forms of entertainment for newly arrived immigrants.*

COLORPLATE 66 *(below, left)*

L. GILROD AND D. MEYROWITZ. *A Boychik Up To Date (An Up-to-Date Dandy).* New York. American Jewish Historical Society, Waltham, Massachusetts. *The cover of this sheet music pictures a faddishly clad "hero." The song is critical of this dandy and through him, the American scene which created him.*

COLORPLATE 67 *(below)*

S. MOGULESCO. *Choson Kale Mazol Tov (Good Luck to the Bride and Groom).* New York. 1909. The Hebraic Section, The Library of Congress. *This was one of the best known songs in the immigrant repertoire.*

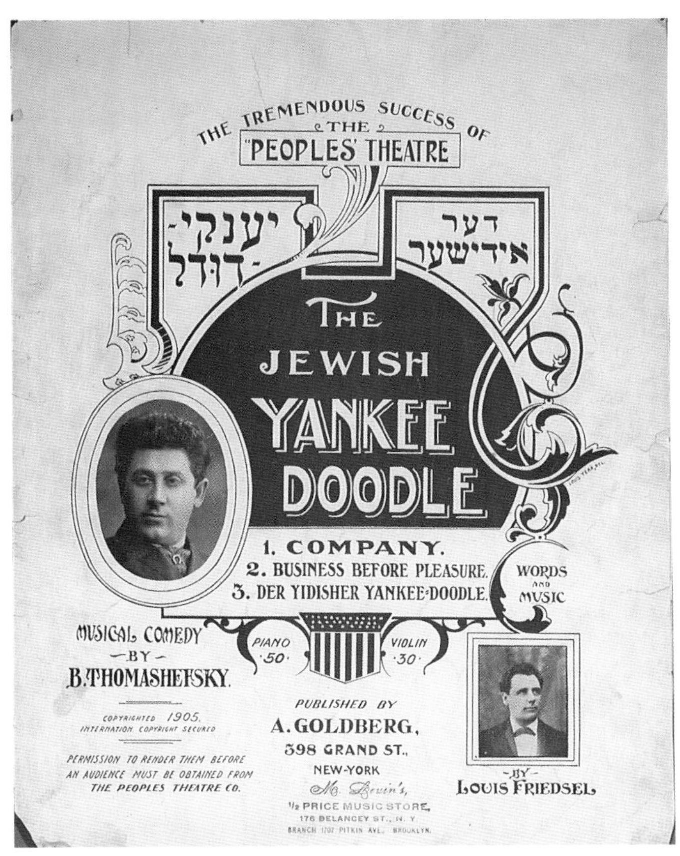

COLORPLATE 68 *(above)*

I'm a Jewish Cowboy. Sheet music cover. 1908. Collection of Peter H. Schweitzer.

COLORPLATE 69 *(above, right)*

Jewish Yankee Doodle. Sheet music cover. 1905. Collection of Peter H. Schweitzer.

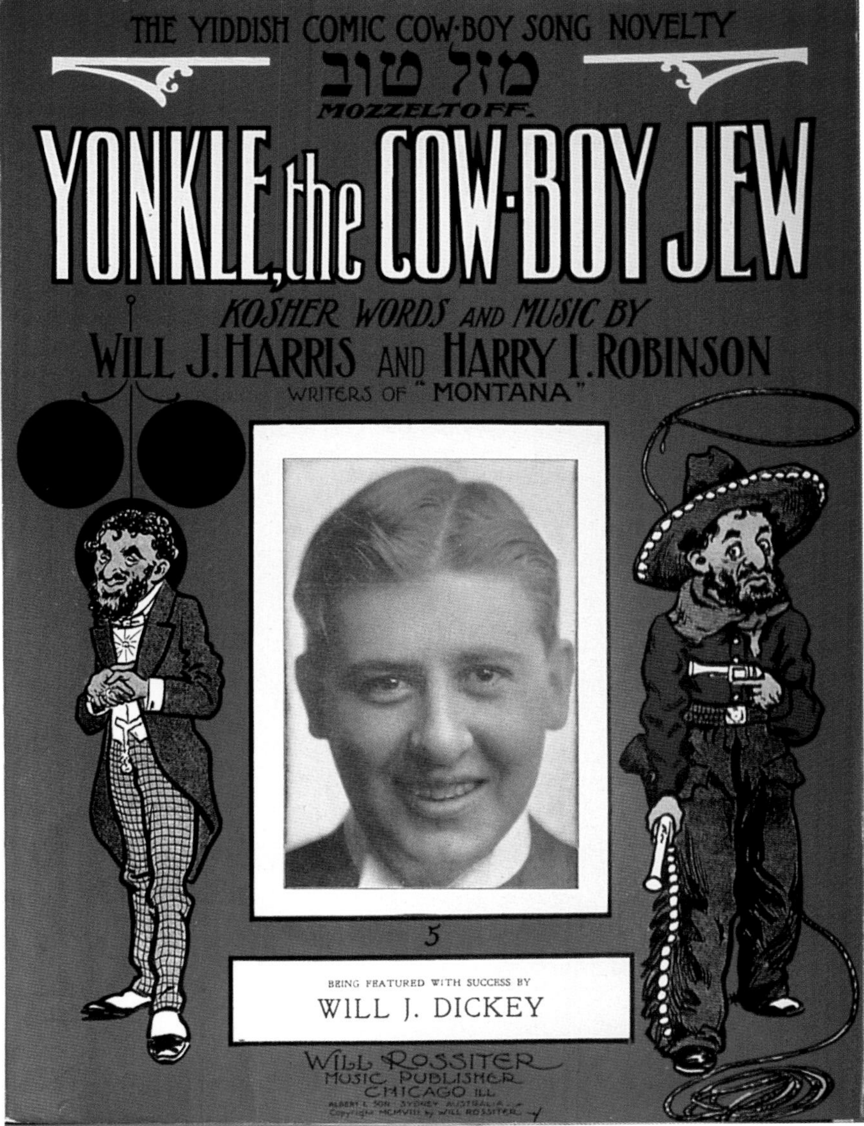

COLORPLATE 70

Yonkle, the Cowboy Jew. Sheet music cover. 1908. Collection of Peter H. Schweitzer.

COLORPLATE 71

Sears Roebuck and Company Catalogue Cover. 1897. The Smithsonian Institution, Washington, D.C.
Julius Rosenwald acquired an interest in the mail order firm of Sears Roebuck and Company. Under his leadership it became the largest retail merchandising organization in the world.

COLORPLATE 72 *(above)*

Share. 1915. Published by The Jewish Relief Campaign. Printed by Sackett and Wilhelms Corporation, Brooklyn, New York. Collection of Peter H. Schweitzer.

COLORPLATE 73 *(above right)*

CHARLES EDWARD CHAMBERS. *Food Will Win the War.* 1918. Color lithograph. 30 x 20 in. Hebrew Union College Skirball Museum, Los Angeles. Gift of Dr. and Mrs. Boris Catz. *Published by the United States Food Administration and printed by Rusling Wood, the message reads: "Food Will Win the War. You Came Here Seeking Freedom. You Must Now Help to Preserve It. Wheat Is Needed for the Allies. Waste Nothing."*

COLORPLATE 74

U.S. War Bonds Poster. Collection of Peter H. Schweitzer. *The message in Yiddish reads "For a Better Tomorrow."*

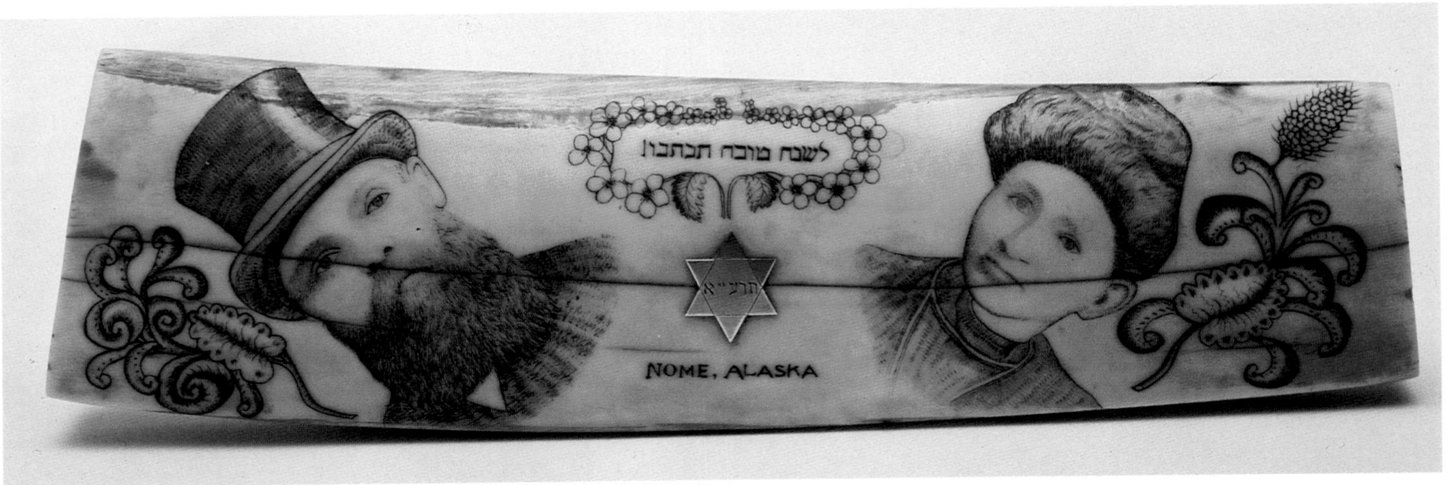

COLORPLATE 75

ATTRIBUTED TO HAPPY JACK (ESKIMO, C. 1870–1918). *Jewish New Year's Greeting.* Nome, Alaska. 1910. Engraved walrus tusk with gold inset. Diameter: 10 x 1 in. The Jewish Museum, New York. Gift of the Kanofsky Family in memory of Minnie Kanofsky. *New Year's greetings were expressed on illustrated cards, photographs, even on metal, wood, and glass—and in Alaska on walrus tusk.*

COLORPLATE 76

Jewish New Year Banner. 1942–1943. Undyed silk, printed. 17 x 13 in. The Jewish Museum, New York. Gift of Menashe Vaxer through Dr. Harry G. Friedman.

COLORPLATE 77 *(top)*

B. Rosenberg & Sons Shoe Trade Sign. 1918. 9 x 13 1/2 in. Collection of Peter H. Schweitzer.

COLORPLATE 78 *(bottom)*

Goldenson Furniture Trade Sign. 27 3/4 x 9 1/2 in. Pittsburgh, Pennsylvania. Collection of Peter H. Schweitzer.

COLORPLATE 79

Frishman's Shoes. Photograph © Bill Aron, 1989. *Harris Frishman, a Russian-Jewish immigrant, opened H. Frishman's in Port Gibson, Mississippi, in the late 1890s. The dry-goods store later became a shoe and department store and served the citizens of Port Gibson for over ninety years. "Red Goose" shoes were a popular brand and the familiar goose was seen on many store signs throughout the South.*

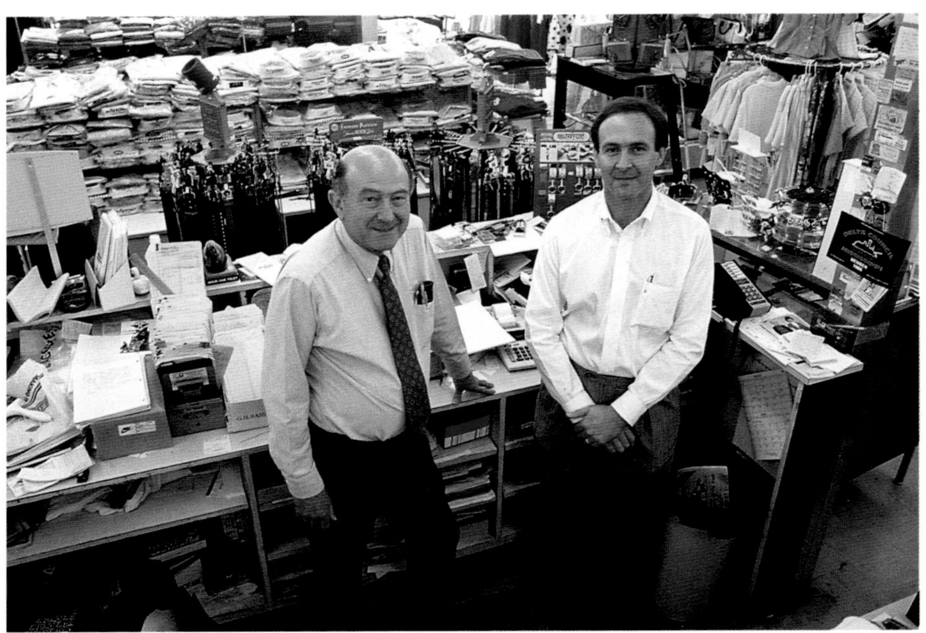

COLORPLATE 80

Goldberg's. Photograph © Bill Aron, 1989. *Joe Goldberg and his son, Charlie, stand behind the counter of Goldberg's in Belzani, Mississippi, which has sold clothing, shoes, and household goods for the entire family since 1917. Typical of general merchandise stores throughout the South, this store and others like it founded by Jewish immigrants were once a common sight on every Main Street in small southern towns. Belzani, a small town in the Mississippi Delta, is known as the "Catfish Capital of the World."*

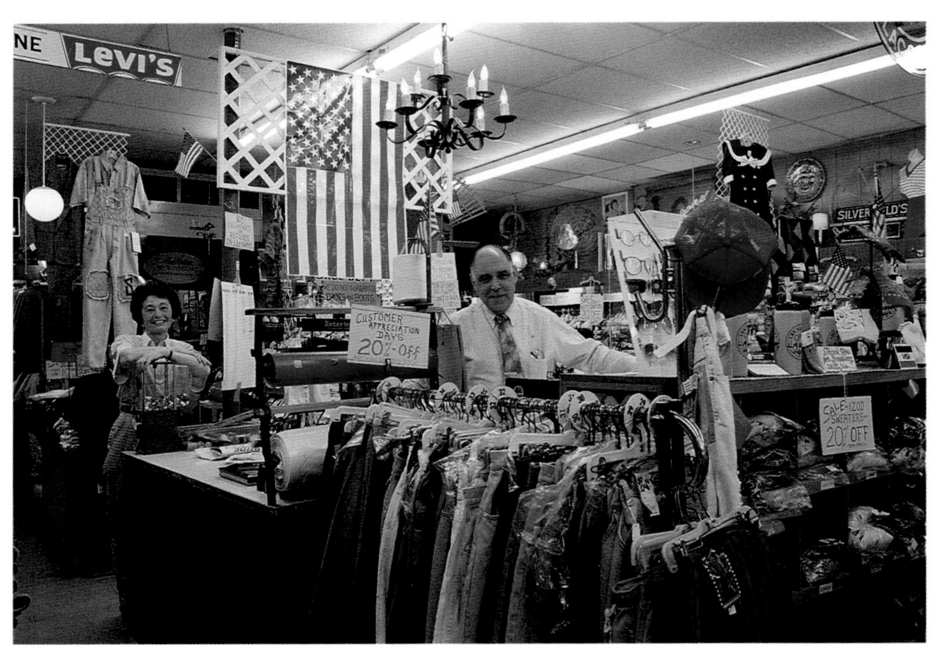

COLORPLATE 81

Silverfield's. Photograph © Bill Aron. *Silverfield's in Osceola, Arkansas, was once one of many Jewish storefronts on the downtown square. Owned and operated by Nora and Lionel Silverfield, pictured here with an American flag in the background, the store survives as a local landmark, known for quality merchandise and personal service for more than seventy-five years.*

William Allen Rogers. *The Candle Merchant.* Drawing. *This poignant depiction appeaerd in* Harper's Weekly, *April 19, 1890.*

Her voice is so weak, that it fails at each word.
Perchance the poor mite in her lap understood,
She hears mother's crying—but where is the good.

I pray you, how long will she sit there and cry
Her candles so feebly to all that pass by?
How long will it be, do you think, ere her breath
Gives out in the horrible struggle with Death?
How long will this frail one in mother-love strong,
Give suck to the babe at her breast? Oh, how long?
The child mother's tears used to swallow before,
But mother's eyes, nowadays, shed them no more.
Oh, dry are the eyes now, and empty the brain,

The heart well-nigh broken, the breath drawn with pain
Yet ever, tho' faintly, she calls out anew:
"Oh buy but two candles, good women, but two!"

In Hester Street stands on the pavement of stone
A small, orphaned basket, forsaken, alone.
Beside it is sitting a corpse, cold and stark:
The seller of candles—will nobody mark?
No, none of the passers have noticed her yet.
The rich ones, on feasting are busily set,
And such as are pious, you well may believe,
Have no time to spare on the gay Sabbath eve.
So no one has noticed and no one has seen.
And now comes the nightfall, and with it, serene,
The Princess, the Sabbath, from Heaven descends,
And all the gay throng to the synagogue wends.

Within, where they pray, all is cleanly and bright,
The cantor sings sweetly, they list with delight.
But why in a dream stands the tall chandelier,
As dim as the candles that gleam round a bier?
The candles belonged to the woman, you know,
Who died in the street but a short time ago.
The rich and the pious have brought them tonight,
For mother and child they have set them alight.
The rich and the pious their duty have done:
Her tapers are lighted who died all alone.
The rich and the pious are nobly behaved:
A body—what matters? But souls must be saved!

O synagogue lights, be ye witnesses bold
That mother and child died of hunger and cold
Where millions are squandered in idle display;
That men, all unheeded, must starve by the way.
Then hold back your flame, blessed lights, hold it fast!
Before the white throne, where imposture is vain,
Ye lights for the soul, ye'll be lighted again!
And upward your flame there shall mount as on wings,
And damn the existing false order of things!

Abraham Shulman
The Yiddish Theater

Abraham Shulman's The New Country *(1976) presents a straightforward account, informative and authentic, of the most popular vehicle of Jewish culture in the immigrant community. At the turn of the century the Yiddish stage offered entertainment—and more. The musicals provided needed relief from the long hours of monotonous labor; historical dramas portraying national sovereignty and power lifted the spirit; plays on current themes offered topics for discussion and argument. The theater as a gathering place made for instant community joined by proximity and a shared experience. It helped infuse life with adventure and excitement—even if vicarious. Like other immigrant institutions, it was a one-generation phenomenon.*

New York very quickly also became a spawning ground for the Yiddish theater, especially along Second Avenue in Manhattan. Soon there were five, eight and, at the peak, twelve Yiddish theaters. They spread to Brooklyn, the Bronx, and many other American cities.

For most of the immigrants, the Yiddish theater was not just a matter of amusement—it was a fulfillment of their cultural needs. The immigrant wanted to become an *Amerikaner* without giving up his tradition or his language. The theater greeted him with a paean to the Statue of Liberty, gave him comedies and dramas about the joys and miseries of immigrant life and, at the same time, allowed him to be nostalgic about the Old Country. Here, the audience could take revenge on traditional Jewish enemies: the Czar, the Cossacks, and the pogromchiks. The theater, with its primitive absurdities, helped the newcomer to get through the period of being a greenhorn—it taught him to be an American.

The repertoire offered was not of a very high quality. In fact, most of the plays were *shund*, a word in the vocabulary of the theater which connoted a vulgar commercialism. But then to write plays for theaters which changed programs every few days

JOSEPH BYRON. *Jacob Adler as Shylock in "The Merchant of Venice."* 1903. Photograph. Museum of the City of New York. The Theater Collection.

was not an easy task. Indeed, it was not a question of art so much as one of manufacturing.

Playwrights concocted plays by stealing from themselves or from other writers. They pinched plots from old operas, and "translated, adapted, and improved" the plays of Shakespeare. There was a *Jewish King Lear,* and a *Jewish Hamlet* in which Hamlet was a yeshiva student whose uncle, a rabbi, informed on his own brother and had him exiled to Siberia so he could seduce Hamlet's mother. Very often a Yiddish playwright went to the American theater to appropriate comedies and dramas, and often he did not know that what he was stealing had already been taken over from Ibsen or Strindberg.

For a long time the Yiddish theater was ruled by its stars—by the Mogulescos, the Boris Tomashevskis, the Bertha Kalishes, the David Kesslers. The star was the absolute monarch; he dictated to the writer what to write and told the director how to direct. The other actors served only one purpose: to give the star cues for his grand scenes. To the audience the star was divine. Each one had his devoted followers, like the Hasidim in the shtetl who were totally devoted to their rebbes. The stars behaved like maharajahs. Boris Tomashevski had his own limousine, his own French chauffeur, and a Japanese valet.

A very important role was played by the prompter. He was often the only member of the cast who could read and write. He not only prompted the words; from his hole in the stage, he often instructed the actors how to move, when to cry, when to laugh, and when to giggle. He sometimes spoke louder than the actors.

The producers of those theaters often went to Europe to hire new actors and new material, or to import entire productions. Since most of the actors came from different parts of Eastern Europe, it often happened that members of a stage "family" would speak in different dialects. The father might say *ikh,* the mother *ekh,* the son *yekh,* and the daughter *yakh*—all meaning "I."

The audience, mostly sweatshop workers and peddlers, came to the theater not only to watch the play but to socialize: to meet *landsleit* and to discuss politics. It was customary to bring along one's supper and to eat it during the show. Hawkers walked down the aisles selling blintzes, knishes, and bottles of seltzer. Matchmakers used the theater by giving one ticket to a young man, and a ticket for the adjoining seat to a young woman. If he liked her, he bought her a bag of peanuts and they walked out together.

The audience reacted with great affection to the plot, crying with the wronged orphan, laughing with the comedian, applauding the idealist, scoffing at the cynic, and hating the evil-doer. Very often the villain had to leave by a back door to avoid being beaten up by a crowd ready to avenge the young orphan. At the end of the play the audience would applaud wildly and demand the appearance of the author. That happened even when the play was *Othello.*

Some of the stage effects were fantastic. When the play demanded rain, there was real water. In plays set on a farm, live goats, chickens, and even a live horse appeared on stage. When the star was on stage, the lights were bright; when he left, half the lights were turned off. To emphasize a tragic scene, the lights were extinguished. Like the commedia dell'arte, the Yiddish theater had its singularly costumed stock characters. The hero always wore a mustache and sideburns; the villain was redheaded; a Hasid carried a colored handkerchief; a matchmaker carried an umbrella; a sexton carried a snuff box; a promoter carried a walking stick; a doctor wore glasses; a capitalist smoked a cigar; a peddler wore tattered pants; a student carried a book.

The audience frequently demanded that the star repeat a monologue, a song, or even a death scene.

Some plays were written collectively by the actors. If one of them contributed a dirge about the destruction of the Temple and the other a Chinese song, the first act would take place in Jerusalem and the second act would take place in Peking. Stage events did not always take place consistently; Abraham made a bigger impression if he smoked a cigar; King David's palace would be lit by electric chandeliers.

The history of the Yiddish theater was a continuous fight against *shund,* a struggle for the education of the public as well as the actors. One of the pioneers of the "better" theater was a gifted playwright and idealist, Jacob Gordin. He was the first to get rid of stock characters, the first to write dramas about real people. He took upon himself the task of reeducating the actors, teaching them respect for the text and respect for the audience. He taught them to stop reciting and start talking, even whispering. He purified the theatrical language. He induced the audience, which had become used to canned spectacles, to sit and watch a real human drama. He even brought the Jewish intelligentsia, which had stayed away from the cheap shows, into the theater. He wrote some forty one-act plays and dramas, including adaptations of plays by Goethe, Schiller, Hauptmann, and Gorki. His influence helped to create serious art theater and important drama clubs, such as the *Artef,* or the *Folksbiene* which exists to this day.

New important playwrights began enriching the repertoire: Peretz Hirshbein, David Pinsky, H. Leivick. And the Yiddish language grew with every play.

Some Yiddish actors, like Joseph Schildkraut, Bertha Kalish, David Kessler, and Paul Muni, were "abducted" by the English-language theater on Broadway. Strange "marriages" took place between the English and the Yiddish theater, as when the great star of Second Avenue, Jacob Adler, played in *The Merchant of Venice* on Broadway. He spoke his part in Yiddish, while the rest of the cast spoke English.

American critics came to the Yiddish theater and were delighted. They admitted that the Yiddish theater often inspired the American. Yiddish troupes imported new artistic styles and introduced new European plays. Other ethnic groups in New York—Poles, Germans, Italians, Greeks—also tried to create their own theater. But only the Jews succeeded, perhaps because Jewish audiences received what they deeply desired: broad humanity, rich color, folklore, inspiration, mysticism—a complete escape.

Hutchins Hapgood

From *The Spirit of the Ghetto*

The Yiddish Actors' Strike

The Yiddish theater, flourishing in the Jewish quarters of the major cities—New York, Chicago, Philadelphia, Boston—offered the immigrant needed escape from daily drudgery and provided a center for social activity. Hutchins Hapgood describes with warmth and understanding the actors and audience at the turn of the century in The Spirit of the Ghetto *(1902). In this account of the actors' strike, we find that respect is worth more than money.*

On the stage curtain are advertisements of the wares of Hester Street or portraits of the "star" actors. On the programmes and circulars distributed in the audience are sometimes amusing announcements of coming attractions or lyric praise of the "stars."

"The Witch" ("The Kyshefmacherin"*) written by Abraham Goldfaden, a Yiddish Art Theatre Production.* 1925. Museum of the City of New York. The Theater Collection. *Identifiable are Paul Muni (fourth from left) as "Hotzmach," Maurice Schwartz (center) as "Bobe Yachne, the witch," and Anna Teitelbaum as "Mirele," center front.*

On the playboards outside the theatre, containing usually the portrait of a star, are also lyric and enthusiastic announcements. Thus, on the return of the great Adler, who had been ill, it was announced on the boards that "the splendid eagle has spread his wings again."

The Yiddish actors, as may be inferred from the verses quoted, take themselves with peculiar seriousness, justified by the enthusiasm, almost worship, with which they are regarded by the people. Many a poor Jew, man or girl, who makes no more than $10 a week in the sweatshop, will spend $5 of it on the theatre, which is practically the only amusement of the Ghetto Jew. He has not the loafing and sporting instincts of the poor Christian, and spends his money for the theatre rather than for drink. It is not only to see the play that the poor Jew goes to the theatre. It is to see his friends and the actors. With these latter he, and more frequently she, try in every way to make acquaintance, but commonly are compelled to adore at a distance. They love the songs that are heard on the stage, and for these the demand is so great that a certain bookshop on the east side makes a specialty of publishing them.

The actor responds to this popular enthusiasm with sovereign contempt. He struts about in the cafés on Canal and Grand Streets, conscious of his greatness. He refers to the crowd as "Moses" with superior condescension or humorous vituperation. Like thieves, the actors have a jargon of their own, which is esoteric and jealously guarded. Their pride gave rise a year or two ago to an amusing strike at the People's Theatre. The actors of the three Yiddish companies in New York are normally paid on the share rather than the salary system. In the case of the company now at the People's Theatre, this system proved very profitable. The star actors, Jacob Adler and Boris Thomashevsky, and their wives, who are actresses—Mrs. Adler being the heavy realistic tragedienne and Mrs. Thomashevsky the star soubrette—have probably received on an average during that time as much as $125 a week for each couple. But they, with Mr. Edelstein, the business man, are lessees of the theatre, run the risk and pay the expenses, which are not small. The rent of the theatre is $20,000 a year, and the weekly expenses, besides, amount to about $1,100. The subordinate actors, who risk nothing, since they do not share the expenses, have made amounts during this favorable period ranging from $14 a week on the average for the poorest actors to $75 for those just beneath the "stars." But, in spite of what is exceedingly good pay in the Bowery, the actors of this theatre formed a union, and struck for wages instead of shares. This however, was only an incidental feature. The real cause was that the management of the theatre, with the energetic Thomashevsky at the head, insisted that the actors should be prompt at rehearsals, and if they were not, indulged in unseemly epithets. The actors' pride was aroused, and the union was formed to insure their ease and dignity and to protect them from harsh words. The management imported actors from Chicago. Several of the actors here stood by their employers, notably Miss Weinblatt, a popular young ingenue, who, on account of her great memory is called the "Yiddish Encyclopedia," and Miss Gudinski, an actress of commanding presence. Miss Weinblatt forced her father, once an actor, now a farmer, into the service of the management. But the actors easily triumphed. Misses Gudinski and Weinblatt were forced to join the union, Mr. Weinblatt returned to his farm, the "scabs" were packed off to Philadelphia, and the wages system introduced. A delegation was sent to Philadelphia to throw cabbages at the new actors, who appeared in the Yiddish performances in that city. The triumphant actors now receive on the average probably $10 to $15 a week less than under the old system. Mr. Conrad, who began the disaffection, receives a salary of $29 a week, fully $10 less than he received for months before the strike. But the dignity of the Yiddish actor is now placed beyond assault. As one of them recently said: "We shall no longer be spat upon nor called 'dog.' "

Letters from *A Bintel Brief*

The immigrant Jew read his Yiddish newspaper for the national and international, general, and Jewish news it contained; studied the cultural articles—history, science, philosophy, politics—for self-education, gulped down the serialized novels, and turned to it for sage advice. In Der Tog (The Day) *the column was called "Men and Women," in the* Morgen Journal (The Morning Journal) *it was "Dr. Klorman," but by far the most widely read and most earnestly discussed was the featured column in* Der Forverts (The Jewish Daily Forward). Dos Bintel Brief, *"A Sheaf of Letters," was pioneered and conducted by the editor, Abraham Cahan. The queries covered the gamut of human experiences, as these three suggest.*

SHNORRING AT A WEDDING
1910

Dear Mr. Editor,

A member of our branch of the *Arbeiter Ring* [Workmen's Circle] got married. We sent a large delegation to the wedding. One of the members spoke on the aims and purpose

The Forward *Building, East Broadway, New York.* Courtesy of YIVO Institute for Jewish Research, New York. *The Yiddish daily,* The Forward, *edited by Abraham Cahan, became the largest daily foreign language newspaper in the United States.*

of the *Arbeiter Ring*. At the wedding dinner, a member of our delegation made an appeal for the strikers in Chicago, who are suffering hunger—they, their wives and their children—and asked for contributions.

The groom rose to protest against "shnorring" [asking for money] at his wedding. So all the members, forty-five in number, rose and left. Only two members, one claiming to be a Russian revolutionary and the other a strong trade unionist, refused to leave.

Mr. Editor, what is your opinion of the conduct of the groom and the two members? We want to point out that the groom was seated next to his boss. Perhaps his enslaved soul forced him to do what he did. The two members claim they did not want to disturb the joy of the celebration . . .

ANSWER:

It is an ancient custom to take up collections for good causes at weddings and other happy occasions. Others consider a good cause a Talmud Torah [Hebrew School] or Hachnosas Kallah [dowering the bride], we consider helping and supporting strikers a good cause. "Shnorring"?

By the Orthodox they "shnorr" at almost every wedding, when the cantor recites the "He who blesses . . ." benediction. And the wealthier the guest the louder the singing. What else is that but "shnorring"? When they take up a collection for the rabbi, the "shamash" [sexton], the "badhan" [bard], the waiters . . . Is this not "shnorring"? Such "shnorring" is for individuals, who did nothing to earn it. But a collection for thousands of strikers—to call that "shnorring" is an insult to the proven fighters who are suffering for the whole laboring class! The simhah [joyous celebration] of a worker cannot be more worthily graced than by such a collection.

At a worker's simhah it is a duty to remember the plight of the thousands sacrificing for our class . . . The Orthodox break a glass at a wedding, so that in the midst of joy, the destruction of the Temple in Jerusalem be not forgotten. In the same spirit progressive workers should remember their brothers locked in strife and struggle.

Naturally, if the worker wants to curry favor with his boss who is at the wedding, he is in an uncomfortable position. The whole incident points out that even at a private affair like a wedding, sharp class distinction is present. Workers can only be comfortable with themselves, and be true to their conscience only in the company of their comrades. The groom was, therefore, wrong. However, this was not the time and place to mount a protest demonstration. The friends should not have left. They should have postponed the protest for another occasion. For everything there is a time and place. The two who remained did not act wrongly. They had the right to maintain that a celebration should not be disturbed.

Labor Rally. Archives of Labor and Urban Affairs, Wayne State University, Detroit, Michigan.

LOVE CONQUERS ALL
1906

Dear Editor,

I am a young man of twenty-one; I have a seventeen-year-old cousin, and she and her parents would like me to marry her. I like the girl. She's educated, American-born, not bad-looking. But she's quite small.

That is the drawback: for her age, she is very short. And I happen to be tall. So when we walk down the street together, people look at us as a poorly matched couple. Another thing: she is very religious, and I am a freethinker. I ask you, esteemed Editor, could this lead to an unpleasant life if we were to marry? I wait impatiently for your answer.

Sympathetic

ANSWER:

Love conquers all. Many such couples live happily, and it is better for the man to be taller and the woman shorter, not the opposite. People are accustomed to seeing the man more developed than the woman. People stare? Let them stare! Also the fact that the girl is religious and the man is not can be overcome if he has enough influence on her.

THE JEWISH FARMER
1909

Dear Editor,

As a reader of the *Forward*, I am writing to you about a matter that will interest other people too. But first I will tell you a little about myself.

I am twenty-seven years of age, have been in the country ten years, and am still

An Outing with the Rabbi, near Helena, Montana. c. 1890. Montana Historical Society. *The Gans, Goldbergs, Sobles, Marks, and Sands picnic with Rabbi Shulkin.*

single. I have worked here at various trades, but never very long at one job. I enjoy traveling and seeing what's going on in the country. Now I've decided it's time to marry and settle down.

I came to North Dakota, where most people make their living from farming. But there are no Jews in this area. I started to work on a farm and I learned farming. I like this kind of life, and after working a year and a half I rented a farm for myself.

My capital was small, but Gentile neighbors helped me. I went into debt for thirteen hundred dollars, but by the end of the summer I had paid back almost all of my debts. I wrote to a friend of mine about joining me. He and his wife came and we work together. We carry on an independent life, have none of the problems of city life because we always have our own potatoes, butter, cheese, milk, chickens, a good home and are content.

This winter I went to Chicago and stayed a few weeks with friends. Most of my friends called me an idiot and told me they could not understand how a young, capable fellow like me became a farmer and leads such a lonely life.

Of all the girls I knew, who would have gladly married me before, not one was interested in going back to the farm with me. But this didn't discourage me. I returned to the farm and I'm now preparing for the spring season.

However, I want to ask you, did my friends have the right to call me "idiot"? Is there any logic in their argument? Please answer me.

Thank you,
The Jewish Farmer

ANSWER:

There is certainly nothing to be ashamed of in living in the lap of Nature. Many people dream of becoming farmers. The cities are full of many diseases that are unheard of on farms. Tuberculosis, for instance, is a disease of the big cities. People in urban areas grow old and gray at forty, but most of the farmers are healthy and strong and live to be eighty and ninety.

Generally, it is a matter of choice. Debates between country people and city people about which have the better life are nothing new.

Sholem Aleichem

"Berl-Isaac Tells the Wonders of America"

Sholom Rabinowitz took the pen name Sholem Aleichem (the standard Jewish greeting: "Peace unto you") when he turned from Hebrew to write in Yiddish in 1883. Under that name he became the most popular of Yiddish writers. His humorous style evoked bitter laughter. Beneath the laughter was sharp satire of the wealthy, the haughty, the pretentious, and the social structure which produced them and fawned upon them. His two stays in America were bitterly disappointing, but he found solace in poking fun at the American way of life and death. This tale of some of the wonders of America first appeared in Yiddish in 1918 and as Berl-Isaac tells it, turns from gentle comedy to deflating farce.

"America is a land of bluff. . ." "American bluffers . . ." That's what the foreigners say. But they are greenhorns and don't know what they're talking about. As far as that's concerned, America doesn't come up to our Kasrilevka—not by a long shot, and all your American bluffers are mere babies compared with our Berl-Isaac.

You can get an idea about what kind of a person Berl-Isaac is if I tell you that in Kasrilevka when anybody lets his imagination run away with him, or, as you would say in your American language, "he raps a teapot," we interrupt him with the words: "Greetings from Berl-Isaac." He gets the hint at once and stops spinning his yarn.

There is a joke they tell in Kasrilevka about a certain Jew of arrogant disposition. On Easter day the custom among the Gentiles in Russia is to greet each other with the glad tidings that Christ has risen again: *Christo voskresse*, and the answer is *Voistinoo voskresse*, meaning: that's right he has risen indeed . . . . So it happened once that a Christian met that arrogant Jew and greeted him with the words: *Christo voskresse*. The Jew was in a quandary: what was he to do? He couldn't answer *Voistinoo voskresse* because he knew that it is a lie and against our religion. . .And he couldn't tell the Gentile: "No, he has not risen," because he might pay dearly for words like those.

So he reflected for a moment and then said to the Christian: "Yes, I've already heard it today from our Berl-Isaac."

Imagine, then, that this very Berl-Isaac went to America, spent a good many years there, and then returned to Kasrilevka. What wonders he has been telling of America ever since!

"To begin with, the country itself," he says, "a land flowing with milk and honey. People make plenty of money; you dig into money with both hands, you pick up gold by the shovelful! And as for 'business,' as they call it in America, there is so much of it that it just makes your head spin! You can do anything you like. You want a factory—so you have a factory; you want to open a store—so you open a store. If you like to push a pushcart, you push a pushcart; and if you don't, you peddle or go to work in a shop—it's a free country! You may starve or drop dead of hunger right in the street—there is nothing to prevent you, nobody will object.

"Then, the size of the cities! The width of the streets! The height of the buildings! They have a building there, they call it the Woolworth—so the top of its chimneypot reaches into the clouds and even higher; it is said that this house has several hundred floors. You want to know, how do they climb up to the attic? By a ladder, which they call an elevator. If you want somebody on the top floor, you sit down in the elevator early in the morning, so you get there towards sunset, just in time for your evening prayers.

"Once I had a notion to take a trip up, just for curiosity, to see what's on the top. Well, I do not regret it. What I saw there I shall never see again. And what I felt—that can hardly be described at all. Just imagine; I stood there on the top, looking down, and all of a sudden I felt something strangely cold touching my left cheek, something smooth like ice, yet not so much like ice as like very chilled jelly—sort of slippery and soft. I slowly turned my head to the left and took a look, and what do you think it was? It was the moon.

"Now take their life—it's all a rushing, a running, and a hustling. 'Urry-hop,' they call it there. Everything is in a hurry, and even when it comes to eating it is also done heels over head. You rush into a restaurant, order a *schnapps*, and as for the meal, I myself once saw a fellow being served something on a plate, something fresh, alive, and kicking, and when he cut it in two, one half of it flew away to one side and the other half to the other side, and the fellow was through with his lunch.

"Still, you ought to see how strong they are! Iron! Regular athletes! They have a custom of boxing with each other right in the streets. Not that they mean to beat you up, kill you, give you a black eye, or knock out some of your teeth for you, as they do

Jacob A. Riis. *Hester Street.* Early 1880s. The Museum of The City of New York.

here. God forbid! It's all just for fun. They roll up their sleeves and hit each other—they want to see who can hit better. They call it 'fightling.' Once, while I was taking a walk in the Bronx, I was carrying some merchandise. I met two boys, loafers, good-for-nothings, as we would say here, who started to dare me: they wanted to fightle with me. I told them: No sir, I don't fightle. I tried to dodge this way and that, but they wouldn't let me go. So I said to myself: If that's the kind of loafers you are, I'm going to show you who's who. And I put down my bundle and took off my coat—and blows began to shower on me so fast it's a miracle I escaped alive. You see, I was only one against two of them. Since then I don't fightle any more—not even if you shower me with gold.

"Now, take their language. It's all turned upside down, as if for spite. If we call somebody a meat-merchant, they call him a butcher; if we say a houseowner, they say a landlord; a neighbor is a next-door-man or a next-door-woman; a hen is a chicken. Everything topsy-turvy. Once I asked the missus to buy a cock to kill for the Day of Atonement. So I couldn't explain to her what I wanted until I hit on the idea of telling her: 'Buy me the gentleman of the chickens.' This she understood, and only then did she deliver herself of that fine word, 'Alright,' which means almost the same as when we say: 'Be it so, why not? Sure, with the greatest of pleasures!'

"Now, take the honor which we Jews enjoy there. No other nation or race in America is so exalted, revered, and glorified as the Jew. A Jew is made a whole fuss about. It's even a distinction to be a Jew. On the Feast of Tabernacles, let us say, you may meet a Jew walking right in the middle of Fifth Avenue carrying a palm leaf and citron, and not afraid that he'll be arrested for it. I'm telling you, they love the Jew in America, so what's the use of talking? They only hate Jewish beards—'whiskers,' they call them there. As soon as they see a Jew with whiskers, they let the Jew go his way in peace, but they do pull at his whiskers, and they keep on pulling until he must get rid of them, shave them off. That's why most of the Jews there have no beards or mustaches, and their faces are as smooth as a plate. You can hardly recognize who's a Jew and who is not, because there are no beards, and their language isn't Jewish, either. Except that you may perhaps tell a Jew by his haste when he walks, or by the way he talks with his hands, there's nothing else to distinguish him . . . . Otherwise they are Jews—Jews in every respect: they observe all Jewish customs, love all Jewish dishes, and celebrate all Jewish holidays. Passover with them is Passover. Matzoth they bake there all year round, and for the Passover mortar, they have a special factory for it—thousands upon thousands of workers sit in that factory and manufacture mortared nuts with apple. Jews made a living even out of the bitter herbs we use on Passover—that's America for you!"

"Yes, Berl-Isaac, all these stories of yours are all very fine. But tell us just one thing that we'd like to know; do people die in America, too, just as they do here, or do they live there forever?"

"They die, why shouldn't they die? In America, when it comes to dying, they die a thousand in one day, ten thousand, twenty thousand, thirty thousand! Whole streets die out at once! Cities are swallowed up by the earth, as Korah was in the Bible! That's America for you!"

"Now, wait a moment, Berl-Isaac. If that's the case, then how, we should like to know, are they better off in America? If, as you say, they die there just as we do here?"

"Yes, they die. But—how do they die? That's the point. And not so much the dying itself. People die the same everywhere—they die of death. The main thing is the burying—that's what it is. In the first place, there is a rule in America that everybody knows beforehand where he is going to buried. Because he himself, while he is still alive, goes to the graveyard—they call it there 'cemeteria'—selects a place for himself and bargains until they settle about the price. Then he takes his wife out for a trip to the 'cemeteria' and tells her: 'See, darling, that's where you are going to lie, and this is where I am going to lie, and there's where our children will lie.' Then he goes to the office of the funerals and orders a funeral for himself—to be held after his death. He orders any class he likes. There are three classes: first, second, and third class.

"A first class funeral—for very rich people, for millionaires—costs a thousand dollars. Well, that's as good a funeral as one could wish. The sun is shining, and the weather is a pleasure. The coffin stands on a black catafalque, inlaid with silver. The horses all wear black trappings and white feathers. The reverends—rabbis, cantors, synagogue beadles—are also dressed in black, with white buttons. And coaches follow the hearse—no end of coaches! Children from all the Hebrew schools walk in front and sing with sonorous voices, as slowly: 'V-i-r-t-u-e m-a-r-c-h-e-s b-e-f-o-r-e h-i-m a-n-d d-i-r-e-c-t-s h-i-s s-t-e-p-s!' The whole town rings with this singing. A thousand dollars is a thousand dollars—it talks!

"Second class is also a fine funeral. But it costs five hundred dollars, and it isn't quite the thing. The weather is not so bright. The coffin is also placed on a black catafalque; but it isn't inlaid with silver. The horses and the reverends are dressed in black, but without feathers and without buttons. Coaches follow the hearse, but not so many. Children of only a few Hebrew schools walk in front, but their singing is in faster movement: 'Vir-tue march-es be-fore him and di-rects his steps!' The singing is bad as you might expect for five hundred dollars.

"Third class—that's quite a common sort of funeral and costs one hundred dollars all in all. It is chilly outside, and cloudy. The coffin is not placed on a catafalque. There are only two horses and two reverends. Not a single coach follows. Children of only one Hebrew school walk in front, and they don't sing but mumble in a hurry, without any tune: 'Vir-tue march b'for'im andirect's steps.' They are sleepy and you can hardly hear them. After all it's only one hundred dollars—what can you expect for a hundred dollars."

"Yes, Berl-Isaac, but what about one who can't afford even a hundred dollars?"

"Well, then he's out of luck! Without money one is hard up everywhere. The poor man always lies nine feet underground! . . . Still, make no mistake! In America they don't allow even a poor man to lie unburied. They give him a funeral for nothing; it doesn't cost him a penny. Of course, it's a rather sad sort of funeral. No ceremonies whatever, not a trace of horses, or of reverends. And it pours cats and dogs. There are only two synagogue beadles; the beadles on each side of the corpse in between, and all three of them—poor fellows—have to walk all the way to the graveyard . . . If you have no money, I am telling you, better don't get born at all—it's a lousy world . . . Can any of you spare a cigarette?"

Edward Field

"Mark Twain and Sholem Aleichem"

Mark Twain (né Samuel L. Clemens) and Sholem Aleichem (né Sholom Rabinowitz), Yankee and Jew, garbed in outlandish fashion, join their beloved simple folk, the poor, playing in the world allotted them, "a sewer full of garbage." The tools they chose for trying to make the world a better place, humor and love, had failed them. What were they now to do, drown and enjoy it? The poem is deceptive. As in the works of his two protagonists, Field's "Mark Twain and Sholem Aleichem" (1963) hides its sadness behind gentle humor.

Mark Twain and Sholem Aleichem went one day to Coney Island—
Mark wearing a prison-striped bathing costume and straw hat,
Sholem in greenish-black suit, starched collar, beard,
Steelrimmed schoolmaster glasses, the whole works,
And an umbrella that he flourished like an actor
Using it sometimes to hurry along the cows
As he described scenes of childhood in the village in Poland,
Or to spear a Jew on a sword like a cossack.

Sitting together on the sand among food wrappers and lost coins,
They went through that famous dialogue
Like the vaudeville routine, After-you-Gaston:
"They tell me you are called the Yiddish Mark Twain."
"Nu? The way I heard it you are the American Sholem Aleichem."
And in this way passed a pleasant day admiring each other,
The voice of the old world and the voice of the new.

"Shall we risk the parachute jump, Sholem?"
"Well, Markele, am I properly dressed for it?
Better we should go in the water a little maybe?"

Beach Scene, Coney Island. 1928. UPI/Bettmann Archives.

So Sholem Aleichem took off shoes and socks (with holes—a shame),
Rolled up stiff-serge pants showing his varicose veins;
And Mark Twain, his bathing suit moth-eaten and gaping
In important places, lit up a big cigar,
And put on a pair of waterwings like an angel.

The two great writers went down where the poor
Were playing at the water's edge
Like a sewer full of garbage, warm as piss.
Around them shapeless mothers and brutal fathers
Were giving yellow, brown, white, and black children
Lessons in life that the ignorant are specially qualified to give:
Slaps and scoldings, mixed with food and kisses.

Mark Twain, impetuous goy, dived right in,
And who could resist splashing a little the good-natured Jew?
Pretty soon they were both floundering in the sea
The serge suit ruined that a loving daughter darned and pressed,
The straw hat floating off on the proletarian waters.

They had both spent their lives trying to make the world a better place
And both had gently faced their failure.
If humor and love had failed, what next?
They were both drowning and enjoying it now,
Two old men of the two worlds, the old and the new,
Splashing about in the sea like crazy monks.

COLORPLATE 82

Interior, Touro Synagogue. Newport, Rhode Island. *The Touro Synagogue of Congregation Yeshuat Israel is the oldest standing synagogue still in use in the United States. It was dedicated in 1763 by a congregation numbering some twenty families. The decline of the city after the Revolutionary War caused the Jewish community to disperse but the building remained and was sustained by bequests by Abraham and Judah Touro, whose father had served as the congregation's* hazzan. *An influx of immigrants at the end of the nineteenth century reestablished it as a house of worship. In 1946 it was declared a National Historic Site.*

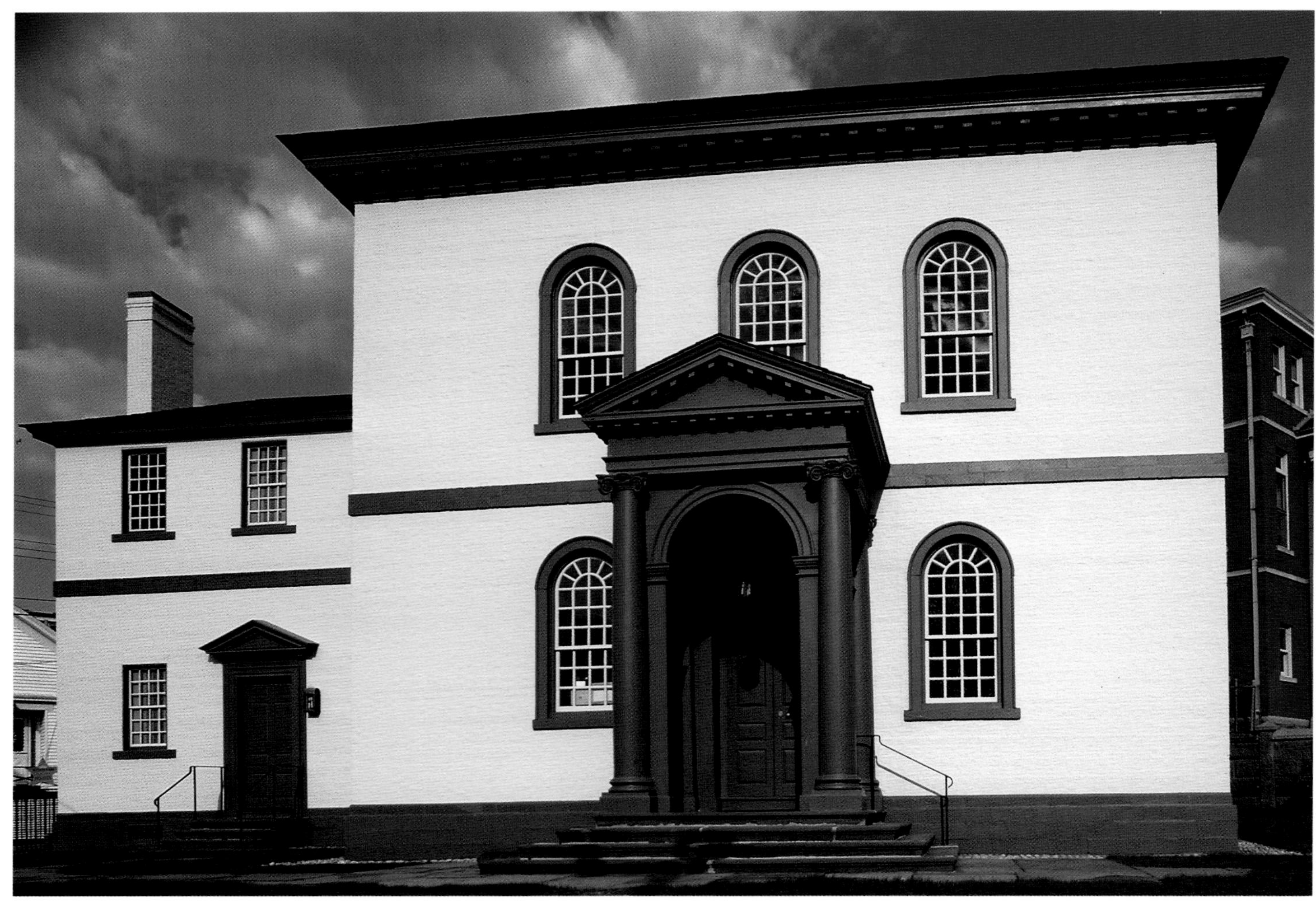

COLORPLATE 83
Exterior, Touro Synagogue. Newport, Rhode Island.

OLORPLATE 84 *(opposite, above)*

ARNOLD W. BRUNNER, ARCHITECT. *Interior View, Congregation Shearith Israel, The Spanish and Portuguese Synagogue.* New York City. 1897. *This interior view of the synagogue shows the reading desk in the center, from which services are conducted. Also visible are the ark, the Ladies Gallery, and Tiffany windows. This is the fifth building of the congregation which was originally founded in 1654.*

COLORPLATE 85 *(opposite, below)*

The Little Synagogue. Congregation Shearith Israel, The Spanish and Portuguese Synagogue. New York City. *The Little Synagogue is a replica of the Mill Street Synagogue of 1730. The interior shows the colonial-style ark and the* ner tamid *(eternal light) which has been in continuous use since 1818. The wooden Ten Commandments and the two candlesticks are thought to be from fifteenth-century Portugal. The bench on the right dates to the Mill Street Synagogue of 1730, the bench on the left from the Crosby Street Synagogue of 1834.*

COLORPLATE 86

FORTUNATO ARRIOLA. *Temple Emanu-El and the San Francisco Armory.* 1866. Oil on board. 18 x 21 1/2 in. California Historical Society. Purchased through Edgar Kahn in memory of Mary-Louise Clayburgh Kahn.

COLORPLATE 87

HENRY MOSLER. *Plum Street Temple. (B'nai Jeshurun Congregation).* Cincinnati, Ohio. 1866. Oil on canvas. 29 1/2 x 24 5/8 in. Hebrew Union College Skirball Museum, Los Angeles. Gift of Mrs. Charles Kenis. *This synagogue is most well known as being the pulpit of Rabbi Isaac Mayer Wise and is architecturally significant as the first Moorish-style synagogue in the United States. Rabbinic ordination services are conducted in its sanctuary by Reform Judaism's seminary, the Hebrew Union College, to this day.*

COLORPLATE 88

Rodef Sholom, Philadelphia. 1869. Chromolithograph. 26 x 20 in. American Jewish Historical Society, Waltham, Massachusetts.

COLORPLATE 89

Khal Adath Jeshuran Synagogue. New York. c. 1884. Watercolor drawing. 8 1/2 x 7 in. The Museum of the City of New York. The J. Clarence Davies Collection. *This is the grandest synagogue built by the immigrant community residing in New York's lower East Side.*

COLORPLATE 90

BARTLETT AND BUDEINEGER, ST. LOUIS, ARCHITECTS. *Temple Gemiluth Chassed, Port Gibson, Missisippi.* 1891. Photograph courtesy of Bill Aron. *The oldest synagogue in the state of Missisippi, Temple Gemiluth Chassed is listed on the National Register of Historic Places. It is of unusual Moorish-Byzantine design. This building still stands in memory of the once vital Jewish community of Port Gibson.*

Morris Raphael Cohen

From *A Dreamer's Journey*

"Brownsville"

Morris Raphael Cohen was a legend in his own time. A philosopher and teacher of philosophers, admired for his keen intellect, revered for his devotion to truth, feared by intellectual foes, and respected by all who were committed to the life of reason, he was the most influential professor at the College of the City of New York, when that institution was arguably the most intellectually exciting school in America. Students flocked to his classes and quaked in his presence. He was a founder of the Conference on Jewish Relations and author of Reflections of a Wondering Jew, *a volume of his essays on Jewish themes. In this selection from his 1949 autobiography,* A Dreamer's Journey, *we can glimpse the earliest influences on his life and intellect.*

Brownsville was at that time a Jewish boom town, whose bloom had been nipped in the bud. It had a number of newly built houses, as well as a scattering of houses belonging to old settlers. Everywhere there were vacant fields and in the direction of Canarsie, meadows, woods, brooks and marshes. Almost all of the natives, old and young, played baseball and so did the Jewish boys of my age.

At the time we moved into our house on Rockaway Avenue my father had some hope of finding work in Brooklyn or in New York, but this turned out to be illusory. He once tried his hand as a glazier, but on his first job he got into some difficulty with the owner of the house where he was to put in a window pane and the latter called him a "sheeny" and threatened to beat him up. My father came home terribly depressed, and though it was Friday night and mother tried to provide the usual Sabbath cheer, father broke down after saying *kiddush* and wept bitterly. After that he was more or less reconciled to the fact of unemployment. Nor was my brother Sam much more successful, though for several weeks during the winter he did find some work. We lived on the little rent that we were occasionally able to collect from some of the tenants, one of the stores being almost always vacant. Despite my mother's wonderful management we often arrived at the state of not having any money or food in the house. I would then walk to New York over the Brooklyn Bridge and ask my brother Tom, who had not lost his position as clerk in Kaufman's Shoe Store, for money to buy bread.

When I applied for admission to the Brownsville Public School I was asked in what grade I had been in New York, and when I told them the truth, that I had just been promoted into the grammar department, they told me that the Brooklyn schools were more advanced and that I would have to enter the last primary grade. This seemed to me an intolerable humiliation, and so I walked a considerable distance to a Brooklyn school on Chauncey Street and applied for admission to its grammar department. When the assistant principal asked me in what class I had been in New York I told her that I had been in the seventh grade, thinking that I would then be placed in the eighth and so avoid losing a grade. She, however, wanted to make sure of my qualifications and asked me what I knew in arithmetic. I told her that I could do fractions and so to my great elation she put me into the seventh grade. My elation, however, subsided when I entered the classroom. A grammar lesson was in progress, and each

Jacob A. Riis. *Getting Ready for Sabbath in a Cellar Dwelling on Ludlow Street.* c. 1890. Photograph. The Museum of the City of New York.

pupil in turn was called upon to parse certain words in sentences which were on the blackboard . . .

For the first half-year I was the only Jew in the school; however I got along fairly well with my schoolmates. Two of them, Mosher and Meyer, invited me to their homes and presented me to their mothers as the brightest boy in the class. But on the way to school I had difficulties. Beyond Dean Street I passed a number of houses inhabited by Germans who delighted to set their young children on me, yelling "sheeny," and running after me as if they were going to attack me from the rear. When I turned around they would retreat, but as soon as I resumed my walk they would return to their annoying pastime. One day I became so irritated that I ran after one of the youngsters and slapped his face. At once, his older brother came out of the house and gave me a good thrashing for hitting someone below my size. But the total result was satisfactory, for the youngsters thereafter left me alone.

Abraham Goldman

From *The Goldman Family Saga*

To Be With His Family

Abraham Goldman, a Jewish businessman in Utica, New York, remembered his life as the son of immigrant parents in upstate New York at the turn of the century. His memoirs, published in

1961, simply written and full of homely details, afford us a glimpse of the hard work, family solidarity, and adaptability demanded of Jewish immigrant life.

Now, Dad is leaving Neustadt [Lithuania] coming to America because he has a brother and sister here. It must have taken every dollar he had to pay for his passage because he was stone broke when reaching New York.

Upon arriving in Castle Garden, there were some Lithuanian farmers on the ship, and they had quite a sum of Russian Rubles which they wanted to exchange for American dollars. They could only speak Litvish but the custom officers could only speak German. As Dad could speak both Litvish and German, he acted as an interpreter for both parties, and in the exchange from Russian rubles to U.S. money Dad made U.S. dollars.

Uncle Hyman Weinberg met Dad at Castle Garden and took him to his apartment on Orchard Street. The next day Dad said he took a walk to see what New York looked like. On East Broadway he saw a bank with a sign printed in Yiddish. It read "Jarmulowsky Bank, Money sent to all parts of Europe." [Sender Jarmulowsky was the leading Jewish banker on the Lower East Side of New York.] Dad went in and sent the $15.00 he made to Mother in Neustadt.

Dad had no intention of remaining in New York, even though Uncle Hyman assured him of a job in the clothing factory where he could learn the trade of a tailor. Dad wanted no part of working for someone else. He was determined to get to Syracuse and start out for himself.

Uncle Hyman advanced Dad the price of a railroad ticket. Upon arriving in Syracuse there was a Jewish truck driver, with a one-horse truck at the station. Dad showed him Uncle Ralph's address and asked how much he would charge to take Dad and his burlap sack to that address. At this point he had exactly 27 cents. After some dickering they agreed on 25 cents.

Now, here is Dad in Syracuse with no trade and no money, but, thanks to God, with good health and a strong body. So, what is there to do but to become a pack-peddler? A Mr. Shimberg had a wholesale notions and dry goods store where most of the peddlers traded. He advanced Dad $35.00 worth of credit, mostly in notions, and with that Dad started peddling. With so little merchandise he confined his travels close to Syracuse. This he did for about six months, until he accumulated a little capital, which enabled him to start out on the road with a fairly complete line of dry goods.

Dad had a special harness built for himself. On his back was the big pack. On both sides of his chest were hooks where small cases were hung; and he had a satchel in each hand. Picture a setup like that, walking from five to ten miles a day over rough country roads. I've had big strong farmers come into our store in Rome and tell me they remembered that when Dad carried the pack it was so heavy that they, as young men, could not lift it off the floor.

I once asked Pa, "In those days horses were cheap, so why didn't you buy a horse and wagon instead of playing the part of a horse?" His answer was that he was so lonesome for Mother and the children that all he could think of was to return to Neustadt. He did not want to tie up any of his money in rigs. He carried the pack for three years and nine months, and then decided that he is in this country to stay, so he swapped or traded three second-hand watches with Dad Fox, the old horse trader, for a small horse and Democrat wagon . . .

How hard Dad worked no one but he knew, but he had a supreme purpose for working and saving. His dream and goal in life was to bring Mother and us three children here so that he could enjoy the pleasure of being with his family. In those days

Ben Taylor and His Peddler's Wagon, Quitman, Georgia. 1908. Photograph. Courtesy of Dr. Louis Schmier, Valdosta State University, Valdosta, Georgia.

the average man earned 10 cents per hour. Milk was 3 cents per quart. Men's socks were 2 for 25 cents. I mention these facts to show how hard a man had to work in order to accumulate any amount of money. So, with the dollar so hard to come by and with Dad here but four years as a pack-peddler, he had saved and had on deposit in the Onondaga County Savings of Syracuse $1400.00.

Now he considered himself an established traveling merchant, for over the wide stretch of territory which he covered he was already acquainted with people and had regular customers. So, he buys steamship tickets and sends for his family.

As there was no railroad in Neustadt, we were all loaded into a horse-drawn wagon and taken to the nearest railroad station in Germany, where we were put aboard a train for Hamburg, the seaport. We had a two day lay-over before the ship sailed, and were housed in army-like barracks . . .

Dad had purchased steamship tickets for a fast boat, which was to make the trip in seven days, but instead we were put on a slow boat which took three weeks. Dad was very angry over the error and received a cash rebate.

Uncle Hyman met us at Castle Garden and took us to their apartment. The next day we were put on the train for Syracuse. Mother knew a few words in English, and on the train was teaching us children what to say . . .

Dad met us at the R.R. station in Syracuse, where he had a hack "carriage" engaged, and we were taken to Uncle Ralph's home. Dad had an apartment rented and furnished ready for us to move into. They were nice rooms but with no inside plumbing, but homes without plumbing were the regular way of living in those days.

We had a hand pump in the kitchen which supplied wash water from a cistern in the cellar. There was an open well a short block from our house, so once every day I or Eli would go to the well and bring back a pail of drinking water . . .

Eli started school one term ahead of me. We both started in the Adam Street School, probably one of the oldest school houses in Syracuse. It was a wooden building with a big, pot-bellied coal burning stove in each room and with a Chick Sales outhouse privy in the yard. I was in the third room, grade 2B, when we moved from Adam to Jackson School, a new modern brick building, with steam heat in each room and flush toilets in the basement. As soon as we became settled, the principal, a motherly woman, went in each room and cautioned us all not to use more than two sheets of tissue paper when we went to the toilet.

Henry Roth

From *Call It Sleep*

Henry Roth's great novel Call It Sleep *(1934) chronicles the immigrant world seen through the eyes of a young boy, bewildered and embittered. The mood is already set in the novel's Prologue.*

PROLOGUE

(I pray thee ask no questions this is that Golden Land)

The small white steamer, Peter Stuyvesant, that delivered the immigrants from the stench and throb of the steerage to the stench and the throb of New York tenements, rolled slightly on the water beside the stone quay in the lee of the weathered barracks and new brick buildings of Ellis Island. Her skipper was waiting for the last of the officials, laborers and guards to embark upon her before he cast off and started for Manhattan. Since this was Saturday afternoon and this the last trip she would make for the week-end, those left behind might have to stay over till Monday. Her whistle bellowed its hoarse warning. A few figures in overalls sauntered from the high doors of the immigration quarters and down the grey pavement that led to the dock.

It was May of the year 1907, the year that was destined to bring the greatest number of immigrants to the shores of the United States. All that day, as on all the days since spring began, her decks had been thronged by hundreds upon hundreds of foreigners, natives from almost every land in the world, the joweled close-cropped Teuton, the full-bearded Russian, the scraggly-whiskered Jew, and among them Slovack peasants with docile faces, smooth-cheeked and swarthy Armenians, pimply Greeks, Danes with wrinkled eyelids. All day her decks had been colorful, a matrix of the vivid costumes of other lands, the speckled green-and-yellow aprons, the flowered kerchief, embroidered homespun, the silver-braided sheepskin vest, the gaudy scarfs, yellow boots, fur caps, caftans, dull gabardines. All day the guttural, the high-pitched voices, the astonished cries, the gasps of wonder, reiterations of gladness had risen from her decks in a motley billow of sound. But now her decks were empty, quiet, spreading out under the sunlight almost as if the warm boards were relaxing from the strain and the pressure of the myriads of feet. All those steerage passengers of the ships that had docked that day who were permitted to enter had already entered—except two, a woman and a young child she carried in her arms. They had just come aboard escorted by a man.

About the appearance of these late comers there was very little that was unusual. The man had evidently spent some time in America and was now bringing his wife and child over from the other side. It might have been thought that he had spent most of his time in lower New York, for he paid only the scantest attention to the Statue of Liberty or to the city rising from the water or to the bridges spanning the East River—or perhaps he was merely too agitated to waste much time on these wonders. His clothes were the ordinary clothes the ordinary New Yorker wore in that period—sober and dull. A black derby accentuated the sharpness and sedentary pallor of his face; a jacket, loose on his tall spare frame, buttoned up in a V close to the throat; and above the V a tightly-knotted black tie was mounted in the groove of a high starched collar. As for his wife, one guessed that she was a European more by the timid wondering look in her eyes as she gazed from her husband to the harbor, than by her clothes. For her clothes were American—a black skirt, a white shirt-waist and a black jacket. Obviously her husband had either taken the precaution of sending them to her while she was still in Europe or had brought them with him to Ellis Island where she had slipped them on before she left.

Only the small child in her arms wore a distinctly foreign costume, an impression one got chiefly from the odd, outlandish, blue straw hat on his head with its polka dot ribbons of the same color dangling over each shoulder.

Except for this hat, had the three newcomers been in a crowd, no one probably, could have singled out the woman and child as newly arrived immigrants. They carried no sheets tied up in huge bundles, no bulky wicker baskets, no prized feather beds, no boxes of delicacies, sausages, virgin-olive oils, rare cheeses; the large black satchel beside them was their only luggage. But despite this, despite their even less than commonplace appearance, the two overalled men, sprawled out and smoking cigarettes in the stern, eyed them curiously. And the old peddler woman, sitting with basket of oranges on knee, continually squinted her weak eyes in their direction.

The truth was there was something quite untypical about their behavior. The old peddler woman on the bench and the overalled men in the stern had seen enough husbands meeting their wives and children after a long absence to know how such people ought to behave. The most volatile races, such as the Italians, often danced for joy, whirled each other around, pirouetted in an ecstasy: Swedes sometimes just looked at each other, breathing through open mouths like a panting dog; Jews wept, jabbered, almost put each other's eyes out with the recklessness of their darting gestures; Poles roared and gripped each other at arm's length as though they meant to tear a handful of flesh; and after one pecking kiss, the English might be seen gravitating toward, but never achieving an embrace. But these two stood silent, apart; the man staring with aloof, offended eyes grimly down at the water—or if he turned his face toward his wife at all, it was only to glare in harsh contempt at the blue straw hat worn by the child in her arms, and then his hostile eyes would sweep about the deck to see if anyone else were observing them. And his wife beside him regarding him uneasily, appealingly. And the child against her breast looking from one to the other with watchful, frightened eyes. Altogether it was a very curious meeting.

They had been standing in this strange and silent manner for several minutes, when the woman, as if driven by the strain into action, tried to smile, and touching her husband's arm said timidly, "And this is the Golden Land." She spoke in Yiddish.

The man grunted, but made no answer.

Ellis Island, The Great Hall. c. 1900. Research Libraries, New York Public Library. Astor, Lenox, and Tilden Foundations. *Until 1890, immigrants arriving in New York disembarked at Castle Garden; after that, Ellis Island served as their doorway to America.*

She took a breath as if taking courage, and tremulously, "I'm sorry, Albert, I was so stupid." She paused waiting for some flicker of unbending, some word, which never came. "But you look so lean, Albert, so haggard. And your mustache—you've shaved."

His brusque glance stabbed and withdrew. "Even so."

"You must have suffered in this land." She continued gentle despite his rebuke. "You never wrote me. You're thin. Ach! Then here in the new land is the same old poverty. You've gone without food. I can see it. You've changed."

"Well that don't matter," he snapped, ignoring her sympathy. "It's no excuse for your not recognizing me. Who else would call for you? Do you know anyone else in this land?"

"No," placatingly. "But I was so frightened, Albert. Listen to me. I was so bewildered, and that long waiting there in that vast room since morning. Oh, that horrible waiting! I saw them all go, one after the other. The shoemaker and his wife. The coppersmith and his children from Strij. All those on the Kaiserin Viktoria. But I—I remained. To-morrow will be Sunday. They told me no one could come to fetch me. What if they sent me back? I was frantic!"

"Are you blaming me?" His voice was dangerous.

"No! No! Of course not Albert! I was just explaining."

"Well then let me explain," he said curtly. "I did what I could. I took the day off from the shop. I called that cursed Hamburg-American Line four times. And each time they told me you weren't on board."

"They didn't have any more third-class passage, so I had to take the steerage—"

"Yes, now I know. That's all very well. That couldn't be helped. I came here anyway. The last boat. And what do you do? You refused to recognize me. You don't know me." He dropped his elbows down on the rail, averted his angry face. "That's the greeting I get."

"I'm sorry, Albert," she stroked his arm humbly. "I'm sorry."

"And as if those blue-coated mongrels in there weren't mocking me enough, you give them that brat's right age. Didn't I write you to say seventeen months because it would save the half fare! Didn't you hear me inside when I told them?"

"How could I, Albert?" she protested. "How could I? You were on the other side of that—that cage."

"Well why didn't you say seventeen months anyway? Look!" he pointed to several blue-coated officials who came hurrying out of a doorway out of the immigration quarters. "There they are." An ominous pride dragged at his voice. "If he's among them, that one who questioned me so much, I could speak to him if he came up here."

"Don't bother with him, Albert," she exclaimed uneasily. "Please, Albert! What have you against him? He couldn't help it. It's his work."

"Is it?" His eyes followed with unswerving deliberation the blue-coats as they neared the boat. "Well he didn't have to do it so well."

"And after all, I did lie to him, Albert," she said hurriedly trying to distract him.

"The truth is you didn't," he snapped, turning his anger against her. "You made your first lie plain by telling the truth afterward. And made a laughing-stock of me!"

"I didn't know what to do." She picked despairingly at the wire grill beneath the rail. "In Hamburg the doctor laughed at me when I said seventeen months. He's so big. He was big when he was born." She smiled, the worried look on her face vanishing momentarily as she stroked her son's cheek. "Won't you speak to your father, David, beloved?"

The child merely ducked his head behind his mother.

His father stared at him, shifted his gaze and glared down at the officials, and then, as though perplexity had crossed his mind he frowned absently. "How old did he say he was?"

"The doctor? Over two years—and as I say he laughed."

"Well what did he enter?"

"Seventeen months—I told you."

"Then why didn't you tell them seventeen—" He broke off, shrugged violently. "Baah! You need more strength in this land." He paused, eyed her intently and then frowned suddenly. "Did you bring his birth certificate?"

"Why—" She seemed confused. "It may be in the trunk—there on the ship. I don't know. Perhaps I left it behind." Her hand wandered uncertainly to her lips. "I don't know. Is it important? I never thought of it. But surely father could send it. We need only write."

"Hmm! Well, put him down." His head jerked brusquely toward the child. "You don't need to carry him all the way. He's big enough to stand on his own feet."

She hesitated, and then reluctantly set the child down toward the bow. Before her the grimy cupolas and towering square walls of the city loomed up. Above the jagged roof tops, the white smoke, whitened and suffused by the slanting sun, faded into the slots and wedges of the sky. She pressed her brow against her child's, hushed him with whispers. This was that vast incredible land, the land of freedom, of immense opportunity, that Golden Land. Again she tried to smile.

"Albert," she said timidly, "Albert."

"Hm?"

"Gehen vir voinen du? In Nev York?"

"Nein. Bronzeville. Ich hud dir schoin geschriben."

She nodded uncertainly, sighed . . .

Screws threshing, backing water, the Peter Stuyvesant neared her dock—drifting slowly and with canceled momentum as if reluctant.

Abraham Cahan

From *The Rise of David Levinsky*

"Am I Happy?"

There is no agreement as to which is the greatest Jewish immigrant novel, but Abraham Cahan's Rise of David Levinsky *(1917), the story of an orphaned, penniless immigrant boy who rose to the top of the clothing industry, surely ranks among the best. At the end of his rise, the clothing king ruefully reflects on his life, which gave him everything but left him nothing.*

Am I happy?

There are moments when I am overwhelmed by a sense of my success and ease. I become aware that thousands of things which had formerly been forbidden fruit to me are at my command now. I distinctly recall that crushing sense of being debarred from everything, and then I feel as though the whole world were mine. One day I paused in front of an old East Side restaurant that I had often passed in my days of need and despair. The feeling of desolation and envy with which I used to peek in its windows came back to me. It gave me pangs of self-pity for my past and a thrilling sense of my present power. The prices that had once been prohibitive seemed so wretchedly low now. On another occasion I came across a Canal Street merchant of whom I used to buy goods for my push-cart. I said to myself: "There was a time when I used to implore this man for ten dollars' worth of goods, when I regarded him as all-powerful and feared him. Now he would be happy to shake hands with me."

I recalled other people whom I used to fear and before whom I used to humiliate myself because of my poverty. I thought of the time when I had already entered the cloak business, but was struggling and squirming and constantly racking my brains for some way of raising a hundred dollars; when I would cringe with a certain East Side banker and vainly beg him to extend a small note of mine, and come away in a sickening state of despair.

At this moment, as these memories were filing by me, I felt as though now there were nobody in the world who could inspire me with awe or render me a service.

And yet in all such instances I feel a peculiar yearning for the very days when the doors of that restaurant were closed to me and when the Canal Street merchant was a magnate of commerce in my estimation. Somehow, encounters of this kind leave me dejected. The gloomiest past is dearer than the brightest present. In my case there seems to be a special reason for feeling this way. My sense of triumph is coupled with a brooding sense of emptiness and insignificance, of my lack of anything like a great, deep interest.

I am lonely. Amid the pandemonium of my six hundred sewing-machines and the jingle of gold which they pour into my lap I feel the deadly silence of solitude.

I spend at least one evening a week at the Benders'. I am fond of their children and I feel pleasantly at home at their house. I am a frequent caller at the Nodelmans', and enjoy their hospitality even more than that of the Benders. I go to the opera, to the theaters, and to concerts, and never alone. There are merry suppers, and some orgies in which I take part, but when I go home I suffer a gnawing aftermath of loneliness and desolation.

I have a fine summer home, with servants, automobiles, and horses. I share it

Louis Block. *Man at a Sewing Machine.* c. 1910. Photograph. Block Brothers Collection. Missouri Historical Society, St. Louis, Missouri.

with the Bender family and we often have visitors from the city, but, no matter how large and gay the crowd may be, the country makes me sad.

I know bachelors who are thoroughly reconciled to their solitude and even enjoy it. I am not.

No, I am not happy.

In the city I occupy a luxurious suite of rooms in a high-class hotel and keep an excellent chauffeur and valet. I give myself every comfort that money can buy. But there is one thing which I crave and which money cannot buy—happiness.

Many a pretty girl is setting her cap at me, but I know that it is only my dollars they want to marry. Nor do I care for any of them, while the woman to whom my heart is calling—Anna—is married to another man.

I dream of marrying some day. I dread to think of dying a lonely man.

Sometimes I have a spell of morbid amativeness and seem to be falling in love with woman after woman. There are periods when I can scarcely pass a woman in the street without scanning her face and figure. When I see the crowds returning from work in the cloak-and-waist district I often pause to watch the groups of girls as they walk apart from the men. Their keeping together, as if they formed a separate world full of its own interests and secrets, makes a peculiar appeal to me.

Once, in Florida, I thought I was falling in love with a rich Jewish girl whose face had a bashful expression of a peculiar type. There are different sorts of bashfulness. This girl had the bashfulness of sin, as I put it to myself. She looked as if her mind harbored illicit thoughts which she was trying to conceal. Her blushes seemed to be full of sex and her eyes full of secrets. She was not a pretty girl at all, but her "guilty look" disturbed me as long as we were stopping in the same place.

But through all these ephemeral infatuations and interests I am in love with Anna.

From time to time I decide to make a "sensible" marriage, and study this woman or that as a possible candidate, but so far nothing has come of it.

There was one woman whom I might have married if she had not been a Gentile—one of the very few who lived in the family hotel in which I had my apartments. At first I set her down for an adventuress seeking the acquaintance of rich Jews for some sinister purpose. But I was mistaken. She was a woman of high character. Moreover, she and her aged mother, with whom she lived, had settled in that hotel long before it came to be patronized by our people. She was a widow of over forty, with a good, intellectual face, well read in the better sense of the term, and no fool. Many of our people in the hotel danced attendance upon her because she was a Gentile woman, but all of them were really fond of her. The great point was that she seemed to have a sincere liking for our people. This and the peculiar way her shoulders would shake when she laughed was, in fact, what first drew me to her. We grew chummy and I spent many an hour in her company.

In my soliloquies I often speculated and theorized on the question of proposing to her. I saw clearly that it would be a mistake. It was not the faith of my fathers that was in the way. It was that medieval prejudice against our people which makes so many marriages between Jew and Gentile a failure. It frightened me.

One evening we sat chatting in the bright lobby of the hotel, discussing human nature, and she telling me something of the good novels she had read. After a brief pause I said:

"I enjoy these talks immensely. I don't think there is another person with whom I so love to talk of human beings."

She bowed with a smile that shone of something more than mere appreciation of the compliment. And then I uttered in the simplest possible accents:

"It's really a pity that there is the chasm of race between us. Otherwise I don't see why we couldn't be happy together."

I was in an adventurous mood and ready, even eager, to marry her. But her answer was a laugh, as if she took it for a joke; and, though I seemed to sense intimacy and encouragement in that laugh, it gave me pause. I felt on the brink of a fatal blunder, and I escaped before it was too late.

"But then," I hastened to add, "real happiness in a case like this is perhaps not the rule, but the exception. That chasm continues to yawn throughout the couple's married life, I suppose."

"That's an interesting point of view," she said, a noncommittal smile on her lips.

She tactfully forbore to take up the discussion, and I soon dropped the subject. We remained friends.

It was this woman who got me interested in good, modern fiction. The books she selected for me interested me greatly. Then it was that the remarks I had heard from Moissey Tevkin came to my mind. They were illuminating.

Most of the people at my hotel are German-American Jews. I know other Jews of

Pushcart Peddler on Lower East Side, New York. 1930. UPI/Bettmann Archives. *Immigrant Jews provided portable stores, in the rural areas as country peddlers, in the large cities as pushcart peddlers.*

this class. I contribute to their charity institutions. Though an atheist, I belong to one of their synagogues. Nor can I plead the special feeling which had partly accounted for my visits at the synagogue of the Sons of Antomir while I was engaged to Kaplan's daughter. I am a member of that synagogue chiefly because it is a fashionable synagogue. I often convict myself of currying favor with the German Jews. But then German-American Jews curry favor with Portuguese-American Jews, just as we all curry favor with Gentiles and as American Gentiles curry favor with the aristocracy of Europe.

I often long for a heart-to-heart talk with some of the people of my birthplace. I have tried to revive my old friendships with some of them, but they are mostly poor and my prosperity stands between us in many ways.

Sometimes when I am alone in my beautiful apartments, brooding over these things and nursing my loneliness, I say to myself:

"There are cases when success is a tragedy."

There are moments when I regret my whole career, when my very success seems to be a mistake.

I think that I was born for a life of intellectual interest. I was certainly brought up for one. The day when that accident turned my mind from college to business seems to be the most unfortunate day in my life. I think that I should be much happier as a scientist or writer, perhaps. I should then be in my natural element, and if I were doomed to loneliness I should have comforts to which I am now a stranger. That's the way I feel every time I pass the abandoned old building of the City College.

The business world contains plenty of successful men who have no brains. Why, then, should I ascribe my triumph to special ability? I should probably have made a much better college professor than a cloak-manufacturer, and should probably be a happier man, too. I know people who have made much more money than I and whom I consider my inferiors in every respect.

Many of our immigrants have distinguished themselves in science, music, or art, and these I envy far more than I do a billionaire. As an example of the successes achieved by Russian Jews in America in the last quarter of a century it is often pointed out that the man who has built the greatest sky-scrapers in the country, including the Woolworth Building, is a Russian Jew who came here a penniless boy. I cannot boast such distinction, but then I have helped build up one of the great industries of the United States, and this also is something to be proud of. But I should readily change places with the Russian Jew, a former Talmud student like myself, who is the greatest physiologist in the New World, or with the Russian Jew who holds the foremost place among American songwriters and whose soulful compositions are sung in almost every English-speaking house in the world. I love music to madness. I yearn for the world of great singers, violinists, pianists. Several of the greatest of them are of my race and country, and I have met them, but all my acquaintance with them has brought me is a sense of being looked down upon as a money-bag striving to play the Maecenas. I had a similar experience with a sculptor, also one of our immigrants, an East Side boy who had met with sensational success in Paris and London. I had him make my bust. His demeanor toward me was all that could have been desired. We even cracked Yiddish jokes together and he hummed bits of synagogue music over his work, but I never left his studio without feeling cheap and wretched.

When I think of these things, when I am in this sort of mood, I pity myself for a victim of circumstances.

At the height of my business success I feel that if I had my life to live over again I should never think of a business career.

I don't seem to be able to get accustomed to my luxurious life. I am always more or less conscious of my good clothes, of the high quality of my office furniture, of the power I wield over the men in my pay. As I have said in another connection, I still have a lurking fear of restaurant waiters.

I can never forget the days of my misery. I cannot escape from my old self. My past and my present do not comport well. David, the poor lad swinging over a Talmud volume at the Preacher's Synagogue, seems to have more in common with my inner identity than David Levinsky, the well-known cloak-manufacturer.

Anzia Yezierska

From "Hunger"

A Heart of Fire

Shenah Pessah is the indomitable Jewish immigrant woman, the person Anzia Yezierska chose to be. "Hunger" (1920) like almost all the rest of her work, is autobiographical—her life's credo. Offered what was almost every immigrant girl's dream, a "home, husband, babies, a breadwin-

ner for life," she hungered for more—to make her mark in America. Her acclaimed books and stories did accomplish that for her. Though at the end of her life she found herself almost destitute and all but forgotten, the works she fashioned still resound with feeling and lustre.

Shenah Pessah paused in the midst of scrubbing the stairs of the tenement. "Ach!" she sighed. "How can his face still burn so in me when he is so long gone? How the deadness in me flames up with life at the thought of him!"

The dark hallway seemed flooded with white radiance. She closed her eyes that she might see more vividly the beloved features. The glowing smile that healed all ills of life and changed her from the weary drudge into the vibrant creature of joy.

It was all a miracle—his coming, this young professor from one of the big colleges. He had rented a room in the very house where she was janitress so as to be near the people he was writing about. But more wonderful than all was the way he stopped to talk to her, to question her about herself as though she were his equal. What warm friendliness had prompted him to take her out of her dark basement to the library where there were books to read!

And then—that unforgettable night on the way home, when the air was poignant with spring! Only a moment—a kiss—a pressure of hands! And the world shone with light—the empty, unlived years filled with love!

She was lost in dreams of her one hour of romance when a woman elbowed her way through the dim passage, leaving behind her the smell of herring and onions.

Shenah Pessah gripped the scrubbing-brush with suppressed fury. "Meshugeneh! Did you not swear to yourself that you would tear his memory out from your heart? If he would have been only a man I could have forgotten him. But he was not a man! He was God Himself! On whatever I look shines his face!"

The white radiance again suffused her. The brush dropped from her hand. "He—he is the beating in my heart! He is the life in me—the hope in me—the breath of prayer in me! If not for him in me, then what am I? Deadness—emptiness—nothingness! You are going out of your head. You are living only on rainbows. He is no more real—

"What is real? These rags I wear? This pail? This black hole? Or him and the dreams of him?" She flung her challenge to the murky darkness.

"Shenah Pessah! A black year on you!" came the answer from the cellar below. It was the voice of her uncle, Moisheh Rifkin.

"Oi weh!" she shrugged young shoulders, wearied by joyless toil. "He's beginning with his hollering already." And she hurried down.

"You piece of earth! Worms should eat you! How long does it take you to wash up the stairs?" he stormed. "Yesterday, the eating was burned to coal; and today you forget the salt."

"What a fuss over a little less salt!"

"In the Talmud it stands a man has a right to divorce his wife for only forgetting him the salt in his soup."

"Maybe that's why Aunt Gittel went to the grave before her time—worrying how to please your taste in the mouth."

The old man's yellow, shriveled face stared up at her out of the gloom. "What has he from life? Only his pleasure in eating and going to the synagogue. How long will he live yet?" And moved by a surge of pity, "Why can't I be a little kind to him?"

"Did you chop me some herring and onions?" he interrupted harshly.

She flushed with conscious guilt. Again she wondered why ugly things and ugly smells so sickened her.

ROE HALPER. *Grief.* 1979. Pen and ink.
13 1/4 x 15 3/4 in. Collection of Mae Schainman.

"What don't you forget?" His voice hammered upon her ears. "No care lays in your head. You're only dreaming in the air."

Her compassion was swept away in a wave of revolt that left her trembling. "I can't no more stand it from you! Get yourself somebody else!" She was surprised at her sudden spirit.

"You big mouth, you! That's your thanks for saving you from hunger."

"Two years already I'm working the nails off my fingers and you didn't give me a cent."

"Beggerin! Money yet, you want? The minute you get enough to eat you turn up your head with freshness. Are you used to anything from home? What were you out there in Savel? The dirt under people's feet. You're already forgetting how you came off from the ship—a bundle of rags full of holes. If you lived in Russia a hundred years would you have lived to wear a pair of new shoes on your feet?"

"Other girls come naked and with nothing to America and they work themselves up. Everybody gets wages in America—"

"Americanerin! Didn't I spend out enough money on your ship-ticket to have a little use from you? A thunder should strike you!"

Shenah Pessah's eyes flamed. Her broken finger-nails pierced the callous flesh of her hands. So this was the end—the awakening of her dreams of America! Her memory went back to the time her ship-ticket came. In her simple faith she had really believed that they wanted her—her father's brother and his wife who had come to the new world before ever she was born. She thought they wanted to give her a chance for happiness, for life and love. And then she came—to find the paralytic aunt—housework—janitor's drudgery. Even after her aunt's death, she had gone on uncomplainingly, till her uncle's nagging had worn down her last shred of self-control.

"It's the last time you'll holler on me!" she cried. "You'll never see my face again if I got to go begging in the street." Seizing her shawl, she rushed out. "Woe is me! Bitter is me! For what is my life? Why didn't the ship go under and drown me before I came to America?"

Through the streets, like a maddened thing, she raced, not knowing where she was going, not caring. "For what should I keep on suffering? Who needs me? Who wants me? I got nobody—nobody!"

And then the vision of the face she worshiped flashed before her. His beautiful kindness that had once warmed her into new life breathed over her again. "Why did he ever come but to lift me out of my darkness into his light?"

Instinctively her eyes sought the rift of blue above the tenement roofs and were caught by a boldly printed placard: "HANDS WANTED." It was as though the sign swung open on its hinges like a door and arms stretched out inviting her to enter. From the sign she looked to her own hands—vigorous, young hands—made strong through toil.

Hope leaped within her. "Maybe I got yet luck to have it good in this world. Ach! God from the sky! I'm so burning to live—to work myself up for a somebody! And why not?" With clenched fist she smote her bosom. "Ain't everything possible in the new world? Why is America but to give me the chance to lift up my head with everybody alike?"

Her feet scarcely touched the steps as she ran up. But when she reached the huge, iron door of Cohen Brothers, a terror seized her. "Oi weh! They'll give a look on my greenhorn rags, and down I go—For what are you afraid, you fool?" she commanded herself. "You come not to beg. They need hands. Don't the sign say so? And you got good, strong hands that can turn over the earth with their strength. America is before you. You'll begin to earn money. You'll dress yourself up like a person and men will fall on their knees to make love to you—even him—himself!"

All fear had left her. She flung open the door and beheld the wonder of a factory—people—people—seas of bent heads and busy hands of people—the whir of machinery—flying belts—the clicking clatter of whirling wheels—all seemed to blend and fuse into one surging song of hope—of new life—a new world—America!

A man, his arms heaped with a bundle of shirts, paused at sight of the radiant face. Her ruddy cheeks, the film of innocence shining out of eyes that knew no guile, carried him back to the green fields and open plains of his native Russia.

"Her mother's milk is still fresh on her lips," he murmured, as his gaze enveloped her.

The bundle slipped and fell to her feet. Their eyes met in spontaneous recognition of common race. With an embarrassed laugh they stooped to gather up the shirts.

"I seen downstairs hands wanted," came in a faltering voice.

"Then you're looking for work?" he questioned with keen interest. She was so different from the others he had known in his five years in this country. He was seized with curiosity to know more.

"You ain't been long in America?" His tone was an unconscious caress.

"Two years already," she confessed. "But I ain't so green like I look," she added quickly, overcome by the old anxiety.

"Trust yourself on me," Sam Arkin assured her. "I'm a feller that knows himself on a person first off. I'll take you to the office myself. Wait only till I put away these things."

Grinning with eagerness, he returned and together they sought the foreman.

EMANUEL
134—Temple Emanu-El, the Jewish House of Worship, Helena, Montana.

COLORPLATE 91

Vintage Postcard Showing Temple Emanu-El in Helena, Montana. Collection of Peter H. Schweitzer.

TEMPLE EMANUEL, 43RD ST. & 5TH AVENUE, NEW YORK CITY.

COLORPLATE 92

Vintage Postcard Showing Temple Emanu-El in New York City at 43rd Street and Fifth Avenue Location. Collection of Peter H. Schweitzer.

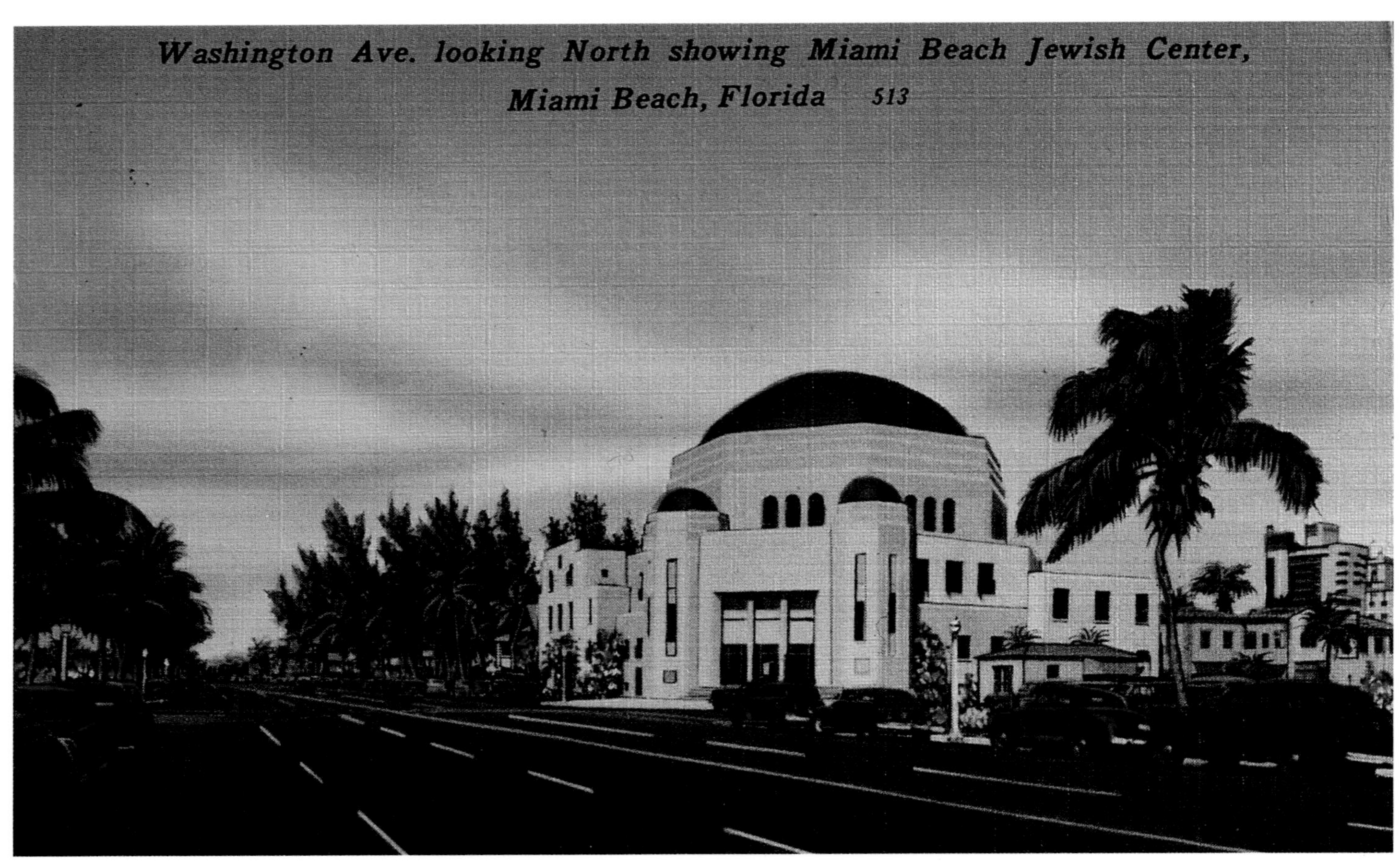

Washington Ave. looking North showing Miami Beach Jewish Center,
Miami Beach, Florida 513

COLORPLATE 93 *(top)*

Vintage Postcard Showing the Miami Beach Jewish Center, Miami, Florida. Collection of Peter H. Schweitzer.

COLORPLATE 94 *(bottom)*

Vintage Postcard (pre-1909) Showing a Synagogue in Hunter, New York (Catskill Region). Collection of Peter H. Schweitzer.

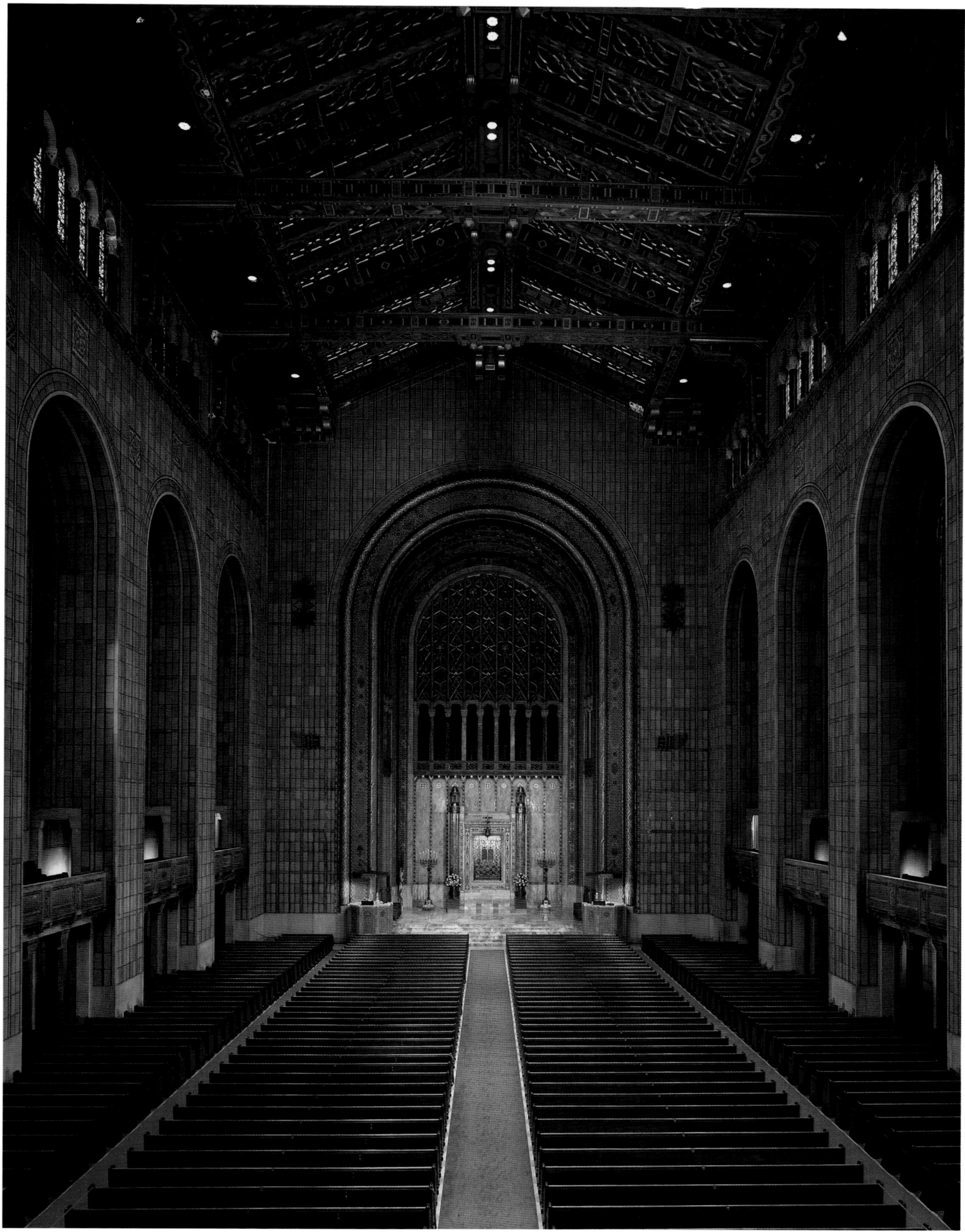

COLORPLATE 95

ROBERT D. KOHN, CHARLES BUTLER, AND CLARENCE S. STEIN, ARCHITECTS. *The Interior of the Main Sanctuary, Temple Emanu-El, New York.* 1929. Photograph courtesy of Congregation Emanu-El of the City of New York. *This photograph shows the interior of the main sanctuary, facing east towards the* bimah *with the organ loft above. The sanctuary seats 2,500 persons and is 103 feet high, 150 feet long, and 100 feet wide. The mosaics in the great arch were designed by Hildreth Meiere, New York, and executed by Ravenna Mosaics of Berlin, 1929.*

לא תרצח
לא תנאף

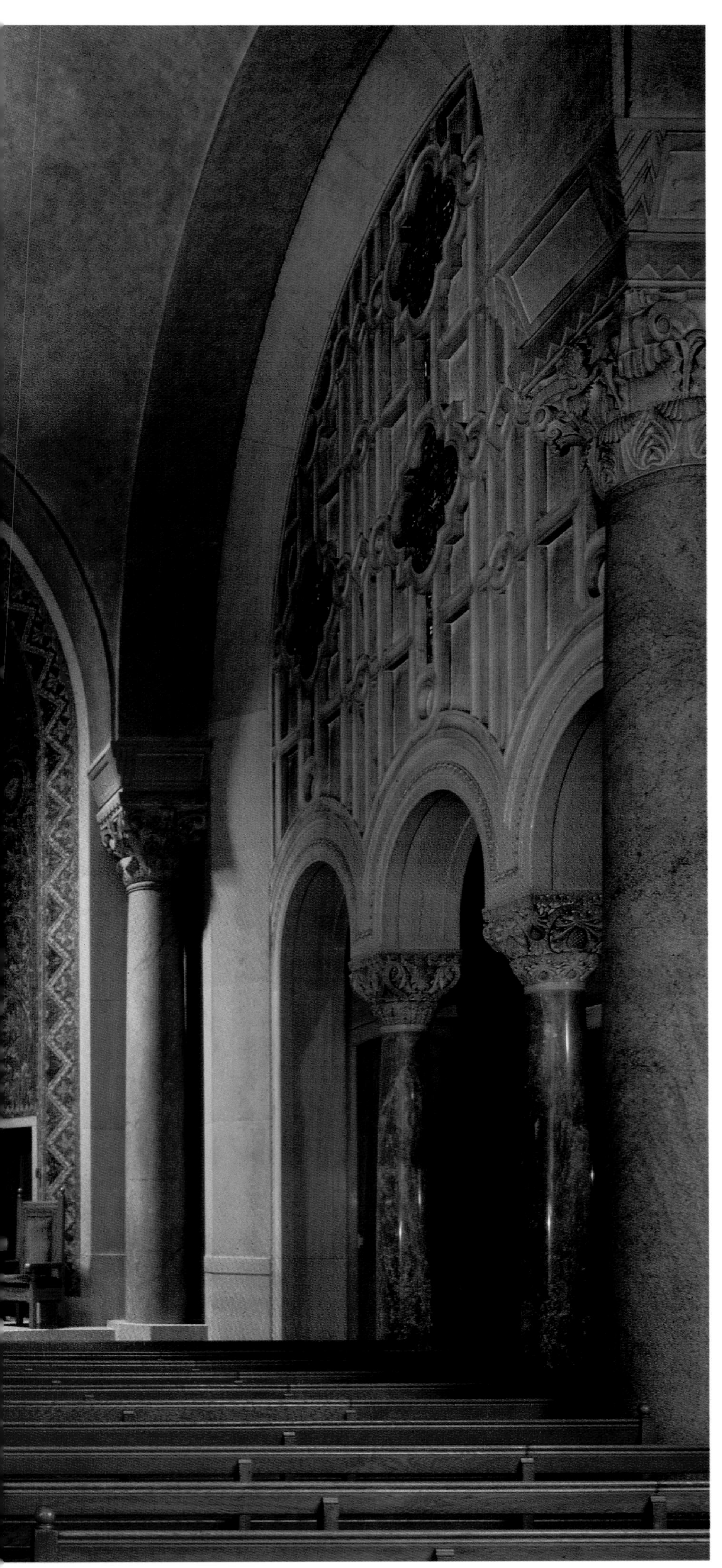

COLORPLATE 96

The Interior of the Beth-El Chapel, Temple Emanu-El, New York. 1929. *The chapel, north of the main sanctuary, is notable for the May Memorial window above the ark. Designed by Louis Comfort Tiffany in 1899, it depicts an idealized Jerusalem landscape. The window was brought from Temple Emanu-El on Fifth Avenue and 43rd Street. The ark was designed by Oscar Bach, a sculptor and metallurgist from New York. The name "Beth-El" meaning "House of God" recalls Congregation Beth-El which was consolidated with Temple Emanu-El in 1927.*

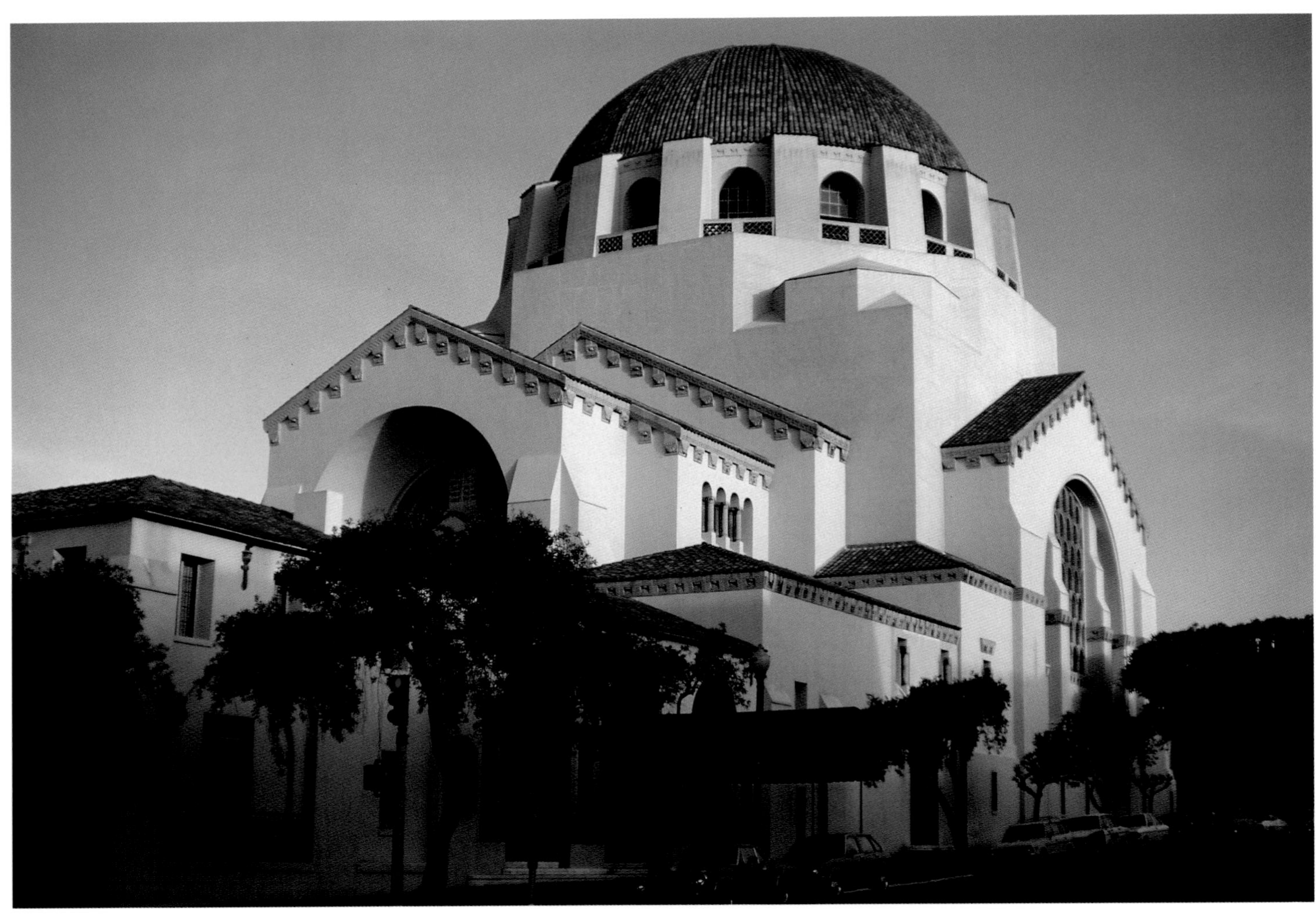

COLORPLATE 97

ARTHUR BROWN, JR., JOHN BAKEWELL, JR., AND SYLVAIN SCHNAITTACHER, ARCHITECTS. *Temple Emanu-El, San Francisco.* 1926. *The style of architecture is Levantine, representing a fusion of the architectural styles of Asia Minor, Palestine, and the Mediterranean world. The central feature of the temple is the great dome, rising 150 feet above the street level and covering the great auditorium or place of worship. It is the foremost point of interest marked by the interplay of masonry and color.*

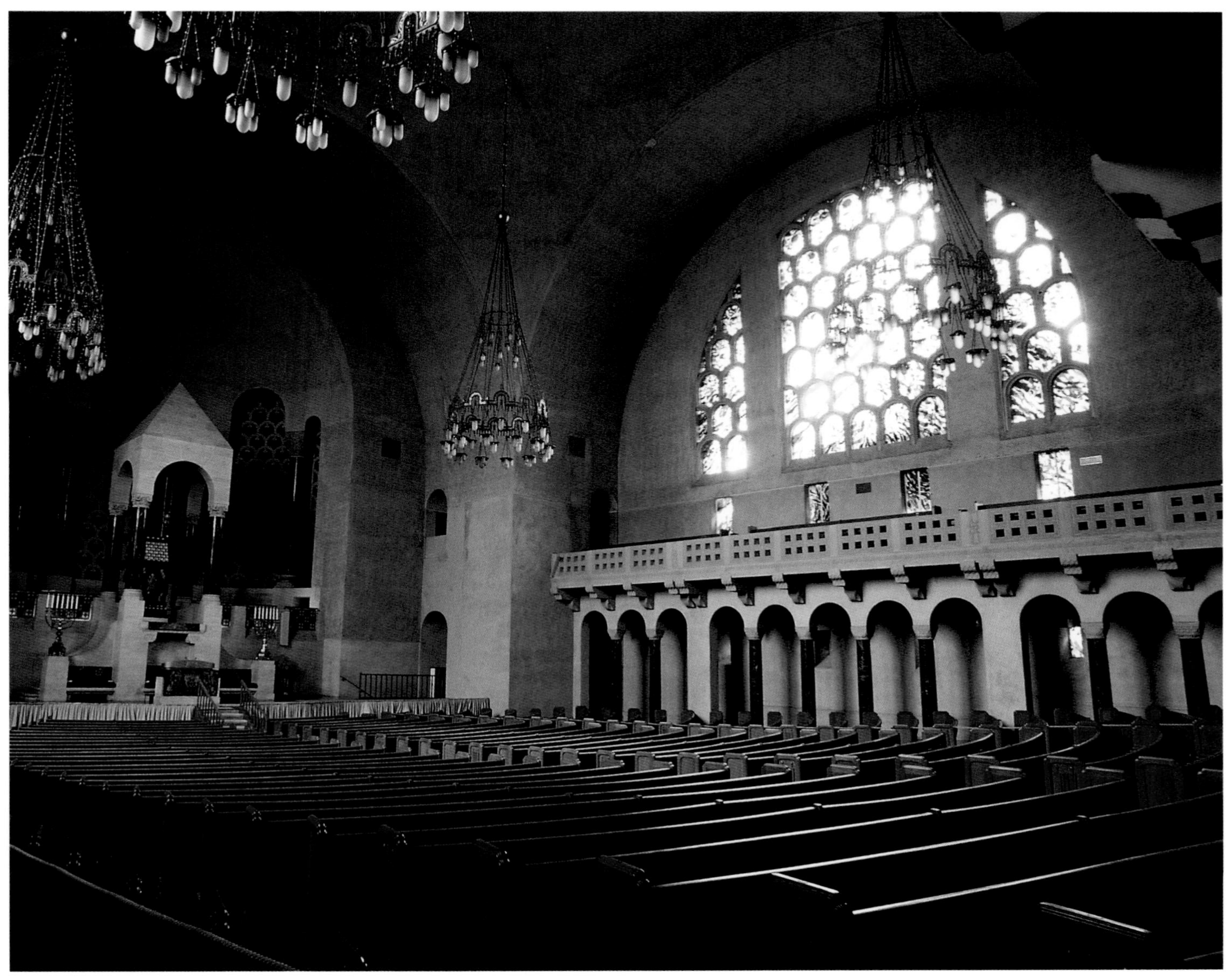

COLORPLATE 98

ARTHUR BROWN, JR., JOHN BAKEWELL, JR., AND SYLVAIN SCHNAITTACHER, ARCHITECTS. *The Interior of the Main Sanctuary, Temple Emanu-El, San Francisco.* 1926. *The great auditorium holds 1,234 seats placed on a sloping floor, enabling worshippers to see from all points. Balconies run on two sides and rear of the temple auditorium, supported by arcades of columns of varicolored marble. These lead to a central niche, richly ornamented, where a series of steps and platforms are located, pointing to the focal objective of the ark. The temple is illuminated by light filtering through the large stained glass windows and four skillfully designed bronze chandeliers suspended from the dome.*

COLORPLATE 99

WARREN PLATNER, ARCHITECT. *Sinai Temple.* Longmeadow, Massachusetts. 1975.

"Good luck to you! I hope you'll be pushed up soon to my floor," Sam Arkin encouraged, as he hurried back to his machine.

Because of the rush of work and the scarcity of help, Shenah Pessah was hired without delay. Atremble with excitement, she tiptoed after the foreman as he led the way into the workroom.

"Here, Sadie Kranz, is another learner for you." He addressed a big-bosomed girl, the most skillful worker in the place.

"Another greenhorn with a wooden head!" she whispered to her neighbor as Shenah Pessah removed her shawl. "Gevalt! All these greenhorn hands tear the bread from our mouths by begging to work so cheap."

But the dumb appeal of the immigrant stirred vague memories in Sadie Kranz. As she watched her run her first seam, she marveled at her speed. "I got to give it to you, you have a quick head." There was conscious condescension in her praise.

Shenah Pessah lifted a beaming face. "How kind it was from you to learn me! You good heart!"

No one had ever before called Sadie Kranz "good heart." The words lingered pleasantly.

"Ut! I like to help anybody, so long it don't cost me nothing. I get paid by the week anyhow," she half apologized.

Shenah Pessah was so thrilled with the novelty of the work, the excitement of mastering the intricacies of her machine, that she did not realize that the day was passed until the bell rang, the machines came to a halt, and the "hands" made a wild rush for the cloak-room.

"Oi weh! Is it a fire?" Shenah Pessah blanched with dread.

Loud laughter quelled her fears. "Greenie! It's six o'clock. Time to go home," chorused the voices.

"Home?" The cry broke from her. "Where will I go? I got no home." She stood bewildered, in the fast-dwindling crowd of workers. Each jostling by her had a place to go. Of them all, she alone was friendless, shelterless!

"Help me find a place to sleep!" she implored, seizing Sadie Kranz by the sleeve of her velvet coat. "I got no people, I ran away."

Sadie Kranz narrowed her eyes at the girl. A feeling of pity crept over her at sight of the outstretched, hungry hands.

"I'll fix you by me for the while." And taking the shawl off the shelf, she tossed it to the forlorn bundle of rags. "Come along. You must be starved for some eating."

As Shenah Pessah entered the dingy hall-room which Sadie Kranz called home, its chill and squalor carried her back to the janitor's basement she had left that morning. In silence she watched her companion prepare the hot dogs and potatoes on the oil-stove atop the trunk. Such pressing sadness weighed upon her that she turned from even the smell of food.

"My heart pulls me so to go back to my uncle." She swallowed hard her crust of black bread. "He's so used to have me help him. What'll he do—alone?"

"You got to look out for yourself in this world." Sadie Kranz gesticulated with a hot potato. "With your quickness, you got a chance to make money and buy clothes. You can go to shows—dances. And who knows—maybe meet a man to get married."

"Married? You know how it burns in every girl to get herself married—that's how it burns in me to work myself up for a person."

"Ut! For what need you to work yourself up. Better marry yourself up to a rich feller and you're fixed for life."

"But him I want—he ain't just a man. He is——" She paused seeking for words and a mist of longing softened the heavy peasant features. "He is the golden hills on the sky. I'm as far from him as the earth is from the stars."

"Yok! Why wills itself in you the stars?" her companion ridiculed between swallows.

Shenah Pessah flung out her hands with Jewish fervor. "Can I help it what's in my heart? It always longs in me for the higher. Maybe he has long ago forgotten me, but only one hope drives in me like madness—to make myself alike to him."

"I'll tell you the truth," laughed Sadie Kranz, fishing in the pot for the last frankfurter. "You are a little out of your head—plain meshugeh."

"Meshugeh?" Shenah Pessah rose to her feet vibrant with new resolve. "Meshugeh?" she challenged, her peasant youth afire with ambition. "I'll yet show the world what's in me. I'll not go back to my uncle—till it rings with my name in America."

She entered the factory, the next day, with a light in her face, a sureness in her step that made all pause in wonder. "Look only! How high she holds herself her head! Has the matchmaker promised her a man?"

Zalman Yoffeh

From "The Passing of the East Side"

"A Completely Jewish World"

At the beginning of the twentieth century, the Jewish population of New York could have been considered the fourth largest "city" in America. That is to say, only the general populations of New York, Chicago, and Philadelphia exceeded that of New York Jewry alone. The greatest portion of that population was crowded into the lower East Side. As Zalman Yoffeh wrote in the Menorah Journal, *American Jewry's leading literary journal, in 1929, the East Side was "a completely Jewish world, in residence, industry, and culture." But in that year, this article tells that the Jews had already dispersed to other areas of residence in Manhattan, Brooklyn, and the Bronx. His autobiographical reminiscences record the way of life, experiences, hopes, and aspirations of its residents with a good memory, a sharp eye, and a warm heart.*

The East Side of my boyhood was a completely Jewish world. The language of our home was Yiddish. The newspapers that came into our home were Yiddish. The store signs were all in Yiddish. The few Gentiles we dealt with spoke to us out of their smattering of Yiddish. Small wonder that after twenty years in America my mother could not speak a complete English sentence. Or that I, born in America, did not know a single English word until I was five years old!

The only holidays we observed were Jewish holidays. Our good clothing was not for Sunday but for Saturday. As Friday night approached, the pushcarts left the street, the stores began to close. Faces were washed and hair was fine-combed. Early Saturday morning found the streets deserted; everybody was in *shul*. In the afternoon the children played in the street, quiet games, not the boisterous games of the week, for one had to keep clothes clean. The restaurant across the street stayed open but served only food warmed over from the day before. The patrons came around in the evening and paid for their meals. After sundown everything would reopen.

The only Gentiles we knew were the janitor in the tenement, the barber around the corner, and the policeman on the beat. Gentiles, we understood, were a race of mental inferiors, fit only for the more menial tasks of life. All the world's wisdom was encompassed in the Jewish brain; when later I met intelligent Gentiles I was astounded. Not only astounded but also suspicious. Something was wrong; either there was some trick about their intelligence or else, very likely, they had Jewish blood in them.

Generally, we kept inside our world. When, occasionally, we left it, we did so with fear and trembling. Once on the other side of the Bowery, we were a marked race. Italian youths would swoop down on us, chase us, beat us, tear our clothing. It was rarely we went. Why take the risk when there was such a complete world right at hand? Let the Italians be physically superior. We readily granted it. We knew that in days to come we would be doctors and lawyers and professors, and they would come around to black our boots and clean our offices.

My father was a pushcart peddler. In the old country, educated beyond the comprehension of the village he lived in, he had found intellectual companionship only with the village priest. He knew Hebrew and the Torah, but could not even become a *melamed.* The Jews refused to trust their children to an *apikoros* who hobnobbed with priests and polished his boots on the Sabbath. So he came to the country of wider opportunity.

He drifted into the clothing shops. There he was very unhappy. Educated for higher things, when a beetle-browed foreman let out on him a string of abuse, my father would just walk out of the shop. This happened several times. Finally he hired a pushcart and became a fruit peddler. This he remained till the end of his life.

Hester Street, New York. c. 1900. Seaver Center for Western History Research. Natural History Museum of Los Angeles County.

The Library of the Pike Street Synagogue. Photograph © Bill Aron. *Synagogues, especially those of the East European Jewish immigrant community, were places for adult Torah study.*

I remember him as slightly above middle height. His hair and beard were black and curly. Most of his face was a deep brick red from exposure to the elements, except that part of his forehead which the hat covered. This was a startingly pure white. His cheeks were sunken and he had high cheek bones. His hands were long and thin and the wrists were very delicate, almost a woman's wrists. Later I was to see his physical counterparts in the Bedouins of Palestine. But I knew nothing of Bedouins then. To me he looked like one of the red men described in my history books. A red man with a black beard. The thought used to tickle me.

We children rarely saw him during the week. He would rise at five in the morning and come home after ten in the evening. Occasionally he sold out his complete stock early in the evening. Then we would have a treat. A pocketful of pennies would cascade onto the table and we would have the pleasure of counting them, and of putting them in stacks of ten. My father would compute the amount and deduct the money he had left with in the morning. There was rarely more than a dollar profit left for the day's work. Occasionally there was less.

His was a terribly lonely life. My mother, a wonderful woman in her way, was no mate for him, never understood him. He was her husband and as such warranted her loyalty and support, but, oh, dear God, why could he not be like other husbands and make a decent living? He had none but business relations with other peddlers, and never exchanged a word with a neighbor. He had a few friends in the synagogue he attended, but even they were not close friends. He was the *Bal Keriyoh*, the reader of the Torah, and they all conceded his piety and learning, but "how could one warm up to an iceberg?" They would have been shocked to learn that he wore no *arba kanfos*, that he did not wind phylacteries, and that he never said his prayers except Saturdays and holidays in the synagogue. A member of the Socialist Labor Party and an ardent revolutionist, he went to the synagogue because that was the one place he knew where men put workaday thoughts out of their minds and worshiped things of the spirit.

Poor man! Undeviating and strict, a despiser of sham and compromise, he saw early that his children were weak, diplomatic, inclined to take the easier way always. He had hoped to see them attain the intellectual heights denied him; when I was graduated from the elementary school with the highest honors he kissed me and cried, the only display of emotion I ever saw in him. Yet he was doomed to see his children, one by one, taken out of school to help supply the needs of the family. Everywhere frustration faced him and overwhelmed him. Even in such an insignificant matter as clothing. He was passionately fond of dressing well. His weekday clothes were always neat. But his Sabbath suit, though old and thread-bare, was scrupulously clean. More than an hour was consumed every Saturday morning in brushing, washing, shining and combing. The one thing he wanted more than anything else was a new suit of clothes. But it could never be managed. He always had to buy old clothes. In the early part of 1919 he finally bought himself a new suit of clothes. Two weeks later he suffered a stroke of paralysis. A week after that he died.

If I say that my mother was a Slavic type, I do not mean she was at all the high cheekboned, sharp-nosed, splay-mouthed type that we usually think of as Slavic. I refer merely to her coloring which was pink and white; to her hair which was blond and had been flaxen; to the sturdy build of her body. I speak of the mother of my youth. She is getting old now. But old men of her town, when they seek a superlative, still say, "as pretty as Chaye Itte was in her youth."

What a glorious match was that between my father and mother. She came from a family of shopkeepers who owned just about everything in Yablonyi. So when her grandfather went to Byalistok and got my father, scion of a long line of rabbis and "learners," the entire district celebrated. Such learning and piety mated to such beauty and wealth. A perfect combination.

But alas, the wealth did not last. Much of it, invested in illegal dealings, was confiscated by the Czar's officers. When it came to making a living, my father was helpless. There was nothing he could do. And when, even in America, the "golden land," he could not earn enough to support a family decently, my mother suffered severely. How could she be expected to realize that it was just because he did no work and could do no work, that my father had been considered such a good match originally? She simply knew that children were coming one after the other, and that it was hard to raise them. Her brothers, when she first came to America, suggested a divorce. But this, too, was beyond her comprehension. Her husband, no matter what happened, was her husband, and to him and her children she must devote her life.

So with our one dollar a day she fed and clothed an ever-growing family. She took in boarders. Sometimes this helped; at other times it added to the burden of living. Boarders were often out of work and penniless; how could one turn a hungry man out? She made all our clothes. She walked blocks to reach a place where meat was a penny cheaper, where bread was a half-cent less. She collected boxes and old wood to burn in the stove instead of costly coal. Her hands became hardened and the lines so begrimed that for years she never had perfectly clean hands. One by one she lost her teeth—there was no money for dentists—and her cheeks caved in. Yet we children always had clean and whole clothing. There was always bread and butter in the house, and, wonder of wonders, there was usually a penny apiece for us to buy candy with. On a dollar and a quarter we would have lived in luxury.

Charles Angoff

From "Memories of Boston"

The *Shul* Shopper

Editor and novelist Charles Angoff set down his "Memories of Boston" for publication in the Menorah Journal *in 1962. Especially moving are his words about the Boston synagogues. It is one of the very few positive descriptions of the role of religion and its institutions—synagogues, schools, rabbis, cantors—in the life of the immigrant Jew in America.*

A word about the Boston synagogues. I knew them all, I loved them all, for from my earliest days I was a *shul* shopper. I loved the variations in the cantorial chants and cantillation, the divergencies in the little and big things that go on in a synagogue. The Boston synagogues were not merely houses of worship, they were also houses of study. The Beth Hamidrash in every synagogue was its main concern, in accordance with the ancient Jewish tradition that if there is a choice between building a chapel and a Talmud Torah, the chapel can wait. I went to many of the study conventicles when I was a boy in Boston. Those that remain in my mind down the years are the North End Shul, the North Russell Street Shul, and the Phillips Street or Vilner Shul. The North Russell Street Shul is still in existence, but its neighborhood is now far different from what it used to be. The Jewish population is tiny, and the great name of the synagogue is now somewhat diminished.

In its days of glory it was one of the great synagogues of America. To me it has special significance on various counts. First of all, its vice-president was a great-uncle of mine, the son of my grandmother. He was the nabob in our family. He ran a soda and candy store on Leverett Street and did handsomely. It was he who first introduced my father and mother to the Yiddish stage in Boston, and it was he who first took them to the band concert in the Boston Common, something that stamped America as truly a "golden land" in my parents' eyes. "Music, and such wonderful music, for nothing, for everybody to hear! What more could a government do? And Jews are allowed just like any other people in America! A blessing on this land!" This great-uncle of mine offered to get my parents into his synagogue on the High Holy Days at a reduced rate, but my father refused. He preferred to go to his little Vilner Shul.

But my father did accept my great-uncle's invitation to come to the North Russell Street Shul to hear great cantors. When the word went around that one was coming, the synagogue naturally filled up quickly, and that's when my great-uncle came in handy. He took my father and me into the synagogue with him, and father and I had, so to speak, orchestra seats. It was there that I got the full meaning of what it meant to get *dem emessen nigun* ("the true melody") into a prayer. Never will I forget Sirota singing "Lecho Dodi" (Come, My Beloved) on Friday night, and Quartin singing "Ovinu Malchaynu" (Our Father, Our King), and Rosenblatt singing "Adon Olam" (Lord of the Universe). I once heard Sirota chant the *Kiddush* on Friday night with such profound sincerity that I felt shivers of delight pass up and down my spine. I was only a boy, under thirteen, but intuitively I grasped what was being done by these great cantors. I grasped, for all time what Jewish prayer meant, and in a vague way I understood why the Jews have lasted all these years and will last to the end of time.

WILLIAM ALLEN ROGERS. *Boston Jewish Quarters at the Turn of the Century.* 1900. Drawing. UPI/ Bettmann Archives.

Rooftop Class, Jewish Training School, Chicago. c. 1910. The Chicago Jewish Archives, Spertus Institute.

There was something else I learned in the North Russell Street Shul. On Saturdays, before I was Bar Mitzvah, I was, so to speak, my Alte Bobbe's *Shabbes goy* (Sabbath gentile). I would go with her to the North Russell Street Shul, carrying her prayer-book, and she would wind her handkerchief around her hand on her wrist. That relieved her from any possible charge of carrying something on the Sabbath, and hence performing manual labor. Now and then I would look upstairs at her, where she sat with the other women, and I saw on her face a joy and a delight such as I have never seen since. She looked at her son, the vice-president of the synagogue, and she was happy, as only a woman of ninety can be happy. Her son was a *gabbai* (important functionary) in a synagogue. What greater joy was there for a mother?

But it was in the Vilner Shul, I think, that I was most deeply imbued with the heart and soul of Jewishness. It was a *kabtzonishe shul* (poor man's synagogue), where people of my father's modest circumstances belonged. Since there was no reason here why one Jew should look down upon another, the morale of the synagogue was good. And this equality did something for the young boys as well. The parents couldn't afford a Sabbath Bar Mitzvah and our own Bar Mitzvahs were on Mondays or Thursdays, when the Torah is read at morning services.

I was Bar Mitzvah on Thursday. My father woke me up at 6:30 in the morning, and took me to *shul.* There were about thirty people at the service. I was called to the Torah for the first time—and that was Bar Mitzvah. Some of the other congregants came over to me and wished me *mazol tov.* My father bashfully put his arm around me and also congratulated me. Then he and I walked a bit and he went off to work. I turned toward home feeling terribly lonely. I had become a full, mature Jew—and most of Boston was asleep, and didn't care. The few people who passed me on the street didn't care either. When I reached our house, as soon as I put my hand on the door knob my mother opened the door and threw her arms around me and kissed me and hugged me and kissed me again. Her arm around me, she took me to the kitchen, which was also our dining room, of course, and there on the table was the *Shabbes* tablecloth. To my mother it was *Yom Tov* (holiday). She had the usual *boolkes* (hot rolls) on a platter, of course, but there was also a platter of the kind of cinnamon cakes I liked, and there was a smaller platter of ginger jam, another favorite of mine. There also was a cup of cocoa. "Eat, Shayel, eat," said my mother. I suggested she have some cocoa too. "No, I'm not hungry." I ate. I was conscious that she was looking at me with great appreciation of what had happened to me. Her oldest son was now a full man in Israel. I was embarrassed, but I was also delighted. I finished my cocoa, and mother said, "Have another cup." The last time she had suggested I have another cup of cocoa was when I was convalescing from a cold that had almost turned into pneumonia. I had another cup. When I was finished with my special breakfast mother said, "Father had to go to work. He had to. You understand."

"Sure," I said.

"But we'll have a small reception on Saturday night, after *mincha* (afternoon prayer). We've invited the relatives and some friends. So we'll have a little reception."

"Oh," I said, too moved to say anything else.

She got up, came to me, patted my head, and then kissed me slowly. "Maybe you're a little sleepy, Shayel. Maybe you want to sleep a little more. I'll wake you up in time for your school."

"Yes, I think I'll have a little more sleep," I said.

I didn't want any more sleep. I lay down on the bed. I was profoundly happy. Everything was good. Everything was very good.

Leo Rosten

From *The Return of H*Y*M*A*N K*A*P*L*A*N*

"Christopher K*a*p*l*a*n"

*Born in Poland, raised in Chicago, Leo Rosten studied at that city's university and at the London School of Economics. He is best known, however, for his stories, satires, and essays of social commentary. The H*Y*M*A*N K*A*P*L*A*N stories, set in a night school where immigrants study English and civics in preparation for their citizenship exams, describe important and worthy components of the immigrant experience. The wonderfully humorous vignettes introduce the reader to melting pot America, to the often bewildering experience of Americanization, and as this story originally published in* The New Yorker *in 1938 indicates, to the immigrants' amazement at and love for their adopted country.*

To Mr. Parkhill the beginners' grade was more than a congregation of students yearning to master English. He took a larger view of his responsibilities: to Mr. Parkhill the American Night Preparatory School for Adults was an incubator of Citizens. To imbue the men and women of a dozen nations with the meaning of America—its past, its traditions, its aspirations—this, to Mr. Parkhill, was the greater work to which he had dedicated himself.

So it was that on the eve of any national holiday, Mr. Parkhill devoted at least half

English Language Class. 1936. AP/Wide World Photos. *Ms. Edith Schnurmacher, 25, instructor of an adult education class in English for the foreign-born, instructs her mother, 54, a student in her class. This was one of the free classes of the Adult Education Project open without charge for adults over 17 at the Educational Alliance, 197 East Broadway, New York.*

an hour to a little excursion into our history. In the spring, it was Decoration Day that enlisted his eloquence. In the fall it was Armistice Day and Thanksgiving. (He always regretted the fact that the Fourth, grandest holiday of them all, fell in a month when the school was not in session.) And this Monday night in October, on the eve of Columbus Day, Mr. Parkhill opened the class with these ringing words: "Tonight, let us set aside our routine tasks for a while to consider the man whose—er—historical achievement the world will commemorate tomorrow."

Expectancy murmured its sibilant path across the room.

"To this man," Mr. Parkhill continued, "the United States—America—owes its very beginning. I'm sure you all know whom I mean, for he—"

"Jawdge Vashington!" Miss Fanny Gidwitz promptly guessed.

"No, no. Not *George* Washington—watch that 'w,' Miss Gidwitz. I refer to———"

"Paul Rewere!" cried Oscar Trabish impetuously.

Mr. Parkhill adjusted his spectacles. Mr. Trabish had formed some peculiar psychic union with "Paul Rewere": he had already written two rhapsodic compositions and made one fiery speech on his beloved alter ego. (The compositions had been called "Paul Revere's House Makes History" and "Paul Revere. One by Land, Two by the Beach." The speech had been announced by Mr. Trabish as "Paul Rewere! Vhy He Vasn't Prazidant?" He had been quite indignant about it.)

Mr. Parkhill shook his head. "Not Paul *'Rewere.'* It's a 'v,' Mr. Trabish, not a 'w.' You spell it correctly when you write but you seem to replace the 'v's with 'w's—and the 'w's with 'v's—when you speak. Class, let's not guess. What *date* is tomorrow?"

"Mine boitday!" an excited voice sang out.

Mr. Parkhill ignored that. "Tomorrow," he said firmly, "is October twelfth. And on October twelfth, 1492—" He got no further.

"Dat's mine *boit*day! October tvalf! I should live so! Honist!" It was (but why, oh why, did it have to be?) the proud, enraptured voice of Hyman Kaplan.

Mr. Parkhill took a deep breath, a slow, deep breath, and said cautiously, "Mr. Kaplan, is October twelfth—er—really your birthday?"

Mr. Kaplan's eyes widened—innocent, hurt. "*Mister* Pockheel!"

Mr. Parkhill felt ashamed of himself.

Stanislaus Wilkomirski growled, "Kaplan too old for have birtday."

"October tvalf I'm born; October tvalf I'm tsalebratink!" Mr. Kaplan retorted. "All mine *life* I'm hevink boitdays October tvalf. No axceptions!"

Mr. Parkhill said, "Well, well, well. That *is* a coincidence. October twelfth. Hmmm." He cleared his throat uneasily. "I'm sure we all wish Mr. Kaplan many happy returns."

Mr. Kaplan beamed, rose, bowed, beamed, and sat down, beaming.

"Phooey," muttered Mr. Plonsky under his breath.

Miss Mitnick, feeling the occasion called for good will and peace among men, stammered "Congratulation."

"Denks," said Mr. Kaplan, all *savoir faire.*

"However," Mr. Parkhill raised his voice, "the particular historical event we are commemorating tomorrow pertains to—Christopher Columbus. For it was on October twelfth, 1492—"

Hester Street, Seen from Clinton Street. c. 1890. The Museum of the City of New York.

"Co*lom*biss!" Mr. Kaplan's rapture passed beyond containment. "Christover Co*lom*biss?!"

Excitement seized the beginners' grade.

"Columbus!"

"Columbia Day," breathed Olga Tarnova. "Romahnteek."

"Colombos discovert America!"

"Oy!" That was Mrs. Moskowitz. No one could groan a "What?" or moan a "Why?" with one-tenth the eloquence Sadie Moskowitz put into her "Oy!" She was the Niobe of the beginners' grade.

"Yes, class, on October twelfth, 1492—"

Mr. Trabish dropped a sneer in the general direction of Fanny Gidwitz. "And you said Jawdge Vashington!"

"*You* said Paul Rewere!"

"On October twelfth, 1492—" Mr. Parkhill persevered.

"By me could avery day in year be somthing about Paul Rewere!" proclaimed Oscar Trabish.

"And by *me* is our foist Prazident vert ten hoss-riders!" scowled Fanny Gidwitz.

Miss Goldberg reached for a nougat.

"On October twelfth, 1492—" Mr. Parkhill's voice rose until it brooked no ignoring—"Christopher Columbus discovered a new continent."

The class simmered down at last, and Mr. Parkhill launched upon the deathless saga of Christopher Columbus and the brave little armada that sailed into the unknown. He spoke slowly, impressively, almost with fervor. (It was not often he was afforded material of such majesty and such momentousness.) And the thirty-odd novitiates of the beginners' grade, caught up in the drama of that great and fearful voyage, hung upon each word. "The food ran low. Water was scarce. Rumors of doom—of disaster—raced through the sailors' ranks . . ."

Goldie Pomeranz leaned forward and sighed moistly into Mr. Kaplan's ear. "You soitinly locky, Mr. Kaplan. Born same day Columbus did."

Mr. Kaplan was in a world of dreams. He kept whispering to himself, "Christover Colombiss," the name a talisman. "My!" He closed his eyes to be alone with his hero. "October tvalf I'm arrivink in de voild, an' October tvalf Colombiss picks ot for discoverink US! Dastiny!"

"Mutiny faced Christopher Columbus," said Mr. Parkhill with feeling.

"My boitday is Motch toity," Miss Pomeranz confided to Mr. Kaplan in a sadness fraught with envy. (Miss Pomeranz was a fitter in a shop that specialized in "bridal gons.") "Not even a *soborb* vas discovered Motch toity."

Mr. Kaplan gave Miss Pomeranz a glance both modest and consoling. "Ufcawss, Colombiss discovert lonk bifore Keplen arrived."

"October twalf is October twalf." cried Mr. Pinsky, his equerry.

Mr. Kaplan allowed the mantle of history to fall upon his shoulders.

Mr. Parkhill, upon whom the Pomeranz-Kaplan-Pinsky symposium was not lost, described the geographical outposts of 1492, the innocent belief that the world was flat as a plate, the mockery to which Columbus had been subjected. He traced the ironic confluence of events through which the new continent had been named after Amerigo Vespucci.

"By *mistake*?" Mr. Kaplan asked incredulously, and at once replied "By mistake!" in indignation.

Mr. Parkhill recounted the course of that immortal voyage, three tiny ships on an ocean infested, in men's minds, by demons of the deep. He sketched the iron resolve of the captain who would not turn back. When he said, "And then a voice from the

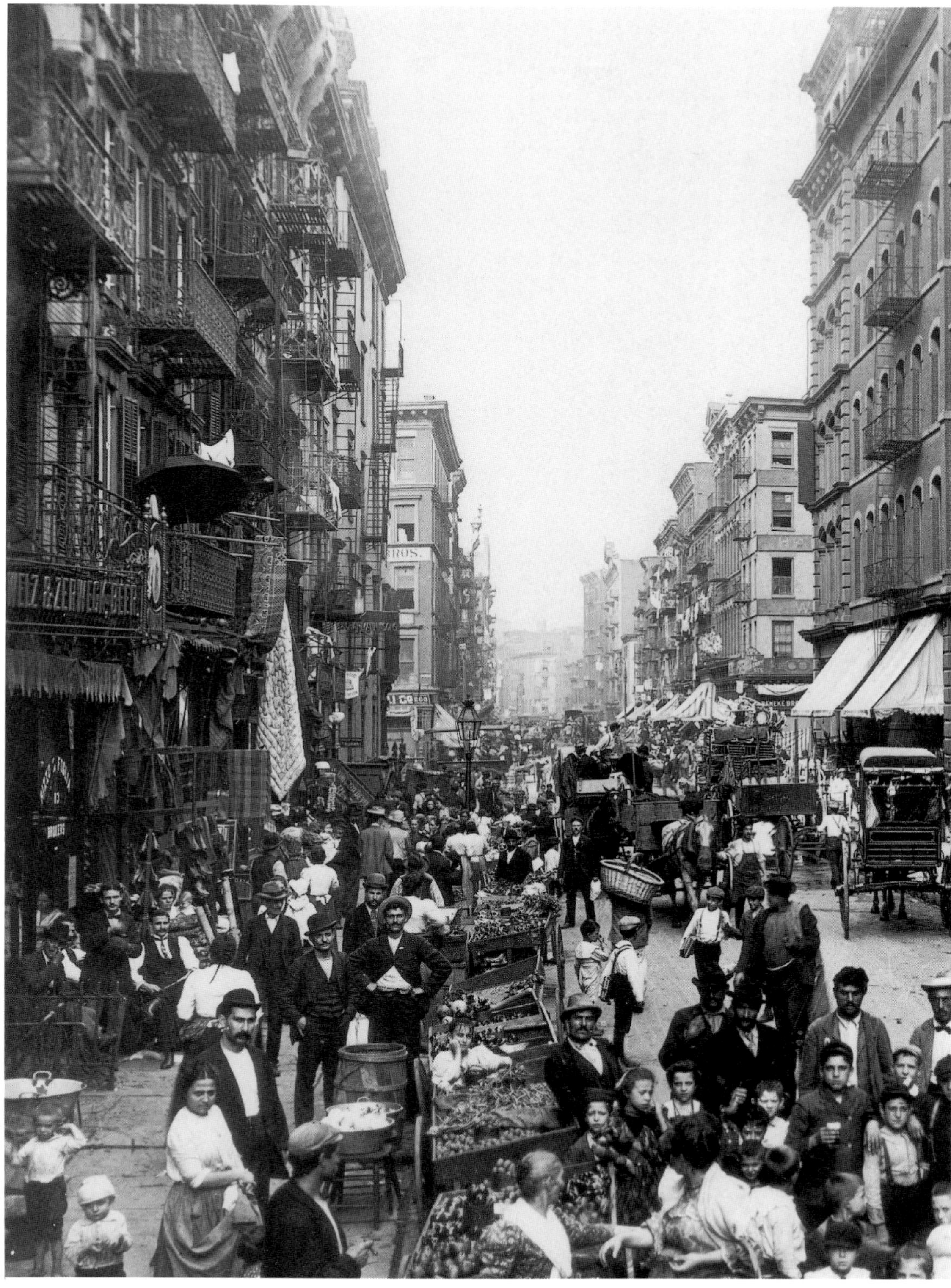

Street Scene, Lower East Side Market. The Library of Congress.

crow's-nest cried 'Land! Land!' " a tear crept into Miss Mitnick's eye. When he described the landing on new soil, Miss Tarnova suppressed a sob. And when he said, "And because Columbus thought he was really in India, he called the natives Indians," the amazement of his flock burst its bonds.

"Vun mistake on top de odder!" cried Mr. Kaplan.

"Dey called Hindyans by *mistake*?" moaned Mrs. Moskowitz. Mrs. Moskowitz could not believe that of history.

"Yes, Mrs. Moskowitz, by mistake," said Mr. Parkhill.

Mr. Kaplan shook his head three times. "Dose poor Indians."

Mrs. Tomasic fingered her crucifix.

Mr. Parkhill hurried on to the role of Ferdinand and Isabella. Just before he completed the absorbing tale, Mr. Kaplan announced, "Ectual, ve ain't Amaricans!"

Street Scene, Lower East Side. The Library of Congress.

Mr. Parkhill paused, "'Actual*ly*,' we '*are*n't' Americans, Mr. Kaplan. There is no such word as—"

"Ectual, ve all Colombians!" Mr. Kaplan exclaimed. A demand for justice—however long overdue—burned in his eyes.

Mr. Parkhill turned the class over to Miss Mitnick for General Discussion. General Discussion, Mr. Parkhill had found, was a most fruitful exercise, particularly when he invited one of the more competent students to lead it. General Discussion was even more productive than Recitation and Speech: it roused fewer anxieties in the breasts of the timid; it spread the burdens of participation.

Miss Mitnick struck the keynote for the evening with a touching, if embarrassed, eulogy of explorers in general and Columbus in particular. She ended her tribute with a deft comparison of Columbus and Admiral Byrd. "Both men fond new places for humanity. Natchelly, in different places."

"Edmiral Boyd?" Mr. Kaplan promptly sniffed in disdain. It was clear that henceforth anyone drawing comparisons between Christopher Columbus and lesser spirits would have to answer to Hyman Kaplan. "Vat kine finder new tings vas dis Edmiral Boyd?"

"It's '*Ad*miral *By*rd,'" Mr. Parkhill suggested from the seat he had taken in the back of the room.

"Admiral Byrd was a kind *modern* Columbus," Miss Mitnick said nervously.

"Vat he discovert could compare mit Columbiss's vunderful didd?" Mr. Kaplan demanded.

"Admiral Byrd discovered Sout Pole!"

"Som discoverink!" said Mr. Kaplan, dismissing all of Antarctica.

"Stop!" roared Mr. Plonsky, his glare thrice magnified by his lenses. "South Pole is important as North, maybe more."

"Ha!" parried Mr. Kaplan. "Averybody *knew* vas a Sot Pole, no? All Edmiral Boyd did vas go dere!"

Miss Mitnick turned white. Mr. Plonsky was so infuriated that he turned his back on Mr. Kaplan and, facing the rear wall, appealed to the gods: "Crazy! Cuckoo! How can you argue with a Mr. Opside Don?"

"Admiral Byrd is big *hero,*" Miss Mitnick faltered, wetting her lips. "He went through terrible things for humanity—cold, icebergs, alone, freezings."

"Edmiral Boyd *vent mit all modinn conweniences*!" ruled Hyman Kaplan.

Miss Mitnick made a strangling sound and shot an S O S to Mr. Parkhill.

"Er—it's '*Ad*miral *By*rd,'" Mr. Parkhill repeated. Nobody paid any attention to him. For Miss Caravello, a never-dormant volcano, had erupted: "Is only da one Columbus. No more lak—before, behinda!" To Miss Caravello, beyond any peradventure of doubt, Columbus would forever be enshrined as a peculiarly Italian phenomenon, unparalleled, incomparable. Admiral Byrd, she said flatly, was a "copying cat." For great Columbus, Miss Caravello concluded hotly, nothing short of a thousand Bravos would do. She proceeded to give three of them: "Bravo! Bravo! Bravo!"

"The Messrs. Kaplan and Pinsky broke into applause.

"Class—"

Now Mr. Gus Matsoukas demanded the floor, and took it before Miss Mitnick could recognize him. "Colomb' good man, no doubts about," he began magnanimously. Columbus was, indeed, worth all that Mr. Kaplan and Miss Caravello had claimed for him. But after all, Mr. Matsoukas insinuated, how could any but the uncultivated regard Columbus as more than a dull descendant of the first and *greatest* explorer—Ulysses? (Ulysses, it turned out, was born no more than seventeen kilometers from Mr. Matsoukas' birthplace.)

"Boit*days* are more important den boit places!" Mr. Kaplan proclaimed.

Mr. Matsoukas, startled, could think of no rejoinder to this powerful and unexpected postulate. He retired, mumbling.

"Anybody else wants to say few words?" asked Miss Mitnick anxiously.

Mr. Kaplan thrust his hand into the air.

"Floor is ebsolutely *open,*" Miss Mitnick announced, keeping her eyes where Mr. Kaplan could not meet them. "*Any*body can talk."

Mr. Kaplan promptly rose, said "Foidinand an' Isabel. Ha!" and sat down.

Uneasy murmurs raced across the room. Miss Mitnick flushed and twisted her handkerchief around her fingers. "Mr. Kaplan," she stammered, "I didn't catch."

Mr. Kaplan got up again, repeated "Foidinand an' Isabel. Ha!" and again sat down.

"Why he is anger?" whispered Mrs. Tomasic.

"He is mod, mod," groaned Olga Tarnova.

"Er—Mr. Kaplan," Mr. Parkhill began, "I do think—"

"Axplain!" Mr. Blattberg sang out. "Describe!" (It was through such clarity and persistence that Aaron Blattberg had become one of the best shoe salesmen on Second Avenue.)

Mr. Kaplan snorted, but said nothing.

"Keplan wants to talk or Keplan *not* wants to talk?" Mr. Plonsky inquired of the rear wall bitterly.

"Y-yes, Mr. Kaplan," Mr. Parkhill frowned, "I do think the class is entitled to some explanation of your—er—comment."

"All of a sodden Mr. Keplen makes fun Foidinand Isabel!" protested Mrs. Moskowitz. "Not even saying 'Axcuse' can he make 'Ha, ha!' on kinks and quinns?!"

This frontal attack stirred the royalists into action.

"Talk, Kaplan?"

"You got the floor, no?"

"Tell awreddy!"

A more formal dialectician cried, "Give your meanink dose remocks!" That was Mrs. Yanoff, an epistemologist dressed, as always, in black.

Mr. Kaplan rose once more and turned to face his challengers. "Ladies an' gantlemen, Mr. Pockheel—an' chairlady." Miss Mitnick lowered her eyes. "Ve all agreeink Colombiss's joiney vas vun de most movellous tings aver heppened in de voild." Cries, calls, grunts of affirmation. *"T'ink* abot det treep, jost *t'ink*. Viks an' viks Colombiss vas sailink—tru storm, lighteninks, tonder. Tru vafes high like Ampire State Buildink. Fodder an' fodder Colombiss vent—alone!" Mr. Kaplan paused to let the awesome data of that ordeal sink home. "Vell, mine frands, in *vat kine boats* Colombiss made det vunderful voyitch?" Mr. Kaplan's eyes narrowed. "In fency sheeps? In fine accommodations? No! In leetle, teentsy chizz boxes! Boats full likks! Boats full doit, joims, vater commink in! *Som* boats for discoverink Amarica! An' det's vy I'm sayink, *'Shame* on you, Foidinand! *Shame* on you, Isabel!'" Mr. Kaplan's eyes flashed. "Couldn't dey give a man like Colombiss batter transportation?"

Outrage exploded in the classroom.

"Viva Columbus!" cried Mrs. Rodriguez, upon whom it had just dawned that Columbus owed much to Iberia.

"Crazy talk," muttered Mr. Matsoukas, thinking of the raft of Ulysses.

"Maybe in 1492 they should manufacture already a SS *Qvinn Lizabeth?"* Mr. Plonsky asked the rear wall sarcastically.

A storm of retorts, defenses, taunts, disclaimers filled the air. Miss Mitnick, staggering under the responsibilities of arbitration, kept pleading, "Mr. Kaplan, please, Mr. Kaplan." Her cheeks kept changing from the flushed to the ashen. "Mr. Kaplan, *please*. The ships Ferdinand and Isabella gave—they were fine for that *time."*

"For de *time*? But not for de *man*!" thundered Hyman Kaplan.

"But in those days—"

"A man like Colombiss should have averyting fromm de bast!"

"Oh migott!" roared Mr. Plonsky.

"Kaplan, give an inch," pleaded Bessie Shimmelfarb.

Miss Tarnova moaned, "Mr. Koplan is no gantlemon."

Mr. Parkhill got up. It seemed to be the only thing to do. "Well, class, I think—"

"Colombiss desoived more den a *Senta Maria*, a *Nina*, an' a *Pintele*!" Mr. Kaplan plunged on in his passion, hacking left and right without mercy in the service of his historical partner. "Ven a man stotts ot to discover Amarica—"

"Columbus didn't go to discover a spacific *place*," Miss Mitnick protested.

"Vat did he go for—axercise?" demanded Hyman Kaplan.

"I mean Columbus didn't *know* was America," she said in desperation. "He didn't know was a continent in middle Atlentic Ocean. Columbus just went *out*. . ."

Mr. Kaplan bestowed upon Miss Mitnick a look of pity laced with scorn. "He 'jost vent ot'? V*y* he vent ot?"

"To—to discover," Miss Mitnick said tearfully.

"Vat to discover?"

Miss Mitnick bit her lip. "Just—to *discover*."

Mr. Kaplan surveyed the ranks of his colleagues, nodding. "Colombiss vent 'jost to discover,' he repeated softly. "'*Jost* to discover.' " He glanced toward heaven, mourning man's naiveté. Then, his face a cloud, he struck. "Som pipple t'ink dat if a man goes ot to mail a latter he only *hopes* maybe he'll find a mailbox!"

"Stop!" howled Mr. Plonsky, smiting his forehead.

And now the battle raged once more—with shouts and cries and accusations; with righteous assaults on the Kaplan logic, and impassioned defenses of the Mitnick

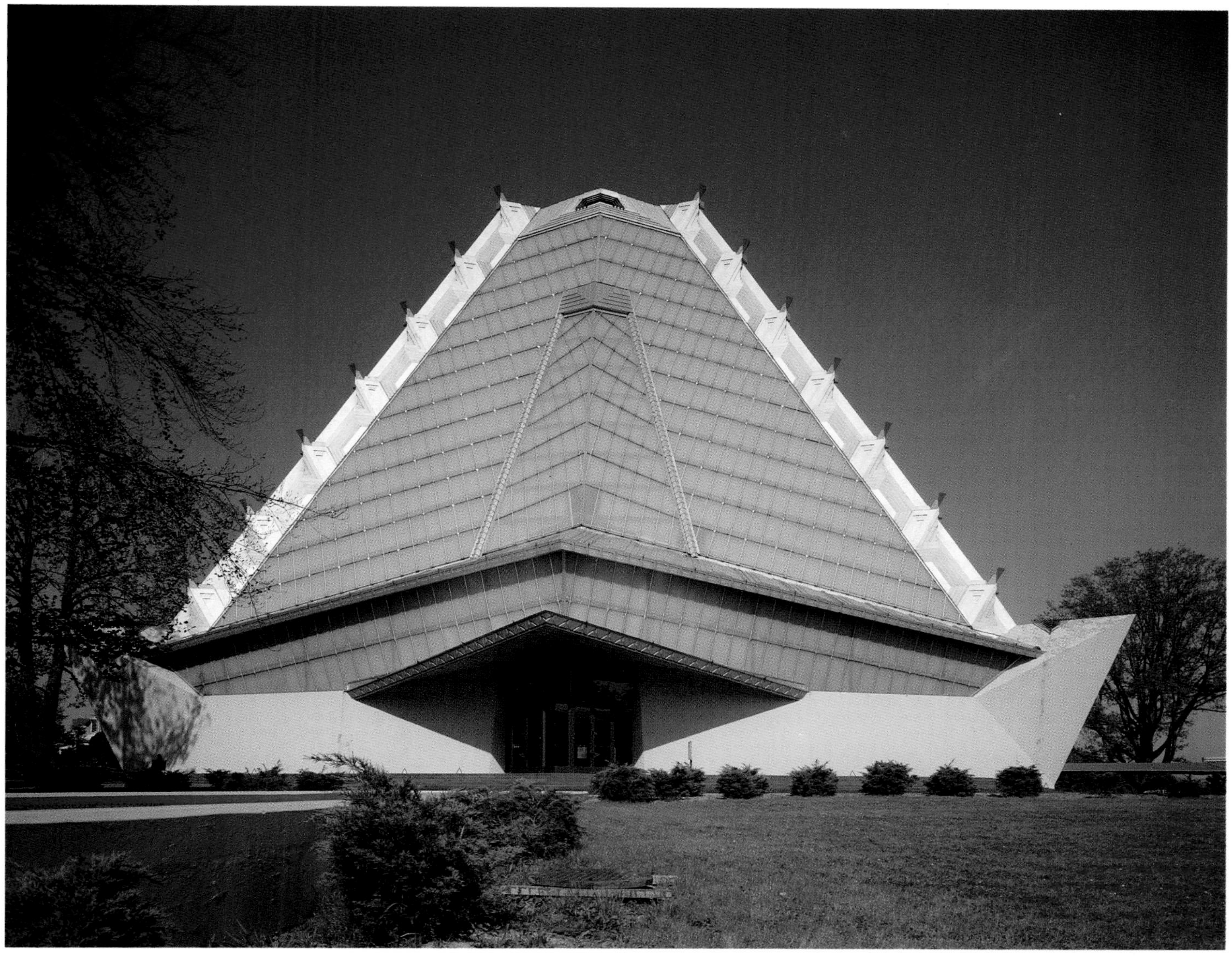

COLORPLATE 100

FRANK LLOYD WRIGHT, ARCHITECT. *Beth Sholom Synagogue.* Elkins Park, Pennsylvania. 1959. *A large steel and glass pyramid from the outside, this synagogue is a hall of light from within. The architect once referred to his design as a "luminous Mt. Sinai." The outer walls are double: wireglass outside, a blue-tinted plastic inside—about an inch of air space between. In the morning the light engulfing the room of worship is crystal-blue; in the afternoon it is golden. At night, viewed from the outside, the building becomes a luminous temple lit from within.*

COLORPLATE 101

SIDNEY EISENSHTAT, FAIA, ARCHITECT, AND CARROLL AND DAEUBLE, ASSOCIATE ARCHITECTS. *Temple Mt. Sinai.* El Paso, Texas. 1962. Photograph courtesy of Julius Shulman. *The slanting tower rises like a* tallit *above a long, low structure composed of blocks, cubes, and curves. The complex sits atop a low hill and blends with an arid mountain backdrop.*

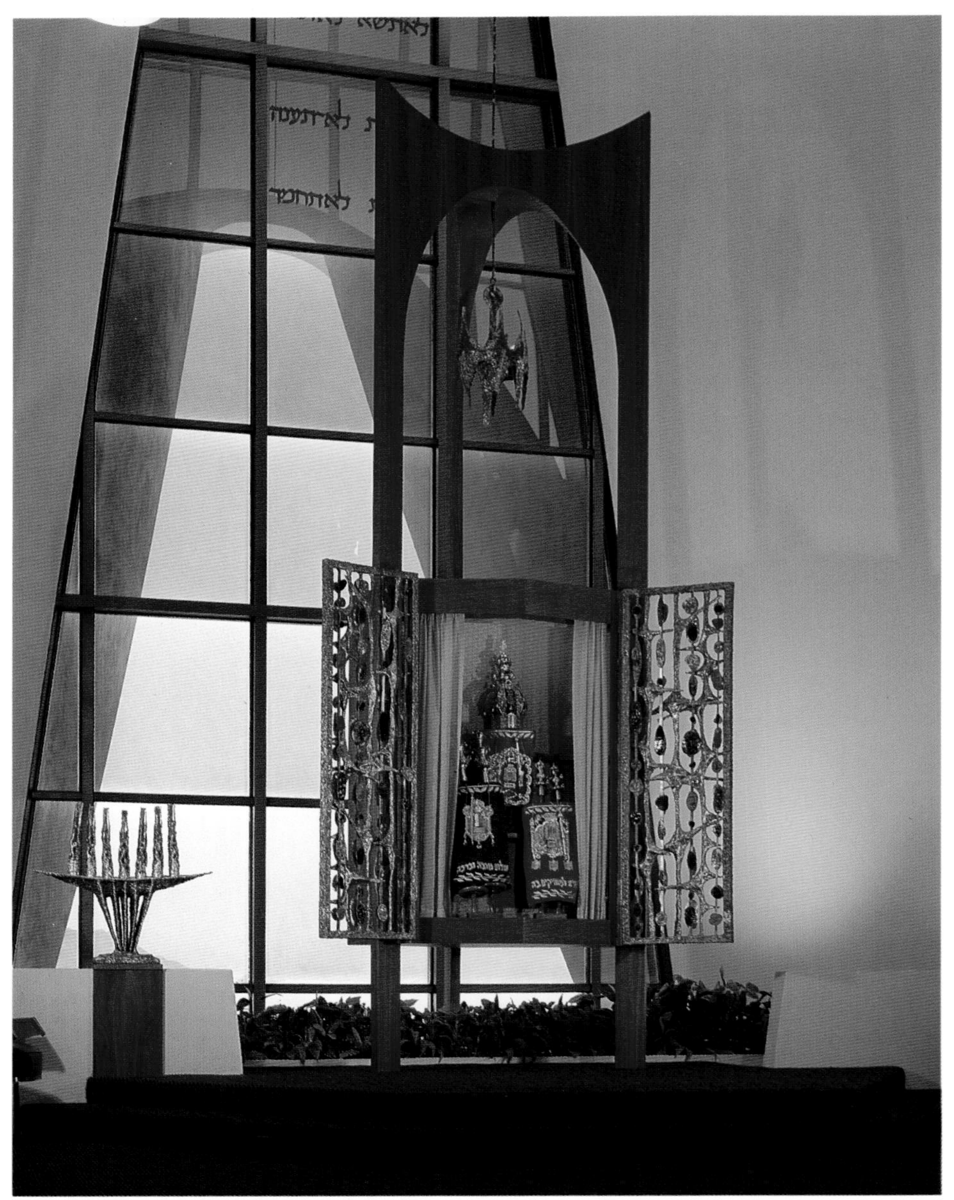

COLORPLATE 102

SIDNEY EISENSHTAT, FAIA, ARCHITECT, AND WILTZ HARRISON, ARTIST. *Temple Mt. Sinai Torah Ark.* 1962. Photograph courtesy of Julius Shulman. *The ark is made of walnut. The open grille doors are bronze, with jewellike colored porcelains attached. The* ner tamid *and the* menorah *are also of bronze. Cutout letters of gray smoked glass, cemented with transparent cement, depict the Ten Commandments which form the window backdrop.*

COLORPLATE 103

PHILLIP JOHNSON, ARCHITECT. *Tiffereth Israel Synagogue.* Port Chester, New York. 1956.

COLORPLATE 104 *(overleaf)*

PHILLIP JOHNSON, ARCHITECT. *Tiffereth Israel Synagogue, Interior, Main Sanctuary.* Port Chester, New York. 1956.

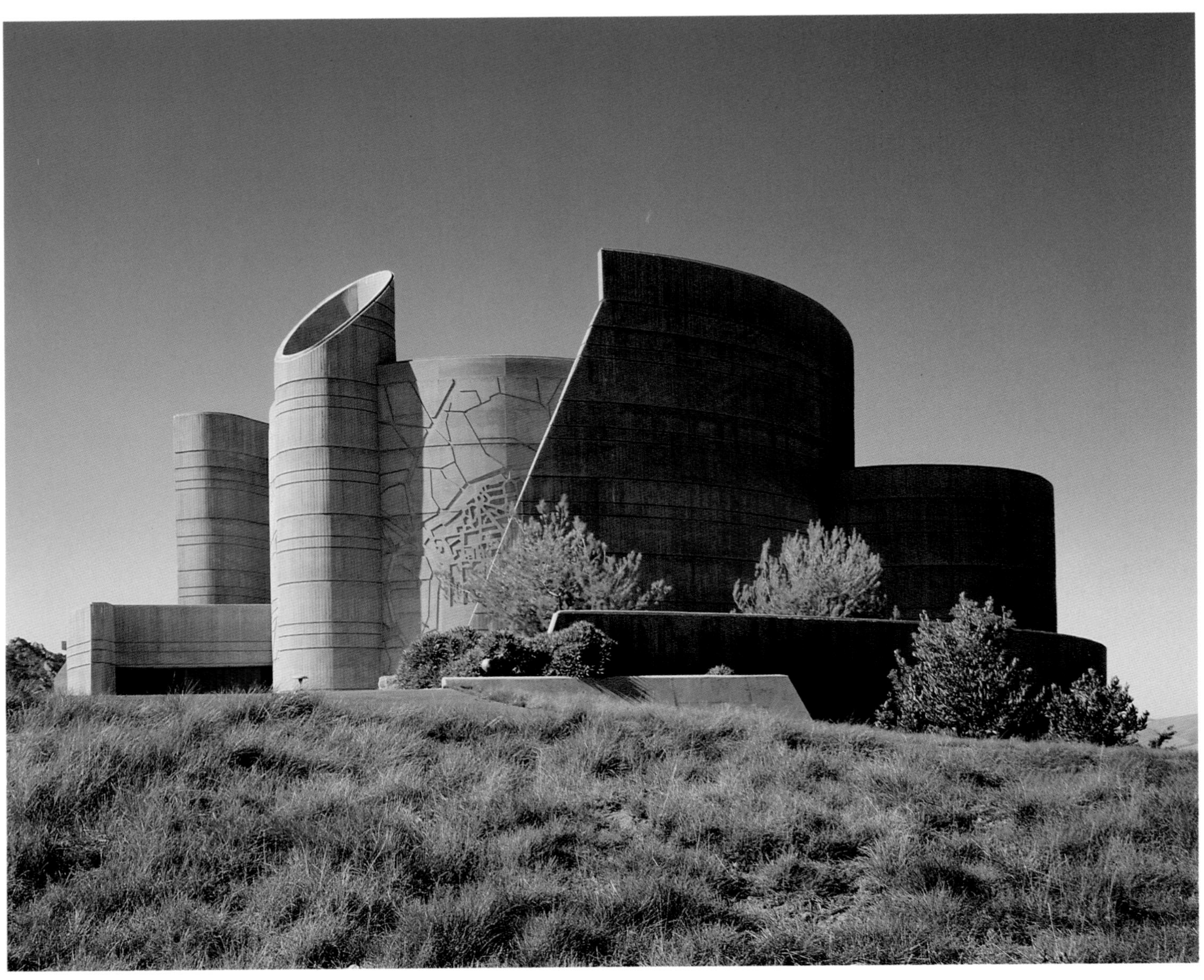

COLORPLATE 105

SIDNEY EISENSHTAT, FAIA, ARCHITECT; CARROLL AND DAEUBLE, ASSOCIATE ARCHITECTS. *House of the Book.* Brandeis/Bardin Camp Institute, Santa Susanna, California. 1973. Photograph courtesy of Julius Shulman. *This chapel is the focal point of an institute which conducts camping and retreats year round. House of the Book grows out a of a hill in the middle of 3,000 acres and overlooks a natural bowl of rocky, almost barren terrain. The long walk from a concealed parking area terminates in the windowless structure, providing complete separation from the grandeur of nature for the intimate act of worship.*

COLORPLATE 106

MAX ABRAMOWITZ, ARCHITECT.
The Jewish Chapel, West Point Academy. Interior. 1983.

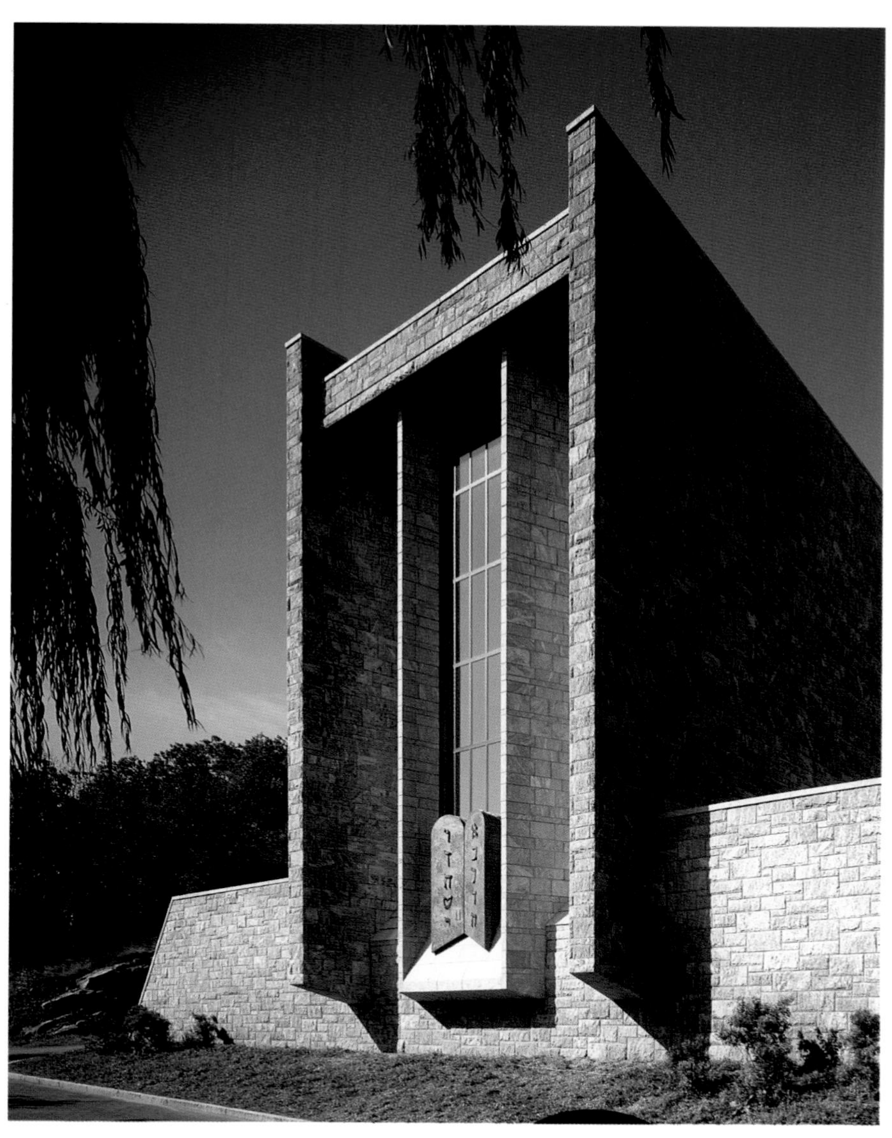

COLORPLATE 107

MAX ABRAMOWITZ, ARCHITECT.
The Jewish Chapel, West Point Academy. Exterior. 1983.

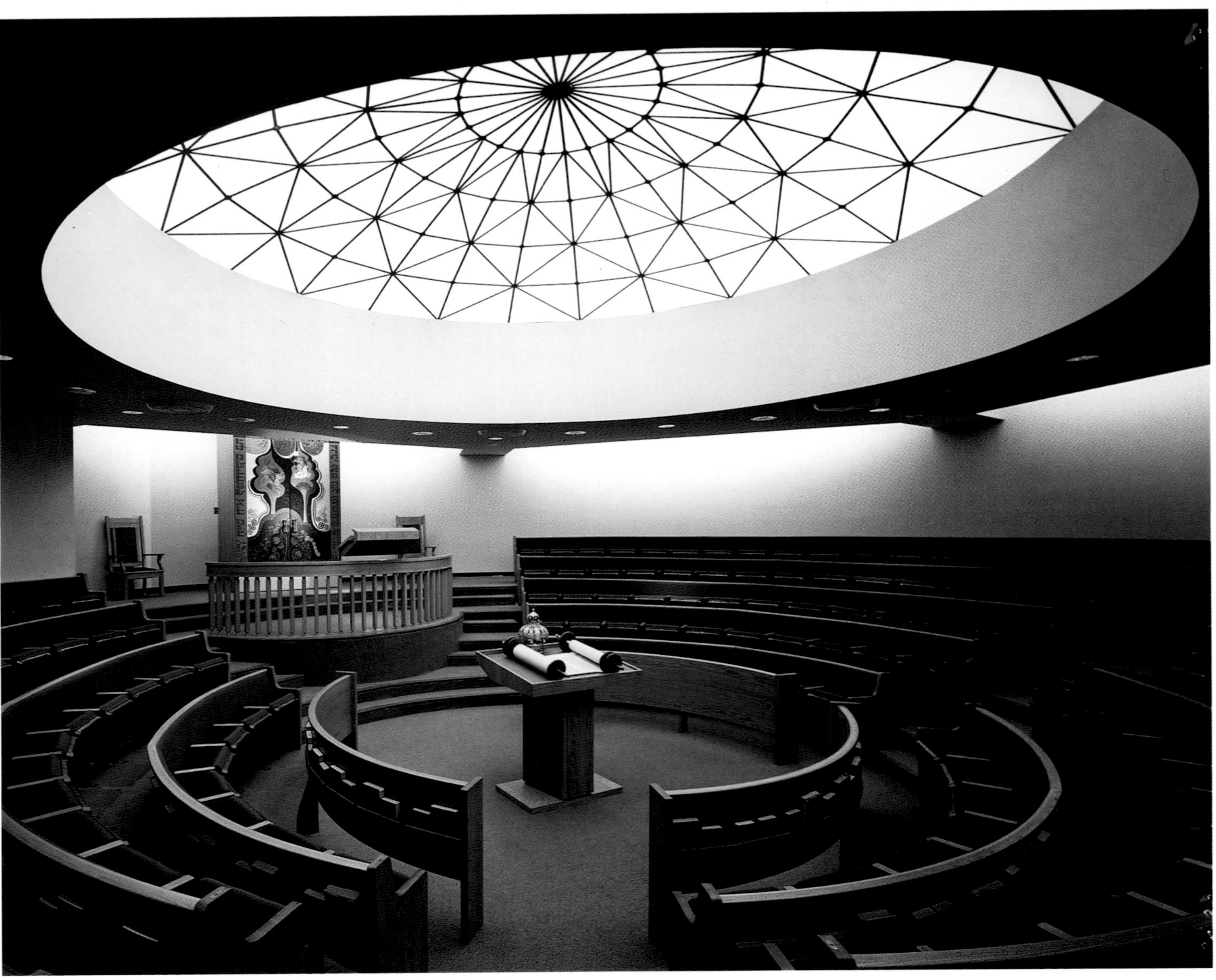

COLORPLATE 108

SIDNEY EISENSHTAT, FAIA, ARCHITECT; CARROLL, DUSANG AND RAND, ASSOCIATE ARCHITECTS. *Congregation B'nai Zion Chapel.* El Paso, Texas. 1984. Photograph courtesy of Julius Shulman. *The round chapel reflects the seating arrangement in the main sanctuary notable for its transparent ark. The ark stands in front of a stained glass wall and roof. Its huge transparent doors slide open and miraculously remain freestanding and unsupported.*

virtue. Mr. Plonsky bellowed that Mr. Kaplan had pulled an unfair rabbit out of an illegal hat; Mr. Pinsky retorted that Mr. Plonsky was too muddle-headed to follow the matchless precision of Mr. Kaplan's reasoning. Mrs. Yanoff charged that Mr. Pinsky was nothing but a Kaplan coolie; Miss Gidwitz rejoined that Mrs. Yanoff was but a myrmidon of Mitnick. Mr. Blattberg warned one and all that Mr. Kaplan could drive normal minds crazy; Mr. Pinsky opined that Mr. Blattberg's mental condition predated exposure to a man of Mr. Kaplan's stature. In a spate of rearguard scuffles on the sidelines, Mr. Wilkomirski raged, Mr. Matsoukas ranted, and Mrs. Moskowitz—abandoned, forlorn—wailed in her Laodicean twilight.

"Class," Mr. Parkhill kept pleading, *"class!"*

In the corridors, the bell rang—but no one heard it. The bell rang again, loud and long—but no one cared.

Mr. Parkhill called, "That will be all for tonight, class." He said it automatically, but he had a worried look. For Mr. Parkhill could not help feeling that General Discussion had not been a complete success this evening. If only Columbus had discovered America on October *eleventh;* if only Hyman Kaplan had been born on October thirteenth . . .

ALLEGIANCES AND CAUSES

Louis D. Brandeis

From "Our Richest Inheritance"

Born in Louisville, Kentucky of immigrant parents and educated at Harvard Law School, Louis D. Brandeis won fame and fortune through his Boston law practice and was affectionately called the "People's Attorney." Appointed to the United States Supreme Court in 1916, he carved out a judicial career of highest distinction. Two years before his appointment, he assumed leadership of the American Zionist movement. A year later, in the first issue of The Menorah Journal, *a periodical for the promotion of Jewish humanism, launched by the intercollegiate Menorah Society, he issued this call and challenge to the educated American Jew.*

While I was in Cleveland a few weeks ago, a young man who has won distinction on the bench told me this incident from his early life. He was born in a little village of Western Russia where the opportunities for schooling were meager. When he was thirteen his parents sent him to the nearest city in search of an education. There—in Bialystok—were good secondary schools and good high schools; but the Russian law,

Louis D. Brandeis.
Culver Pictures, Inc.

which limits the percentage of Jewish pupils in any school, barred his admission. The boy's parents lacked the means to pay for private tuition. He had neither relative nor friend in the city. But soon three men were found who volunteered to give him instruction. None of them was a teacher by profession. One was a newspaper man; another was a chemist; the third, I believe, was a tradesman; all were educated men. And throughout five long years these three men took from their leisure the time necessary to give a stranger an education.

The three men of Bialystok realized that education was not a thing of one's own to do with as one pleases—not a personal privilege to be merely enjoyed by the possessor—but a precious treasure transmitted upon a sacred trust to be held, used and enjoyed, and if possible strengthened—then passed on to others upon the same trust. Yet the treasure which these three men held and the boy received in trust was much more than an education. It included that combination of qualities which enabled and impelled these three men to give and the boy to seek and to acquire an education. These qualities embrace: first, *intellectual capacity;* second, *an appreciation of the value of education;* third, *indomitable will;* fourth, *capacity for hard work.* It was these qualities which enabled the lad not only to acquire but to so utilize an education that, coming to America, ignorant of our language and of our institutions, he attained in comparatively few years the important office he has so honorably filled.

Now whence comes this combination of qualities of mind, body and character? These are qualities with which every one is familiar, singly and in combination; which you find in friends and relatives, and which others doubtless discover in you. They are qualities possessed by most Jews who have attained distinction or other success; and in combination they may properly be called Jewish qualities. For they have not come to us by accident; they were developed by three thousand years of civilization, and nearly two thousand years of persecution; developed through our religion and spiritual life; through our traditions; and through the social and political conditions under which our ancestors lived. They are, in short, the product of Jewish life.

THE FRUIT OF THREE THOUSAND YEARS OF CIVILIZATION

Our intellectual capacity was developed by the almost continuous training of the mind throughout twenty-five centuries. The Torah led the "People of the Book" to intellectual pursuits at times when most of the Aryan peoples were illiterate. And religion imposed the use of the mind upon the Jews, indirectly as well as directly, and demanded of the Jew not merely the love, but the understanding of God. This necessarily involved a study of the Laws. And the conditions under which the Jews were compelled to live during the last two thousand years also promoted study in a people among whom there was already considerable intellectual attainment. Throughout the centuries of persecution practically the only life open to the Jew which could give satisfaction was the intellectual and spiritual life. Other fields of activity and of distinction which divert men from intellectual pursuits were closed to the Jews. Thus they were protected by their privations from the temptations of material things and worldly ambitions. Driven by circumstances to intellectual pursuits, their mental capacity gradually developed. And as men delight in that which they do well, there was an ever widening appreciation of things intellectual.

Is not the Jews' indomitable will—the power which enables them to resist temptation and, fully utilizing their mental capacity, to overcome obstacles—is not that quality also the result of the conditions under which they lived so long? To live as a Jew during the centuries of persecution was to lead a constant struggle for existence. That struggle was so severe that only the fittest could survive. Survival was not possible except where there was a strong will—a will both to live and to live a Jew. The weaker ones passed either out of Judaism or out of existence.

And finally, the Jewish capacity for hard work is also the product of Jewish life—a life characterized by temperate, moral living continued throughout the ages, and protected by those marvellous sanitary regulations which were enforced through the religious sanctions. Remember, too, that amidst the hardship to which our ancestors were exposed it was only those with endurance who survived.

So let us not imagine that what we call our achievements are wholly or even largely our own. The phrase "self-made man" is most misleading. We have power to mar; but we alone cannot make. The relatively large success achieved by Jews wherever the door of opportunity is opened to them is due, in the main, to this product of Jewish life—to this treasure which we have acquired by inheritance—and which we are in duty bound to transmit unimpaired, if not augmented, to coming generations.

But our inheritance comprises far more than this combination of qualities making for effectiveness. These are but means by which man may earn a living or achieve other success. Our Jewish trust comprises also that which makes the living worthy and success of value. It brings us that body of moral and intellectual perceptions, the point of view and the ideals, which are expressed in the term Jewish spirit; and therein lies our richest inheritance.

THE KINSHIP OF JEWISH AND AMERICAN IDEALS

Is it not a striking fact that a people coming from Russia, the most autocratic of countries, to America, the most democratic of countries, comes here, not as to a strange land, but as to a home? The ability of the Russian Jew to adjust himself to America's essentially democratic conditions is not to be explained by Jewish adaptability. The explanation lies mainly in the fact that the twentieth-century ideals of America have been the ideals of the Jew for more than twenty centuries. We have inherited these ideals of democracy and of social justice as we have the qualities of mind, body and character to which I referred. We have inherited also that fundamental longing for truth on which all science—and so largely the civilization of the twentieth century—rests; although the servility incident to persistent oppression has in some countries obscured its manifestation.

Among the Jews democracy was not an ideal merely. It was a practice—a practice made possible by the existence among them of certain conditions essential to successful democracy, namely:

FIRST: *An all-pervading sense of the duty in the citizen.* Democratic ideals cannot be attained through emphasis merely upon the rights of man. Even a recognition that every right has a correlative duty will not meet the needs of democracy. Duty must be accepted as the dominant conception in life . . .

SECOND: *Relatively high intellectual attainments.* Democratic ideals cannot be attained by the mentally undeveloped . . .

THIRD: *Submission to leadership as distinguished from authority.* Democratic ideals can be attained only where those who govern exercise their power not by alleged divine right or inheritance, but by force of character and intelligence . . .

FOURTH: *A developed community sense.* The sense of duty to which I have referred was particularly effective in promoting democratic ideals among the Jews, because of their deep-seated community feeling. To describe the Jew as an individualist is to state a most misleading half-truth. He has to a rare degree merged his individuality and his interests in the community of which he forms a part . . . Of all the nations, Israel "takes precedence in suffering"; but, despite our national tragedy, the doctrine of individual immortality found relatively slight lodgment among us. As Ahad Ha'-Am so beautifully said:

> Judaism did not turn heavenward and create in Heaven an eternal habitation of souls. It found 'eternal life' on earth, by strengthening the social feeling in the individual; by making him regard himself not as an isolated being with an existence bounded by birth and death, but as part of a larger whole, as a limb of the social body. This conception shifts the center of gravity not from the flesh to the spirit, but from the individual to the community; and concurrently with this shifting, the problem of life becomes a problem not of individual, but of social life. I live for the sake of the perpetuation and happiness of the community of which I am a member: I die to make room for new individuals, who will mould the community afresh and not allow it to stagnate and remain forever in one position. When the individual thus values the community as his own life, and strives after its

happiness as though it were his individual well-being, he finds satisfaction, and no longer feels so keenly the bitterness of his individual existence, because he sees the end for which he lives and suffers.

Is not that the very essence of the truly triumphant twentieth-century democracy?

THE TWO-FOLD COMMAND OF NOBLESSE OBLIGE

Such is our inheritance; such the estate which we hold in trust. And what are the terms of that trust; what the obligations imposed? The short answer is *noblesse oblige;* and its command is two-fold. It imposes duties upon us in respect to our own conduct as individuals; it imposes no less important duties upon us as part of the Jewish community or race. Self-respect demands that each of us lead individually a life worthy of our great inheritance and of the glorious traditions of the race . . .

But from the educated Jew far more should be exacted. In view of our inheritance and our present opportunities, self-respect demands that we live not only honorably but worthily; and worthily implies nobly. The educated descendants of a people which in its infancy cast aside the Golden Calf and put its faith in the invisible God cannot worthily in its maturity worship worldly distinction and things material . . .

And yet, though the Jew makes his individual life the loftiest, that alone will not fulfill the obligations of his trust. We are bound not only to use worthily our great inheritance, but to preserve and, if possible, augment it; and then transmit it to coming generations. The fruit of three thousand years of civilization and a hundred generations of suffering may not be sacrificed by us. It will be sacrificed if dissipated. Assimilation is national suicide. And assimilation can be prevented only by preserving national characteristics and life as other peoples, large and small, are preserving and developing their national life . . . must we not . . . have a land where the Jewish life may be naturally led, the Hebrew language spoken, and the Jewish spirit prevail? Surely we must, and that land is our fathers' land: it is Palestine.

A LAND WHERE THE JEWISH SPIRIT MAY PREVAIL

The undying longing for Zion is a fact of deepest significance—a manifestation in the struggle for existence. Zionism is, of course, not a movement to remove all the Jews of the world compulsorily to Palestine . . . It is essentially a movement to give to the Jew more, not less, freedom—a movement to enable Jews to exercise the same right now exercised by practically every other people in the world—to live at their option either in the land of their fathers or in some other country . . .

Zionism seeks merely to establish in Palestine for such Jews as choose to go and remain there, and for their descendants, a legally secured home, where they may live together and lead a Jewish life; where they may expect ultimately to constitute a majority of the population, and may look forward to what we should call home rule.

The establishment of the legally secured Jewish home is no longer a dream. For more than a generation brave pioneers have been building the foundations of our new old home. It remains for us to build the superstructure. The ghetto walls are now falling, Jewish life cannot be preserved and developed, assimilation cannot be averted, unless there be re-established in the fatherland a center from which the Jewish spirit may radiate and give to the Jews scattered throughout the world that inspiration which springs from the memories of a great past and the hope of a great future.

Felix Frankfurter

"The Obligation of the Jews in America"

Friend and disciple of Louis D. Brandeis, Vienna-born Felix Frankfurter was a co-worker with his mentor in Zionist activities and like him, was appointed to the United States Supreme Court. Educated at the College of the City of New York and Harvard University, where he was appointed to the faculty of its law school, he taught for a quarter of a century till his ascent to the bench. In an article in the Menorah Journal *in 1918, he calls upon the Jews of America as "the last reservoir of Jewry" in the war-torn world to make the dream of a Jewish homeland a reality.*

But the life of a nation is not given to you by other people. Neither England nor France, nor the United States, can give Palestine to the Jewish people. It must be desired. It must be sought for. It must be earned. In good truth, it must be taken—not

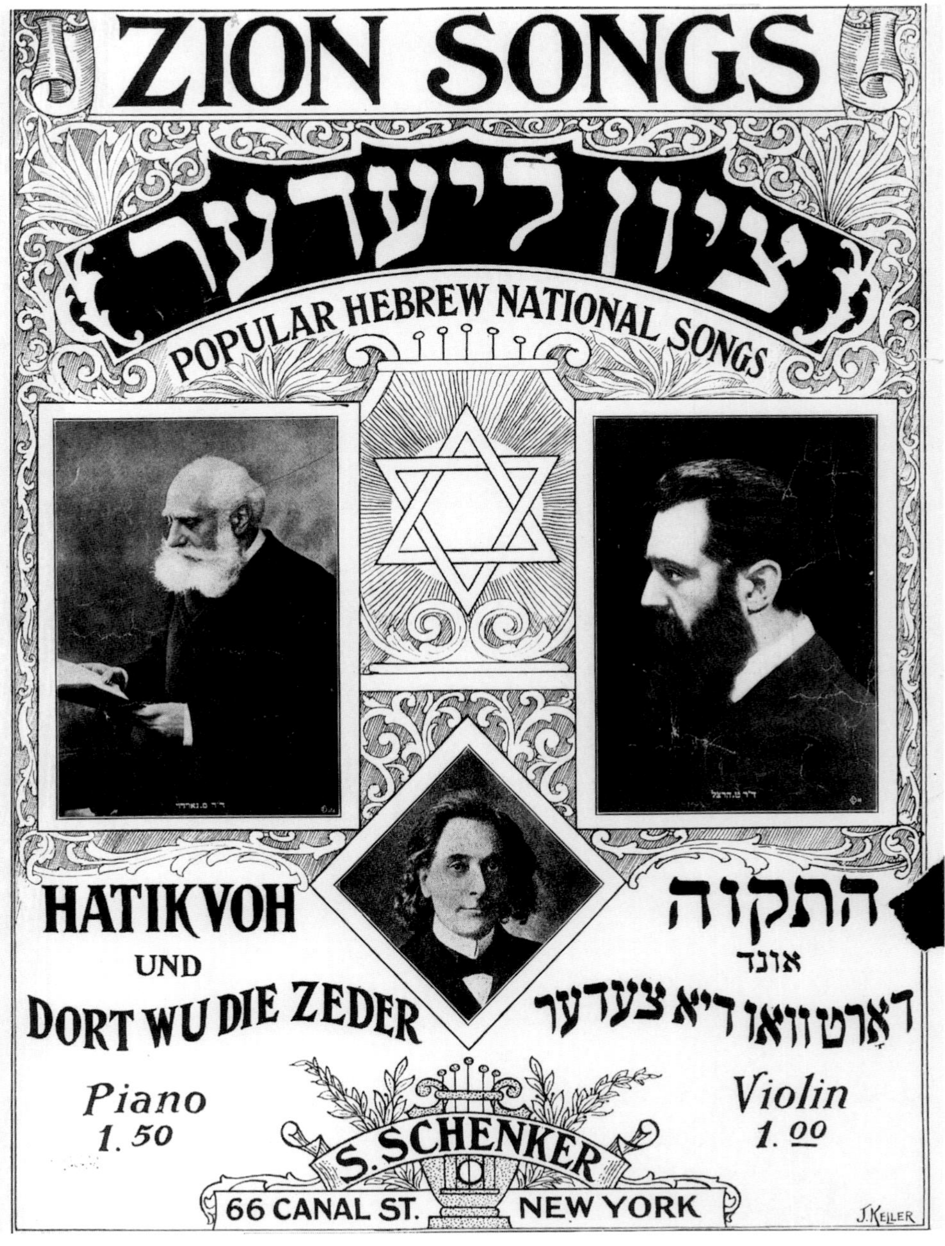

Zion Songs. Sheet music cover. Collection of Abraham and Deborah Karp. *At the right is Dr. Theodore Herzl, founder of modern Zionism and president of the World Zionist Organization; at the left is his vice president, Dr. Max Nodau. At lower center is Naphtali Herz Imber, author of "The Zionist" and the Israeli national anthem "Hatikvah."*

Voter Registration During the Roosevelt Campaign. 1936. Courtesy International Ladies Garment Workers Union of America, Labor-Management Documentation Center, Cornell University. *Franklin D. Roosevelt and Herbert Lehman were endorsed by the American Labor Party.*

merely by arms, though arms are essential—not by talk, but by the conviction impressed upon the world that the Jews really demand Palestine as an outlet for those Jews who want to return, and also as the permanent abiding-place of Jewish culture and the Jewish spirit.

From all this has come the specific inquiry: "What does this all mean to the American Jew?" It does not mean that you and I should, of necessity, go there. Of course not! In the beginning, only a very small tide of those who will want to go there will be able to be accommodated, because, if the life is to be a healthy life, if the community is to grow wisely, population must be conservative in its influx. There must not be an overwhelming horde—only such numbers must be allowed to come in as can wisely be assimilated by the land and the resources of the land. This, therefore, does not mean either that we should desire to go there or that we should be forced to go there. There are sufficient Jews in the world who are longing to go there, and economic and political conditions should be created which shall make this possible. Instead of struggling against a government that is corrupt and ignorant and obstructive, Jews should be enabled to live there under the same conditions that we live under here—those of a free life, a healthy life, a life which is recognized as liberal and democratic by the standards of democracy to which we subscribe. And we Jews particularly in the United States must help to achieve it. It is hard to realize, but it is a fact, nevertheless, that America is the last reservoir of Jewry. Jews the world over have suffered beyond all telling, and it depends upon our numbers and our strength here in America, particularly our spiritual and intellectual strength, whether the dream of Palestine is to be realized.

If you are silent and indifferent it will react against Jews the world over, because the American Jews count in number and influence. You are asked, in effect, to participate in the re-creation of a nation, and that means wise statesmanship. That requires knowledge, the knowledge of thinkers and the knowledge of practical men; the knowledge, as that knowledge is now mobilized, of doctors and engineers and chemists, and even lawyers and architects. It requires the combined Jewish brain and the combined Jewish resources.

What, after all, is this war about? The rights of free nations and of small nations is a phrase much used, and I am not sure that we do not insist too much on rights and too little on obligations. But what is it that is really struggling on that Western front today? It is this: a denial of the German theory of the absolute. It is a denial of the theory that any people has reached such wisdom and such goodness that it is an answer to the world's enigma. It is a denial of the German claim that their philosophy and life and culture is superior to the life and traditions and desires of any other people. The struggle on the Western front is a struggle for the claim of diversity. It is an assertion of the differences in peoples. It is a claim that the Frenchman and the German and the Belgian and the Serbian and the Jew and the Englishman, all and each, is a chosen people if he lives a chosen life. The fight on the Western front means that no one people is wise enough or good enough, to paraphrase Lincoln, "to dictate its life to another people." Through the ages there has developed a certain tradition, certain ways of looking at life, certain literature, certain music, certain art which becomes the personal possession of a group large enough to be called a nation. Through the ages many such peoples have come and gone, and many have come and stayed. Among the peoples that have come and stayed is the Jewish people. They have endured with an extraordinary persistence because it has been a life preserved against unheard-of and untold-of opposition, and out of it all has come the continued Jewish strain; out of it has come the continued Jewish culture; out of it, in short, has come that difference which makes us Jews.

The war means that any nation which has attained such tradition, be it Belgian or Serbian, or Jewish, is too valuable to the world to be crushed. Life is a harmony produced by many notes and many instruments, each nation playing its own instrument. The question that confronts us Jews is a very simple one. Do we think that the Jews scattered the world over, who dream of a life in the traditional Jewish way, have no right to that dream? That the mission of the Jewish people in the culture of the world has been spent, that the longing of Jews with genius and aspiration to live their lives in Zion must be suppressed and unsatisfied? No American can say that that is his position, because that is the Prussian military position. On the contrary, we must say that just as we want the Belgian nation to remain vital and give what it has got to give to the world, and all the other small nations, so those Palestinian pioneers should live and grow and fructify. It is the bounden duty of Jews particularly to encourage those pioneers and make it possible by the great inescapable accident of the relationship of birth. And in so helping we are not merely acting as Jews. We are giving practical effect to the Allied doctrine that is at stake in this war, the right of a small, gallant and ancient people to continue the ancient traditions and to live in the world, not only as it has in the past, but in a great new future.

It is not merely a small little nation that is desired in Palestine, but a great little nation. We Jews in America, by declaring our faith vigorously and supporting our faith by thought and deed, can help to make such a nation possible. Not to make it possible is to be unworthy of a great duty and of a noble privilege, that of rebuilding an old nation into a new nation—the traditional people which is ours.

Jessie Sampter

From "A Confession"

Finding God and My People

Her place of birth, New York City, and her place of death, Palestine, mark the trajectory of Jessie Sampter's journey through life and spiritual quest. Her fascinating journey took her from Ethical Culture to Unitarianism to traditional Judaism. Her "religious confession," published in The Reconstructionist Magazine *in 1937, unfolds before the reader the roads taken and the landmarks and guides that showed her the way, chief among them being Henrietta Szold, Mordecai M. Kaplan, and the Jewish people.*

I was born into a German-Jewish, third-generation-American, upper middle class, well-to-do, completely assimilated, highly cultured bourgeois and individualistic family in New York City, where *trefah* meat was eaten as often as three times a day, where Christmas trees and Easter eggs obliterated all traces of Chanukkah and Passover, whose prophet was not Moses but Darwin. My maternal grandfather ate on Yom Kippur and my paternal grandmother made fun of people who kept kosher. I am now a citizen of Palestine, a vegetarian. I am a member of a Socialist-Zionist commune of agricultural and industrial but highly cultured workers, the chief aim of whose rapidly growing and penurious settlement is to bring as many Jews as possible, as quickly as possible, to our ancient homeland. Having crossed continents, literally and figuratively, from one civilization to another, I know into the depths of my being what civilization means and what it does not mean. I know what are the eternally human and what are the transiently provincial things, what is international and what is national, what in me is human and what in me is Jewish.

In a godless household of Ethical Culturists, I got God from the servants by the time I was seven. I knew him quite intimately and prayed to him nightly to beg him to make a good girl of me. I also got from these same servant girls an ineradicable sense of human equality. But if they, or anyone, ever told me I was Jewish, it made no impression. When I was seven years old, some children in the street told me I was Jewish, which impressed me exactly as if they had told me I was a rag-picker, a gypsy or an idiot. I denied it hotly. I went home to be enlightened, to pass through the fire of indignation into a defender of my race, but to continue to hang up my Christmas stocking and to paint my Easter eggs.

When I was fifteen, having already tasted tragedy and swallowed it down, the childish religion with which I tried to sugarcoat bitter reality split and broke under the pressure of maturing thought. I became an atheist, who had loved God and had lost him. Life was an empty and horrible void. I sought a way out. I sought above all to understand first the pain and grief of life, second, the absence of God who was supposed to have made this now meaningless and fatherless world. The world and I—we were both orphans; yet we were. It became necessary to explain not only death and pain but life and joy, thought, beauty and love. I remember, as a turning point, one night on the seashore realizing first the vast sea, then the stars—each star a sun larger than our sun, this earth a grain of dust and I, dust of dust—and suddenly realizing who was thinking this thought. It was I. This infinity which terrified me lived in my own mind. And terror became awe. I remember seeing a woman's red hat flash among

First Graduating Class of Hadassah Nurses. 1922. The Hadassah Archives, New York. *Henrietta Szold, founder of Hadassah, the first women's Zionist organization in America, is seen in the center of the photograph.*

green trees in a park near Paris, and the instantaneous realization that beauty justifies life. My mind that day was a raw sore, and the flash of color was a balm, as of a loving healer's hand. To me that which replaced God, the God recreated in turmoil out of the night emptiness, the realization of Being as in the beginning out of the chaos of my own heart, could never become that symbol of fatherhood, of clanhood, of nationality, and later of humanity to which the peoples prayed and pray. Such a God has his place in history; he is responsible for and created by civilizations and changes with them. He is a symbol like a flag, a concrete something which smaller minds need, in order to realize the unseen whole, a handle for the emotion to grasp and hold fast. His "Thou shalt" and "Thou shalt not," his morality, is the morality of the people or peoples he represents. My God refound was not a moral God, though morality be a necessary part of that universe—or of that part of that universe called humanity—whose very existence proclaims him. My God was an inner experience, a Presence felt and understood but not to be expressed in prose, an overwhelming realization to be experienced incompletely but passionately in poetry, music, art and in the way of life itself. Half my life ago in crisis, terror, sacrifice, and resurrection, I found the answer to the questions I had asked after my childish world crashed, and though the name may not have been well chosen, I then called the answer God.

Today I do not care to use that name.

My God was neither Jewish nor Christian. He needed no congregation. Yet I found him reflected in humanity, in great art and literature, and therefore also in parts of both sections of the Bible. But my solitary heart needed a congregation. Personal life had failed me, left me empty yet over-rich with spent and unspent love. So I went to seek for a congregation and I found a Unitarian Church. The words of the minister and the psalms he had tallied with the words in which I might and did express what I felt. But the ways of this congregation did not tally with what I needed. This congregation was not mine. Their societies were polished surfaces. Their charity was not love. All their ways were comfortable, self-satisfied and superior. This people was not my people. Then, one Sunday, when I had almost left them, I heard read from this pulpit parts of a modern Jewish book. Suddenly, as I had seen myself in the stars, I saw myself in the Jewish people. This was my congregation, this scattered, persecuted, poverty-stricken and divided people. My people, my congregation. At that moment I passed over from one kind of life into another. My God had spoken.

My first step, then, into my heritage was not Zionism nor Judaism; it was the acceptance of the Jewish people as my congregation. Through what I knew of the Bible—and I then knew the Bible well in English—and through this one modern poem which I had heard, the *Book of Pain Struggle* by Hyman Segal, and no doubt at all also through something in my direct spiritual inheritance, I experienced the Jewish people as my people and as historically and inevitably engaged in seeking to understand and to do what life has predestined within man and what, for want of a clearer expression, I now called the will of God. At first I rejected Zionism. What could geography have to do with an inner struggle? Very soon, however, I saw the connection, the need for earth under our feet and the meaning of history to a people. Before this, being absorbed in biology, psychology and philosophy, history had meant nothing to me. I had been a theoretical, a "parlor Socialist," I could not find contact with the materialism of the Socialist party. Now I found my Socialism in Zionism which meant to me the resettlement of Palestine by the Jew—whose Prophets were to my mind the first Socialists—in the spirit of social and economic equality. I found that spirit among the Zionists of New York's East Side.

From the acceptance of Zionism, I passed quickly to my own interpretation of Judaism. In this I had three teachers, three who stand out from many. Henrietta Szold, in whose household I saw the grace and beauty of traditional forms and who initiated me into an understanding of the synagogue service which made it possible for me to find truth, goodness, and beauty, that is, poetry, in the set prayers, and to penetrate the depths of feeling among a mixed and distracting group of worshipers; Dr. Mordecai Kaplan, who opened my eyes to the true place of the Bible in Jewish life, not as history, not as miracle, not as religion, but as the history of the unfoldment of the Jewish spirit. My third teacher was the Jewish people itself, as I found it on the East Side of New York City, where I went to live in order to be among my own. I learned Hebrew, and as I learned I had the distinct feeling that I was remembering something known long since and long forgotten. I entered into rich treasures of thought, old and new; and as I came to know my people better, I saw that those who had preserved these treasures and those who were creating new values for Jewish life in America and Palestine were embodying the traditional Jewish customs and ceremonies in their daily lives. I saw these customs ridiculed or neglected by those who were carried along by other customs just as rigid but different, unintegrated and mechanical. Chanukkah replacing Christmas; Passover, Easter; and Saturday the Sunday Sabbath, gave meaning and distinction to the fact of my Jewishness. The sufferings of the Jews were as my sufferings, their weakness as mine, their power and overcomings and their future were mine. In the space of a few years I lived through intensively what I had missed for generations. In synagogue service, in diligent study and in traditional living among the poor of my people, I recapitulated my lost history.

Abraham J. Karp

"Jewish Religious Thought in America"

Born in Poland in 1921, Abraham Karp arrived in America nine years later speaking Yiddish, Hebrew, and Polish but not a word of English. He was educated in New York public schools and at Yeshiva University and was ordained by the Jewish Theological Seminary of America.

He served as a rabbi for a quarter of a century and for two decades thereafter as professor of history and religion at the University of Rochester. A leading historian of the American Jewish experience, he has served as president of the American Jewish Historical Society. In this excerpt from an article in the Encyclopedia of the American Religious Experience *(1988), he briefly presents his perception of the spiritual history of the Jews in America.*

The challenge of modernity confronted the Jew in the New World as in the Old. The earliest Jewish religious ideologists, all European born and trained, saw America through European spectacles. At first they perceived the confrontation to be the same that they had experienced in Europe and responded with the ideological formulations fashioned there. Later they saw that America was different. In Europe emancipation was a gift granted at the end of a long struggle; in America it was an "inalienable right." In Europe enlightenment—i.e., participation in the larger culture—was grudgingly granted; in "melting-pot" America it was readily extended. The American Jew quickly learned that the same America that urged cultural assimilation, accepted religious differentiation. Here no justification was demanded of him for his persistence in corporate identity. But he just as quickly perceived that the identity which was most readily acceptable, and which helped his integration into America, was a religious identity. So, as in nineteenth-century Western Europe, the American Jews adopted the posture of a "religious community."

Later, in the twentieth century, when the American Jews felt more at home in America, they discarded the melting-pot image of America for that of cultural pluralism, which permitted the free expression of ethno-national sentiments and the retention of a creative ethnic culture. In post-World War II America, the American Jew welcomed sociologist Will Herberg's description of America as the "Land of the Three Great Faiths," for it lifted Judaism to equal partnership in the American triad of—in Herberg's title—*Catholic, Protestant, Jew.* Feeling fully at home in America, Jewish religious leaders could now turn from formulations of justification to theological consideration of God and man, and the world they shared. Among the theological concerns they addressed were the God in and of history in the post-Holocaust world, and the covenantal relationship of God and man as seen from an existentialist perspective. At home in America, Jewish religious thinkers turned from the *why* of continued Jewish existence to the *how* of creative Jewish living.

Mordecai M. Kaplan
A Moment of Personal Discovery

Mordecai M. Kaplan "reinvented" Judaism as an evolving religious civilization in which the centrality of God and Torah was replaced by the Jewish people and the folkways they had sanctified. Reconstructionism, as this religious view is called, has taken its place alongside Orthodox, Reform, and Conservative Judaism as a religious movement in America—the only one of the four to have been wholly founded and fashioned in America. Its founder shares his personal confrontation with his faith in an essay published in Moments of Personal Discovery *(1952) from which the following excerpts are taken.*

During my adolescent years, in the midst of my college and theological studies I came under the influence of the greatest modern Jewish exegete, Arnold B. Ehrlich. He opened my eyes to the Bible as a composite human document, the original meaning of which lies buried, for the most part, under the many layers of commentary. Ancient commentators generally read meanings into the texts rather than out of it. In addition, I became acquainted with the works of Higher Criticism, which destroyed for me not only the strictly traditional assumption that the Pentateuch was dictated by God to Moses, but even the more modern one that it was all the work of Moses. For a few years I struggled with that problem, upon a satisfactory solution to which depended my continuing in the rabbinate. Loss of belief in the Mosaic authorship of the Torah and in the historicity of the miracles recorded in it seemed to me then as ominous to the survival of Judaism as the destruction of the First and Second Temples of Jerusalem must have appeared to those who witnessed them. I went through my storm and stress period during the first decade of this century, when the Zionist movement, despite its seemingly quixotic character was beginning to make headway in this country. From the very start that movement had an ambivalent character. The Zionism promulgated by Theodore Herzl, as a movement to establish a Jewish state, was a reactive response to anti-semitism. As such it was a means of salvaging *the Jews* from impending doom by finding for them a haven of refuge. The Zionism promulgated by Ahad Haam was a *creative* response to the disintegration of Judaism. As such it spelled the rebirth of Judaism in the land of its origin.

As an American Jew, removed from the European scene, I was troubled much less by the menace of anti-semitism than by the disintegration of Judaism. I experienced that disintegration in my own person, when the Bible and the Talmud lost their authority for me. At that juncture in my life Ahad Haam came, as it were, to my rescue. His series of essays, entitled *At the Crossroads*, made me realize that Judaism did not depend upon the authoritative character of the Bible and the Talmud but upon the will of the Jews to live as a people. That was an most illuminating moment in my life. It opened up new vistas of thought and spirit. It revealed to me the existential reality of the Jewish people. I became poignantly aware of the Jewish people, in the same way as we become aware of our country when it is threatened by invasion. This poignant awareness then afforded me the spiritual anchorage I sorely needed.

I discovered that the essence of living as a Jew was the acceptance of belonging to, and self-involvement in, the life of a people animated by a common will-to-live. The potency of that common will-to-live of the Jewish people was such as to find expression in a common history, in a common tradition, and in a sense of common destiny. No matter how much I doubted the historicity of the miracles and the supernatural origin of the Torah, I could not doubt the existence of the Jewish people and its claim upon me to help it live creatively. It was at that point that the nature of my conditioning during the first seven years of my young life bore fruit. It helped to give body to the notion of the existential reality of the Jewish people, for it convinced me that the Jews had enough in their own unsupplemented way of life, all that was necessary for living a full and good life, all that we associate with the term, "civilization."

Our inner problem as Jews was, therefore, not how to maintain the infallibility of a tradition but how to save our people from dissolution. The problem was how to get its men and women and children to retain and maintain their sense of oneness. That sense of oneness had never been challenged before the advent of modern nationalism. For, as long as Jews were kept out of the general body politic, their very segregation reinforced their will-to-live as a people. But with the advent of the modern nation that no longer required church affiliation as a condition of citizenship, and with the incorporation of Jews into the general body politic, their status as a people has become increasingly ambiguous. That ambiguity has had a corroding effect on the will-to-live as a Jew, an effect that mere religious revival, whether orthodox or modernist, cannot counteract. It is impossible for Judaism to exist without Jews, and it is impossible for Jews to exist without an identifiable, status-possessing Jewish people. Jews today are actually like veterans of a disbanded army, mistaking their periodic parades for military service.

It was this interpretation of the crisis in our inner life as Jews that opened my eyes to the need of effecting a Copernican revolution in the very understanding of Judaism. More important than modernizing it was seeing it in its proper relation to the Jewish people. Instead of Judaism occupying the center of the constellation of Jewish values, with peoplehood revolving around it, I discovered that peoplehood always had held and should continue to hold the center, with Judaism revolving around it. I thus came to see Judaism as the creation of the Jewish people as well as its molder, in the same way as the character which a person achieves gives meaning and direction to his life. So viewed, Judaism cannot possibly be limited merely to what is generally spoken of as a religion. The land of Israel, for example, which the Jewish people has made into a house word of its own religion as well as of Christendom and Islam, or the Hebrew language into which it has breathed its own spirit, are as integral a part of Judaism as its religious beliefs and practices. On the other hand, those religious beliefs and practices have been able to keep the Jewish people alive throughout the centuries that it has been a wanderer in many lands where it evolved vernaculars other than Hebrew. If the Jewish people is to recover its capacity for creative living, especially outside the land of Israel, its religious beliefs and practices will again have an indispensable role to play.

It is thus evident that, from the standpoint of creative Jewish survival, we are in need of two distinct though integrally related categories to operate with, one for the entire complex of land, language, laws, folkways, mores, institutions, and agencies through which Jews have been interacting individually and collectively and experiencing their sense of oneness as a people. That is the Jewish civilization. Judaism is as appropriate a term for that as Hellenism for Greek civilization and Americanism for American civilization. On the other hand, the particular aspect of the Jewish civilization which relates to the belief in God should be specifically designated as Jewish religion. A religion embodies universal truth in particular circumstances.

Abraham Joshua Heschel

From *Man Is Not Alone*

"The Awareness of Grandeur"

Born in Poland, scion of a distinguished family of Hasidic rabbi scholars, and educated in Germany, Abraham Joshua Heschel became in America what Reinhold Niebuhr predicted for him on publication of his first work in English, Man Is Not Alone: A Philosophy of Religion *(1951): "A commanding voice not only in the Jewish community but in the religious life of America." His subsequent publications, his social activism, and his teaching at the Hebrew Union College and the Jewish Theological Seminary of America made him the most productive and most influential Jewish theologian in post-World War II America.*

There are three aspects of nature which command man's attention: power, loveliness, grandeur. Power he exploits, loveliness he enjoys, grandeur fills him with awe. We take it for granted that man's mind should be sensitive to nature's loveliness. We take it equally for granted that a person who is not affected by the vision of earth and sky, who has no eyes to see the grandeur of nature and to sense the sublime, however vaguely, is not human.

Dr. Martin Luther King, Jr., Ralph Bunche, and Abraham Joshua Heschel at the march from Selma, Alabama to the state capitol in Montgomery. 1965.

But why? What does it do for us? The awareness of grandeur does not serve any social or biological purpose; man is very rarely able to portray his appreciation of the sublime to others or to add it to his scientific knowledge. Nor is its perception pleasing to the sense or gratifying to our vanity. Why, then, expose ourselves to the disquieting provocation of something that defies our drive to know, to something which may even fill us with fright, melancholy or resignation? Still we insist that it is unworthy of man not to take notice of the sublime.

Perhaps more significant than the fact of our awareness of the cosmic is our consciousness of *having to* be aware of it, as if there were an *imperative,* a compulsion to pay attention to that which lies beyond our grasp.

THE SENSE OF THE INEFFABLE

The power of expression is not the monopoly of man. Expression and communication are, to some degree, something of which animals are capable. What characterizes man is not only his ability to develop words and symbols, but also his being compelled to draw a distinction between the utterable and the unutterable, to be stunned by that which is but cannot be put into words.

It is the sense of the sublime that we have to regard as the root of man's creative activities in art, thought and noble living. Just as no flora has ever fully displayed the hidden vitality of the earth, so has no work of art ever brought to expression the depth of the unutterable, in the sight of which the souls of saints, poets and philosophers live. The attempt to convey what we see and cannot say is the everlasting theme of mankind's unfinished symphony, a venture in which adequacy is never achieved. Only those who live on borrowed words believe in their gift of expression. A sensitive person knows that the intrinsic, the most essential, is never expressed. Most—and often the best—of what goes on in us is our own secret; we have to wrestle with it ourselves. The stirring in our hearts when watching the star-studded sky is something no language can declare. What smites us with unquenchable amazement is not that which we grasp and are able to convey but that which lies within our reach but beyond our grasp; not the quantitative aspect of nature but something qualitative; not what is beyond our range in time and space but the true meaning, source and end of being, in other words, the ineffable.

THE ENCOUNTER WITH THE INEFFABLE

The ineffable inhabits the magnificent and the common, the grandiose and the tiny facts of reality alike. Some people sense this quality at distant intervals in extraordinary events; others sense it in the ordinary events, in every fold, in every nook; day after day, hour after hour. To them things are bereft of triteness; to them being does not mate with non-sense. They hear the stillness that crowds the world in spite of our noise, in spite of our greed. Slight and simple as things may be—a piece of paper, a morsel of bread, a word, a sigh—they hide and guard a never-ending secret: A glimpse of God? Kinship with the spirit of being? An eternal flash of a will?

Part company with preconceived notions, suppress your learning to reiterate and to know in advance of your seeing, try to see the world for the first time with eyes not dimmed by memory or volition . . . Piety, finally, is allegiance to the will of God. Whether that will is understood or not, it is accepted as good and holy, and is obeyed in faith. Life is a mandate, not the enjoyment of an annuity; a task, not a game; a command, not a favor. So to the pious man life never appears as a fatal chain of events following necessarily one on another, but comes as a voice with an appeal. It is a flow of opportunity for service, every experience giving the clue to a new duty, so that all that

COLORPLATE 109

Stained Glass Windows. Temple Emanu-El, New York. Courtesy of Congregation Emanu-El of the City of New York. *These windows are in the arcades beside the sanctuary. On the 65th Street aisle, are two pairs of windows that depict previous homes of Congregation Emanu-El. The windows, designed by Oliver Smith, show the previous locations of Temple Emanu-El at 56 Chrystie Street (1848–1854) and 110 East 12th Street (1854–1868).*

COLORPLATE 110

Stained Glass Windows. Temple Emanu-El, New York. Courtesy of Congregation Emanu-El of the City of New York. *These arcade windows depict Temple Emanu-El on Fifth Avenue and 43rd Street, designed by Leopold Eidlitz and Henry Fernbach (dedicated in 1868), and Temple Beth-El on Fifth Avenue and 78th Street, designed by Arnold Brunner and completed in 1891. The present building is the congregation's fifth home.*

COLORPLATE 111 *(opposite)*

Oliver Smith. *The Great Wheel Window.* Temple Emanu-El, New York. 1929. Courtesy of Congregation Emanu-El of the City of New York. *This window is the focus of the entrance wall. Its design has its roots in ancient Jewish art. The twelve spokes of the wheel recall mosaic synagogue floors built in the Holy Land during the second to sixth centuries of the Common Era. In ancient maps, the world was depicted as a great circle with Jerusalem as its center.The Great Wheel Window, with its suggestion of the cosmos, has as its center the six-pointed star variously called the Jewish Star, the Seal of Solomon, or the Star of David. The numerical references are to Jewish mysticism: twelve spokes for the Jewish tribes or months of the year; eighteen segments in the surrounding arch for the* Amidah, *the eighteen-part daily prayer.*

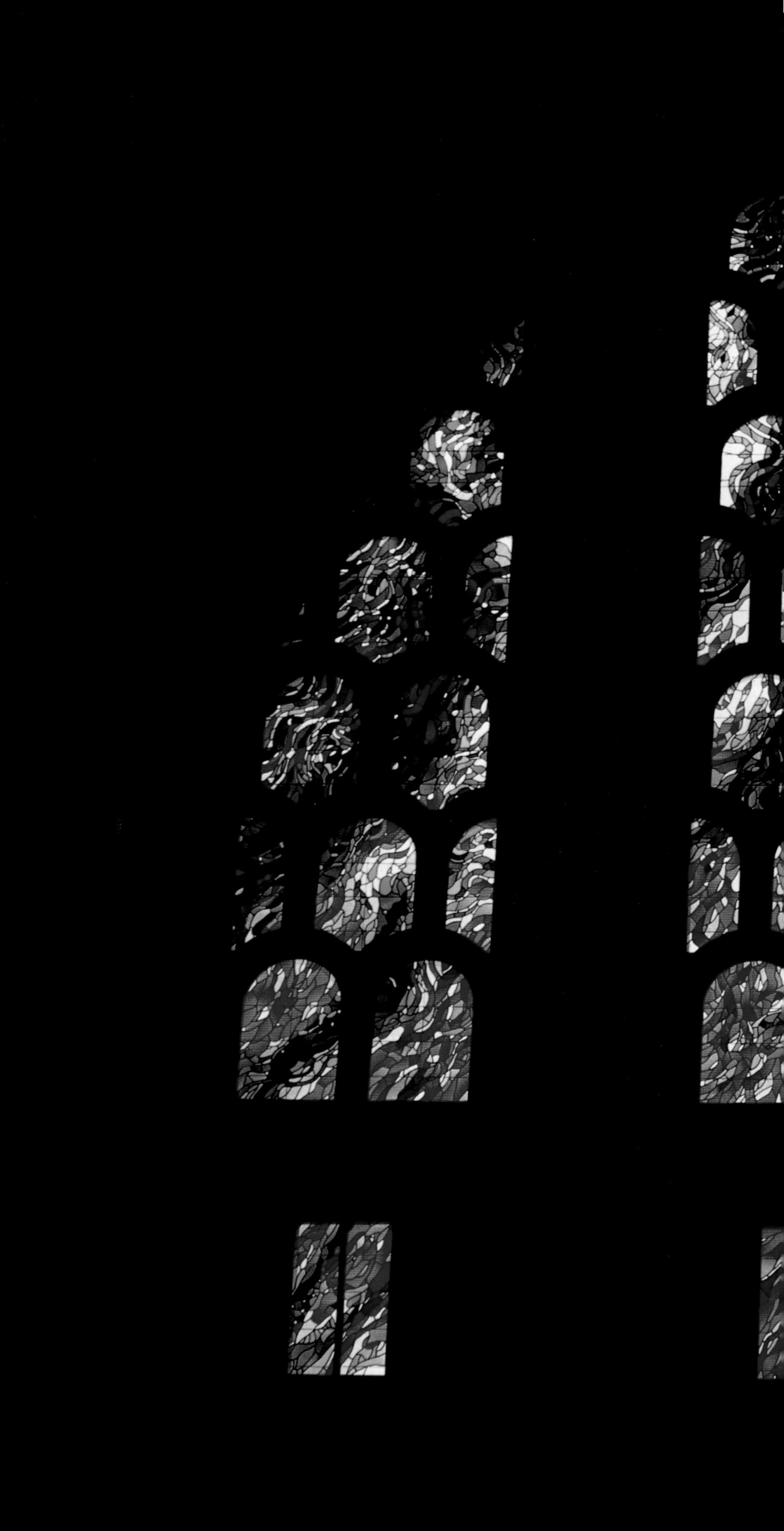

COLORPLATE 112

MARK ADAMS, DESIGNER, AND GEORGE McKEEVER, ARTIST. *Stained Glass Window, "Fire."* Temple Emanu-El, San Francisco. *This photograph depicts one of the two stained glass windows, together entitled "Fire and Water"—the two mystical elements of creation. These two windows are on the west ("Fire") and east ("Water") walls of the synagogue and face each other in the sanctuary. Each window is a complex of seven levels of segments, aligned under a soaring arch with a set of detached rectangular windows beneath. Each window is fashioned from 2,000 pieces of selected types of glass from European factories, leaded together and comprising a spectrum of over 200 radiant colors, shapes, and transparent luminosity. Fabrication was accomplished single-handedly by George McKeever. After a year of studio work on each window, he installed each panel during the summers of 1972 and 1973.*

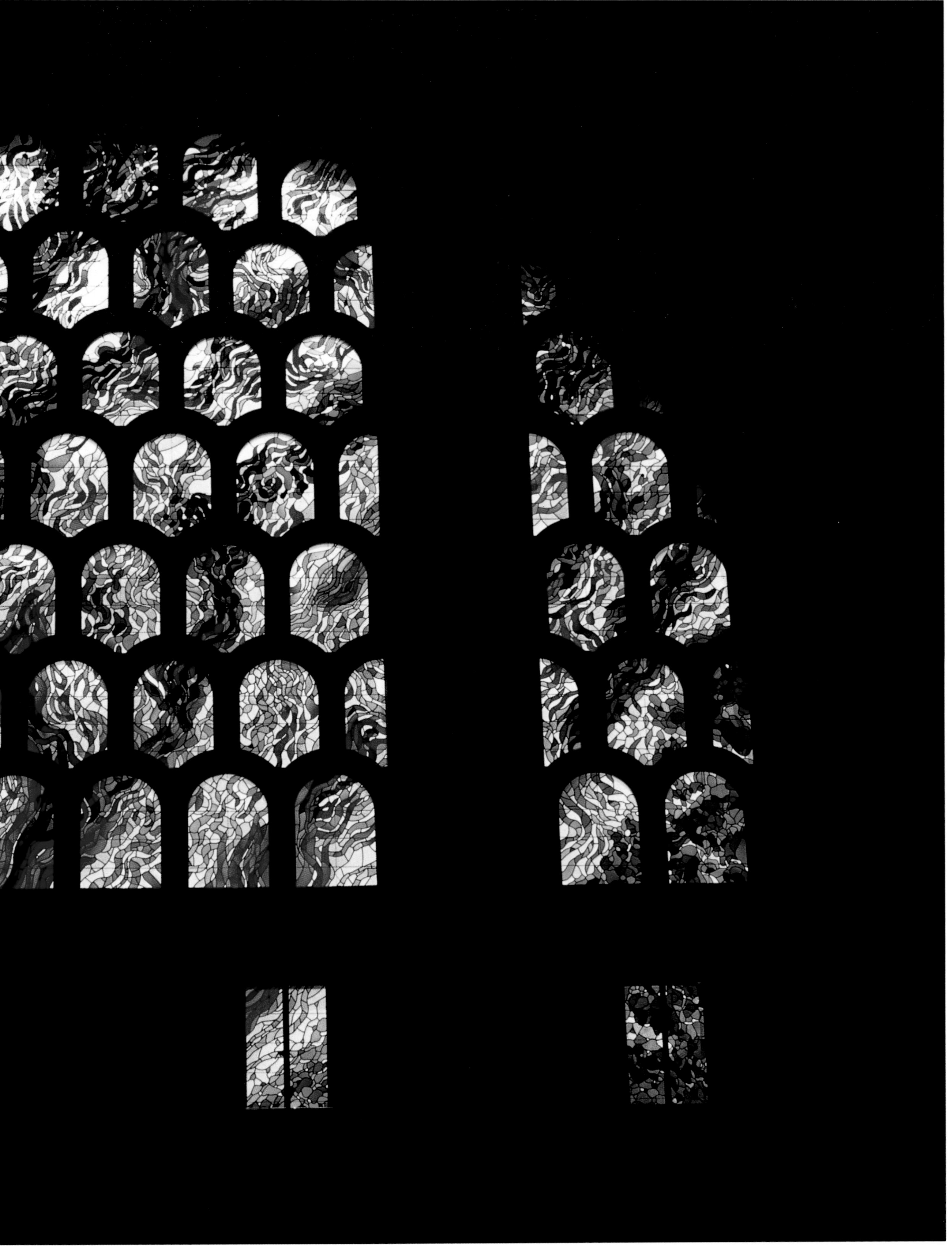

COLORPLATE 113

BENOIT GILSUL. *Clerestory Windows of Beth El Synagogue-Center.* New Rochelle, New York. Photograph courtesy of Stanley Batkin. *These windows picture the* shofar *and the flute: "With trumpets and the sound of the horn, Shout ye before the King, the Lord" (Psalm 98:6);."And the harp and the lyre, the tambourine, the flute and the wine are at their feasts" (Isaiah 5:12).*

COLORPLATE 114

ABRAHAM RATTNER. *And God Said, Let There Be Light And There Was Light.* 1960. Stained glass window, east wall, The Chicago Loop Synagogue. Photograph courtesy George A. Lane, S.J. *Abraham Rattner took as his theme that moment in the biblical Creation when God created light. "I tried to make this design a reflection of the presence of God through the shimmering light of the stained glass for I wanted very much to succeed in creating an atmosphere of contemplation and meditation where man might experience that feeling of hope and a renewed faith in a higher elevation of being."*

COLORPLATE 115

Wallace Harrison and Max Abramowitz, architects. *Beth Zion.* Buffalo, New York. 1965.

enters life is for him a means of showing renewed devotion. Piety is, thus, not an excess of enthusiasm, but implies a resolve to follow a definite course of life in pursuit of the will of God. All the pious man's thoughts and plans revolve around this concern, and nothing can distract him or turn him from the way. Whoever sets out on this way soon learns how imperious is the spirit. He senses the compulsion to serve, and though at times he may attempt to escape, the strength of this compulsion will bring him back inevitably to the right way in search of the will of God. Before he acts, he will pause to weigh the effects of his act in the scales of God. Before he speaks, he will consider whether his words will be well pleasing to Him. Thus, in self-conquest and earnest endeavor, with sacrifice and single-mindedness, through prayer and grace, he proceeds on his way, and to him the way is more important than the goal. It is not his destiny to accomplish but to contribute, and his will to serve shapes his entire conduct. His preoccupation with the will of God is not limited to a section of his activities, but his great desire is to place his whole life at the disposal of God. In this he finds the real meaning of life. He would feel wretched and lost without the certainty that his life, insignificant though it be, is of some purpose in the great plan, and life takes on enhanced value when he feels himself engaged in fulfilling purposes which lead him away from himself. In this way, he feels that in whatever he does, he is ascending step by step a ladder leading to the ultimate. In aiding a creature, he is helping the Creator. In succoring the poor, he fulfills a concern of God. In admiring the good, he reveres the spirit of God. In loving the pure, he is drawn to Him. In promoting the right, he is directing things toward His will, in which all aims must terminate. Ascending by this ladder, the pious man reaches the state of self-forgetfulness, sacrificing not only his desires but also his will; for he realizes that it is the will of God that matters, and not his own perfection or salvation. Thus, the glory of man's devotion to the good becomes a treasure of God on earth.

Chaim Potok

From *The Chosen*

In his partly autobiographical first novel, The Chosen *(1967), Chaim Potok writes of the growing friendship of two gifted boys growing up in New York. What unites them is their religious orthodoxy, both living a life of devotion to religious study and observance. What separates them is that one is the son of a rabbi in the insular, anti-Zionist Hasidic community, the other the son of a worldly Zionist activist. What they can and do share to the fullest is traditional Talmud study in the class conducted by Rav Gershenson.*

Rav Gershenson was a tall, heavy-shouldered man in his late sixties, with a long, pointed gray beard and thin, tapered fingers that seemed always to be dancing in the

air. He used his hands constantly as he talked, and when he did not talk his fingers drummed on his desk or on the open Talmud in front of him. He was a gentle, kindly person, with brown eyes, an oval face, and a soft voice, which at times was almost inaudible. He was an exciting teacher, though, and he taught Talmud the way my father did, in depth, concentrating for days on a few lines and moving on only when he was satisfied that we understood everything thoroughly. He laid heavy emphasis on the early and late medieval Talmudic commentators, and we were always expected to come to class knowing the Talmud text and these commentators in advance. Then he would call on one of us to read and explain the text—and the questions would begin. "What does the Ramban say about Rabbi Akiva's question?" he might ask of a particular passage, speaking in Yiddish. The rabbis spoke only Yiddish in the Talmud classes, but the students could speak Yiddish or English. I spoke English. "Everyone agrees with the Ramban's explanation?" Rav Gershenson might go on to ask. "The Me'iri does not. Very good. What does the Me'iri say? And the Rashba? How does the Rashba explain Abaye's answer?" And on and on. There was almost always a point at which the student who was reading the text would become bogged down by the cumulative intricacies of the questions and would stare down at his Talmud, drown-

ILYA SCHOR. *Hanukkah Lamp.* 1958. Silver, pierced, chased, and engraved. Height: 10 7/8 in. Private collection. *A master silversmith, Schor recreated the world of Eastern Europe. This silver Hanukkah* menorah *is peopled with children in celebration, women offering holiday treats, and musicians adding their songs to the joy of the season.*

ing in the shame produced by his inability to answer. There would be a long, dreaded silence, during which Rav Gershenson's fingers would begin to drum upon his desk or his Talmud. "Nu?" he would ask quietly. "You do not know? How is it you do not know? Did you review beforehand? Yes? And you still do not know? There would be another long silence; and then Rav Gershenson would look around the room and say quietly, "Who does know?" and, of course, Danny's hand would immediately go up, and he would offer the answer. Rav Gershenson would listen, nod, and his fingers would cease their drumming and take to the air as they accompanied his detailed review of Danny's answer. There were times, however, when Rav Gershenson did not nod at Danny's answer but questioned him on it instead, and there would then ensue a lengthy dialogue between the two of them, with the class sitting by and listening in silence. Most often these dialogues took only a few minutes, but by the end of September there had already been two occasions when they had lasted more than three quarters of an hour. I was constantly being reminded by these dialogues of the way Danny argued Talmud with his father. It made it not only difficult to forget him but quite impossible. And now it was also I and not only Reb Saunders who was able to listen to Danny's voice only through a Talmudic disputation.

The hours of the Talmud classes in the school were arranged in such a way that we were able to spend from nine in the morning to noon preparing the material to be studied with Rav Gershenson. We would then eat lunch. And from one to three we would have the actual Talmud session itself, the shiur, with Rav Gershenson. No one in the class knew who would be called on to read and explain, so all of us worked feverishly to prepare. But it never really helped, because no matter how hard we worked there would always be that dreaded moment of silence when the questions could no longer be answered and Rav Gershenson's fingers would begin their drumming.

There were fourteen students in the class, and each one of us, with the exception of Danny, sooner or later tasted that silence personally. I was called on in the first week of October and tasted the silence briefly before I managed to struggle through with an answer to an almost impossible question. The answer was accepted and amplified by Rav Gershenson, thereby forestalling Danny's poised hand. I saw him look at me briefly afterward, while Rav Gershenson dealt with my answer. Then he looked away, and a warm smile played on his lips. My anger at him melted away at the sight of that smile, and the agony of not being able to communicate with him returned. But it was a subdued agony now, a sore I was somehow able to control and keep within limits. It was no longer affecting my schoolwork.

By the middle of October everyone in the class, except me, had been called on at least twice. I prepared feverishly, expecting to hear my name called any day. But it wasn't. By the end of October, I began to feel uneasy. By the middle of November I still hadn't been called on again. I took part in the class discussions, asked questions, argued, raised my hand almost as frequently as Danny raised his in response to Rav Gershenson's "Who does know?"—but I was not called on to read. I couldn't understand it, and it began to upset me. I wondered if this was his way of participating in Reb Saunders' ban against me and my father.

There were other things, too, that were upsetting me at the time. My father had begun to look almost skeletal as a result of his activities, and I dreaded the nights he came wearily home, drank his glass of tea, spent some minutes with me in my room, looking hollow-eyed and not really listening to what I told him, and then went into his study. Instead of studying Talmud with him on the Shabbat, I studied alone while he slept. The Palestine issue was being debated now by the United Nations, and the Partition Plan would soon be voted upon. Every day there were headlines announcing new acts of terror and bloodshed; every week, it seemed, there was another massive rally in

Madison Square Garden. I was able to attend two of those rallies. The second time I went I made sure to arrive early enough to get a seat inside. The speeches were electrifying, and I joined in the applause and the cheering until my hands were sore and my voice was hoarse. My father spoke at that rally, his voice booming out clearly through the public address system. He seemed so huge behind the microphones, his voice giving his body the stature of a giant. When he was done, I sat and listened to the wild applause of the crowd, and my eyes filled with tears of pride.

In the midst of all this, Reb Saunders' League for a Religious Eretz Yisroel continued putting out its anti-Zionist leaflets. Everywhere I went I found those leaflets—on the streets, in the trolley cars, in my classroom desks, on my lunch table, even in the school bathrooms.

It became clear as November went by that the United Nations vote on the Partition Plan would take place sometime at the end of the month. My father was at a meeting on Sunday evening, November 29, when the vote was finally held, and I listened to it over the kitchen radio. I cried like a baby when the result was announced, and later, when my father came home, we embraced and wept and kissed, and our tears mingled on our cheeks. He was almost incoherent with joy. The death of the six million Jews had finally been given meaning, he kept saying over and over again. It had happened. After two thousand years, it had finally happened. We were a people again, with our own land. We were a blessed generation. We had been given the opportunity to see the creation of the Jewish state. "Thank God!" he said. "Thank God! Thank God!" We alternately wept and talked until after three in the morning when we finally went to bed.

I woke groggy from lack of sleep but still feeling the sense of exhilaration, and was eager to get to school to share the joy with my friends. My exhilaration was dampened somewhat during breakfast when my father and I heard over the radio that a few hours after the United Nations vote a bus on its way from Tel Aviv to Jerusalem had been attacked by Arabs and seven Jews had been killed. And my exhilaration was snuffed out and transformed into an almost uncontrollable rage when I got to school and found it strewn with the leaflets of Reb Saunders' anti-Zionist league.

The leaflets denounced the United Nations vote, ordered Jews to ignore it, called the state a desecration of the name of God, and announced that the league planned to fight its recognition by the government of the United States.

Only the Dean's threat of immediate expulsion prevented me from engaging in a fistfight that day. I was tempted more than once to scream at the groups of anti-Zionist students huddling together in the halls and classrooms that they ought to go join the Arabs and the British if they were so opposed to the Jewish state. But I managed somehow to control myself and remain silent.

In subsequent weeks, I was grateful for that silence. For as Arab forces began to attack the Jewish communities of Palestine, as an Arab mob surged through Princess Mary Avenue in Jerusalem, wrecking and gutting shops and leaving the old Jewish commercial center looted and burned, and as the toll of Jewish dead increased daily, Reb Saunders' league grew strangely silent. The faces of the anti-Zionist Hasidic students in the school became tense and pained, and all anti-Zionist talk ceased. I watched them every day at lunch as they read to each other the accounts of the bloodshed reported in the Jewish press and then talked about it among themselves. I could hear sighs, see heads shaking and eyes filling with sadness. "Again Jewish blood is being spilled," they whispered to one another. "Hitler wasn't enough. Now more Jewish blood, more slaughter. What does the world want from us? Six million isn't enough? More Jews have to die?" Their pain over this new outbreak of violence against the Jews of Palestine outweighed their hatred of Zionism. They did not

become Zionists; they merely became silent. I was glad during those weeks that I had restrained my anger.

Tiferet Yerushalayim Yeshiva. Photograph © Bill Aron.

I received straight A's in my college courses at the end of that semester. I also received an A in Talmud, despite the fact that Rav Gershenson had only called on me once during the entire four-month period I had spent in his class. I planned to talk to him about it during the inter-semester break, but my father suffered a second heart attack on the first day of that break.

He collapsed at a Jewish National Fund meeting and was rushed to the Brooklyn Memorial Hospital by ambulance. He hovered tenuously between life and death for three days. I lived in a nightmare of hallucinatory dread, and if it hadn't been for Manya constantly reminding me with gentle kindness that I had to eat or I would get sick, I might well have starved.

My father was beginning to recover when the second semester began, but he was a shell of a man. Dr. Grossman told me that he would be in the hospital at least six weeks, and that it would take from four to six more months of complete rest before he would be able to return to his work.

My classmates had all heard the news by the time the semester began, but their words of consolation didn't help very much. The look on Danny's face, though, when I saw him for the first time, helped a little. He passed me in the hallway, his face a suffering mask of pain and compassion. I thought for a moment he would speak to me, but he didn't. Instead, he brushed against me and managed to touch my hand for a second. His touch and his eyes spoke the words that his lips couldn't. I told myself it was bitter and ironic that my father needed to have a heart attack in order for some contact to be established once again between myself and Danny.

Herman Wouk

From *This Is My God*

"My Sabbath"

Herman Wouk, one of America's most popular novelists and a Pulitzer Prize winner for fiction, is an observant Orthodox Jew. In the midst of his busy work schedule he paused to compose This Is My God *(1959), a highly personal, autobiographical affirmation of his faith and a most readable handbook of Judaism as well. In it he describes his observance of the sabbath in the traditional manner, which becomes as much advocacy as description.*

The Sabbath has cut most sharply athwart my own life when one of my plays has been in rehearsal or in tryout. The crisis atmosphere of an attempt at Broadway is a legend of our time, and a true one; I have felt under less pressure going into battle at sea. Friday afternoon, during these rehearsals, inevitably seems to come when the project is tottering on the edge of ruin. I have sometimes felt guilty of treason, holding to the Sabbath in such a desperate situation. But then, experience has taught me that a theatre enterprise almost always is in such a case. Sometimes it does totter to ruin, and sometimes it totters to great prosperity, but tottering is its normal gait, and cries of anguish are its normal tone of voice. So I have reluctantly taken leave of my colleagues on Friday afternoon, and rejoined them on Saturday night. The play has never yet collapsed in the meantime. When I return I find it tottering as before, and the anguished cries as normally despairing as ever. My plays have encountered in the end both success and failure, but I cannot honestly ascribe either result to my observing the Sabbath.

Leaving the gloomy theatre, the littered coffee cups, the jumbled scarred-up scripts, the haggard actors, the shouting stagehands, the bedevilled director, the knuckle-gnawing producer, the clattering typewriter, and the dense tobacco smoke and backstage dust, I have come home. It has been a startling change, very like a brief

return from the wars. My wife and my boys, whose existence I have almost forgotten in the anxious shoring up of the tottering ruin, are waiting for me, gay, dressed in holiday clothes, and looking to me marvellously attractive. We have sat down to a splendid dinner, at a table graced with flowers and the old Sabbath symbols: the burning candles, the twisted loaves, the stuffed fish, and my grandfather's silver goblet brimming with wine. I have blessed my boys with the ancient blessing; we have sung the pleasantly syncopated Sabbath table hymns. The talk has had little to do with tottering ruins. My wife and I have caught up with our week's conversation. The boys, knowing that the Sabbath is the occasion for asking questions, have asked them. The Bible, the encyclopedia, the atlas, have piled up on the table. We talk of Judaism, and there are the usual impossible boys' queries about God, which my wife and I field clumsily but as well as we can. For me it is a retreat into restorative magic.

Saturday has passed in much the same manner. The boys are at home in the synagogue, and they like it. They like even more the assured presence of their parents. In the weekday press of schooling, household chores, and work—and especially in a play-producing time—it often happens that they see little of us. On the Sabbath we are always there, and they know it. They know too that I am not working, and that my wife is at her ease. It is their day.

It is my day, too. The telephone is silent. I can think, read, study, walk, or do nothing. It is an oasis of quiet. When night falls, I go back to the wonderful nerve-racking Broadway game. Often I make my best contribution of the week then and there to the grisly literary surgery that goes on and on until opening night. My producer one Saturday night said to me, "I don't envy you your religion, but I envy you your Sabbath."

Havdalah Service. Late 19th century. From *The Century Magazine,* January 1892, to accompany the article "Jews in New York" by Richard Wheatly. *In the Havdalah service of separation at the conclusion of the sabbath, a separation of the holiness of that day from the rest of the days of the week, special benedictions are recited over wine, spices, and light. In this depiction the father is dousing the candle, the mother is savoring the spices, while their children look on.*

The Troy Jewish Relief Committee Seeks Contributions

On October 25, 1915, representatives of Jewish organizations, reaching across the entire gamut of the American Jewish community, met and formed the American Jewish Relief Committee to aid needy fellow Jews in war-torn Europe. The Committee of One Hundred launched a vigorous campaign of organization and individual solicitation and turned to Jewish communities across the nation to do the same. Typical of their response is this letter of solicitation circulated in Troy, New York, to Jews and non-Jews as well. Typical too is the poignant appeal: "Bread for the Living—Shrouds for the Dead."

BREAD FOR THE LIVING—SHROUDS FOR THE DEAD

Headquarters
TROY JEWISH RELIEF COMMITTEE
FOR THE RELIEF OF JEWISH WAR SUFFERERS
166 RIVER STREET
TROY, N. Y.

Jewish War Sufferers Poster. Collection of Peter H. Schweitzer. *The first major united, nationwide, overseas relief effort by the American Jewish community was launched during World War I.*

January 22nd, 1916.

My Dear Sir:-

President Wilson, in compliance with a resolution of the Senate, designated January 27th

> "as a day upon which the people of the United States may make such contributions as they feel disposed for the aid of the stricken Jewish people."

Of the Nine Million Jews in the war zones of Europe a majority of them are destitute of food, shelter and clothing. They have been driven from their homes without any warning and suffer from starvation and disease.

The Troy Jewish Relief Committee was appointed the official representative of the American Jewish Relief Committee to receive contributions to the $5,000,000 fund being raised by the Jews of the United States.

Thus far we have met with very encouraging success from all, regardless of race or creed, and we assure you that the Jews of Troy feel deeply appreciative for the generous assistance offered them by their neighbors.

We trust that you will feel inclined to answer this call of humanity and extend a helping hand to relieve the suffering of our brethren in the war-stricken countries.

Contributions may be mailed to Mr. Charles Laub, Treasurer, 46 Third Street, Troy, N.Y.

H. H. Butler, Chairman,

Mayor Cornelius F. Burns,
Rev. Dr. H.R. Freeman,
Rev. Dr. H.R. Lasker,
Rev. Dr. D. Kleinfeld,
Rt. Rev. John Walsh,
Mr. Henry Gross,
Mr. Thomas Vail,
Mr. Wm. Leland Thompson,
Mr. H. G. Hammett,
Mr. Joseph A. Leggett,
Mr. Jacob Ellis,
Mr. James Goldstone,
Mr. B. Kraus,
Mr. Joseph T. Foxell.

Promptness Spells Success—Delay Spells Suffering

Joseph Opatoshu

"Lampshade King"

How to respond to the "modern Haman"; how to defeat the enemy of the Jews? Joseph Opatoshu's short, short story about a Jew in New York and a Jew in Paris, joining to strike a blow in defiance, is, in retrospect, a painfully pathetic response in the darkening days before World War II. But at the time and even later, what could a Jew in New York and a Jew in Paris do but fight back in their own small way?

Silence reigned—the silence of a cathedral.

Irving Treves, alone, contemplated the deep-set, arched windows, the two marble columns, the paneled walls that absorbed all sound, repelling the din rising from Fifth

Avenue and Broadway in New York City. The arched ceiling and the muted light streaming from the walls like the glow of waxed candles emphasized the shadows around the columns. Were it not for the black oak desk that occupied one entire wall, this might have been taken for a house of prayer, rather than Treves' business office.

Three maps hung on the wall—the United States, Asia and Africa, and Europe. The American map, the largest of the three, resembled a battlefield. The places where Treves' customers were located were pinned with American flags, red, white and blue. Flags dotted the states, heavily in certain areas, more sparsely in others.

Treves rose and gazed at the map of the United States, like a victorious field marshal. The profusion of flags was conclusive evidence that the war was long since won, the enemy defeated. The few competitors who had moved their factories to the hinterlands, to undercut Treves with cheap labor, were languishing.

Treves had achieved the position of the biggest manufacturer of lampshades in the United States. The small flags represented the hundreds of cities where Treves supplied merchants, where he had customers in the thousands. It was Treves who dictated prices, dictated fashions in lampshades. Broadway called him the Lampshade King. His factory in New Jersey, with two thousand hands working around the clock on day and night shifts, needed to be enlarged. This was a problem Treves did not discuss with his managers. He was a man who did not care to ask for advice. When a new project presented itself to his attention, he would first work it through in his own mind—a process that took days, sometimes weeks. Once he decided on a program, it was up to his managers to execute it faithfully. That was Treves' method of operation. In order to plan, Treves required solitude. He had sectioned off one-third of the entire floor he occupied and had it renovated. The result was a suite that was a cross between a temple and a cathedral, where every thought was converted into prayer.

Treves moved over to the second map. His gaze swept over the few flags in Asia and Africa. There were no flags at all in the third map, that of Europe. Treves was determined to gain a foothold in France. Treves was disturbed by the fact that the Germans had flooded the European lampshade market.

He knew that competing with Germany was madness. German labor was dirt cheap, the cost of raw material practically zero. Driving out the Germans would mean throwing away one hundred thousand dollars, one-tenth of Treves' fortune. And afterward? When Treves set about raising prices again, what certainty would he have that the French would not go back to the Germans? This was a risky venture, it meant gambling with the devil. Treves knew that no one but a hotheaded idiot would even consider it. But he could not help himself. He was impelled, painfully impelled, to take the measure of Germany. And he had the means to put up a stake. At this point it did not matter to him that he might lose a tenth, or a third, or even half of his entire fortune. Disagreeing with the Communists, it was his position that, like the proletariat, capital was not truly international. The World War had proved that. If the capitalists of the democratic world opposed Nazi Germany, it would collapse, as Treves' opponents had collapsed. Nor did Treves put much faith in the iron laws of economics. He did not believe that overproduction necessarily caused economic crisis. There had been overproduction in the automobile market for years. Twice as many cars as were needed were being produced. Every automobile was produced for the luxury market—and *luxury* was giving employment to millions of workers. As for Nazi Germany, what about the emotional considerations—the anger and bitterness and hostility—that are always capable of upsetting so-called economic laws? Treves knew that he did not stand alone. There were men like him in England and France and Holland. They must think like him, too. With their backing, Treves was certain he would not only drive the Germans out of the lampshade business; he would dominate the entire French market, as he had dominated the American one.

Stamp Distributed by the Jewish Anti-Fascist League of Winnipeg, Canada. 1938. Courtesy of Canadian Museum of Civilization, Québec, Canada.

The very thought bred a restlessness in Treves; his office all at once grew too confining. He opened a massive door and began to pace the entire seventeenth floor.

Treves moved through two rows of typewriters, past steel filing cabinets. He entered the showroom, as big as an Oriental bazaar. Dozens of burning floor lamps barely lit up the lampshades piled high on show like pyramids, cones with their apexes cut.

It was quiet. The staff had all left at five o'clock; only Treves and his chauffeur remained. The time was six. In ten minutes Treves was to be connected with Paris by telephone. Bijour, with more than one hundred shops in France, was to make his first order, for fifty thousand dollars. In filling it, Treves would lose ten thousand dollars.

Sitting among the lampshade pyramids like a carved Buddha, was a fat Korean—Treves' chauffeur. He was staring into the half-lit room, disregarding his master, his lips moving, as if in silent debate.

Treves had passed his chauffeur when he suddenly turned around. The Korean was still opening and shutting his mouth like a frog. Treves asked him: "Whom are you cursing, Chen?"

"The enemy of my country, Japan."

"Listen, Chen: How much would you pay me to drive the Japanese out of Korea?"

"All the money I have in the world, master."

The Korean rose. His face glowed, his small eyes turned into slits. He spoke rapidly, swallowing the difficult English words:

"My countrymen are holding six hundred dollars for me. I give you all of it, master."

Treves was not listening. He had walked a distance away from the Korean when he replied in good humor:

"Good, Chen. That's good, Chen Sin Sen! Very good!"

Through the seventeenth floor resounded the persistent ringing of a telephone. Treves entered his office and shut the door behind him. Seating himself in the padded chair, he coughed, as though about to address his employees. The ringing seemed to grow louder, rattling the window panes. With outward calm, Treves raised the receiver to his ear:

"Hello?"

The telephone operator sang out:

"You are connected with Paris. Bijour and Company calling."

A distant, pregnant silence. The silence lasted for a moment or two. In the next three minutes two people who had never seen each other and were uncertain in what language to converse, suddenly felt very near, despite the three thousand miles of ocean separating them.

"Hello? Monsieur Treves?" The voice from Paris was a familiar one; it could have been a New York friend speaking. "Two months ago, I would have considered your proposition mad. Now I think it perfectly sane—in fact, the only course of action possible. Send the order right off. If we have to, I'll sell the goods below the market price. Let that modern Haman know that we Jews are not at anybody's mercy!"

The three minutes ended. Treves kept the receiver to his ear, listening for an echo—like a man standing in the railroad station after the departure of someone dear to him. Joy rose in him, the joy of creation. When the three thousand mile distance between them that had been broken for three minutes, was resumed, and buzzing assailed his ear, Treves hung up the receiver, and leaned back in his chair.

What matter that he had just lost ten thousand dollars? He was happy because the Jew in France had spoken with such contempt of the modern Haman; he was happy because Bijour too was ready to lose money in order to defeat the enemy of the Jews.

When Treves rose, night had fallen. Taking a small red flag out of a box, he approached the map of Europe. In the darkness he located Paris and stuck the flag in it.

Neil Simon

From *Brighton Beach Memoirs*

Neil Simon is probably the most prolific and popular playwright of the twentieth century. In thirty years, he has written twenty-seven plays and musicals and eighteen screenplays and has won more Academy Awards and Tony nominations than any other writer. But who would have thought to look for an average American Jewish family's reaction to the oncoming Holocaust in his Drama Critics Circle Award-winning Brighton Beach Memoirs *(1984)? But it is there, as we now can see.*

JACK: Somebody has something to discuss? If there's a problem, this is the time to bring it up. This is the family hour.

EUGENE: What a great idea for a radio show. *The Family Hour.* Every Wednesday night you hear a different family eating dinner discussing their problems of the week. And you get to hear different recipes. *(As announcer)* "WEAF presents dinner at Brighton Beach starring the Jacob Jerome Family and featuring tonight's specialty, liver and cabbage, brought to you by Ex-Lax, the mild laxative."

KATE: The whole country's going to hear about a fifteen-year-old boy gagging on liver?

JACK: Nothing to discuss? Nobody has any problems? Otherwise I want to turn on the news.

STANLEY: Well, as a matter of fact . . .

Judaica Store Window. The Library of Congress. *The dual allegiances expressed in the window display are love and appreciation for America and reverence for the Holy Land and the holy faith.*

Portable Ark and Altar Used in World War II. The National Museum of American Jewish Military History, Washington, D.C. *Chaplain Martin Weitz conducted services all over the South Pacific with this portable ark and altar. The altar is unique, having been made from a medical department foot-locker and remnants found in the battle-field. (The Ten Commandments are carved from an aluminum remnant of a Japanese Zero plane.) It was Chaplain Weitz's version of beating swords into plowshares.*

JACK: What?

STANLEY: Nothing.

EUGENE: I'll help with the dishes.

KATE: You sit there and finish your liver.

EUGENE: I can't swallow it. It won't go down. Remember the lima-bean catastrophe last month? Does anybody want to see a repeat of that disgusting episode?

JACK: Why does he always talk like it's a Sherlock Holmes story?

STANLEY: He thinks he's a writer.

EUGENE: And what do you think *you* are?

KATE: Eat half of it.

EUGENE: Which half? They're both terrible.

Kate: A quarter of it. Two bites.

EUGENE: *One* bite.

KATE: *Two* bites.

EUGENE: I know you. If I eat one bite, you'll make me eat another bite. . . I'll take it to my room. I'll eat it tonight. I need time to chew it.

JACK: These are not times to waste food. If you didn't want it, Eugene, you shouldn't have taken it.

EUGENE: I didn't take it. They gave it to me. It comes attached to the plate.

NORA: If it's so important to everybody, I'll eat your liver, Eugene.

(They all look at her)

EUGENE: You *will?*

NORA: It seems to be the only thing this family is worried about. *(She takes his plate)* Give me your liver so we can get on with more important things in our lives.

JACK: Nora's right. Take the liver away. If nobody likes it, why do you make it?

KATE *(Angrily)*: Because we can't afford a roast beef for seven people.

(She heads for the kitchen)

EUGENE *(To the audience)*: I suddenly felt vulgar and cheap.

JACK: Stanley, turn on the news. Blanche. Laurie, get off your feet. You look tired to me.

STANLEY: Can I talk to you a minute, Pop? It's something really important.

JACK: More important than what's going on in Europe?

(He turns on the radio)

STANLEY: It's not more important. It's just coming up sooner.

JACK *(Fiddles with the dial)*: Hitler's already moved into Austria. In a couple of months the whole world will be in it. . . What's the matter with this radio?

(It is barely audible)

KATE *(Comes out of the kitchen)*: Someone's been fooling around with it. Haven't they, Eugene?

EUGENE: Why "Eugene"? Pop had the news on last night.

KATE: You weren't listening to the ball game this afternoon?

JACK: He's talking about Poland. . . Dammit! I don't want anyone touching this radio anymore, you understand?

EUGENE *(To the audience)*: Guess who's gonna get blamed for the war in Europe?

KATE: Eugene! Bring in the knives and forks.

(He does. JACK turns off the radio)

STANLEY: You really think there'll be war, Pop? I mean, America too?

JACK: We're already in it. Not us maybe. But friends, relatives. If you're Jewish, you've got a cousin suffering *somewhere* in the world.

KATE *(Wiping the table)*: Ida Kazinsky's family got out of Poland last month. The stories she tells about what's going on there, you don't even want to hear.

STANLEY: How many relatives do we have in Europe?

KATE: Enough. Uncles, cousins. I have a great-aunt. Your father has nephews.

JACK: I have a cousin, Sholem, in Poland. His whole family.

BLANCHE: Dave had relatives in Warsaw. That's where his mother was born.

STANLEY: What if they got to America? Where would they live?

JACK: Who?

STANLEY: Your nephews. Mom's cousins and uncles. Would we take them in?

JACK *(Looks at Kate)*: What God gives us to deal with, we deal with.

ELIE WIESEL

From *The Gates of the Forest*

The Hasidim and God

Toward the end of his fifth and final autobiographical novel, The Gates of the Forest *(1966), Elie Wiesel in the person of Holocaust survivor Gregor, after a long and shattering quest, visits Brooklyn where whole communities of Hasidic Jews live the paradox of having had their faith strengthened by their brush with death. There he confronts a Hasidic rabbi of whom he demands that he, the man of God, restore faith and sanity to this Holocaust survivor who has seen death at Auschwitz and cannot escape it. The confrontation between the man of God and the survivor of Auschwitz offers the author the opportunity to rise to his fullest artistic and moral power. In recognition of his vocation to force humankind to confront its conscience, and for having in the process become that conscience, Wiesel in 1986 was awarded the Nobel Prize for Peace.*

The celebration was at its height. It seemed as if it would never come to an end. The *hasidim* were dancing, vertically, as if not moving from their place, but forcing the rhythm down into the earth. What did it matter if the walls gave way except to show that no enclosure was large enough to contain their fervor? They sang; and the song gave them life and caused the sap to well up in them and bind them together. Ten times, fifty times, they repeated the same phrase, taken from the Psalms or some other portion of Scripture, and every time the fire would be renewed again with primordial passion: yes, once God and man were one, then their unity was broken; ever since they have sought each other, pursued each other, and before each other have proclaimed themselves invincible. As long as the song and dance go on, they are.

The *hasidim* sang. the song burst their chests and lit a thousand flames in their eyes. "If I could sing," said the famous Rebbe Pinchas of Koritz," I'd force God to leave his throne and to come down among us to be at our side." The hall was stifling as if God filled it; he was the interval that separated the words and then brought them together into prayer or melody; he was the *hasid* listening with closed eyes or his com-

COLORPLATE 116

ABRAHAM WALKOWITZ. *In the Street.* 1909. Oil on canvas. 14 1/8 x 11 1/8 in. Hirshhorn Museum and Sculpture Garden, Smithsonian Institution, Washington, D.C. Gift of Joseph H. Hirshhorn, 1966.

COLORPLATE 117

George Luks. *Houston Street.* 1917. Oil on canvas. 24 x 42 in. The Saint Louis Art Museum. Bequest of Marie Setz Hertslet.

COLORPLATE 118

JENNINGS TOFEL *Family Reunion.* 1929. Oil on canvas. 18 x 21 3/4 in. Hirshhorn Museum and Sculpture Garden, Smithsonian Institution, Washington, D.C. Gift of Joseph H. Hirshhorn, 1966.

COLORPLATE 119 *(overleaf)*

MAYER KIRSHENBLATT. *Simchat Torah.* 1993. Oil on canvas. 24 x 36 in. Courtesy of the artist. *The "Joy of the Law" celebration marks the conclusion of the annual reading of the Pentateuch from the Torah scroll. Men danced holding Torah scrolls; children carried special flags often topped by an apple with a lit candle inserted.*

SYMKHAS TORA #2
OPATOW CIRCA 1930
M KIRSHENBLATT
TORONTO 1993

COLORPLATE 120

THERESA BERNSTEIN. *Zionist Meeting, New York.* 1923. Oil on canvas. 34 1/2 x 44 1/2 in. Courtesy of the National Jewish Fund, New York. *This meeting took place in 1921 when Albert Einstein, Chaim Weizmann, president of the World Zionist Organization, and Menahem Ussishkin, head of the Zionist Commission in Palestine, toured America soliciting funds for Zionist work and for the projected Hebrew University in Jerusalem. They are in the first row, right to left.*

COLORPLATE 121

RAPHAEL SOYER. *The Artist's Parents.* 1932. Oil on canvas. 28 x 30 in.
The Metropolitan Museum of Art, New York. Gift of the artist, 1979.

COLORPLATE 122

Moses Soyer. *Lover of Books*. 1934. Oil on canvas. 42 x 23 in.
The Jewish Museum, New York. Gift of Ida Soyer.

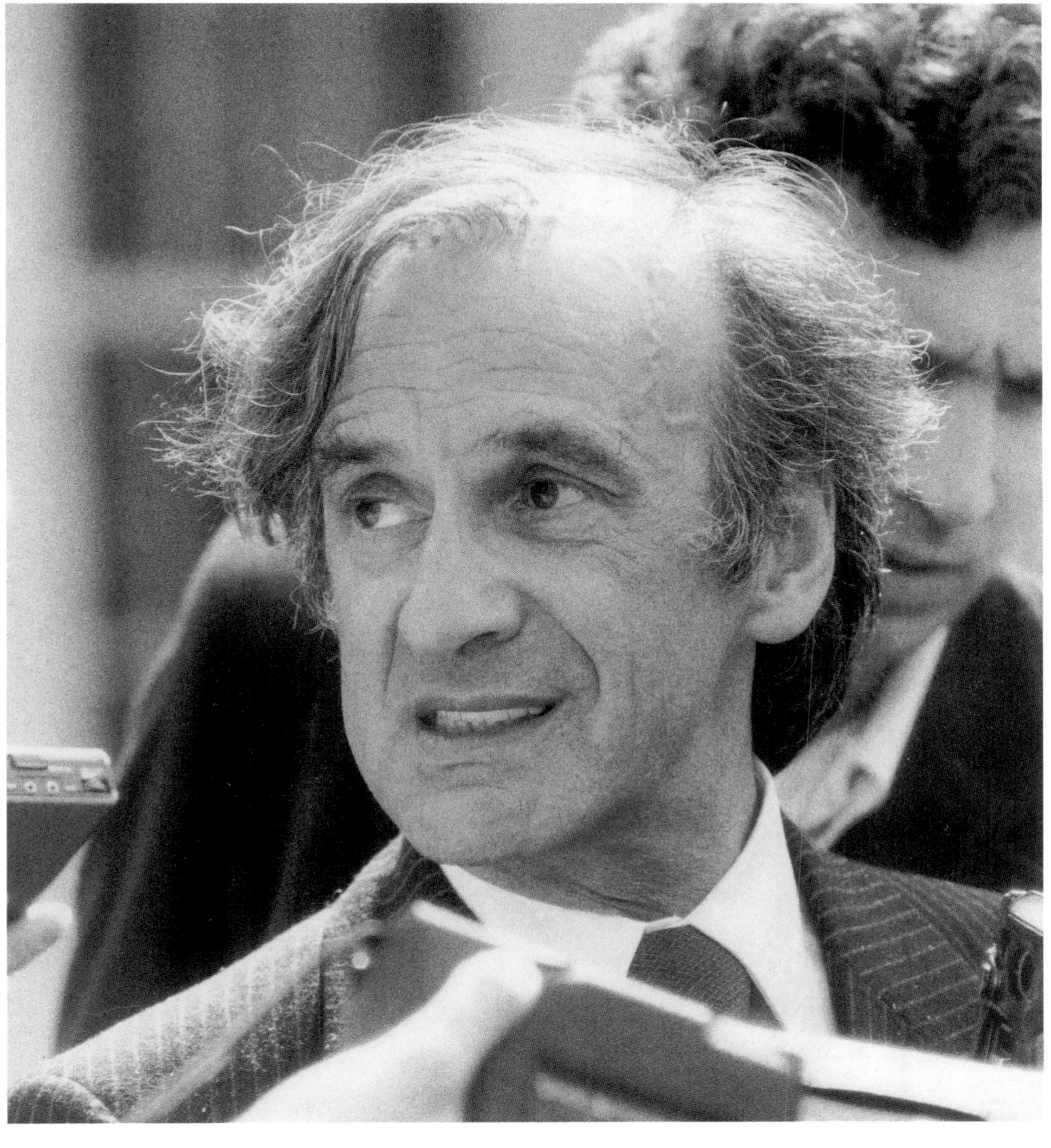

Elie Wiesel. 1985.
UPI/Bettman Archives.
Holocaust survivor, author, Nobel Peace Laureate, Elie Wiesel became the post-World War II era's "keeper of the conscience."

panion who was clapping his hands as if to applaud a victory. He was there, let that suffice; he is there and that surely sufficed. Let the Angel of Death arrive if he chose and he would be disposed of forever. But he did not dare to come; he hid himself, awaiting his hour, for the angel of death is patient and knows that his hour will come.

At the far end of the room, facing the door, the Rebbe surrounded by his court presided over the table of honor. A royal person of the line of David the Conqueror, he joined past glory with future promise. All those present feared and admired him and pledged him fidelity without limit, limning the forces which converted in his person and which he alone could put to use. With a single look he could destroy buildings and raise them up again. With a word he could deny the power of fate and substitute his own for it. *Hatzadik gozer vehakadosh baruch hu mekayem,* says the Talmud. The righteous decree and the Holy One, blessed be He, obeys. If the Rebbe had willed it, he could alter the course of history. But the Rebbe sat silent. His disciples sang louder and louder as if to provoke him to action, but he remained unprovoked. The hand of the Lord must not be forced; let him act when he will, choosing the hour and the instrument. We offer him only his freedom. If he exacts of his people a million children, it is because, in truth, he requires them to exalt his name (may it be blessed) and his power, for he is all of life as he is all of death. If he needs rivers of blood, let him be pitied for it is only that he lacks imagination. For man the infinite is God; for God the infinite is man.

Karl Shapiro

From *Poems of a Jew*

"The 151st Psalm"

"We are in America," Karl Shapiro sings in "The 151st Psalm" (the Bible has 150). "We have been here three hundred years." This new psalm for the New World in his Poems of a Jew *echoes the midrashic conceit that at the destruction of the Temple and Jerusalem, God went into exile with His people. Shapiro was the first American Jew to receive the Pulitzer prize for poetry—in 1945, for his* V-Letter and Other Poems.

Are You looking for us? We are here.
Have You been gathering flowers, Elohim?
We are Your flowers, we have always been.
When will You leave us alone?
We are in America.
We have been here three hundred years.
And what new altar will You deck us with?

Whom are You following, Pillar of Fire?
What barn do You seek shelter in?
At whose gate do You whimper

Jacob A.Riis. *Talmud School on Hester Street.* Turn of the century. Photograph. Museum of the City of New York. *After attending public school til mid afternoon, boys of the immigrant Jewish community then began Hebrew classes.*

In this great Palestine?
Whose wages do You take in this New World?
But Israel shall take what it shall take,
Making us ready for Your hungry Hand!

Immigrant God, You follow me;
You go with me, You are a distant tree;
You are the beast that lows in my heart's gates;
You are the dog that follows at my heel;
You are the table on which I lean;
You are the plate from which I eat.
Shepherd of the flocks of praise.
Youth of all youth, ancient of days,
Follow us.

AT HOME IN AMERICA

Eli N. Evans

From *The Provincials*

The Jewish Mayor of Durham

An intimate portrayal of Jewish life in the South is found in The Provincials: A Personal History of Jews in the South *by Eli N. Evans. He served as an aide in the Johnson administration and a senior program officer with the Carnegie Corporation concentrating on civil rights. Evans is currently president of the Charles H. Revson Foundation. Here he tells of his father's campaign for the mayoralty of Durham, North Carolina in 1950.*

For our family 1950 was a special year—a new home and my father's first campaign for mayor of Durham.

My father always cared about his town, and it seemed that any time money had to be raised, Durham called on him. He was part of the generation that was too young

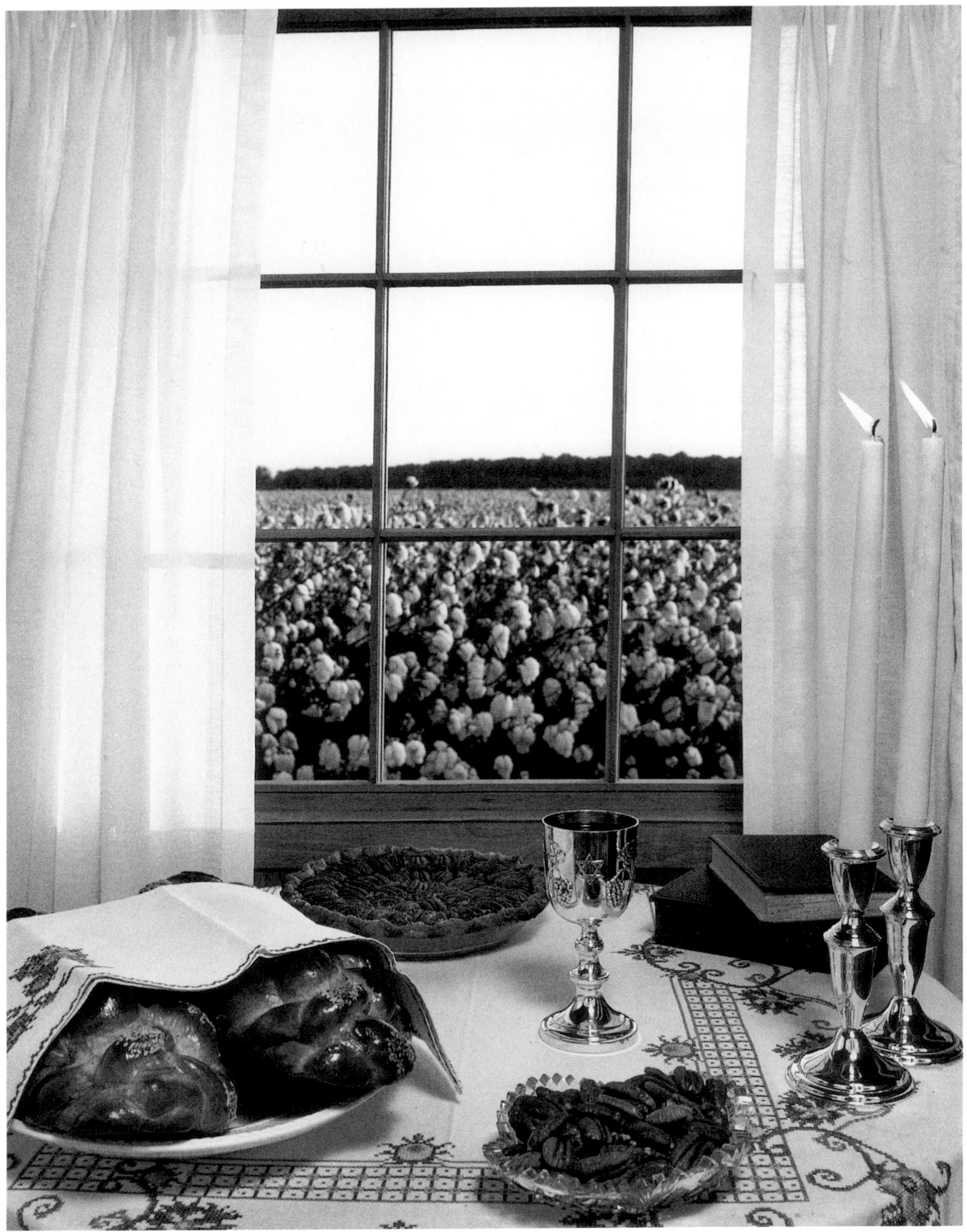

Shabbat Table, Cary, Mississippi. Photograph © Bill Aron. *The tradition of Shabbat when the family gathers at the table before Friday evening services is represented here in a uniquely southern setting—challah, silver kiddush cup and candlestick, prayer books, and pecan pie against a backdrop of cotton fields. Courtesy of the Museum of the Southern Jewish Experience, Jackson, Mississippi.*

for World War I and too old for World War II, the men left at home to carry the brunt of community work to buttress the war effort. He headed the Community Chest campaigns; he brought all the hostile political groups together to pass the bond issue for the new wings on the white and Negro hospitals; he twice headed the war bond campaign; and he even persuaded Judge Spears to serve as chairman of the United Jewish Appeal and raised $8,000 from the gentiles when other Jewish leaders in North Carolina were too timid to ask non-Jews for money.

* * *

My father was the only candidate that all the factions could agree on, but after the meeting the conservative members of the business group balked at endorsing anyone that the Negroes and labor trusted. They decided to run Judge James R. Patton against him, a canny corporation lawyer who had served as chairman of the Democratic Party in Durham until he was ousted by a new labor-Negro coalition several years before.

The newspapers announced the potential candidates, and some alarmed members of the Jewish community began calling my father to beg him not to run. They feared that if anything happened in the city, the whites would blame the Jews and that a divisive campaign might sink into an anti-Semitic slugfest that could cause racial unrest, threats to their business, and ugly incidents.

He decided to run anyway, on a platform of bringing the city together, but the "downtown crowd," of which he, ironically, was a leader, opposed him vigorously. As election day approached, *The Public Appeal*, a small local paper with a workingman's readership and run by vitriolic "Wimpy" Jones, published the fake Protocols of Zion, under a headline that suggested Durham was becoming part of a Jewish plot for world domination. When Joe Brady from New York, an old family friend whose father had been one of Buck Duke's cigarette rollers, sent a contribution, a whispering campaign started to the effect that Evans was the "puppet" of a group of wealthy New York Jews.

The Sunday before the election, two ministers from the largest Baptist churches preached sermons deploring the inclusion of racial and religious issues in the campaign, and said they personally intended to vote for Evans. The night before the election, Dad went on the radio and was introduced by Frank Hickman, the most popular professor in the Duke Divinity School, who said, "I want to introduce a friend of mine, a great humanitarian, and invite you to vote for him for mayor tomorrow." Dr. Hickman taught preaching to student ministers, and his voice reverberated with the righteousness of the hills of Judea.

Dad came on strong. "I ran to instill the same harmony in government affairs as we have had in civic affairs," he said to emphasize his chairmanship of two successful war bond campaigns. "If we are to attain unity in Durham, each individual must be judged on his merit alone, and we must stop arraying class against class, labor against management, race against race in a vicious cycle of resentment. If I am fortunate enough to go into office on May eighth, I will go as a representative of *all* the people, regardless of faith, creed, or position in life." Mom and I sat in the living room listening; she touched my arm as the band struck up "Marching along together, no one's gonna stop us now."

On election day, our black maid Zola voted early and Dad asked her at breakfast how things were going at the Hillside High precinct. She was so excited she could barely get it out. "Mister Evans, they's lined up from here to Jerusalem, and everybody's votin' for *you*."

We came back home in the late afternoon to sweat out the rest of the day with Gene Brooks, a crafty former state senator whose father had been one of the most progressive leaders in behalf of Negro education in the state. He was our family lawyer, political adviser, and campaign manager. Today, he had turned our living room into a command post with an extra phone to dramatize its new purpose, and both phones were jangling away.

"It's for you," he said, handing the phone to Dad.

Dad went pale listening and told the caller that he would talk to Gene and get right back to him. "He says there's a guy at the Fuller School precinct giving out razor blades to every voter and telling them to cut the Jew off the ticket."

Fuller School was a workingman's precinct where the struggling labor unions might sway a few poor white voters back from the reaction against any candidate with black support. Gene called Leslie Atkins, the controversial labor leader who had brought the Negroes into Democratic Party politics, put them in charge of their own precincts, and generally held the always frail Negro-labor coalition together. An hour later, Leslie called back.

"One of the boys took care of it," Gene said. And then with a puckish grin, he admitted, "They just slipped that fellow a bottle of liquor and he's finished for today—passed out."

The ballots were counted by hand, and at eleven o'clock Dad was far behind. Then the Hillside precinct came in: Evans 1,241 and Patton 64. Gene whooped, "I bet Jackie Robinson couldn't have done better." Then he added, "I wonder where those sixty-four votes came from. I'll have to get after somebody about that."

Pearson School, the other large Negro precinct, came rolling in at 833 to 29, and Dad was also doing well at the Duke University precincts where the "innylekchals," as Gene teasingly called them, were voting more heavily than usual.

When the radio announcer gave the final results in the mayor's race at 6,961 to 5,916, officially confirming the phoned reports from the precincts, Dad turned to my mother and kissed her. "I told you that it would all work out. How does it feel to be the first lady of Durham?"

Mother was heading for the kitchen to put some food on the table for the few friends who might drop by when suddenly the door burst open and a gang of people from the Jewish community came thundering through, straight from an election night party at Hannah Hockfield's. Fifty or sixty strong, buzzing with excitement, kissing me and messing my hair, they went roaring through the kitchen and out to the dining room, like a starving army of locusts, and just as suddenly, they were gone, the table in the dining room stripped totally bare.

The next morning when the phone rang at breakfast, Zola answered with a resounding, "Mayor Evans' resee-*dense*," and Mother blushed at Dad across the table. Nobody had instructed Zola in the new greeting, but nobody ever corrected her either.

George Burns

From *All My Best Friends*

Milton Berle, one of early television's greatest stars; the Marx Brothers beloved by the literati and glitterati as by the common folk; Al Jolson who left his father's cantorial pulpit for honky-tonk vaudeville and lucrative concert hall; Georgie Jessel who elevated the "tumler" to "Toastmaster General"—George Burns knew them all, loved them, and writes of them with warmth and high good humor in his All My Best Friends *(1989). Let the interlocutor depart; bring on the star.*

When Milton Berle was five years old he cut a piece of fur from his mother's hand-warmer, pasted it under his nose, picked up a cane then walked like a drunken sailor—and won a quarter and a loving cup for his imitation of Charlie Chaplin. This was a very famous moment in show business history: the first time Milton Berle did somebody else's act.

Milton was born to be in show business. That was his mother's plan. Milton's mother, Sarah Berlinger, was probably the most famous stage mother of all time. Almost before Milton could walk she had him modeling as the boy in the Buster Brown shoe ads. When he was six she took him to Fort Lee, New Jersey, to work at the Biograph Studios in the silent films. Milton was the little boy on top of the moving train with Pearl White in *The Perils of Pauline*. He worked with great stars like Marie

The Marx Brothers: Harpo, Chico, and Groucho. c. 1935. The Museum of Modern Art, New York.

Dressler, Mabel Normand, Ruth Roland and Douglas Fairbanks, Senior. Fairbanks "saved" Milton's life in several serials, something a lot of people never forgave him for. Then Milton went to Hollywood and worked with Chaplin in *Tillie's Punctured Romance* and Mary Pickford in *Little Lord Fauntleroy* and *Rebecca of Sunnybrook Farm.* He made about fifty films.

Milton's mother dedicated her life to his career. Once, when he was working in the Catskills, she broke up a baseball game to tell the other kids, "Milton has to be captain because it's his bat and ball, and besides, he's going to be a big Broadway star someday."...

Sarah Berle would hire people to sit in the audience and laugh at Milton's jokes. When Berle was working in Brooklyn one day, she paid a young comedian named Henny Youngman fifty cents to laugh at Berle. Youngman said that Berle was so good he would have done it for forty cents. Berle came onstage and said, "Good evening, ladies and gentlemen . . ."

"Oh no," Youngman said to the person sitting next to him, "he stole my opening."

* * *

Harpo and Groucho were good friends of mine, but I knew all five Marx Brothers. They were also born into show business. Their grandfather had been a German magician and ventriloquist who had toured Europe in a covered wagon for fifty years.

Their uncle, Al Shean, who started as a pants presser on my block, Rivington Street, was one of vaudeville's great comedians, Shean of "Gallagher and Shean." It was Minnie Marx, the boys' mother, who was determined that they would be in show business.

Chico was the oldest and he was a talented piano player. Harpo was born next and he could play two songs on the piano, "Love Me and the World Is Mine," and "Waltz Me Around Again, Willie." Chico and Harpo looked very much alike and whenever a piano-playing job came up Chico would go audition for it. If he got it, Harpo would show up for the job and play his two songs over and over, fast, slow, medium, fast and slow, while Chico was busy auditioning for the next job. By the time Harpo got fired, Chico already had another job lined up for him. Groucho started his career as a soprano in the Episcopal Church—he was the only Jewish kid in the whole choir—but was suspended for puncturing the organ bellows with the alto's hatpin. That shouldn't have surprised anyone, Groucho spent his whole life letting the hot air out of windbags. Groucho made his professional debut in North Beach, New Jersey, standing on a beer barrel to sing "Don't Break the News to Mother."

Minnie Marx put together a singing act called "Fun in Hi-Skule" starring Groucho, Harpo and Gummo Marx, and featuring a pretty girl she hired. Chico, meanwhile, was playing piano in honky-tonks and wrestling all challengers at one dollar a match. When he was fired for throwing a paying customer through the front window, he went to Waukegan, Illinois, to catch up with the rest of the family. While the Marx Brothers were singing in Waukegan, Minnie Marx offered the job of musical director of the act to a member of the local house orchestra. And if that young man's father had let him take the job, the world might never have heard of . . . Benny Kubelsky.

Okay, maybe the world never heard of Benny Kubelsky. But everyone had heard of . . . you'd better imagine a little drumroll here, this is a very dramatic part. . . Jack Benny! Jack's real name was Benny Kubelsky. He was also Ben K. Benny for a little while. I think he might have also been Brown of "Brown and Williams" just after Thomas J. Wooley, the great peg-legged dancer, had been Brown.

But can you imagine that, Minnie Marx wanting to hire Jack Benny as musical director of the Marx Brothers act? That would be like hiring Durante to be grammar coach.

The Marx Brothers really did start as a musical act. No kidding. Minnie wouldn't allow it. The best thing that could be said about their singing ability was that they always showed up on time. In Springfield, Ohio, for example, the tenor in an illustrated song bit didn't show up and Harpo volunteered to fill in for him. The theater manager accepted, and after hearing Harpo sing he fined him ten dollars.

Even the boys couldn't take their singing seriously, and sometimes when Minnie wasn't around they'd burlesque their own act. When she showed up unexpectedly in Cedar Rapids, Iowa, and caught them, she started screaming. She reminded them that the mortgage to their house was held by a tough landlord named Greenbaum, and if the act was canceled she wouldn't be able to pay Greenbaum and they'd lose their house. "Don't forget Greenbaum," she warned. And they never did. So from that time on, whenever their act started to get out of control, one of them would shout, "Don't forget Greenbaum!" And then things would really get out of control.

The real inspiration for their act, which I guess you can describe as indescribable, came from a wild mule in Nacogdoches, Texas. The Marx Brothers were onstage singing when somebody ran into the theater and announced that an angry mule was kicking a store apart. Given a choice between the Marx Brothers and a wild mule, the entire audience walked out. Groucho was furious, and when the audience came back inside he started insulting them. "Nacogdoches," he told them, "is full of roaches. " The audience thought Groucho's insults were almost as good as watching that mule kick the store apart.

* * *

Al Jolson's father also wanted him to go into the family business; he wanted him to be a cantor. Religion was very important to many of the immigrants, in a lot of cases they'd left Europe and Russia to escape religious persecution. Jack Benny's father, for example, was an Orthodox Jew. One Yom Kippur Jack embarrassed him by showing up in the middle of the service. Meyer Kubelsky picked up a prayer book, a siddur, and smacked Jack in the face with it. That night, Mr. Kubelsky, trying to apologize, walked into his son's room and told him, "You know, in our religion it's considered a great blessing to be hit by a siddur on Yom Kippur."

Jolson sang in his father's choir, but he used to sneak away to work in Baltimore burlesque houses like the Bijou and Kernan's, singing songs with lyrics like "I'll leave my happy home for you, for you're the nicest girl I ever knew . . ."

Jolie ended up running away from home to serve as a mascot for a regiment in the Spanish-American War. He must have done a pretty good job, we won the war. He never personally claimed credit for that though, and knowing Jolson, that was surprising. Jolson was a lot of things, none of them were "shy." He ran away from home three times and ended up living in the St. Mary's Home for Boys, the same place that Babe Ruth lived.

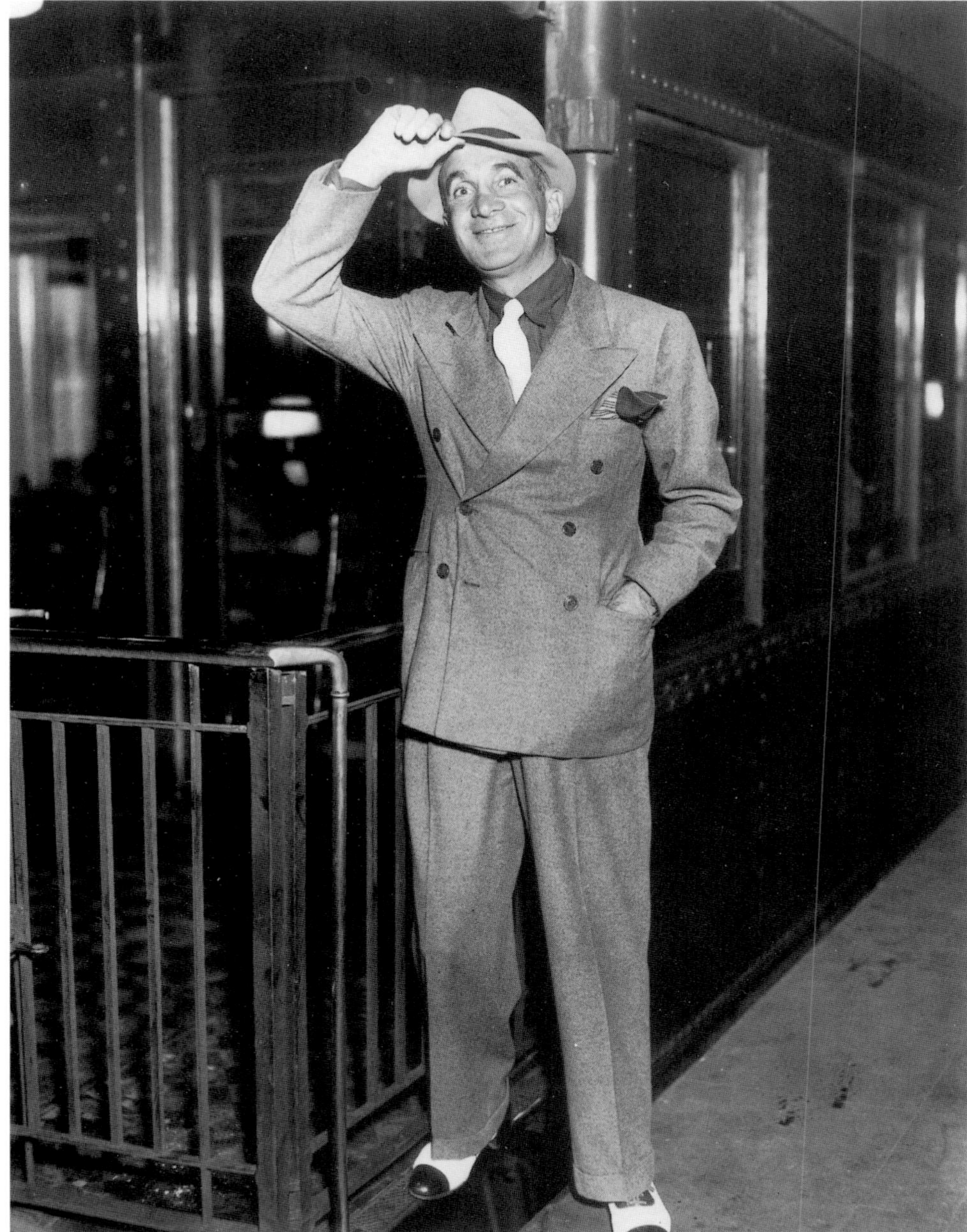

Al Jolson. 1927. The Museum of Modern Art, New York. *Son of a cantor, Jolson began his show business career in circuses, minstrel shows, and vaudeville and later became famous in the theater and films.*

Like the rest of us, Jolson had some tough times when he was starting out. He did whatever he had to do to eat. For example, whistling was very popular at that time and Joliè was a wonderful whistler, so after moving to New York he earned throw money by imitating the whistle of the Italian organ-grinders. For a while he worked in a circus sideshow as a ballyhoo man, bringing in the rubes by promising to show them wonders like The Incredible Lizard Man, The Amazing Tattooed Lady, The Unbelievable Headless Horse, Milton Berle doing his own material. . . Okay, I lied about the headless horse.

Jolson hung around outside the theaters like we all did, just waiting for a chance. He finally made his stage debut as a member of the mob in Zangwill's *Children of the Ghetto* at the Herald Square Theatre. I wasn't there, but I'll bet Jolson was the best mobster in theater history.

* * *

I finally did get to meet Jessel, and Cantor, and Jolson, and we became friends. When I started working with Gracie they were great to us; Georgie pushed us in vaudeville and Cantor gave us our first break on the radio. Jolson gave us tickets to his concert.

This was the beginning of the Roaring Twenties and it was an incredibly exciting time to be young and a vaudevillian in New York. Jessel would often invite me to tag along with him, and he always seemed to have somebody important with him. Maybe it would be "Gentleman Jimmy" Walker, the dapper Mayor of New York, or Pola Negri, with whom he was having a fling, or Irving Berlin or George M. Cohan. It was hard for me to believe I was there; just a few years earlier I'd been playing stooge to a seal, now I was having dinner with George M. Cohan. Jessel only gave me two words of advice: "Don't sing."

There was something great to do every night. Sometimes a group of us who stayed at the Forrest Hotel on 49th Street would get together and go to a show or to one of the hundreds of speakeasies in the city to see performers like Lou Clayton, who was then working with Ukulele Ike, or "Ragtime Jimmy" Durante, who was starting to make a name for himself.

A lot of nights we wouldn't go out at all; after the theaters had closed we'd meet in somebody's room and send out to the Gaiety Delicatessen for sandwiches and sodas while we played cards or charades all night long.

Sam Levenson

From *In One Era and Out the Other*

A Brief Career in Music

In the decades following World War II, humorist Sam Levenson entertained his public with an affectionate vision of American Jewish life and values. He did so through sharp, often hilarious, yet tender vignettes of the lives of ordinary people. Consider this account of a mother's dreams and hopes for her son's brilliant success, thwarted by the annoying reality—talent not commensurate with aspiration.

Sam Levenson. Mid 1950s.
Movie Star News.

It was on my fifth birthday that Papa put a hand on my shoulder and said, "Remember, my son, if you ever need a helping hand, you'll find one at the end of your arm." So I took my arm by the hand and off we went to seek my fortune. Show business was the last place in the world I expected to find it.

I almost made it as a child star, but it was not yet to be. My debut was in a kindergarten play at Public School 86, Manhattan. It was on the eve of Chanukah that I brought home the glad tidings. "Ma, tomorrow I'm gonna be the last 's' in Merry Christmas."

"Oy," Mama groaned gratefully.

I got one curtain call, but didn't get another until about twenty-five years later.

In the meantime Mama and I dreamed of my becoming a great violinist—a dream we shared every night. We saw me stage center, in Carnegie Hall, delivering a brilliant performance of a simplified Minuet in G to the cheering and swooning of thirty-five hundred Mama Levensons, one in each seat, and hundreds more on borrowed kitchen chairs all around me on the stage.

My brothers (who never even dreamed of being mothers) found me somewhat less inspiring. "Sammy has such a wonderful memory. He makes the same mistakes over and over again."

They compared me with Heifetz. "A Heifetz he ain't!"

The family next door had a dog who sang along with me. "Do us a favor, Sammy. Play something he doesn't know."

They appointed me "company violinist." If there was company that stayed on too long they turned to me: "Sammy, play the violin."

As in all my careers (I think I'm now in my fourth), I was a late bloomer in music. In junior high school I got to be concertmaster of the orchestra and fiddled well enough to earn spending money with my own dance band, Sam's Snazzy Syncopators. We were "Available for All Occasions," but hired only for a few. Good Old Max, our political leader, engaged us for rallies. We always marched on just ahead of him, blaring out "Mother Machree," "Mamma Mia" or "My Yiddisheh Mama," depending on the neighborhood. He paid very little, but he hinted a lot about getting me into West Point.

The day our synagogue acquired a new Torah, it was paraded through the streets not with the biblical zithers, harps, pipes, flutes, horns, castanets and cymbals, but with Sammy on the solo violin. This time I worked for free. You can't charge God. (Professional courtesy.) Besides, only God could ever get me into West Point.

Perhaps it was in payment for previous services rendered gratis, but a short while later an act of God did occur—a professional booking in St. Gregory's Roman Catholic Church. Neither my parents nor I had ever been inside a church. For me to be invited there was implausible, but to get paid ten dollars for being there was incredible.

Ruth Byrne, my history teacher, hired me to play the Bach-Gounod "Ave Maria" at her wedding. It was an overwhelming experience. I cried throughout the performance, partly because of Bach, Gounod, and St. Gregory, but mostly from inhaling incense. By the second chorus I was ready for my last rites. When I finally made it home, Mama asked only whether the church was bigger than Carnegie Hall; Papa asked whether the priest had worn his skullcap, and my brothers asked if I had noticed any small miracles, like maybe I had played in tune.

Thanks to my band I got to spend a whole summer in the country at a small resort hotel. I must have possessed the quality that soothes the breast of savage beasts. This time it was not a dog but the owner's horse that got carried away by my playing. When I practiced he would stick his head through the broken window of my ground-floor room and neigh along with Sam. When I proudly reported this to the boss he said, "It's not you; that's his room in the winter."

By the time I got out of high school the Depression had set in (I never noticed the change), and unemployed symphony men were underbidding me for jobs. I gave up the dream of ever making it to Carnegie Hall "live" and took the next dream, to college and schoolteaching.

Emmanuel Winters

From "God's Agents Have Beards"

The young hero of Emmanuel Winters's, gentle and humorous "growing up" story written in 1963 wants to meet God. He needs God's help in his endeavors to skip the sixth grade, so he plays his games with the Almighty. The enterprise blessed with success, the young philosopher makes his peace with his Maker. A warm tale of familial love, is it also a critical comment on the nature of the relationship to God, in a nation so certain of His existence? The author, a graduate of Cornell and its law school, has also served as first violinist in symphony orchestras.

One hot June night, after having simultaneously eaten two hundred and fifty peanuts and read two hundred and fifty pages of *The Three Musketeers* by Dumas—which is at the average rate of one peanut a page—I slammed the book shut, stood up to face my father, and announced:

"I want to meet God."

Every beautiful, dark-haired, book-loving member of my amazing family, gathered as usual around the dining-room table, stopped reading. Everyone, that is, except my father, who instead of reading had been composing music. For over two hours, the only sounds in the room had been the turning of pages, the cracking of brittle peanut shells in the learned, book-salted mouths of my impassioned family, and the scratching of my father's goose quill on the stiff white music paper before him on the dining-room table. Now everyone stared at me in horror, and there was a ghastly stillness that was broken finally, as expected, by waves of hacking laughter from my tubercular uncle, Amos.

"The boy has gone crazy all of a sudden," he said, simultaneously laughing, gasping, coughing, retching, and finally breaking into tears.

"Amos," my father said, "close your mouth to senseless laughter. Boys who express interest in God should not be laughed at unless, of course, they express immoderate interest in God." Then he turned to me. "What are you reading?" he asked gently. My father was the gentlest man alive. Sweetness, kindness and goodness dripped all over him like the warm wax on a great luminous candle.

"*The Three Musketeers* by Alexandre Dumas," I said. "A very exciting if poorly written book."

My father shook his head. "Very interesting," he said. "Extremely interesting."

Uncle Amos let some more laughter, coughing, and mockery escape from his bitter lungs again. "The boy is *meshugeh*-mad," he insisted. "Here he is quietly reading *The Three Musketeers* by Alexandre Dumas, as generations of us have done each in our turn, and all of a sudden he stands up and says he wants to meet God—and at the same time, he gives a book review! Did you ever heard of such a thing before in your whole history of book reading? May I cackle like a jackal full of moldy *potato-kugel* if I ever did!" . . .

"Oh, be quiet," my father said. "This emergency calls for some important concentration. Let me think."

Everyone obeyed my father. We were all as quiet as the corpse at a funeral. Nobody cracked peanuts, nobody read, nobody even dared breathe. Except me. I dared do everything with my father . . .

Finally, my father said: "Well, little children, I have decided. The boy's interest in God is not immoderate."

He got up and put on his hat. "Come outside with me," he said, beckoning.

We went out of doors into the warm brilliance of the June evening, and began to walk in utter silence.

After we had walked around the block twice without saying a word, my father said: "Now tell me all over again so I'll be sure."

"Pa," I said, "I want to meet God."

We walked around the block once more.

"How do you mean you want to *meet* God? You mean you want proof there is a God?"

"Excuse me, Pa," I said. "I don't go for second-hand things. I'm a philosopher. I want to meet God personally, face to face."

My father looked amazed. He was wonderful. He didn't say a word. Of course, I knew he wouldn't take me by the left ear and twist my head around. But sometimes, if you did something wrong, or, what was worse, something foolish, he would laugh at you in a gentle kind way. This time, my father did not even laugh in a gentle way.

We took another walk around the block, then we sat down under a huge elm on the soft sweet grass of June, far away from the lights.

"Do you see the stars up there?" my father asked.

"Yes, Pa," I said. "I see them."

"There's millions," my father said.

"I know it," I said.

"They move exactly on schedule," he said. "They never change."

"Like a clock," I said. This was an old routine.

"Suppose," my father went on, "there was no traffic system to keep the cars downtown moving right. They'd bump into each other all the time."

"Yes," I said.

"Well, there's a traffic system that keeps the stars moving the same way. It's God."

I thought for a while.

"Maybe," I said, "they don't bump into each other because they are so far apart. Maybe once upon a time there used to be more of them, closer together. So they destroyed each other, and what's left has all the room it needs. That's why, maybe, they don't bump now."

My father pulled up some grass by the roots and meditated. I did the same . . . .

My father took me by the hand and we got up from the soft green grass and began to walk home. Before we reached the house, my father said:

"I'm going to tell you something. But I don't want you to breathe it to a soul, especially not to Uncle Amos." My father wasn't afraid of Uncle Amos. He just didn't like to keep telling him he was wrong all the time.

"Sure, Pa," I said. "I can keep a secret just as good as the next fellow."

"Then," my father said, lowering his voice to a whisper, "if you really want to see God face to face, you can."

"I can?"

"Yes, you can, if you keep asking God long enough, and God is sure you really mean it."

"You're not kidding me just because I'm only ten years old, are you, Pa?" I said.

"No," my father said. "I never kid anyone—unless it's your mother once in a while."

We started to climb the stairs. "There's something else you should know if you're going to meet God," my father whispered. "Sometimes, God's too busy seeing somebody else; then he sends his personal representative. Will that be OK?"

I thought a while.

"Sure, Pa," I said. "I guess that will be OK—so long as I know it *is* his representative."

"You'll know when the time comes," my father said. "But remember, not a word of this to anyone."

"Not a word, Pa," I said.

The next morning at nine o'clock I went down to Union Street School and signed up for summer school. You attended summer school for six weeks, and if you passed, you skipped a whole grade. That meant a whole year saved.

I was the most ambitious kid in town, and I knew that I knew more than anybody else, but I was scared stiff of flunking. That's why I usually came out first in my class. I was so scared of not passing that I worked hard enough to be considered the most brilliant and promising boy in the history of the school system. But being the most promising and brilliant boy in the school system still didn't stop me from being scared to death.

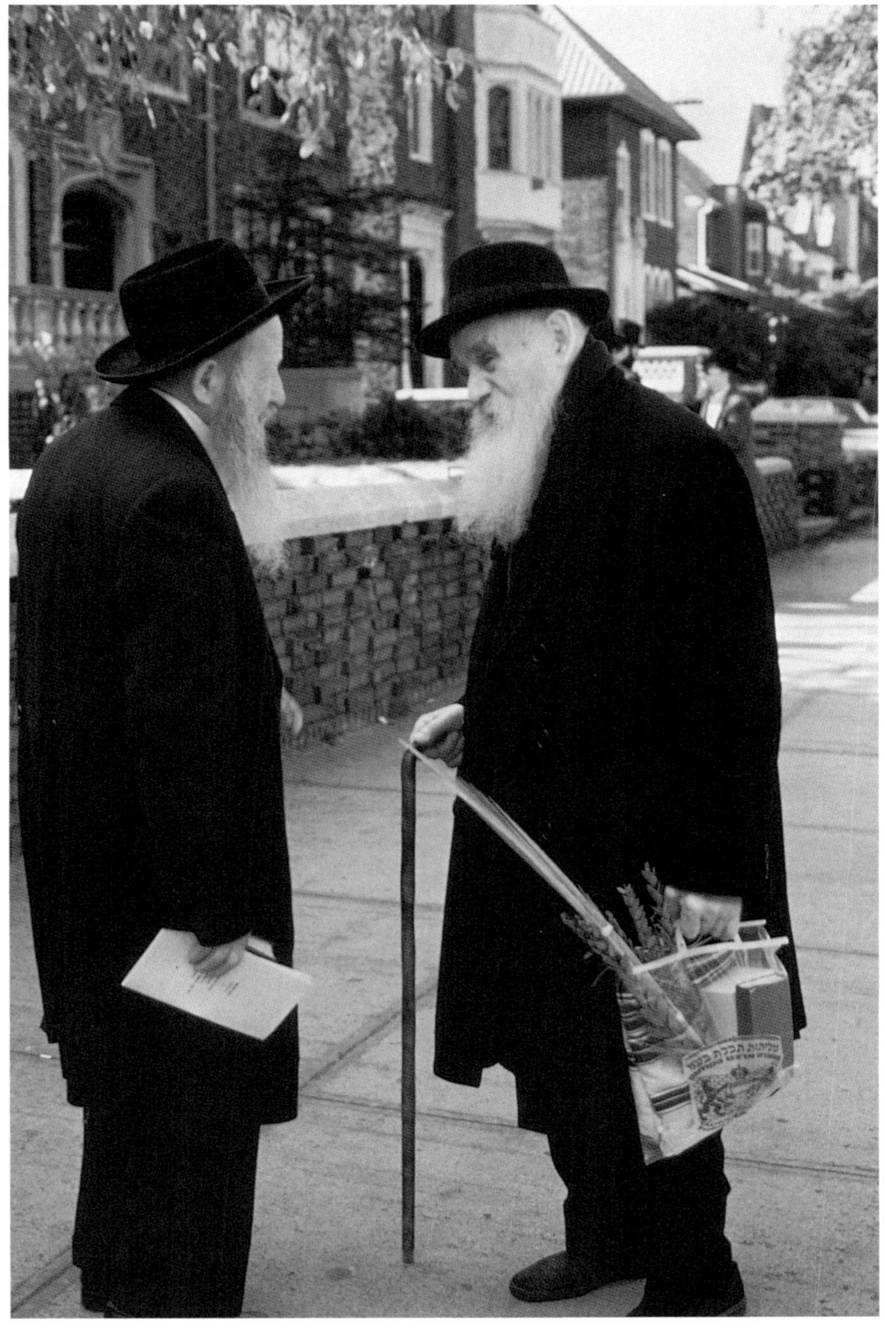

Eve Arnold. *Two Hasidic Men, Brooklyn, New York.* 1980s. Photograph. Magnum Photos.

Each day on my way to school, I prayed to God to let me pass. "Dear God," I said, "just think of the disgrace to my whole book-reading family if I don't pass the sixth grade in six weeks. My mother will say, 'Oh, it was too hard for him,' but you and I know it isn't too hard. Uncle Amos will laugh his head off and that isn't too good for his consumption because every time he laughs the blood comes out. So, for the sake of my poor book-devouring family, let me pass to my just reward, the seventh grade, O God!" I said it over and over. That was just one prayer.

I had a second. "O God," I said, "don't let me waste my valuable time praying to you if you aren't real. Let me see you face to face like the old prophets in the Bible. Just one look, O God!"

I kept repeating this every day. I knew them so well that I was even able to say them under my breath during class . . .

At length I took the final examination and was told to report the following morning to find out if I'd passed or not.

That morning, I started out for school earlier than usual. I wanted to give myself and God a good last chance. I crossed the South Street bridge, praying hard all the way. As I turned on Washington Street and headed for school, I said: "O God, in just three minutes I'm going to turn the corner at Union where the traffic light is broken, and walk into school. You've got just three minutes, O God, to save me and my family from a terrible everlasting disgrace. Incidently, O God," I said, "those three minutes are important to you, too, because if you don't show yourself to me, then I'll have to stop believing in you, and that means I'll have to stop believing in my father, too, because he said I would see you if I prayed hard and long enough. So, please God, let me see you now—this minute!"

I stopped walking—scared stiff. If I didn't see God, I knew I had flunked. If I saw God—what would I do or say? After all, I had never met God before; he was a perfect stranger to me. But there wasn't a soul on the street, not even a sparrow.

I started walking again, very slowly. Ahead of me was the corner of Washington and Union. Once I turned that, it was all over.

"O God," I said, "maybe I've been asking too much. Maybe you're too busy, like my father said. If you are, O God, why not send your representative? Any old representative will do."

I came to the corner.

"O God," I said. "I'm going to turn the corner now. Send a representative. Let him be right around the corner. Let him have a long black beard. Please, God, please!"

I took a deep breath, clenched my fists, and turned the corner.

There *was* a man there. He *did* have a long black beard.

I didn't know what to do. I just stared wildly at him. When he saw how excited I was, he smiled at me, and asked me in Jewish:

"What time is it, son?"

I knew it was just nine o'clock because the school bell was ringing.

"It's nine o'clock, O mighty sir," I replied in my best chosen Jewish. Of course, I knew he was checking up on the time so he could tell God what time he had done his job.

He stroked his long black beard, hoisted to his shoulder a huge pack that looked as though it contained carpets, and walked away. I didn't know what to do, so I simply bowed from the waist and watched him until he turned the corner. Then I went inside.

Sure enough, I had passed the sixth grade. I was number one in my class. Miss Regan smiled for the first time in six weeks, and said that I was the most brilliant and promising boy in the school system. She said I would have a happy future, but that I must be careful of trains.

That night at home I joined my amazing book-devouring family. In the center of the dining-room table was a fresh, five-pound sack of peanuts. In front of each member of the family was a plate for shells. From the shelf I took down *The Three Musketeers* and opened it to page 251.

On the way to my place at the table I stopped and whispered to my father as he scratched musical notes with his goose quill on a shiny sheet of paper.

"I passed, Pa," I said.

My father nodded his head sweetly.

"I expected you would," he said.

I paused for a while, and my father waited patiently.

"I also saw His personal representative today," I said. "He had a long black beard and asked me what time it was."

My father nodded again.

"I expected you would," he said, pulling at his short goatee.

"You two, there, what are you gloating about?" Uncle Amos cried from his couch in the corner. He alone was not reading; he had already read every book in the world in three or four different languages. "If it's something we should know, tell us and

COLORPLATE 123

MARK ROTHKO. *Street Scene XX*. c. 1936–1939. Oil on canvas. 29 x 40 in. National Gallery of Art, Washington, D.C. Gift of the Mark Rothko Foundation. © Kate Rothko-Prizel and Christopher Rothko/Artists Rights Society, New York.

COLORPLATE 124

MORRIS SHULMAN. *Tompkins Square Park.* 1938. Oil on canvas. 26 x 30 in.
The Jewish Museum, New York. Gift of Mrs. Sarah Shulman.

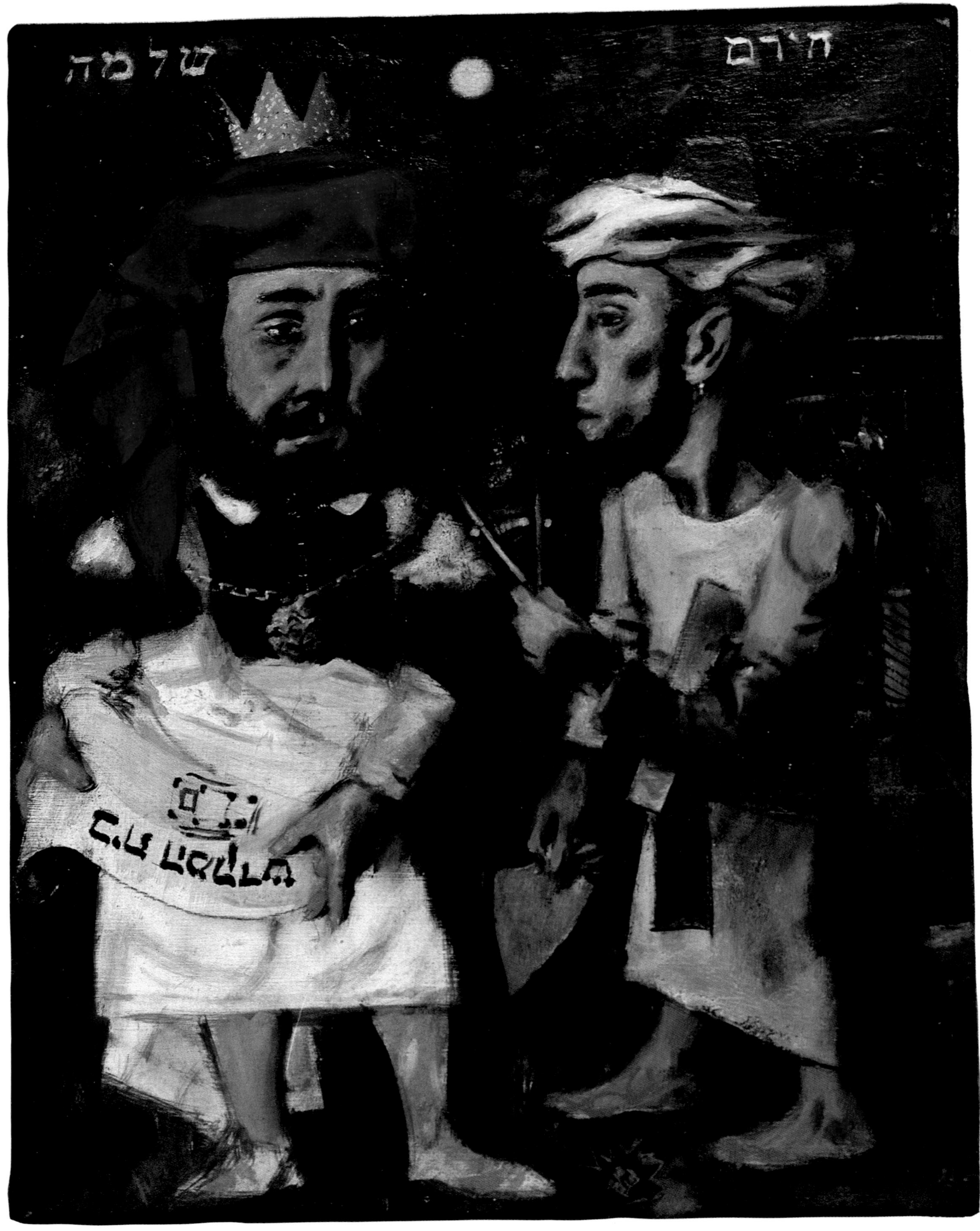

COLORPLATE 125

JACK LEVINE. *Planning Solomon's Temple.* c. 1940. Oil on masonite. 10 1/16 x 7 15/16 in. Israel Museum, Jerusalem. Gift of Rebecca Shulman, New York, 1955. © Jack Levine / VAGA, New York, 1994. *Jack Levine, who at one time was a W.P.A. artist, is known for his expressionistic canvasses, with their themes of social criticism. In this painting, Levine turns to the biblical subject of King Solomon's building of the First Temple.*

COLORPLATE 126 *(above)*

William Gropper. *The Tailor.* 1940. Oil on canvas. 20 1/4 x 26 1/4 in. Hirshhorn Museum and Sculpture Garden, Smithsonian Institution, Washington, D.C. Gift of Joseph H. Hirshhorn, 1966.

COLORPLATE 127

Max Weber. *Rabbi.* 1940. Oil on canvas. 20 1/8 x 16 1/4 in. The Phillips Collection, Washington, D.C.

COLORPLATE 128

HYMAN BLOOM. *The Synagogue*. c. 1940. Oil on canvas. 65 1/4 x 46 3/4 in. The Museum of Modern Art. Acquired through the Lillie P. Bliss Bequest. © 1994 The Museum of Modern Art, New York.

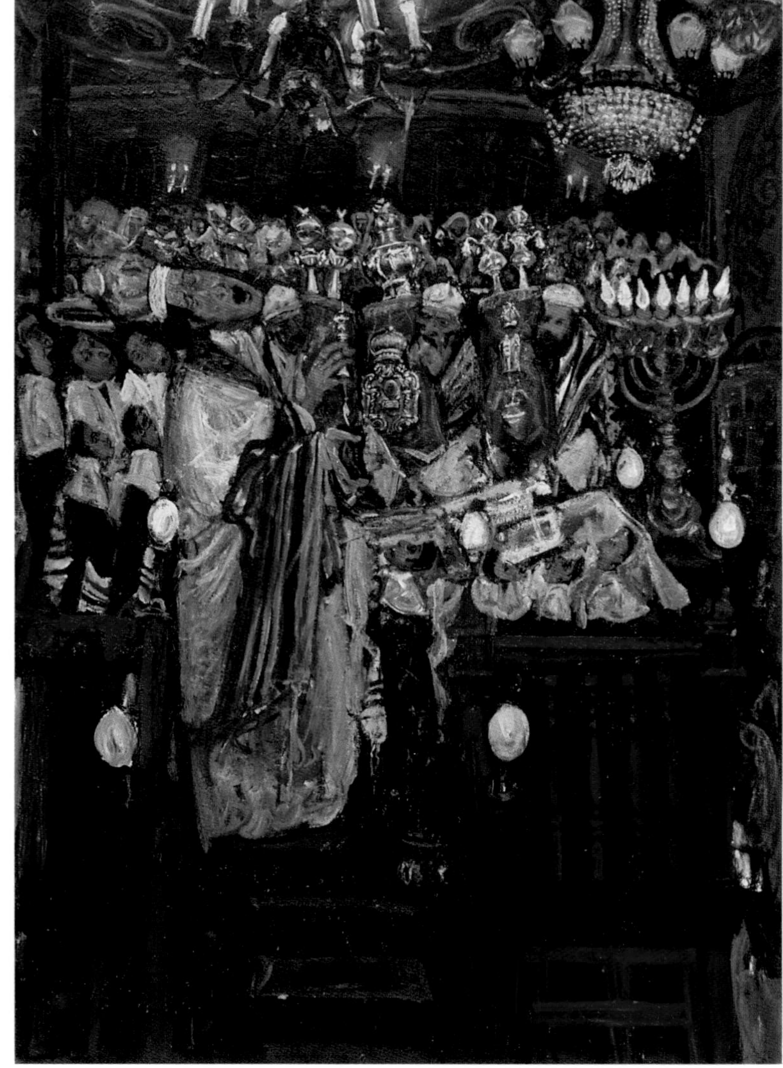

COLORPLATE 129 *(below)*

MORRIS HIRSCHFIELD. *Moses and Aaron*. 1944. Oil on canvas. 28 x 40 in. Courtesy of the Sidney Janis Gallery, New York. © Estate of Morris Hirschfield / VAGA, New York, 1994.

COLORPLATE 130

MEICHEL PRESSMAN. *The Seder.* 1950. Watercolor on paper. 22 x 19 in. The Jewish Museum, New York. Gift of Henry Pressman. *The Hebrew phrase reads "Next year in Jerusalem."*

COLORPLATE 131 *(above)*

GRACE HARTIGAN. *Grand Street Brides.* 1954. Oil on canvas. 72 x 102 1/2 in. The Whitney Museum of American Art, New York. Gift of an anonymous donor.

COLORPLATE 132

LEO SCHUTZMAN. *The Wedding.* c. 1960. Oil on canvas. 30 x 24 in. The Jewish Museum, New York. Gift of Betty Comden Kyle.

COLORPLATE 133

ILYA SCHOR. *The Crown.* 1950. Watercolor. 8 x 6 1/2 in. Courtesy of Stanley Batkin.

stop gloating secretly like two kittens with a bellyful of well-spiced gefilte fish," he said.

My father smiled at me and I smiled to him. "It's nothing, Amos," he said gently. "The boy tells me he has passed the sixth grade in six weeks, that's all."

"Well, why shouldn't he pass?" Uncle Amos grumbled. "Haven't generations of us passed the sixth grade—like maggots through the small eyes of a sieve?"

I waited for the family's applause to die down. Then I went to my place at the table and began to read and eat peanuts.

It was still an exciting if poorly written book. But I felt somewhat superior to Alexandre Dumas. He, to, had undoubtedly passed the sixth grade, but had God's personal representative with a long black beard smiled at *him?*

Grace Paley

"The Loudest Voice"

Grace Paley, a noted writer of short stories, taught at Sarah Lawrence College and Columbia University. In "The Loudest Voice" (1959), Miss Paley's gifts as a writer are apparent. Her characters come alive in this gently humorous story of Jewish children in the school Christmas play.

There is a certain place where dumb-waiters boom, doors slam, dishes crash; every window is a mother's mouth bidding the street shut up, go skate somewhere else, come home. My voice is the loudest.

There, my own mother is still as full of breathing as me and the grocer stands up to speak to her. "Mrs. Abramowitz," he says, "people should not be afraid of their children."

"Ah, Mr. Bialik," my mother replies, "if you say to her or her father 'Ssh,' they say 'In the grave it will be quiet.' "

"From Coney Island to the cemetery," says my papa. "It's the same subway; it's the same fare."

I am right next to the pickle barrel. My pinky is making tiny whirlpools in the brine. I stop a moment to announce: "Campbell's Tomato Soup. Campbell's Vegetable Beef Soup. Campbell's S-c-otch Broth . . ."

"Be quiet," the grocer says, "the labels are coming off."

"Please, Shirley, be a little quiet," my mother begs me.

In that place the whole street groans: Be quiet! Be quiet! but steals from the happy chorus of my inside self not a tittle or a jot.

There, too, but just around the corner, is a red brick building that has been old for many years. Every morning the children stand before it in double lines which must be straight. They are not insulted. They are waiting anyway.

I am usually among them. I am, in fact, the first, since I begin with an "A."

One cold morning the monitor tapped me on the shoulder. "Go to Room 409, Shirley Abramowitz," he said. I did as I was told. I went in a hurry up a down stair-

ARTHUR ROTHSTEIN. *Bathgate Avenue, Bronx, New York.* 1936. Photograph. The Library of Congress.

case to Room 409, which contained sixth-graders. I had to wait at the desk without wiggling until Mr. Hilton, their teacher, had time to speak.

After five minutes he said, "Shirley?"

"What?" I whispered.

He said, "My! My! Shirley Abramowitz! They told me you had a particularly loud, clear voice and read with lots of expression. Could that be true?"

"Oh yes," I whispered.

"In that case, don't be silly; I might very well be your teacher some day. Speak up, speak up."

"Yes," I shouted.

"More like it," he said. "Now, Shirley, can you put a ribbon in your hair or a bobby pin? It's too messy."

"Yes!" I bawled.

"Now, now, calm down." He turned to the class. "Children, not a sound. Open at page 39. Read till 52. When you finish, start again." He looked me over once more. "Now, Shirley, you know, I suppose, that Christmas is coming. We are preparing a beautiful play. Most of the parts have been given out. But I still need a child with a strong voice, lots of stamina. Do you know what stamina is? You do? Smart kid. You know, I heard you read 'The Lord is my shepherd' in Assembly yesterday. I was very impressed. Wonderful delivery. Mrs. Jordan, your teacher, speaks highly of you. Now listen to me, Shirley Abramowitz, if you want to take the part and be in the play, repeat after me, 'I swear to work harder than I ever did before.'"

I looked to heaven and said at once, "Oh, I swear." I kissed my pinky and looked at God.

"That is an actor's life, my dear," he explained. "Like a soldier's, never tardy or disobedient to his general, the director. Everything," he said, "absolutely everything will depend on you."

That afternoon, all over the building, children scraped and scrubbed the turkeys and the sheaves of corn off the schoolroom windows. Goodbye Thanksgiving. The next morning a monitor brought red paper and green paper from the office. He made new shapes and hung them on the walls and glued them to the doors.

The teachers became happier and happier. Their heads were ringing like the bells of childhood. My best friend Evie was prone to evil, but she did not get a single demerit for whispering. We learned "Holy Night" without an error. "How wonderful!" said Miss Glacé, the student teacher. "To think that some of you don't even speak the language!" We learned "Deck the Halls" and "Hark! The Herald Angels" . . . . They weren't ashamed and we weren't embarrassed.

Oh, but when my mother heard about it all, she said to my father: "Misha, you don't know what's going on there. Cramer is the head of the Tickets Committee."

"Who?" asked my father. "Cramer? Oh yes, an active woman."

"Active? Active has to have a reason. Listen," she said sadly. "I'm surprised to see my neighbors making tra-la-la for Christmas."

My father couldn't think of what to say to that. Then he decided: "You're in America! Clara, you wanted to come here. In Palestine the Arabs would be eating you alive. Europe you had pogroms. Argentina is full of Indians. Here you got Christmas . . . Some joke, ha?"

"Very funny, Misha. What is becoming of you? If we came to a new country a long time ago to run away from tyrants, and instead we fall into a creeping pogrom, that our children learn a lot of lies, so what's the joke? Ach, Misha, your idealism is going away."

"So is your sense of humor."

"That I never had, but idealism you had a lot of."

"I'm the same Misha Abramowitz. I didn't change an iota. Ask anyone."

"Only ask me," says my mama, may she rest in peace. "I got the answer."

Meanwhile the neighbors had to think of what to say too.

Marty's father said: "You know, he has a very important part, my boy."

"Mine also," said Mr. Sauerfeld.

"Not my boy!" said Mrs. Klieg. "I said to him no. The answer is no. When I say no, I mean no!"

The rabbi's wife said, "It's disgusting!" But no one listened to her. Under the narrow sky of God's great wisdom she wore a strawberry-blond wig.

Every day was noisy and full of experience. I was Right-Hand Man. Mr. Hilton said: "How could I get along without you, Shirley?"

He said: "Your mother and father ought to get down on their knees every night and thank God for giving them a child like you."

He also said: "You're absolutely a pleasure to work with, my dear, dear child."

Sometimes he said: "For God's sake, what did I do with the script? Shirley! Shirley! Find it."

Then I answered quietly: "Here it is, Mr. Hilton."

Once in a while, when he was very tired, he would cry out: "Shirley, I'm just tired of screaming at those kids. Will you tell Ira Pushkov not to come in till Lester points to that star the second time?"

Then I roared: "Ira Pushkov, what's the matter with you? Dope! Mr. Hilton told you five times already, don't come in till Lester points to that star the second time."

The Max Levine College, Grand Concourse and Fordham Road. Bronx, New York. c. 1949. The Bronx County Historical Society, Bronx, New York. *This section of the Bronx was the center of the uptown Bronx Jewish neighborhood.*

"Ach, Clara," my father asked, "what does she do there till six o'clock she can't even put the plates on the table?"

"Christmas," said my mother coldly.

"Ho! Ho!" my father said. "Christmas. What's the harm? After all, history teaches everyone. We learn from reading this is a holiday from pagan times also, candles, lights, even Chanukah. So we learn it's not altogether Christian. So if they think it's a private holiday, they're only ignorant, not patriotic. What belongs to history, belongs to all men. You want to go back to the Middle Ages? Is it better to shave your head with a secondhand razor? Does it hurt Shirley to learn to speak up? It does not. So maybe someday she won't live between the kitchen and the shop. She's not a fool."

I thank you, Papa, for your kindness. It is true about me to this day. I am foolish but I am not a fool.

That night my father kissed me and said with great interest in my career, "Shirley, tomorrow's your big day. Congrats."

"Save it," my mother said. Then she shut all the windows in order to prevent tonsillitis.

In the morning it snowed. On the street corner a tree had been decorated for us by a kind city administration. In order to miss its chilly shadow our neighbors walked three blocks east to buy a loaf of bread. The butcher pulled down black window shades to keep the colored lights from shining on his chickens. Oh, not me. On the way to school, with both my hands I tossed it a kiss of tolerance. Poor thing, it was a stranger in Egypt.

I walked straight into the auditorium past the staring children. "Go ahead,

Shirley!" said the monitors. Four boys, big for their age, had already started work as propmen and stagehands.

Mr. Hilton was very nervous. He was not even happy. Whatever he started to say ended in a sideward look of sadness. He sat slumped in the middle of the first row and asked me to help Miss Glacé. I did this, although she thought my voice too resonant and said, "Show-off!"

Parents began to arrive long before we were ready. They wanted to make a good impression. From among the yards of drapes I peeked out at the audience. I saw my embarrassed mother.

Ira, Lester, and Meyer were pasted to their beards by Miss Glacé. She almost forgot to thread the star on its wire, but I reminded her. I coughed a few times to clear my throat. Miss Glacé looked around and saw that everyone was in costume and on line waiting to play his part. She whispered, "All right . . ." Then:

Jackie Sauerfeld, the prettiest boy in the first grade, parted the curtains with his skinny elbow and in a high voice sang out:

"Parents dear
We are here
To make a Christmas play in time.
It we give
In narrative
And illustrate with pantomime."

He disappeared.

My voice burst immediately from the wings to the great shock of Ira, Lester, and Meyer, who were waiting for it but were surprised all the same.

"I remember, I remember, the house where I was born . . ."

Miss Glacé yanked the curtain open and there it was, the house—an old hayloft, where Celia Kornbluh lay in the straw with Cindy Lou, her favorite doll. Ira, Lester, and Meyer moved slowly from the wings toward her, sometimes pointing to a moving star and sometimes ahead to Cindy Lou.

It was a long story and it was a sad story. I carefully pronounced all the words about my lonesome childhood, while little Eddie Braunstein wandered upstage and down with his shepherd's stick, looking for sheep. I brought up lonesomeness again, and not being understood at all except by some women everybody hated. Eddie was too small for that and Marty Groff took his place, wearing his father's prayer shawl. I announced twelve friends, and half the boys in the fourth grade gathered around Marty, who stood on an orange crate while my voice harangued. Sorrowful and loud, I declaimed about love and God and Man, but because of the terrible deceit of Abie Stock we came suddenly to a famous moment. Marty, whose remembering tongue I was, waited at the foot of the cross. He stared desperately at the audience. I groaned, "My God, my God, why hast thou forsaken me?" The soldiers who were sheiks grabbed poor Marty to pin him up to die, but he wrenched free, turned again to the audience, and spread his arms aloft to show despair and the end. I murmured at the top of my voice, "The rest is silence, but as everyone in this room, in this city—in this world—now knows, I have life eternal."

That night Mrs. Kornbluh visited our kitchen for a glass of tea.

"How's the virgin?" asked my father with a look of concern.

"For a man with a daughter, you got a fresh mouth, Abramovitch."

"Here," said my father kindly, "have some lemon, it'll sweeten your disposition."

They debated a little in Yiddish, then fell in a puddle of Russian and Polish. What I understood next was my father, who said, "Still and all, it was certainly a beautiful affair, you have to admit, introducing us to the beliefs of a different culture."

"Well, yes," said Mrs. Kornbluh. "The only thing . . . you know Charlie Turner—that cute boy in Celia's class—a couple others? They got very small parts or no part at all. In very bad taste, it seemed to me. After all it's their religion."

"Ach," explained my mother, "what could Mr. Hilton do? They got very small voices; after all, why should they holler? The English language they know from the beginning by heart. They're blond like angels. You think it's so important they should get in the play? Christmas . . . the whole piece of goods . . . they own it."

I listened and I listened until I couldn't listen any more. Too sleepy, I climbed out of bed and kneeled. I made a little church of my hands and said,
"Hear, O Israel . . ." Then I called out in Yiddish, "Please, good night, good night. Ssh."

My father said, "Ssh yourself," and slammed the kitchen door.

I was happy. I fell asleep at once. I had prayed for everybody: my talking family, cousins far away, passers-by, and all the lonesome Christians. I expected to be heard. My voice was certainly the loudest.

Susan Merson

From *Reflections of a China Doll*

"Chicken Noodle Night Flights"

Laurel Rixton Montague, as described by Susan Merson in her solo autobiographical play Reflections of a China Doll *(1978), is a lovely, gifted, generous friend—from a totally different home environment. Her Jewish girl friend, whose mother sings Yiddish lullabies to her, is warmly welcomed into Laurel's home for a sleepover. Everything is quiet and lovely, but she feels so alone and lonely that before the night is over, she begs to return home.*

I remember being a little girl at the top of the stairs in somebody else's house on Grandmont Street in Detroit. A dark-haired, pajama-ed visitor sitting perched and listening/glistening for a sound to soothe her and make her feel familiar in this alien atmosphere. This was Laurel's house. I often played and sometimes slept over here because Laurel was my very best friend.

We would do wonderful things together. She, the blondie Spam-eating, sensible Singer sewing machine addict of age seven and me, the pudged prisoner of chicken soup and egg challah.

Laurel could do everything that the Louisa May Alcott heroines could do. She made all her own clothes, she played the piano like Amy in *Little Women*, she sang in the church choir. I remember going with her one Sunday to Sunday school and writing Hebrew words on the blackboard for her class.

Laurel would make Christmas cookies even in the heat of July. Santa Clauses or green Christmas trees. And we would eat them while drinking pink lemonade in her perfect kitchen, smiled on by her Donna Reed-like mother, her cat named Spook, her dog named Mitzi, her bird named Hi Fi, and her garden with perfect marigolds. Laurel was my romantic dreamed child. She was everything that I wasn't and I adored her for it.

It was never quite right seeing Laurel munch bagels and overstuffed tuna sandwiches. Somehow, she was made for one slice of presliced ham on thin white bread with French's mustard and a glass of mustache-making milk. I hated milk, white bread, ham, and mustard and though I adored Laurel, I could never feel quite comfortable with the food in her house. I would always carefully explain to her mother that the reason I couldn't eat white bread and milk, Mrs. Montague, was because I was Jewish and of course, white bread and milk were not kosher. And neither was Cheerios. Or bananas. Or eggs with loose yolks or anything else I didn't want to be eating. Being Jewish had its great advantages. Mrs. Montague would just smile in her rapturous Donna Reed way and let me do as I pleased.

I remember the sleep-over times the most though. We would always sleep in her sister Barbara's room. It had the soft affluent roar of an air conditioner, and I would always feel very properly tucked in (though somehow sterilized) in the matching twin beds with their matching dust ruffles and the picture of Jesus watching over me from the wall.

"Pssst. Hey Laurel! Are you sleeping? Psst! Hey Laurel! Can you hear me? I guess she's asleep! Uh . . . hello Jesus. You sure are glowing. I learned a song about you the other day. It goes:

Jesus loves the little children
All the children of the world
Red or yellow, black or white
Children singing in the night
Jesus loves the little children of the world.

Confirmation Class, New Jersey. 1960s. Private collection.

"Phew. You know, it's hard for me to sleep here. I miss my Mom. She sings to me. She sings to me just like I sing to you.

> In dem bait ha mikdash
> in a vinkele cheder
> zizst de almone bat tziyon alayne
> raisins, almonds and honey
> shluf, kinderlach, shluf . . .

"That's Yiddish. You know that language? Nope. I guess not.

"Y'know Jesus, it sure is quiet here. Not like my house. I bet they're still up. I bet they're watching Jack Paar. Bet they're up right now, bet they're having tea and black bread and butter. It tastes real good. Not at all like Wonder Bread. Maybe somebody is up downstairs. I'll just go see. Uh . . . bye-bye Jesus.

"Nope. Nobody else here. It's all quiet. The carpet sure is scratchy.

"Ding dong ding dong—ding dong ding dong! DONG! It's one o'clock. I can just barely see the top of the grandfather clock. It sure is dark here. Sure glad the piano light is on because I guess I am pretty much all alone and I think . . . I think I better I think better wanna GO HOME! MRS. MONTAGUE I WANNA GO HOME!"

And Mrs. Montague would come graciously, bathrobedly forward and ask me what my pain was. Try to convince me that the crisp, cool sheets inside were inviting and finally induce me to swallow an aspirin buried in a mound of strawberry jam. But that did not work. The strawberry jam here only reminded me of the jam that my grandfather put into his glass of tea, and I knew that tea and jam here, in Laurel's house, had never even been dreamt of together. No. I had to go home.

So phone calls and late night whispers agreed that that was best and my daddy, in a one a.m. face, drove his Buick up to the Wasp mansion of my very best friend and wrapped me up and took me home.

Bernard Malamud

From *The Assistant*

The Assistant *(1957) is Malamud's finest work. It is both parochial and universal. In his suffering and compassion Morris Bober is the quintessential Jew; Frank Alpine, his Italian assistant, becomes a Jew through these qualities before his formal conversion to Judaism. In Malamud's world the Jews are the heart of the world, first to suffer its pain, and first to be redeemed by the compassion it evokes.*

Ida was very unhappy that she had kept Frank on when she could have got rid of him so easily. She was to blame and she actively worried. Though she had no evidence, she suspected Helen was interested in the clerk. *Something* was going on between them. She did not ask her daughter what, because a denial would shame her. And though she had tried she felt she could not really trust Frank. Yes, he had helped the business, but how much would they have to pay for it? Sometimes when she came upon him alone in the store, his expression, she told herself, was sneaky. He sighed often, mut-

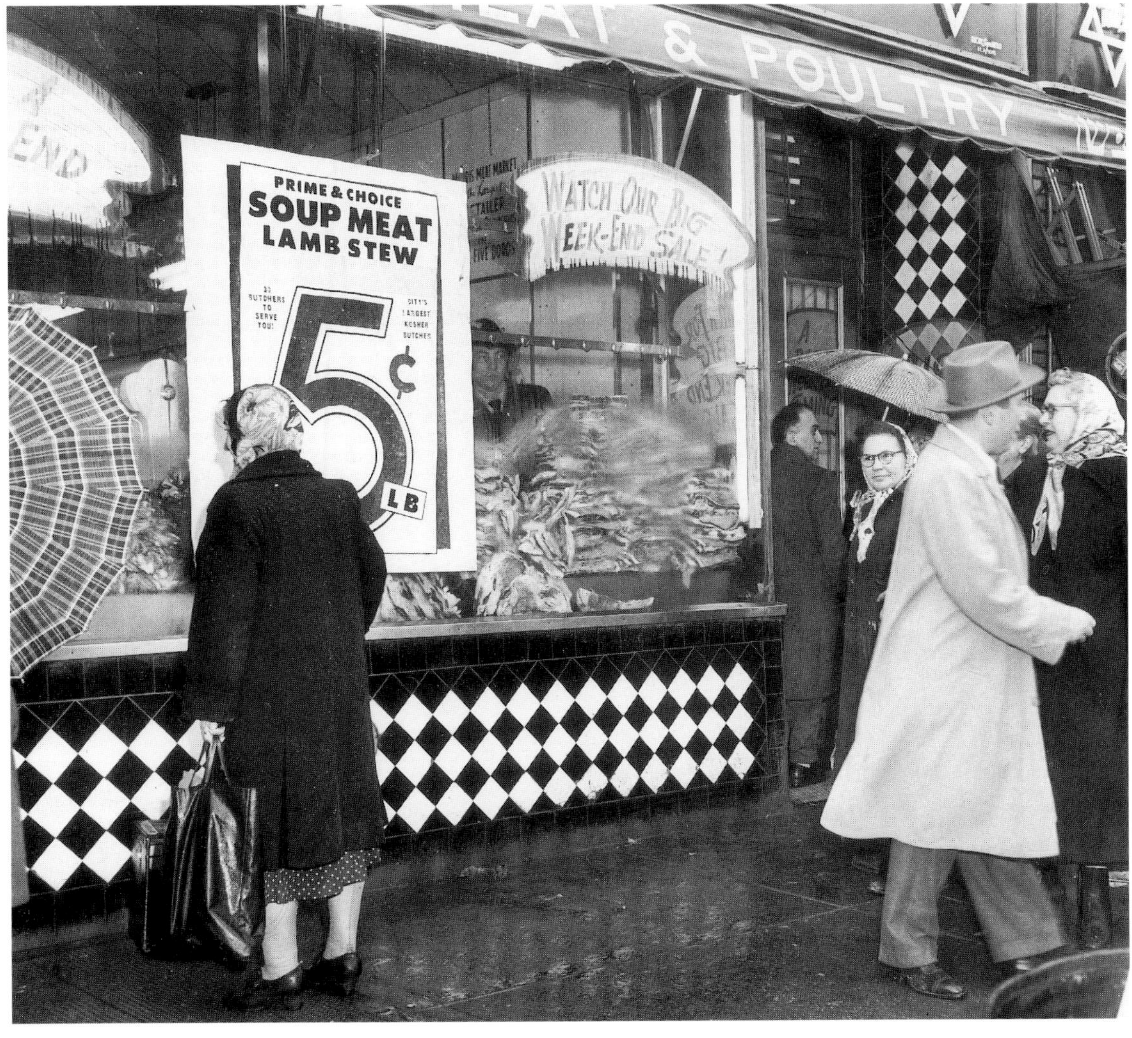

Morris Meat Market, Brooklyn, New York. Opening Day. 1957. UPI/Bettmann Archives. *As an opening day bonanza, 8,000 pounds of flank steak, normally selling at 45 cents a pound, went on sale for 5 cents.*

tered to himself, and if he saw he was observed, pretended he hadn't. Whatever he did there was more in it than he was doing. He was like a man with two minds. With one he was here, with the other someplace else. Even while he read he was doing more than reading. And his silence spoke a language she couldn't understand. Something bothered him and Ida suspected it was her daughter. Only when Helen happened to come into the store or the back while he was there, did he seem to relax, become one person. Ida was troubled, although she could not discover in Helen any response to him. Helen was quiet in his presence, detached, almost cold to the clerk. She gave him for his restless eyes, nothing—her back. Yet for this reason, too, Ida worried . . .

She spoke to Morris and cautiously asked if he had noticed anything developing between Helen and the clerk.

"Don't be foolish," the grocer replied. He had thought about the possibility, at times felt concerned, but after pondering how different they were, had put the idea out of his head.

"Morris, I am afraid."

"You are afraid of everything, even which it don't exist."

"Tell him to leave now—business is better."

"So is better," he muttered, "but who knows how will be next week. We decided he will stay till summer."

"Morris, he will make trouble."

"What kind trouble will he make?"

"Wait," she said, clasping her hands, "a tragedy will happen."

Her remark at first annoyed, then worried him.

The next morning the grocer and his clerk were sitting at the table, peeling hot potatoes. The pot had been drained of water and dumped on its side; they sat close to the steaming pile of potatoes, hunched over, ripping off the salt-stained skins with small knives. Frank seemed ill at ease. He hadn't shaved and had dark blobs under his eyes. Morris wondered if he had been drinking but there was never any smell of liquor about him. They worked without speaking, each lost in his thoughts.

After a half-hour, Frank squirming restlessly in his chair, remarked, "Say, Morris, suppose somebody asked you what do the Jews believe in, what would you tell them?"

The grocer stopped peeling, unable at once to reply.

"What I like to know is what is a Jew anyway?"

Because he was ashamed of his meager education Morris was never comfortable with such questions, yet he felt he must answer.

"My father used to say to be a Jew all you need is a good heart."

"What do you say?"

"The important thing is the Torah. This is the Law—a Jew must believe in the Law."

"Let me ask you this," Frank went on. "Do you consider yourself a real Jew?"

Morris was startled, "What do you mean if I am a real Jew?"

"Don't get sore about this," Frank said, "But I can give you an argument that you aren't. First thing, you don't go to the synagogue—not that I have ever seen. You don't keep your kitchen kosher and you don't eat kosher. You don't even wear one of those little black hats like this tailor I knew in South Chicago. He prayed three times a day. I even hear the Mrs say you kept the store open on Jewish holidays, it makes no difference if she yells her head off."

"Sometimes," Morris answered, flushing, "to have to eat, you must keep open on holidays. On Yom Kippur I don't keep open. But I don't worry about kosher, which is to me old-fashioned. What I worry is to follow the Jewish Law."

"But all those things are the Law, aren't they? And don't the Law say you can't eat any pig, but I have seen you taste ham."

"This is not important to me if I taste pig or if I don't. To some Jews is this important but not to me. Nobody will tell me that I am not Jewish because I put in my mouth once in a while, when my tongue is dry, a piece ham. But they will tell me, and I will believe them, if I forget the Law. This means to do what is right, to be honest, to be good. This means to other people. Our life is hard enough. Why should we hurt somebody else? For everybody should be the best, not only for you or me. We ain't animals. This is why we need the Law. This is what a Jew believes."

"I think other religions have those ideas too," Frank said. "But tell me why it is that the Jews suffer so damn much, Morris? It seems to me that they like to suffer, don't they?"

"Do you like to suffer? They suffer because they are Jews."

"That's what I mean, they suffer more than they have to."

"If you live, you suffer. Some people suffer more, but not because they want. But I think if a Jew don't suffer for the Law, he will suffer for nothing."

"What do you suffer for, Morris?" Frank said.

"I suffer for you," Morris said calmly.

Frank laid his knife down on the table. His mouth ached. "What do you mean?"

"I mean you suffer for me."

The clerk let it go at that.

"If a Jew forgets the Law," Morris ended, "he is not a good Jew, and not a good man."

Frank picked up his knife and began to tear the skins off the potatoes. The grocer peeled his pile in silence. The clerk asked nothing more.

When the potatoes were cooling, Morris, troubled by their talk, asked himself why Frank had brought up this subject. A thought of Helen, for some reason, crossed his mind.

"Tell me the truth," he said, "why did you ask me such questions?"

Frank shifted in his chair. He answered slowly, "To be truthful to you, Morris, once I didn't have much use for the Jews."

Morris looked at him without moving.

"But that was long ago," said Frank, "before I got to know what they were like. I don't think I understood much about them."

His brow was covered with sweat.

"Happens like this many times," Morris said.

But his confession had not made the clerk any happier.

* * *

They sat on folding chairs facing the bereaved and talked in whispers. Frank Alpine stood for a moment, his hat uncomfortably on, in a corner of the room. When the place grew crowded he left and seated himself among the handful of mourners already assembled in the long narrow chapel, dimly lit by thick, yellow wall lamps. The rows of benches were dark and heavy. In the front of the chapel, on a metal stand, lay the grocer's plain wooden coffin . . .

The rabbi then prayed, a stocky man with a pointed black beard. He stood on the podium near the coffin, wearing an old Homburg, a faded black frock coat over brown trousers, and bulbous shoes. After his prayer in Hebrew, when the mourners were seated, in a voice laden with sorrow he spoke of the dead man.

"My dear friends, I never had the pleasure to meet this good grocery man that he now lays in his coffin. He lived in a neighborhood where I didn't come in. Still and all I talked this morning to people that knew him and I am now sorry I didn't know him also. I would enjoy to speak to such a man. I talked to the bereaved widow, who lost her dear husband. I talked to his poor beloved daughter Helen, who is now without a father to guide her. To them I talked, also to landsleit and old friends, and each and all told me the same, that Morris Bober, who passed away so untimely—he caught double pneumonia from shoveling snow in front of his place of business so people could pass by on the sidewalk—was a man who couldn't be more honest. Such a person I am sorry I didn't meet sometime in my life. If I met him somewhere, maybe when he went to visit in a Jewish neighborhood—maybe at Rosh Hashana or Pesach—I would say to him, 'God bless you, Morris Bober.' . . .

The rabbi paused and gazed over the heads of the mourners.

"He was also a very hard worker, a man that never stopped working. How many mornings he got up in the dark and dressed himself in the cold, I can't count. After, he went downstairs to stay all day in the grocery. He worked long long hours. Six o'clock every morning he opened and he closed after ten every night, sometimes later. Fifteen, sixteen hours a day he was in the store, seven days a week, to make a living for his family . . . And for this reason that he worked so hard and bitter, in his house, on his table, was always something to eat. So besides honest he was a good provider."

The rabbi gazed down at his prayer book, then looked up.

"When a Jew dies, who asks if he is a Jew? He is a Jew, we don't ask. There are many ways to be a Jew. So if somebody comes to me and says, 'Rabbi, shall we call such a man Jewish who lived and worked among the gentiles and sold them pig meat, trayfe, that we don't eat it, and not once in twenty years comes inside a synagogue, is such a man a Jew, rabbi?' To him I will say, 'Yes, Morris Bober was to me a true Jew because he lived in the Jewish experience, which he remembered, and with the Jewish heart.' Maybe not to our formal tradition—for this I don't excuse him—but he was true to the spirit of our life—to want for others that which he wants also for himself. He followed the Law which God gave to Moses on Sinai and told him to bring to the people. He suffered, he endu-red, but with hope. Who told me this? I know. He asked for himself little—nothing, but he wanted for his beloved child a better existence than he had. For such reasons he was a Jew. What more does our sweet God ask his poor people? So let Him now take care of the widow, to comfort and protect her, and give to the fatherless child what her father wanted her to have. 'Yiskadal v'yiskadash shmey rabo. B'olmo divro . . .' "

* * *

Her thoughts were heavy. She remembered Ida saying Frank worked some place at night but the news had meant nothing to her. Now that she had seen him there, groggy from overwork, thin, unhappy, a burden lay on her, because it was no mystery who he was working for. He had kept them alive. Because of him she had enough to go to school at night.

In bed, half-asleep, she watched the watcher. It came to her that he had changed. It's true, he's not the same man, she said to herself. I should have known by now. She had despised him for the evil he had done, without understanding the why of aftermath, or admitting there could be an end to the bad and a beginning of good.

It was a strange thing about people—they could look the same but be different. He had been one thing, low, dirty, but because of something in himself—something she couldn't define, a memory perhaps, an ideal he might have forgotten and then remembered—he had changed into somebody else, no longer what he had been. She should have recognized it before. What he did to me he did wrong, she thought, but since he has changed in his heart he owes me nothing.

On her way to work one morning a week later, Helen, carrying her brief case, entered the grocery and found Frank hidden behind the tissue paper of the window, watching her. He was embarrassed, and she was curiously moved by the sight of his face.

"I came in to thank you for the help you're giving us," she explained.

"Don't thank me," he said.

"You owe us nothing."

"It's just my way."

They were silent, then he mentioned his idea of her going to day college. It would be more satisfying to her than at night.

"No, thank you," Helen said, blushing. "I couldn't think of it, especially not with you working so hard."

"It's no extra trouble."

"No, please."

"Maybe the store might get better, then I could do it on what we take in here?"

"I'd rather not."

"Think about it," Frank said.

She hesitated, then answered she would.

He wanted to ask her if he still had any chance with her but decided to let that wait till a later time.

Before she left, Helen, balancing the brief case on her knee, unsnapped it and took out a leather-bound book. "I wanted you to know I'm still using your Shakespeare."

He watched her walk to the corner, a good-looking girl, carrying his book in her brief case. She was wearing flat-heeled shoes, making her legs slightly more bowed, which for some reason he found satisfying . . .

* * *

Frank had only six customers all morning. To keep from getting nervous he took out a book he was reading. It was the Bible and he sometimes thought there were parts of it he could have written himself.

As he was reading he had this pleasant thought. He saw St. Francis come dancing out of the woods in his brown rags, a couple of scrawny birds flying around over his head. St. F. stopped in front of the grocery, and reaching into the garbage can, plucked the wooden rose out of it. He tossed it into the air and it turned into a real flower that he caught in his hand. With a bow he gave it to Helen, who had just come out of the house. "Little sister, here is your little sister the rose." From him she took it, although it was with the love and best wishes of Frank Alpine. One day in April Frank went to the hospital and had himself circumcised. For a couple of days he dragged himself around with a pain between his legs. The pain enraged and inspired him. After Passover he became a Jew.

Saul Bellow

From *Herzog*

On Napoleon Street

In 1976 the Nobel Prize for Literature was awarded to Canadian-born Saul Bellow, long an American citizen and clearly America's premier novelist in the post-war period. His most accomplished work was Herzog, *published in 1964. The carefully chosen name of its protagonist—Moses (the liberator and lawgiver) Herzog (a nobleman)—is not descriptive but ironic. This alienated, brooding intellectual would like to be what the name demands, but he fails at the enterprises which mean most to him. The account of the Herzog family, excerpted here, is a tale of enterprise and failure brought on by the vicissitudes of history.*

As for my late unlucky father, J. Herzog, he was not a big man, one of the small-boned Herzogs, finely made, round-headed, keen, nervous, handsome. In his frequent bursts of temper he slapped his sons swiftly with both hands. He did everything quickly, neatly, with skillful Eastern European flourishes: combing his hair, buttoning his shirt, stropping his bone-handled razors, sharpening pencils on the ball of his thumb, holding a loaf of bread to his breast and slicing toward himself, tying parcels with tight little knots, jotting like an artist in his account book. There each canceled page was covered with a carefully drawn X. The 1s and 7s carried bars and streamers. They were like pennants in the wind of failure. First Father Herzog failed in Petersburg, where he went through two dowries in one year. He had been importing onions from Egypt. Under Pobedonostsev the police caught up with him for illegal residence. He was convicted and sentenced. The account of the trial was published in a Russian journal printed on thick green paper. Father Herzog sometimes unfolded it and read aloud to the entire family, translating the proceedings against Ilyona Isakovitch Gerzog. He never served his sentence. He got away. Because he was nervy, hasty, obstinate, rebellious. He came to Canada, where his sister Zipporah Yaffe was living.

John Foster Carr. *Guide to the United States for the Jewish Immigrant.* 1912. Jewish Division, The New York Public Library. Astor, Lenox, and Tilden Foundations.

In 1913 he bought a piece of land near Valleyfield, Quebec, and failed as a farmer. Then he came into town and failed as a baker; failed in the dry-goods business; failed as a jobber; failed as a sack manufacturer in the War, when no one else failed. He failed as a junk dealer. Then he became a marriage broker and failed—too short-tempered and blunt. And now he was failing as a bootlegger, on the run from the provincial Liquor Commission. Making a bit of a living.

In haste and defiantly, with a clear tense face, walking with mingled desperation and high style, a little awkwardly dropping his weight on one heel as he went, his coat, once lined with fox, turned dry and bald, the red hide cracking. This coat sweeping open as he walked, or marched his one-man Jewish march, he was saturated with the odor of the Caporals he smoked as he covered Montreal in his swing—Papineau, Mile-End, Verdun, Lachine, Point St. Charles. He looked for business opportunities—bankruptcies, job lots, mergers, fire sales, produce—to rescue him from illegality. He could calculate percentages mentally at high speed, but he lacked the cheating imagination of a successful businessman. And so he kept a little still in Mile-End, where goats fed in the empty lots. He traveled on the tramcar. He sold a bottle here and there and waited for his main chance . . . . American rum-runners would buy the stuff from you at the border, any amount, spot cash, if you could get it there. Meanwhile he smoked cigarettes on the cold platforms of streetcars. The Revenue was trying to catch him. Spotters were after him. On the roads to the border were hijackers. On Napoleon Street he had five mouths to feed. Willie and Moses were sickly. Helen studied the piano. Shura was fat, greedy, disobedient, a plotting boy. The rent, back rent, notes due, doctors' bills to pay, and he had no English, no friends, no influence, no trade, no assets but his still—no help in all the world. His sister Zipporah in St. Anne was rich, very rich, which only made matters worse.

* * *

My ancient times. Remoter than Egypt. No dawn, the foggy winters. In darkness, the bulb was lit. The stove was cold. Papa shook the grates, and raised an ashen dust. The grates grumbled and squealed. The puny shovel clinked underneath. The Caporals gave Papa a bad cough. The chimneys in their helmets sucked in the wind. Then the milkman came in his sleigh. The snow was spoiled and rotten with manure and litter, dead rats, dogs. The milkman in his sheepskin gave the bell a twist. It was brass, like the winding-key of a clock. Helen pulled the latch and went down with a pitcher for the milk. And then Ravitch, hung-over, came from his room, in his heavy sweater, suspenders over the wool to keep it tighter to the body, the bowler on his head, red in the face, his look guilty. He waited to be asked to sit.

The morning light could not free itself from gloom and frost. Up and down the street, the brick-recessed windows were dark, filled with darkness, and schoolgirls by twos in their black skirts marched toward the convent. And wagons, sledges, drays, the horses shuddering, the air drowned in leaden green, the dung-stained ice, trails of ashes. Moses and his brothers put on their caps and prayed together,

> *"Ma tovu ohaleha Yaakov . . ."*
> "How goodly are thy tents, O Israel."

Napoleon Street, rotten, toylike, crazy and filthy, riddled, flogged with harsh weather—the bootlegger's boys reciting ancient prayers. To this Moses' heart was attached with great power. Here was a wider range of human feelings than he had ever again been able to find. The children of the race, by a never-failing miracle, opened their eyes on one strange world after another, age after age, and uttered the same prayer in each, eagerly loving what they found. What was wrong with Napoleon Street? thought Herzog. All he ever wanted was there. His mother did the wash, and mourned. His father was desperate and frightened, but obstinately fighting. His brother Shura with staring disingenuous eyes was plotting to master the world, to become a millionaire. His brother Willie struggled with asthmatic fits. Trying to breathe he gripped the table and rose on his toes like a cock about to crow. His sister Helen had long white gloves which she washed in thick suds. She wore them to her lessons at the conservatory, carrying a leather music roll. Her diploma hung in a frame. *Mlle. Hélène Herzog . . . avec distinction.* His soft prim sister who played the piano.

Philip Roth

From *The Ghost Writer*

Philip Roth's first book, Goodbye Columbus, *won the National Book Award for Fiction. His second,* Portnoy's Complaint, *was a runaway bestseller, but was widely criticized in the Jewish community. Its central character was a lecherous young Jew, whose depiction, it was claimed, not only shamed the Jewish community but betrayed its welfare as well. Roth, deeply hurt, rose to his own defence. The hurt apparently festered, for he returns to the affair in his* Ghost Writer *(1979) and dramatizes it as a confrontation with his critical father.*

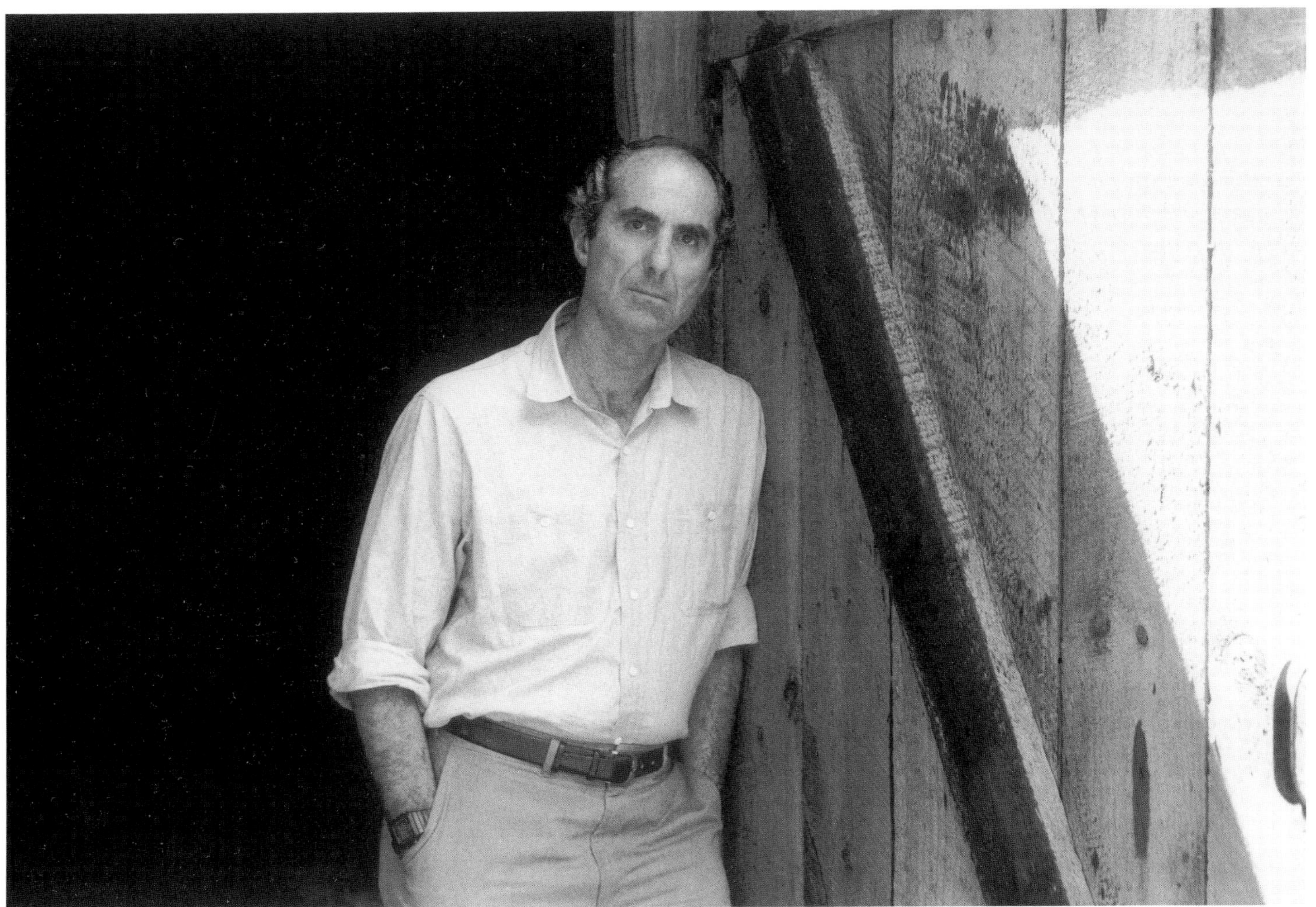

Philip Roth. Photograph courtesy of Nancy Crampton.

"So," he said, when at last, in my own sweet time, I came back up on the curb, "what do you do with the story now? Send it to a magazine?"

"It's long for a magazine. Probably no magazine will publish it."

"Oh, they'll publish it. The *Saturday Review* has put you on the map. That was a wonderful write-up, a terrific honor to be chosen like that at your age."

"Well, we'll see."

"No, no. You're on your way. The *Saturday Review* never sold so many copies in North Jersey as when your picture was in it. Why do you think everybody came by today, Frieda and Dave, Aunt Tessie, Birdie, Murray, the Edelmans? Because they saw your picture and they're proud."

"They all told me."

"Look, Nathan, let me have my say. Then you can go, and up there at the artists' colony maybe you'll think over in peace and quiet what I'm trying to get you to understand. If you were going to turn out to be nobody, I wouldn't be taking this seriously. But I do take you seriously—and you have to take yourself seriously, and what you are doing. Stop looking for that goddam bus and listen to me, *please.* You can catch the *next* bus! Nathan, you are not in school any more. You are the older brother and you are out in the world and I am treating you accordingly."

"I understand that. But that doesn't mean that we can't disagree. That's what it *does* mean."

"But from a lifetime of experience I happen to know what ordinary people will think when they read something like this story. And you don't. You can't. You have been sheltered from it all your life. You were raised here in this neighborhood where you went to school with Jewish children. When we went to the shore and had the house with the Edelmans, you were always among Jews, even in the summertime. At

COLORPLATE 134

"GRANDPA" ZELIG TEPPER. *Czar Nicholas II Thumbing His Nose at President Roosevelt Over the Kishineff Pogrom.* 1954. Watercolor on paper. The Jewish Museum , New York. Purchased with funds from the Joshua Lowenfish Estate Bequest.

COLORPLATE 135

BEN SHAHN. *Ram's Horn and Menorah.* 1958. Tempera and gold leaf. 16 1/2 x 27 1/4 in. Courtesy of Sid Deutsch Gallery, New York. © Estate of Ben Shahn / VAGA, New York, 1994.

COLORPLATE 136

HARRY LIEBERMAN. *East Side Market*. c. 1970. Acrylic on canvas. 40 x 30 in. Collection of Arlene R. Popkin. Courtesy of Frank Miele Gallery, New York.

COLORPLATE 137

LARRY RIVERS. *Bar Mitzvah Photograph Painting*. 1961. Oil on canvas. 80 x 72 in.
Private collection. © Larry Rivers / VAGA, New York, 1994.

COLORPLATE 138 *(overleaf)*

BEN SHAHN. *Roosevelt Mural*. 1937–1938. Fresco. 12 x 45 ft.
© Estate of Ben Shahn / VAGA, New York, 1994.

Dr. med.
Besuch
verboten!
Euch!
nicht
bei Juden!
48
87
76

COLORPLATE 139

WILLIAM KURELEK. *Bender Hamlet, the Farming Colony That Failed.* 1975. Oil on masonite. 30 3/4 x 33 in. Reproduced courtesy of the estate of William Kurelek and the Isaacs / Innuit Gallery, Toronto.

COLORPLATE 140

WILLIAM KURELEK. *Jewish Immigrants Arriving on the Prairies*. 1975. Oil on masonite. 20 x 22 1/2 in. Reproduced courtesy of the estate of William Kurelek and The Isaacs/Innuit Gallery, Toronto.

COLORPLATE 141

NATHAN HILU. *Sukkot in Brooklyn*. c. 1976. Acrylic and collage on paper. 22 1/4 x 29 3/4 in. Private collection.

Chicago your best friends who you brought home were Jewish boys, always. It's not your fault that you don't know what Gentiles think when they read something like this. But I can tell you. They don't think about how it's a great work of art. They don't know about art. Maybe I don't know about art myself. Maybe none of our family does, not the way that you do. But that's my point. People don't read art—they read about *people.* And they judge them as such. And how do you think they will judge the people in your story, what conclusions do you think they will reach? Have you thought about that?"

"Yes."

"And what have you concluded?"

"Oh, I can't put it into one word, not out here in the street. I didn't write fifteen thousand words so as now to put it into one word."

"Well, I can. And the street isn't a bad place for it. Because I know the word. I wonder if you fully understand just how very little love there is in this world for Jewish people. I don't mean in Germany, either, under the Nazis. I mean in run-of-the-mill Americans, Mr. and Mrs. Nice Guy, who otherwise you and I consider perfectly harmless. Nathan, it is there. I guarantee you it is there. I *know* it is there. I have seen it, I have felt it, even when they do not express it in so many words."

"But I'm not *denying* that. Why did Sidney throw that redneck off his ship—?"

"Sidney," he said furiously, "never threw any redneck off any ship! Sidney threw the bull, Nathan! Sidney was a petty hoodlum who cared about nobody and nothing in this world but the good of Sidney!"

"And who actually existed, Dad—and no better than I depict him!"

"Better? He was worse! How rotten he was you don't *begin* to know. I could tell you stories about that bastard that would make your hair stand on end."

"Then where *are* we? If he was *worse*— Oh, look, we're not getting anywhere. Please, it's getting dark, it's going to snow—*go home*. I'll write when I get up there. But there is no more to say on this subject. We just disagree, period."

"All right!" he said crisply, "all right!" But only, I knew, to defuse me for the moment.

"Dad, go home, please."

"It won't hurt if I wait with you. I don't like you waiting out here by yourself."

"I can manage perfectly well out here by myself. I have for years now."

Some five minutes later, blocks away, we saw what looked like the lights of the New York bus.

"Well," I said, "I'll be back down in a few months. I'll keep in touch—I'll phone—"

"Nathan, your story, as far as Gentiles are concerned, is about one thing and one thing only. Listen to me, before you go. It is about kikes. Kikes and their love of money. That is all our good Christian friends will see, I guarantee you. It is not about the scientists and teachers and lawyers they become and the things such people accomplish for others. It is not about the immigrants like Chaya who worked and saved and sacrificed to get a decent footing in America. It is not about the wonderful peaceful days and nights you spent growing up in our house. It is not about the lovely friends you always had. No, it's about Essie and her hammer, and Sidney and his chorus girls, and that shyster of Essie's and his filthy mouth, and, as best I can see, about what a jerk I was begging them to reach a decent compromise before the whole family had to be dragged up in front of a *goyisher* judge."

"I didn't depict you as a jerk. Christ, far from it. I thought," I said angrily, "I was administering a bear hug, to tell you the truth."

"Oh, did you? Well, it didn't come out that way. Look, son, maybe I *was* a jerk, trying to talk sense to such people. I don't mind being made a little fun of—that couldn't bother me less. I've been around in life. But what I can't accept is what you don't see—what you don't *want* to see. This story isn't us, and what is worse, it isn't even *you*. You are a loving boy. I watched you like a hawk all day. I've watched you all your life. You are a good and kind and considerate young man. You are not somebody who writes this kind of story and then pretends it's the truth."

"But I *did* write it." The light changed, the New York bus started toward us across the intersection—and he threw his arms onto my shoulders. Making me all the more belligerent. "I *am* the kind of person who writes this kind of story!"

"You're not," he pleaded, shaking me just a little.

But I hopped up onto the bus, and then behind me the pneumatic door, with its hard rubber edge, swung shut with what I took to be an overly appropriate thump, a symbol of the kind you leave out of fiction. It was a sound that suddenly brought back to me the prize fights at the Laurel Garden, where once a year my brother and I used to wager our pennies with one another, each of us alternately backing the white fighter or the colored fighter, while Doc Zuckerman waved hello to his few acquaintances in the sporting crowd, among them, on one occasion, Meyer Ellenstein, the dentist who became the city's first Jewish mayor. What I heard was the heartrending thud that follows the roundhouse knockout punch, the sound of the stupefied heavyweight hitting the canvas floor. And what I saw, when I looked out to wave goodbye for the winter, was my smallish, smartly dressed father—turned out for my visit in a new "fingertip" car coat that matched the coffee-toned slacks and the checkered peaked cap, and wearing, of course, the same silver-rimmed spectacles, the same trim little mustache that I had grabbed at from the crib; what I saw was my bewildered father, alone on the darkening street-corner by the park that used to be our paradise, thinking himself and all of Jewry gratuitously disgraced and jeopardized by my inexplicable betrayal.

* * *

Hadn't Joyce, hadn't Flaubert, hadn't Thomas Wolfe all been condemned for disloyalty or treachery or immorality by those who saw themselves as slandered in their works? . . .

But what about sons? It wasn't Flaubert's father or Joyce's father who had impugned me for my recklessness—it was my own. Nor was it the Irish he claimed I had maligned and misrepresented, but the Jews. Of which I was one. Of which, only some five thousand days past, there had been millions more.

Isaac Bashevis Singer

From "The Son"

It is ironic but deeply satisfying that the Nobel Prize for Literature in 1978 was awarded to a writer in a language long since pronounced dead, Yiddish. Isaac Bashevis Singer was the recipient, but in honoring him, homage was paid to the great literature—in quality and quantity—created in that language, and to which he made a signal contribution. "The Son" (1962) is perhaps his most personal writing, filled with the feelings one experiences when one feels all alone in the midst of a great multitude—apprehension and expectation.

The ship from Israel was due to arrive at twelve o'clock, but it was late.

It was evening before it docked in New York, and then I had to wait quite a while before any passengers were let off. Outside, it was hot and rainy. A mob of people had come to wait for the ship's arrival. It seemed to me that all the Jews were there—assimilated ones, and rabbis with long beards and sidelocks; girls with numbers on their arms from Hitler's camps; officers of Zionistic organizations with bulging portfolios; Yeshiva boys in velvet hats, with wildly growing beards; and worldly ladies with rouged faces and red toenails.

I realized I was present at a new epoch in Jewish history. When did the Jews have ships? And if so, their ships went to Tyre and Sidon, and not to New York . . .

The New York women fanned themselves, spoke all at once with hoarse voices, refreshed themselves with chocolate and Coca-Cola. A non-Jewish toughness stared out of their eyes. It was hard to believe that only a few years ago, their brothers and sisters in Europe went like sheep to the slaughter. Modern Orthodox young men with tiny skullcaps hidden like plasters in their dense hair spoke loudly in English and cracked jokes with the girls, whose behavior and clothes showed no sign of religion. Even the rabbis here were different, not like my father and grandfather. To me, all these people appeared worldly and clever. Almost all, except myself, had secured permits to board the boat. And they got acquainted unusually fast, shared information, shook their heads knowingly.

The ship's officers began to descend, but they seemed stiff in their uniforms, which had epaulettes and gilded buttons. They spoke Hebrew, but they had accents like Gentiles.

I stood and waited for a son whom I hadn't seen in twenty years.

He was five years old when I parted with his mother. I went to America, she to Soviet Russia. But apparently one revolution was not enough for her. She wanted "the permanent revolution." And they would have liquidated her in Moscow if she hadn't had someone who could reach the ear of a high official. Her old Bolshevik aunts who had sat in Polish prisons for Communist activity had interceded for her, and she was deported, together with the child, to Turkey. From there, she managed to reach Palestine, where she had brought up our son in a kibbutz.

Now he had come to visit me.

He had sent me one photograph taken when he had served in the army and fought the Arabs. But the picture was blurred, and in addition he was wearing a uniform. Only now, as the first passengers began to come down, did it occur to me that I did not have a clear image of what my son looked like.

Was he tall? Was he short? Had his blond hair turned dark with the years?

This son's arrival in America pushed me back to an epoch which I had thought of as already belonging to eternity. He was emerging out of the past like a dream or a phantom. He did not belong in my present home, nor would he fit into any of my relationships outside. I had no room for him, no bed, no money, no time. Like that ship flying the white and blue flag with the Star of David, he constituted a strange combination of the past and the present. He had written me that of all the languages he had spoken in his childhood—Yiddish, Polish, Russian, Turkish—he now spoke only Hebrew. So I knew in advance that, with what little Hebrew I possessed from the Pentateuch and the Talmud, I would not be able to converse with him. Instead of talking to my son, I would stammer and have to look up words in dictionaries.

The pushing and noise increased. The dock was in a tumult. Everyone screamed and shoved themselves forward with the exaggerated joy of people who have lost the standard to measure achievement in this world. Women cried hysterically; men wept hoarsely. Photographers took pictures, and reporters rushed from person to person, conducting hurried interviews.

A Brivele Dem Taten (A Letter to the Father). Sheet music. 1911. Collection of Abraham and Deborah Karp. *Refrain: The father's plea: Write a letter to your father each week, a sheaf of paper send. This will ease my loneliness. Oh, how I long to have you near. If I will be able to survive it, it will be a miracle indeed. May God send His fullest blessing, to you my child. But don't forget: A letter to your father! (Trans.: AJK).*

Then occurred the same thing that always occurs when I am part of a crowd. Everyone became one family, while I remained an outsider. Nobody spoke to me, and I didn't speak to anybody. The secret power which had joined them kept me apart. Eyes measured me absent-mindedly, as if to ask: What is *he* doing here? After some hesitation, I tried to ask someone a question, but the other didn't hear me, or at least he moved away in the middle of my sentence.

I might just as well have been a ghost.

After a while, I decided what I always do decide in such cases, to make peace with fate. I stood out of the way in a corner and watched everyone as they came off the boat, sorting them out in my mind. My son could not be among the old or middle-aged. He could not have pitch-black hair, broad shoulders, and fiery eyes—one like that could not have stemmed from my loins.

But suddenly a young man emerged strangely familiar to that soldier in the snapshot, tall, lean, a little bent, with a longish nose and a narrow chin. This is he, something screamed in me. I tore myself from my corner to run to him. He was searching for someone. A fatherly love awoke in me. His cheeks were sunken, and a sickly pallor lay on his face. He is sick, he has consumption, I thought anxiously. I had already opened my mouth to call out "Gigi" (what his mother and I had called him as a small boy), when suddenly a thick woman waddled over to him and locked him in her arms. Her cry turned into a kind of barking; soon a whole bunch of other relatives came up.

They had snatched a son from me, who was not mine!

There was a kind of spiritual kidnapping in the whole thing. My fatherly feelings became ashamed and stepped back in a hurry into that hiding place where emotions can stay for years without a sound.

I felt that I had turned red with humiliation, as if I had been struck in the face. I decided to wait patiently from now on, and not to allow my feelings to come out prematurely. Then, for a while, no more passengers emerged.

I thought: What is a son after all? What makes my semen more to me than somebody else's? What value is there in a flesh and blood connection? We all foam from the same caldron. Go back a number of generations and all this crowd of strangers probably had a common grandfather. And two or three generations hence, the descendents of those who are relatives now will be strangers. It's all temporary and passing—we're bubbles on the same ocean, moss from the same swamp. If one cannot love everybody, one should not love anybody.

The passengers again began to come out.

Three young men appeared together, and I examined them. None was Gigi, and, even if one were, no one would snatch him from me anyhow. It was a relief when each of the three went away with someone else. None of them had pleased me. They belonged to the rabble. The last one had even turned around and thrown a bellicose look at me, as if he had in some mysterious way caught my deprecating thoughts about him and those like him.

* * *

Suddenly I saw him.

He came out slowly, hesitantly, and with an expression that said he didn't expect anybody would have waited for him. He looked like the snapshot, but older. There were youthful wrinkles in his face, and his clothes were mussy. He showed the shabbiness and neglect of a homeless young man who had been years in strange places, who had gone through a lot and become old before his time. His hair was tangled and matted, and it seemed to me there were wisps of straw and hay in it—like the hair of those who sleep in haylofts. His light eyes, squinting behind whitish eyebrows, had the half-blind smile of an albino. He carried a wooden satchel like an army recruit, and a package wrapped in brown paper.

Instead of running to him immediately, I stood and gaped. His back was already bent a little, but not like a Yeshiva boy's, rather like that of someone who is used to carrying heavy burdens. He took after me, but I recognized traits of his mother—the other half that could never blend with mine. Even in him, the product, our contrary traits had no harmony. The mother's lips did not pair with the father's chin. The protruding cheekbones did not suit the high forehead. He looked carefully on both sides, and his face said good-naturedly: Of course, he didn't come to meet me.

I approached him and asked unsurely, *"Atah,* Gigi?"

He laughed. "Yes, I'm Gigi."

We kissed and his stubble rubbed my cheeks like a potato grater. He was strange to me yet I knew at the same time that I was as devoted to him as any other father to his son. We stood still with that feeling of belonging together that needs no words. In one second I knew how to treat him. He had spent three years in the army, had gone through a bitter war. He must have had God knew how many girls, but he had remained as bashful as only a man can be. I spoke to him in Hebrew, rather amazed at my own knowledge.

I immediately acquired the authority of a father, and all my inhibitions evaporated. I tried to take his wooden box, but he wouldn't let me. We stood outside looking for a taxi, but all the taxis had already gone. The rain had stopped. The avenue along the docks stretched out—wet, dark, badly paved, the asphalt full of ditches and with puddles of water reflecting pieces of the glowing sky, which was low and red like a metal cover. The air was choking. There was lightning but no thunder. Single drops of water fell from above but it was hard to know whether these were spray from the former rain or a new gust beginning. It hurt my dignity that New York should show itself to my son so gloomy and dingy. I had a vain ambition to have him see immediately the nicer quarters of the city. But we waited for fifteen minutes without a taxi appearing. Already I had heard the first sounds of thunder.

There was nothing else to do but walk.

Cynthia Ozick

From *The Pagan Rabbi and Other Stories*

"Yiddish in America"

Cynthia Ozick is an artist of the English language. More than that, she is a learned, devoted, and passionate Jew. The trimillennial Jewish literary heritage is dear to her. And she has a creative imagination and a keen ear for dialogue. All this comes to the fore in "Envy; or, Yiddish in America" (1969). The writer Edelshtein is holding the fort for Yiddish, but recognizing that literature needs an audience, he seeks to preserve it through translation and becomes frantic for a translator who would become the transmitter.

Edelshtein, an American for forty years, was a ravenous reader of novels by writers "of"—he said this with a snarl—"Jewish extraction." He found them puerile, vicious, pitiable, ignorant, contemptible, above all stupid. In judging them he dug for his deepest vituperation—they were, he said, "*Amerikanergeboren.*" Spawned in America, pogroms a rumor, *mamaloshen* a stranger, history a vacuum. Also many of them were still young, and had black eyes, black hair, and red beards. A few were blue-eyed, like the *cheder-yinglach* of his youth. Schoolboys. He was certain he did not envy them, but he read them like a sickness. They were reviewed and praised, and meanwhile they were considered Jews, and knew nothing. There was even a body of Gentile writers in reaction, beginning to show familiarly whetted teeth: the Jewish Intellectual Establishment was misrepresenting American letters, coloring it with an alien dye, taking it over, and so forth. Like Berlin and Vienna in the twenties, *Judenrein ist Kulturrein* was Edelshtein's opinion. Take away the Jews and where, O so-called Western Civilization, is your literary culture?

Mastheads from Jewish Press in America. 1917–1918. *Among the newspaper and journals are* The Forward, *the largest of the Yiddish dailies;* Der Tog, *for the Yiddish cultural elite; the* Yiddishes Tageblatt, *for the Orthodox;* The Zionist Maccabean; *and* The Menorah Journal, *as fine a journal as America has had.*

For Edelshtein Western Civilization was a sore point. He had never been to Berlin, Vienna, Paris, or even London. He had been to Kiev, though, but only once, as a young boy. His father, a *melamed*, had traveled there on a tutoring job and had taken him along. In Kiev they lived in the cellar of a big house owned by rich Jews, the Kirilovs. They had been born Katz, but bribed an official in order to Russify their name. Every morning he and his father would go up a green staircase to the kitchen for a breakfast of coffee and stale bread and then into the schoolroom to teach *chumash* to Alexei Kirilov, a red-cheeked little boy. The younger Edelshtein would drill him while his father dozed. What had become of Alexei Kirilov? Edelshtein, a widower in New

York, sixty-seven years old, a Yiddishist (so-called), a poet, could stare at anything at all—a subway car-card, a garbage can lid, a streetlight—and cause the return of Alexei Kirilov's face, his bright cheeks, his Ukraine-accented Yiddish, his shelves of mechanical toys from Germany—trucks, cranes, wheel-barrows, little colored autos with awnings overhead. Only Edelshtein's father was expected to call him Alexei—everyone else, including the young Edelshtein, said Avremeleh. Avremeleh had a knack of getting things by heart. He had a golden head. Today he was a citizen of the Soviet Union. Or was he finished, dead, in the ravine at Babi Yar? Edelshtein remembered every coveted screw of the German toys. With his father he left Kiev in the spring and retuned to Minsk. The mud, frozen into peaks, was melting. The train carriage reeked of urine and dirt seeped through their shoelaces into their socks.

And the language was lost, murdered. The language—a museum. Of what other language can it be said that it died a sudden and definite death, in a given decade, on a given piece of soil? Where are the speakers of ancient Etruscan? Who was the last man to write a poem in Linear B? Attrition, assimilation. Death by mystery not gas. The last Etruscan walks around inside some Sicilian. Western Civilization, that pod of muck, lingers on and on. The Sick Man of Europe with his big globe-head, rotting, but at home in bed. Yiddish, a littleness, a tiny light—oh little holy light!—dead, vanished. Perished. Sent into darkness.

This was Edelshtein's subject. On this subject he lectured for a living. He swallowed scraps. Synagogues, community centers, labor unions underpaid him to suck on the bones of the dead. Smoke. He traveled from borough to borough, suburb to suburb, mourning in English the death of Yiddish. Sometimes he tried to read one or two of his poems. At the first Yiddish word the painted old ladies of the Reform Temples would begin to titter from shame, as at a stand-up television comedian. Orthodox and Conservative men fell instantly asleep. So he reconsidered, and told jokes:

Before the war there was held a great International Esperanto Convention. It met in Geneva. Esperanto scholars, doctors of letters, learned men, came from all over the world to deliver papers on the genesis, syntax, and functionalism of Esperanto. Some spoke of the social value of an international language, others of its beauty. Every nation on earth was represented among the lecturers. All the papers were given in Esperanto. Finally the meeting was concluded, and the tired great men wandered companionably along the corridors, where at last they began to converse casually among themselves in their international language: *"Nu, vos macht a yid?"*

After the war a funeral cortège was moving slowly down a narrow street on the Lower East Side. The cars had left the parking lot behind the chapel in the Bronx and were on their way to the cemetery in Staten Island. Their route took them past the newspaper offices of the last Yiddish daily left in the city. There were two editors, one to run the papers off the press and the other to look out the window. The one looking out the window saw the funeral procession passing by and called to his colleague: "Hey, Mottel, print one less!"

But both Edelshtein and his audiences found the jokes worthless. Old jokes. They were not the right kind. They wanted jokes about weddings—spiral staircases, doves flying out of cages, bashful medical students—and he gave them funerals. To speak of Yiddish was to preside over a funeral. He was a rabbi who had survived his whole congregation. Those for whom his tongue was no riddle were specters.

Norman Podhoretz

From *Making It*

"The Brutal Bargain"

Norman Podhoretz, long-time editor of Commentary, *one of America's leading intellectual periodicals, notes that "one of the longest journeys in the world is the journey from Brooklyn to Manhattan." In his autobiographical* Making It *(1967), he recalls how he made that journey, who helped him "across the river," and the price he had to pay.*

One of the longest journeys in the world is the journey from Brooklyn to Manhattan—or at least from certain neighborhoods in Brooklyn to certain parts of Manhattan. I have made that journey, but it is not from the experience of having made it that I know how very great the distance is, for I started on the road many years before I realized what I was doing, and by the time I did realize it I was for all practical purposes already there. At so imperceptible a pace did I travel, and with so little awareness, that I never felt footsore or out of breath or weary at the thought of how far I still had to go. Yet whenever anyone who has remained back there where I started—remained not physically but socially and culturally, for the neighborhood is now a Negro ghetto and the Jews who have "remained" in it mostly reside in the less affluent areas of Long Island—whenever anyone like that happens into the world in which I now live with such perfect ease, I can see that in his eyes I have become a fully acculturated citizen of a country as foreign to him as China and infinitely more frightening.

That country is sometimes called the upper middle class; and indeed I am a member of that class, less by virtue of my income than by virtue of the way my speech is accented, the way I dress, the way I furnish my home, the way I entertain and am entertained, the way I educate my children—the way, quite simply, I look and I live. It appalls me to think what an immense transformation I had to work on myself in order to become what I have become: if I had known what I was doing I would surely not have been able to do it, I would surely not have wanted to. No wonder the choice had to be blind; there was a kind of treason in it: treason toward my family, treason toward my friends. In choosing the road I chose, I was pronouncing a judgment upon them, and the fact that they themselves concurred in the judgment makes the whole thing sadder but no less cruel.

When I say that the choice was blind, I mean that I was never aware—obviously not as a small child, certainly not as an adolescent, and not even as a young man already writing for publication and working on the staff of an important intellectual magazine in New York—how inextricably my "noblest" ambitions were tied to the vulgar desire to rise above the class into which I was born; nor did I understand to what an astonishing extent these ambitions were shaped and defined by the standards and values and tastes of the class into which I did not know I wanted to move. It is not that I was or am a social climber as the term is commonly used. High society interests me, if at all, only as a curiosity; I do not wish to be a member of it; and in any case, it is not, as I have learned from a small experience of contact with the very rich and fashionable, my "scene." Yet precisely because social climbing is not one of my vices (unless what might be called celebrity climbing, which very definitely *is* one of my vices, can be considered the contemporary variant of social climbing), I think there

Raphael Soyer. *The Williamsburgh Bridge.* 12 x 8 in. Lithograph. Collection, Abraham and Deborah Karp.

may be more than a merely personal significance in the fact that class has played so large a part both in my life and in my career.

But whether or not the significance is there, I feel certain that my long-time blindness to the part class was playing in my life was not altogether idiosyncratic . . . .

In my own case, the blindness to class always expressed itself in an outright and very often belligerent refusal to believe that it had anything to do with me at all. I no longer remember when or in what form I first discovered that there was such a thing as class, but whenever it was and whatever form the discovery took, it could only have coincided with the recognition that criteria existed by which I and everyone I knew were stamped as inferior: we were in the *lower* class. This was not a proposition I was willing to accept, and my way of not accepting it was to dismiss the whole idea of class as a prissy triviality.

Given the fact that I had literary ambitions even as a small boy, it was inevitable that the issue of class would sooner or later arise for me with a sharpness it would never acquire for most of my friends. But given the fact also that I was on the whole very happy to be growing up where I was, that I was fiercely patriotic about Brownsville (the spawning-ground of so many famous athletes and gangsters), and that I felt genuinely patronizing toward other neighborhoods, especially the "better" ones like Crown Heights and East Flatbush which seemed by comparison colorless and unexciting—given the fact, in other words, that I was not, for all that I wrote poetry and read books, an "alienated" boy dreaming of escape—my confrontation with the issue of class would probably have come later rather than sooner if not for an English teacher in high school who decided that I was a gem in the rough and who took it upon herself to polish me to as high a sheen as she could manage and I would permit.

I resisted—far less effectively, I can see now, than I then thought, though even then I knew that she was wearing me down far more than I would ever give her the satisfaction of admitting. Famous throughout the school for her altogether outspoken snobbery, which stopped short by only a hair, and sometimes did not stop short at all, of an old-fashioned kind of patrician anti-Semitism, Mrs. K. was also famous for being an extremely good teacher; indeed, I am sure that she saw no distinction between the hopeless task of teaching the proper use of English to the young Jewish barbarians whom fate had so unkindly deposited into her charge and the equally hopeless task of teaching them the proper "manners." (There were as many young Negro barbarians in her charge as Jewish ones, but I doubt that she could ever bring herself to pay very much attention to them. As she never hesitated to make clear, it was punishment enough for a woman of her background—her family was old-Brooklyn and, she would have us understand, extremely distinguished—to have fallen among the sons of East European immigrant Jews.)

For three years, from the age of thirteen to the age of sixteen, I was her special pet, though that word is scarcely adequate to suggest the intensity of the relationship which developed between us . . . .

Childless herself, she worked on me like a dementedly ambitious mother with a somewhat recalcitrant son; married to a solemn and elderly man (she was then in her early forties or thereabouts), she treated me like a callous, ungrateful adolescent lover on whom she had humiliatingly bestowed her favors. She flirted with me and flattered me, she scolded me and insulted me. Slum child, filthy little slum child, so beautiful a mind and so vulgar a personality, so exquisite in sensibility and so coarse in manner. What would she do with me, what would become of me if I persisted out of stubbornness and perversity in the disgusting ways they had taught me at home and on the streets?

To her the most offensive of these ways was the style in which I dressed: a tee shirt, tightly pegged pants, and a red satin jacket with the legend "Cherokees, S.A.C." (social-athletic club) stitched in large white letters across the back. This was bad enough, but when on certain days I would appear in school wearing, as a particular ceremonial occasion required, a suit and tie, the sight of those immense padded shoulders and my white-on-white shirt would drive her to even greater heights of contempt and even lower depths of loving despair than usual. *Slum child, filthy little slum child.* I was beyond saving; I deserved no better than to wind up with all the other horrible little Jewboys in the gutter (by which she meant Brooklyn College). If only I would listen to her, the whole world could be mine: I could win a scholarship to Harvard, I could get to know the best people, I could grow up into a life of elegance and refinement and taste. Why was I so stupid as not to understand?

In those days it was very unusual, and possibly even against the rules, for teachers in public high schools to associate with their students after hours. Nevertheless, Mrs. K. sometimes invited me to her home, a beautiful old brownstone located in what was perhaps the only section in the whole of Brooklyn fashionable enough to be intimidating. I would read her my poems and she would tell me about her family, about the schools she had gone to, about Vassar, about writers she had met, while her husband, of whom I was frightened to death and who to my utter astonishment turned out to be Jewish (but not, as Mrs. K. quite unnecessarily hastened to inform me, my kind of Jewish), sat stiffly and silently in an armchair across the room, squinting at his newspaper through the first *pince-nez* I had ever seen outside the movies. He spoke to me but once, and that was after I had read Mrs. K. my tearful editorial for the school newspaper on the death of Roosevelt—an effusion which provoked him into a full five-minute harangue whose blasphemous contents would certainly have shocked me into insensibility if I had not been even more shocked to discover that he actually had a voice.

But Mrs. K. not only had me to her house; she also—what was even more unusual—took me out a few times, to the Frick Gallery and the Metropolitan Museum, and once to the theater, where we saw a dramatization of *The Late George Apley*, a play I imagine she deliberately chose with the not wholly mistaken idea that it would impress upon me the glories of aristocratic Boston.

One of our excursions into Manhattan I remember with particular vividness because she used it to bring the struggle between us to rather a dramatic head. The familiar argument began this time on the subway. Why, knowing that he would be spending the afternoon together "in public," had I come to school that morning improperly dressed? (I was, as usual, wearing my red satin club jacket over a white tee shirt.) She realized, of course, that I owned only one suit (this said not in compassion but in derision) and that my poor parents had, God only knew where, picked up the idea that it was too precious to be worn except at one of those bar mitzvahs I was always going to. Though why, if my parents were so worried about clothes, they had permitted me to buy a suit which made me look like a young hoodlum she found it very difficult to imagine. Still, much as she would have been embarrassed to be seen in public with a boy whose parents allowed him to wear a zoot suit, she would have been somewhat less embarrassed than she was now by the ridiculous costume I had on. Had I no consideration for her? Had I no consideration for myself? Did I want everyone who laid eyes on me to think that I was nothing but an ill-bred little slum child?

My standard ploy in these arguments was to take the position that such things were of no concern to me: I was a poet and I had more important matters to think about than clothes. Besides, I would feel silly coming to school on an ordinary day dressed in a suit. Did Mrs. K. want me to look like one of those "creeps" from Crown Heights who were all going to become doctors? This was usually an effective counter, since Mrs. K. despised her middle-class Jewish students even more than she did the "slum children," but probably because she was growing desperate at the thought of how I would strike a Harvard interviewer (it was my senior year), she did not respond according to form on that particular occasion. "At least," she snapped, "they reflect well on their parents."

I was accustomed to her bantering gibes at my parents, and sensing, probably, that they arose out of jealousy, I was rarely troubled by them. But this one bothered me; it went beyond banter and I did not know how to deal with it. I remember flushing, but I cannot remember what if anything I said in protest. It was the beginning of a very bad afternoon for both of us.

We had been heading for the Museum of Modern Art, but as we got off the subway, Mrs. K. announced that she had changed her mind about the museum. She was going to show me something else instead, just down the street on Fifth Avenue. This mysterious "something else" to which we proceeded in silence turned out to be the college department of an expensive clothing store, de Pinna. I do not exaggerate when I say that an actual physical dread seized me as I followed her into the store. I had never been inside such a store; it was not a store, it was enemy territory, every inch of it mined with humiliations. "I am," Mrs. K. declared in the coldest human voice I hope I shall ever hear, "going to buy you a suit that you will be able to wear at your Harvard interview." I had guessed, of course, that this was what she had in mind, and even at fifteen I understood what a fantastic act of aggression she was planning to commit against my parents and asking me to participate in. Oh no, I said in a panic (suddenly realizing that I *wanted* her to buy me that suit), I can't, my mother wouldn't like it. "You can tell her it's a birthday present. Or else I will tell her. If I tell her, I'm sure she won't object." The idea of Mrs. K. meeting my mother was more than I could bear: my mother, who spoke with a Yiddish accent and of whom, until that sickening moment, I had never known I was ashamed and so ready to betray.

To my immense relief and my equally immense disappointment, we left the store, finally, without buying a suit, but it was not to be the end of clothing or "manners" for me that day—not yet. There was still the ordeal of a restaurant to go through. Where I came from, people rarely ate in restaurants, not so much because most of them were

Famous 4th Street Delicatessen. Philadelphia Jewish Archives Center at the Balch Institute, Philadelphia.

too poor to afford such a luxury—although most of them certainly were—as because eating in restaurants was not regarded as a luxury at all; it was, rather, a necessity to which bachelors were pitiably condemned. A home-cooked meal was assumed to be better than anything one could possibly get in a restaurant, and considering the class of restaurants in question (they were really diners or luncheonettes), the assumption was probably correct. In the case of my own family, myself included until my late teens, the business of going to restaurants was complicated by the fact that we observed the Jewish dietary laws, and except in certain neighborhoods, few places could be found which served kosher food; in midtown Manhattan in the 1940's, I believe there were only two and both were relatively expensive. All this is by way of explaining why I had had so little experience of restaurants up to the age of fifteen and why I grew apprehensive once more when Mrs. K. decided after we left de Pinna that we should have something to eat.

The restaurant she chose was not at all an elegant one—I have, like a criminal, revisited it since—but it seemed very elegant indeed to me: enemy territory again, and this time a mine exploded in my face the minute I set foot through the door. The hostess was very sorry, but she could not seat the young gentleman without a coat and tie. If the lady wished, however, something could be arranged. The lady (visibly pleased by this unexpected—or was it expected?—object lesson) did wish, and the so recently defiant but by now utterly docile young gentleman was forthwith divested of his so recently beloved but by now thoroughly loathsome red satin jacket and provided with a much oversized white waiter's coat and a tie—which, there being no collar to a tee shirt, had to be worn around his bare neck. Thus attired, and with his face supplying the touch of red which had moments earlier been supplied by his jacket, he was led into the dining room, there to be taught the importance of proper table manners through the same pedagogic instrumentality that had worked so well in impressing him with the importance of proper dress.

Like any other pedagogic technique, however, humiliation has its limits, and Mrs. K. was to make no further progress with it that day. For I had had enough, and I was not about to risk stepping on another mine. Knowing she would subject me to still more ridicule if I made a point of my revulsion at the prospect of eating nonkosher food, I resolved to let her order for me and then to feign lack of appetite or possibly even illness when the meal was served. She did order—duck for both of us, undoubtedly because it would be a hard dish for me to manage without using my fingers.

The two portions came in deep oval-shaped dishes, swimming in a brown sauce and each with a sprig of parsley sitting on top. I had not the faintest idea of what to do—should the food be eaten directly from the oval dish or not?—nor which of the many implements on the table to do it with. But remembering that Mrs. K. herself had once advised me to watch my hostess in such a situation and then to do exactly as she did, I sat perfectly still and waited for her to make the first move. Unfortunately, Mrs. K. also remembered having taught me that trick, and determined as she was that I should be given a lesson that would force me to mend my ways, she waited too. And so we both waited, chatting amiably, pretending not to notice the food while it sat there getting colder and colder by the minute. Thanks partly to the fact that I would probably have gagged on the duck if I had tried to eat it—dietary taboos are very powerful if one has been conditioned to them—I was prepared to wait forever. And in fact it was Mrs. K. who broke first.

"Why aren't you eating?" she suddenly said after something like fifteen minutes had passed. "Aren't you hungry?" Not very, I answered. "Well," she said, 'I think we'd better eat. The food is getting cold." Whereupon, as I watched with great fascination, she deftly captured the sprig of parsley between the prongs of her serving fork, set it aside, took up her serving spoon and delicately used those two esoteric implements to transfer a piece of duck from the oval dish to her plate. I imitated the whole operation as best I could, but not well enough to avoid splattering some partly congealed sauce onto my borrowed coat in the process. Still, things could have been worse, and having more or less successfully negotiated my way around that particular mine, I now had to cope with the problem of how to get out of eating the duck. But I need not have worried. Mrs. K. took one bite, pronounced it inedible (it must have been frozen by then), and called in quiet fury for the check.

Several months later, wearing an altered but respectably conservative suit which had been handed down to me in good condition by a bachelor uncle, I presented myself on two different occasions before interviewers from Harvard and from the Pulitzer Scholarship Committee. Some months after that, Mrs. K. had her triumph: I won the Harvard scholarship on which her heart had been so passionately set. It was not, however, large enough to cover all expenses, and since my parents could not afford to make up the difference, I was unable to accept it. My parents felt wretched but not, I think, quite as wretched as Mrs. K. For a while it looked as though I would wind up in the "gutter" of Brooklyn College after all, but then the news arrived that I had also won a Pulitzer Scholarship which paid full tuition if used at Columbia and a small stipend besides. Everyone was consoled, even Mrs. K.: Columbia was at least in the Ivy League.

The last time I saw her was shortly before my graduation from Columbia and just after a story had appeared in the *Times* announcing that I had been awarded a fellowship which was to send me to Cambridge University. Mrs. K. had passionately wanted to see me in Cambridge, Massachusetts, but Cambridge, England was even better. We met somewhere near Columbia for a drink, and her happiness over my fellowship, it seemed to me, was if anything exceeded by her delight at discovering that I now knew enough to know that the right thing to order in a cocktail lounge was a very dry martini with lemon peel, please.

Murray Schumach

From *The Diamond People*

"The Street"

A long history of expulsions and exile, which made the Jews the most mobile of peoples, impressed upon generations the wisdom of portable assets. And what is more portable than precious stones? This may account for the significant Jewish presence in the diamond trade, an industry disciplined by a self-imposed "code of honor unparalleled in American business." Today, a surprisingly high percentage of diamond merchants are ultra-Orthodox Jews whose adherence to a most demanding religious code would make it normal for them to establish and accept a rigorous code of business ethics.

In the heart of Manhattan, a world persists that is very different from anything in the United States; a world that has maintained a lifestyle that is unique. It is Alice's Wonderland, with electronic calculators. Peter Pan's Never-Never Land, rewritten by Adam Smith. This is the block of West Forty-seventh Street, from Fifth Avenue to the Avenue of the Americas, which is the heart of the nation's multibillion-dollar diamond business, handling the bulk of all diamonds sold in the United States with the whimsical slogan: "There's a customer for everything."

Sometimes referred to by the media as the Street of Diamonds, it is known to its own people simply as "the Street." This strip of some six hundred feet, bounded by store windows ablaze with gems, topped by grimy offices containing an incalculable treasure of diamonds, is a shrine of individualism in a nation drifting toward corporate conglomerates. Like other businesses, it should long ago have been squeezed into cold, computerized modules manipulated by lawyers, accountants, and statisticians. But it hasn't. This tiny realm of free enterprise may be the most exciting and mysterious block in the United States. It has the glamour of Broadway, the daring of Wall Street, and the secrecy of the C.I.A. Dealers bicker over a pittance, but make handshake deals over millions. There are paneled offices with full-time cooks. There are sweatshops that are a throwback to the Lower East Side at the turn of the century. The industry thrives in a frenzy of competition, but lives in the long shadow of the omnipotent South African monopoly—the De Beers Syndicate—that long ago set the pattern for multinational cartels. It is a bizarre world that combines the crassness of the coldest commerce with the ethics of the Old Testament and the Talmud; the free-wheeling independence of a medieval marketplace with the latest technology of the twentieth century. It makes a virtue of guile, but lives by a code of honor unparalleled in American business.

The Street is introverted, but its people roam the world. They concentrate on the present, but are fully informed of any scientific or political developments that may affect their future. Most important, the Street exudes a sense of freedom, self-confidence, ambition, and limitless hope. The assurance of the men and women behind the counters of the jewel-laden showcases in diamond exchanges and stores; the aggressiveness of diamond dealers in their offices or over the green tables of the Diamond Dealers Club, where parcels of diamonds are opened and closed in endless bargaining sessions; the deft fingers of the men in workshops where diamonds are shaped and put in settings: everywhere is the feeling that hard work and resourcefulness will bring success, perhaps riches . . . .

This bazaar of precious stones and negotiations in many languages has been more than a thousand years in the making. Born of centuries of persecution, pogroms, forced emigrations, and concentration camps, the diamond people are a paradox.

Diamond Dealers on 47th Street, New York City. Photograph. © 1979 Werner Wolff, Black Star.

COLORPLATE 142

JULIE STALLER-PENTELNIK. *Ha Motzi.* 1987. Serigraph with center portion hand-painted in ink. 20 x 20 1/2 in. © Julie Staller-Pentelnik. Courtesy the American Guild of Judaic Art, New York.

COLORPLATE 143

JULIE STALLER-PENTELNIK. *Ha Gafen.* 1988. Serigraph with center portion hand-painted in ink. 20 x 20 1/2 in. © Julie Staller-Pentelnik. Courtesy the American Guild of Judaic Art, New York.

COLORPLATE 144

EDITH ALTMAN. *The Black Fire, the White Fire, the Red Fire, the Green Brings the Gold.* 1989. Oil sticks on board. 45 x 60 in. Collection of the artist.

COLORPLATE 145

BRAHNA YASSKY. *Family Values.* 1994. Oil on photo transfer on canvas. 24 x 18 in. Collection of the artist.

COLORPLATE 146

MARILYN COHEN. *Feed and Hay (Fargo, North Dakota).* 1993. Dyes and torn paper; entire surface in collage. 30 x 42 in. © Marilyn Cohen/Morgan Rank Gallery, 1993.

AND
HAY
GOLDBERG
FLOUR
&
FEED

COLORPLATE 148

LINDA DAYAN FRIMER AND GEORGE LITTLECHILD. *Persecute Us Not, In Honor of Our Grandmothers.* 1993. Left panel: Watercolor, gouache, and gold illumination on paper. Right panel: Acrylic and mixed media on paper. Each panel, 30 x 40 in. Collection of the artists. *This collaboration, created by Frimer, a Jew now living in Vancouver, and Littlechild, a Canadian Cree Indian, is a tribute to both of their grandmothers. Frimer's grandmother, Fene, was an observant Jew, who endured a hard life in the wilderness of Canada, yet remained steadfast to her culture and traditions. Frimer remembers hearing of the Torah her grandmother kept in the kitchen, and of the deliveries of kosher meat via sled from Winnipeg during the winter months. The two paintings shown together are an expression of shared respect, dignity, and reverence for both women's individual journeys through oppression.*

COLORPLATE 149

LYNNE FELDMAN. *Purim.* 1992. Oil on canvas. 50 x 84 in. Commission from Temple Beth David, Westwood, Massachusetts.

Although their telephone calls cross the world, their behavior is suggestive of an invisible wall. The people of the Street are part of a tight community, suspicious of strangers because of their tragic history. The vast majority of the fifteen to twenty thousand people who work on this block—only a handful live there—are either children of Jewish immigrants or Jewish immigrants themselves. This block of extensive wealth is a Diamond Ghetto.

The eyes of these people are always alert and intense. The faces may break into smiles. The voices may soften. The heads may incline. But the eyes remain watchful. They may speak in English, Yiddish, Hebrew, Dutch, Flemish, Spanish, French, German, Hungarian, or Hindustani. Yet, the language of the eyes is always the same, as sharp over the counter of a noisy restaurant as over a mound of diamonds at the Diamond Dealers Club.

The reason for this vigilance is the key to the apparent chaos of Forty-seventh Street—everyone is buying and selling diamonds, or hoping to do so. Not just the diamond dealer or the diamond broker who sells on commission, or the retailer at booth or in store. Everyone. The cutter at his wheel is always on the lookout for a stone to buy from the dealers who bring him work. The woman, sorting stones with a tweezer in a dealer's office and grading them, is always alert for a chance to act as a broker on her own. The old man who runs errands, the youth who fetches coffee, the itinerant jeweler with a store in some other part of the city or suburbs—they all have diamond fever. It is a contagious dream, perhaps an illness, the sort of senseless hope that produces a mirage. Yet constantly, every day, many make a profit. Every year, some men step away from the toil of the wheel forever, to buy, sell, and pay others to grind their stones . . .

An outsider to Forty-seventh Street, making an occasional purchase in a store or at a booth in an exchange, may think his or her trade is important. It isn't. Even at the booths of the exchanges, most of the business is wholesale. Many retailers say that the majority of their business is with persons they know, or who are sent by satisfied customers. The business that comes in off the street, though enormous by the standards of the average jewelry store, is very small for Forty-seventh Street as a whole. It is almost insignificant compared to the volume transacted in the offices of dealers above, secluded in the buildings where dealers tap calculators while they talk on the phone to London, Antwerp, Tel Aviv, Johannesburg, Amsterdam, Bombay, and Hong Kong. Often, in these phone conversations, the dealer switches in mid-sentence from English to Yiddish, Hebrew, French, Flemish, German, Italian, or Spanish. There are many people in the diamond business who speak five languages and some who speak ten.

Diamonds can pass with astonishing rapidity from dealer to dealer without leaving the block.

A dealer smiles as he waves a visitor to a chair. "See the man who just left?" he asks. "He brought me a stone I sold early today for forty-eight thousand dollars. A profit of maybe two thousand. That stone went from dealer to dealer today. Six dealers in one day. This man just wanted to sell it to me. He wanted seventy thousand."

Phones are rarely silent in a dealer's office for more than a minute. Conversations are brief to the point of rudeness. But no one in the business is offended. An individual negotiation may be prolonged over days with each phase of the deal a sprint of just a few minutes.

The enormous volume of transactions, often without records, is possible on Forty-seventh Street only because of the Code. In the diamond business, you never go back on your word. A deal closed with a handshake and the Yiddish words "mazel und brucha"—luck and blessing—is inviolate. It is a ritual that goes back centuries and, as we shall see, is probably ingrained in the Jewish tradition passed along by the Old Testament, the Talmud, and the teachings of Maimonides.

John Gruen
From *The Private World of Leonard Bernstein*

For almost four decades, charismatic conductor, wide-ranging composer, masterful teacher Leonard Bernstein held center stage in the contemporary musical world. Throughout his career, his Jewish identity has been manifest. His first symphonic work, the Jeremiah Symphony *(1944), uses the traditional cantillations in which the prophetic portions are chanted in the synagogue and the traditional melody in which the book of* Lamentations *is sung. His oratorio,* Kaddish, *was first presented in Tel Aviv; the* Chichester Psalms *are sung in Hebrew, the language of their ancient authors. In this passage, he discusses the resistance of his father, a Talmudic scholar, to Bernstein's choice of career.*

"Picasso's private world made a perfectly wonderful book because Picasso lives absolutely openly. He lives in a bikini in the south of France; his morality is absolutely free. I myself have a much more bourgeois background. After all, I'm the son of a rather puritanical, Mosaic-oriented Talmudic scholar. And as free as I have been, especially in my youthful years, I have never been able to escape from that strong puritan morality which comes to me both by way of the Talmudic father and the New England I grew up in, which make a very puritanical combination indeed.

"Although you may spend your youth fighting your environmental morality, protesting it, and showing what a rebel you are, it stays with you—even through some abortive attempts at psychoanalysis. I still have this bourgeois streak and I will always have it. It's a streak which is reinforced by my need to protect people I love. So there's a limit to how much I can reveal myself. . .

"Of course, it all ties back to Daddy. That whole tremendous influence. It's pure ambivalence. I think the two poles of the ambivalence are not just poles, but are interdependent and mutually influential, if you know what I mean. I'm sure that if you investigate it, it becomes a tangled neurotic knot.

"For example, I must feel a certain guilt about my father, about having resented him, feared him so when I was a child. Because he opposed my music, because he didn't seem to understand me.

"It doesn't mean I had a compensating, equivalent dependence, or an elaborate, exaggerated love for my mother. I was very fond of her. But it isn't that I threw myself completely on my mother's side and rejected my father, although she did have much greater sympathy for the music, for the whole artistic idea.

"And yet my father impressed me enormously. I admired him. I learned so much from him. His knowledge was enormous—extremely limited and circumscribed by Talmudic studies, yet within that limited area his knowledge was enormous. His intelligence was equally enormous. The breadth of his reasoning—which is a Talmudic quality—made him in every sense a man of God. He is a deeply religious man. Highly moral." . . .

Lenny told me that from the very first his father had pinned his hopes on one of two things for him. Either to go into his business or become a rabbi. The idea of Lenny becoming a musician was both distasteful and depressing to him. It had to do with his own somewhat limited points of reference. In his day, to be a musician meant somebody sitting in the lobby of a hotel, playing in a trio. In eastern Europe a musician was a *klesmer*, a sort of wandering minstrel little better than a beggar, who would go from

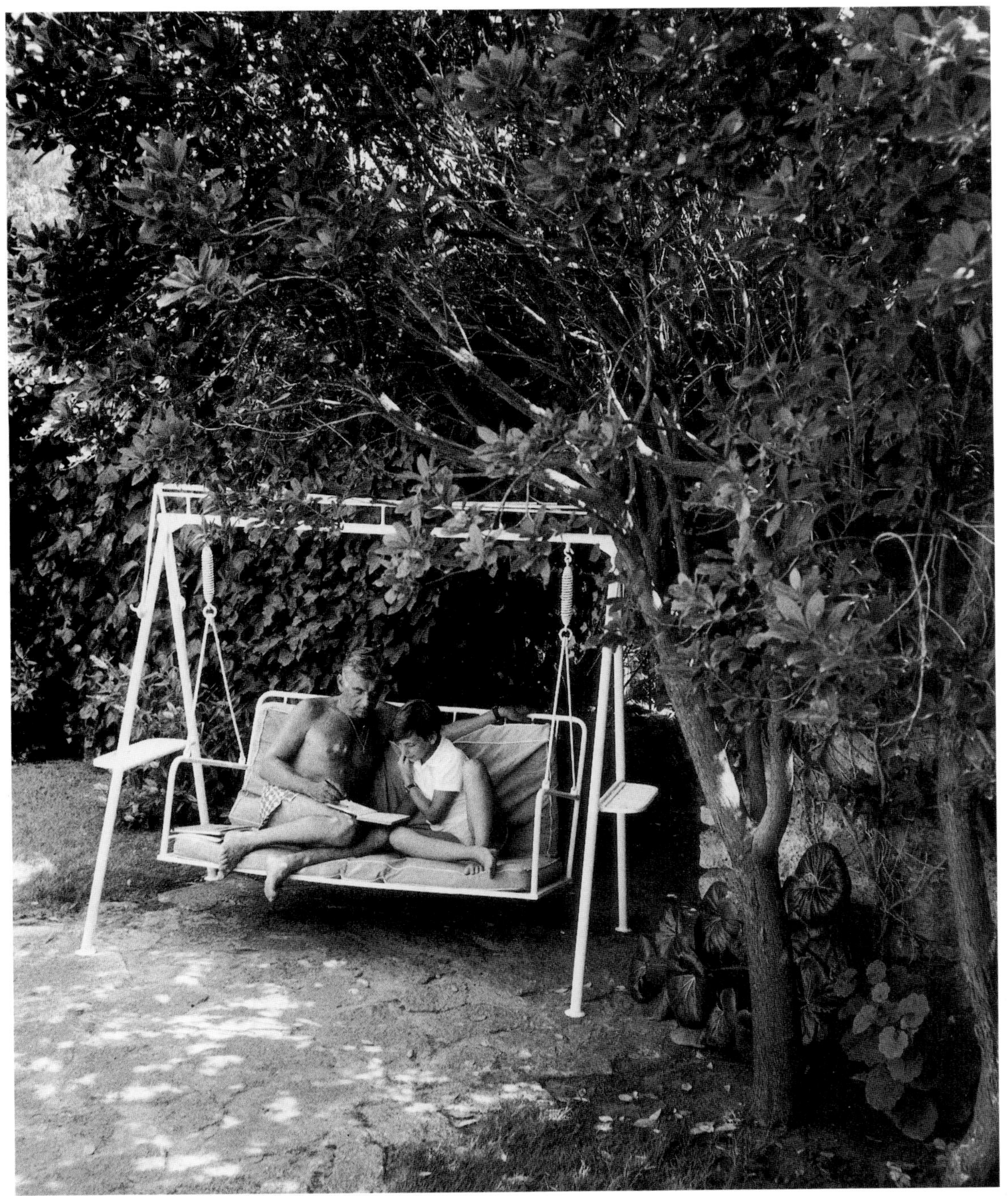

Leonard Bernstein Preparing His Son, Alexander, for His Bar Mitzvah Lesson. Photograph. Ken Heyman/Woodfin Camp. *The Bernstein family, father, mother, two daughters, and a son, spent the summer of 1967 at a villa near Rome. Here, Bernstein trained his twelve-year-old son to chant his Bar Mitzvah haftorah.*

town to town looking for weddings and feasts, and be thrown a crust, or be invited to sit down and have something to eat for his labors. A *klesmer!* His son was going to be a *klesmer!* Never! . . .

"I know it would have pleased my father deeply if I had become a rabbi," he said. "And there is a certain amount of rabbi in me which I get from him, of course. He is the son of a rabbi and he is very rabbinical in nature himself. If you say to him 'pass the salt,' he's already teaching you something: 'You know, Moses said about salt . . .' or whatever. I must say, I've inherited some of that. I do tend to be lecture-y and I love to teach. I also, I'm sure, bore people to death by giving lectures when all they want is a simple answer. I know this is true of my children. I do it constantly. It's part of my rabbinical streak.

"I suppose I could have made a passably good rabbi. However, there was no question of it, because music was the only thing that consumed me.

"I loved other things. I loved other studies. I was particularly taken with English literature and poetry. And languages. But music was a whole other thing. It wasn't a study, you see. It was a way of life."

David Amram

From *Vibrations*

Sacred Service

His great-grandfather was the owner of Philadelphia's first matzah bakery. His grandfather, an attorney, was an authority on Jewish law and Hebrew books, whose books and articles are still read and consulted. David Amram has had a distinguished career as a composer, conductor, and musician. Among many distinctions, he was the first artist in residence at the New York Philharmonic (1966–1967) and served as the Musical Director of the International Jewish Arts Festival (1992). In his autobiography, Vibrations *(1968), he writes of the composition of* Sacred Service *and its presentation at New York's Park Avenue Synagogue.*

I had promised Stuart Vaughan that I would do the music for *Hamlet,* which opened March 16. But every other second of my time day and night was devoted to my sacred service. I didn't answer one letter, go to any parties, movies, concerts or bars. By April it was completed and we were ready to begin rehearsals.

The opening three notes of the service provided the unifying motif for the entire work. I imagined them as being symbolic of some kind of giant ram's horn. I realized when the service was nearly completed that these three notes were similar to what I had heard the old man singing in the synagogue in Frankfort seven years before. Somehow his croaking voice in the middle of a prayer had stayed in my mind. His old, craggy face and the whole scene of that service returned to me again as I completed the final pages.

In spite of our many arguments, philosophic discussions and constant concern about how the prayers could be most effectively set to music, Cantor Putterman and I always agreed about one thing: Maurice Peress would be the ideal conductor for my sacred service. Maurice seemed to have an instinctive feeling for liturgical music. His father was an Arab-speaking Jew from Iraq who played and sang beautifully. His mother was from a very religious family in Poland. Maurice, like myself, was a runaway from home who had come up the hard way in music. He had worked in every area of music but never lost his direction. He had that old lyric feeling when he played the trumpet and when he conducted.

Maurice began to accompany me each week as I worked with Cantor Putterman. The cantor was a man who was a truly old soul. Even if we never got together without arguing, I loved him like a second father and he treated me like his third son. His knowledge of Hebrew and the subtle inflection of the prayers, the accents and drama of the religious text was extraordinary. When he sang the traditional music to the prayers, and especially "the counting of the Omer," it sounded as if he were going back five thousand years in a time machine. I always felt I was listening to a voice out of the desert. Even though he was in his sixties, his tenor had a quality that could reduce you to tears within a second. It had a melancholy, wailing-wall sound.

It had been a long time since my grandfather had taught me Hebrew as a little boy. My father had taught us Sunday school on our farm. I remembered how we had talked about the men who wrote the Bible. My father felt they were probably Hebrew shepherds who lay in the fields with their sheep, staring up at the stars to think about God. Hearing Cantor Putterman talk and sing brought back that old mystical feeling.

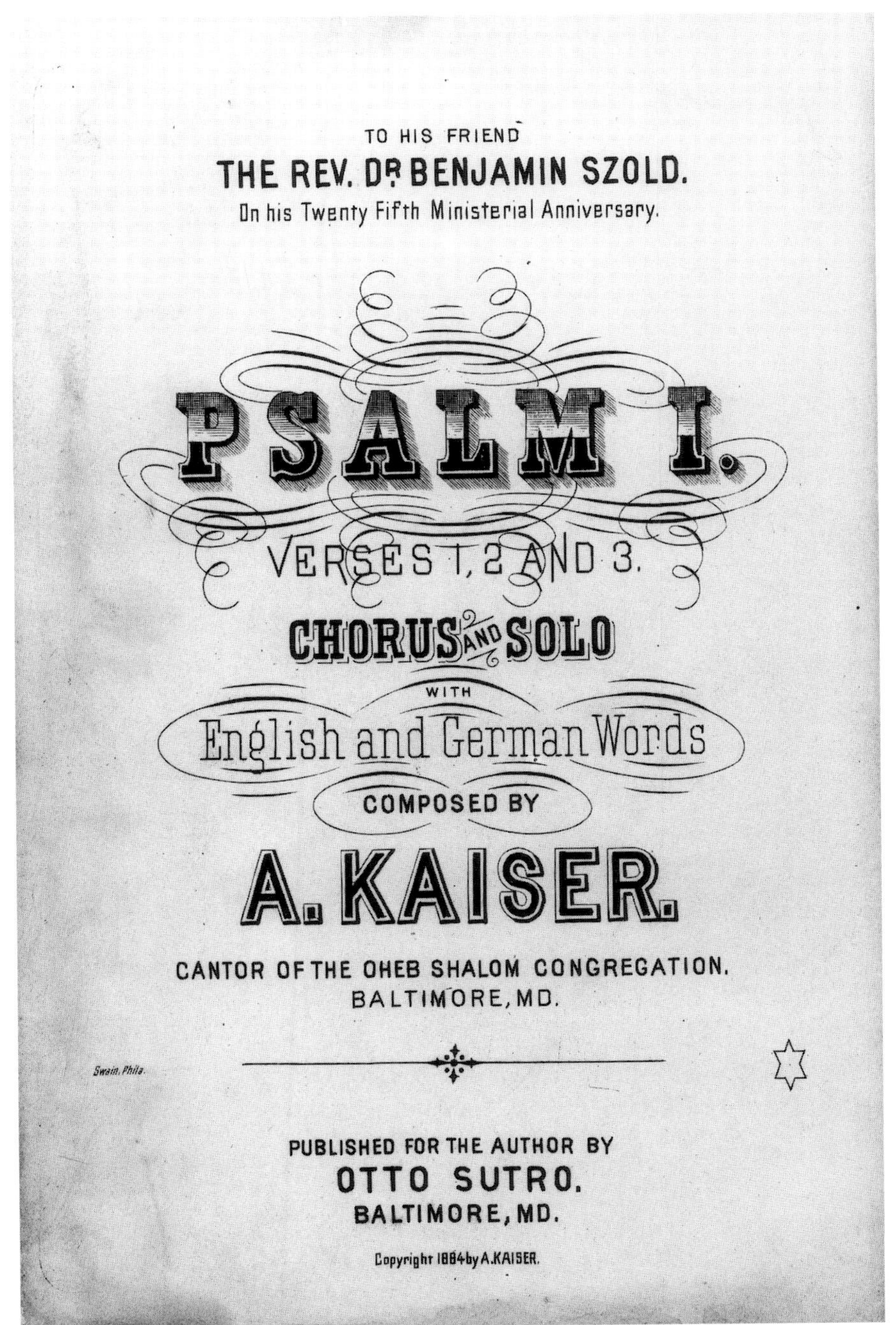

Psalm I. 1884. Collection of Abraham and Deborah Karp. *Title page of a musical setting for Psalm 1, verses 1, 2, and 3 by Cantor Alois Kaiser, composed in honor of the 25th anniversary of the Rev. Dr. Benjamin Szold's ministry at the Oheb Shalom Congregation in Baltimore, Maryland.*

He made me aware of the poetry and soul of Jewish music and consequently made me look deeper into the eyes and souls of my fellow Jews and non-Jews alike. In a certain way I went through what so many other people in America go through when they find the greatness and poetry in their own heritage. I could just be more me than ever, and enjoy it.

The experience of writing the service was like a delayed Bar Mitzvah for me. I had never had one because my father was away during the war. When my mother and I wanted to join a synagogue in Washington, the admission fee was almost half my father's yearly salary as a government worker. As a result, I became a temple drop-out for the next seventeen years.

But during the time that I wrote the sacred service I gained a new part of my manhood, even though I was thirty instead of thirteen. It didn't make me suddenly feel like a professional Jew. I was a professional musician. It didn't make me want to go out and slaughter the goyim, although there was certainly enough precedent for that kind of violence in the Old Testament. Nor did it make me want to renounce my American citizenship and join the Israeli army. What it did do was to make me aware of the great brotherhood that I had with all men. It made me understand that the love of nature, the joy of the physical as well as the spiritual world, was a natural part of my tradition. I saw that the Calvinistic attitudes of so many assimilated Jews no longer had to bug me because they were values designed for someone else, not me. I saw that my feeling of always being an outsider was something that was natural and that by acknowledging my own ancestral vibrations I could enjoy life every second just by knowing more who I was.

As the months went by my whole life began to make more sense. I realized as I got into the core of my own feelings that Allen Ginsberg, while he looked like Karl Marx and came on like Buddha, was like me. I had felt a kinship with him when we worked together on *Pull My Daisy* the year before. Even though we had different habits of living, there was a certain Talmudic rhythm and great yea-saying energy in his finer works that predated his debt to Walt Whitman. He had the old Jewish wail.

I really looked forward to the first performance of my sacred service. With Cantor Putterman's unique artistry, the rehearsals and the fine choir, we had prospects of an excellent performance. I was given unlimited free passes because the temple held almost two thousand people. So I went down to the Village with friends of mine a few days before the premier, spreading the news and the passes around.

The night of the performance there was a fantastic turn-out. People from the theater whom I had worked with, many concert musicians, like Felix Galimir, who was to help me so much at Marlboro, the great jazz pianist Randy Weston, Dan, Seymour, Emma, my druid maiden, Spike, Midhat, Malcolm, painters, writers, poets and pals. It was a beautiful event. Afterward we had an *Oneg Shabbat,* a kind of reception with cookies and tea in the basement of the temple. My father was called up on the platform with Maurice. He looked so pleased, some people thought he was me. Mel Brooks came up with Anne Bancroft and whispered in my ear, "Man, you're the Jewish Bach!" Friends from the Village and the Lower East Side who had never even been that far uptown in their lives were there. Jewish hipsters who hadn't been in a temple since they were children were there. It was a wild event and somehow very meaningful in a contemporary way. The non-Jews enjoyed it as much as the Jews and as Horty Lambert said to me afterward when we all went down to Dillon's tavern in the Village, "Old friends that pray together, stay together." It was really a treat and that's part of what religion should be.

Simon Finkelstein

"Slobodka and America"

This evocative essay was written by European-born and educated Rabbi Simon J. Finkelstein, who came to America in 1896 and served congregations in Baltimore, Cincinnati, Syracuse, and Brooklyn. But it is equally the product of his son, Cincinnati-born and American-trained rabbi and scholar, Louis Finkelstein who, as head of the Jewish Theological Seminary of America, became one of America's leading religious personalities. The essay appeared in Spiritual Autobiographies *(1952) edited by Louis Finkelstein.*

America has been my adopted country for more than sixty years. Though I still pronounce the English language imperfectly and speak it with difficulty, I feel that I am thoroughly American, loving my country with a passion possible only for one who has known autocracy. My heart swells with gratitude at the words: "I am an American." Among the many benefits which kind Providence has showered on me, none, it seems to me, outweighs that which guided me to the shores of this blessed land. I know of no merit on my part which can have justified this remarkable grace to me denied to so many of my kindred; it was like God's gifts to man generally, an undeserved expression of love. Nothing that I can do in the service of God can begin to reflect the thankfulness and sense of obligation which comes over me, when I consider that He has redeemed me from the dungeon of Czarism into which I was born and in which I was reared, and brought me to these shores.

I love America not primarily for its plenty, its high standard of living, its magnificent resources and power. The vast material improvement in my life which America has meant is secondary to the joy I derive from the spirit of the land. America's liberty and human equality, the friendship and sociability of its people, is comparative freedom from petty self-seeking, hostilities, and rivalries, are perhaps not easily recognizable by those who have known no other world. I hear my fellow citizens complain of the flaws in America's standards of social behavior. I recognize our imperfections in that regard, but the difference between America and the Lithuania in which I was reared, so far as arbitrary rule, class distinctions, irrational dislikes, group discrimination, sectarian and ethnic arrogance are concerned, is so vast as to be beyond compare. The feelings which overwhelmed me when I was admitted to American citizenship, when I first voted for an American president, when I watched my eldest child being registered in a public school, are ineffable. It was the breaking of a dawn after a long dark night. America represents for me a closer fulfillment of the Biblical doctrine of human equality and the commandment to love one's neighbor as oneself than I had expected to see on earth, short of the coming of the Messiah himself. The very lilt of

WULF KAHN. *Professor Louis Finkelstein (detail).* 1970. Oil on canvas. 46 x 53 in. The Jewish Theological Seminary of America. *Louis Finkelstein was Chancellor of The Jewish Theological Seminary of America from 1940 to 1971.*

the word "America" gives me peace and comfort and hope. If the spirit which binds Americans to one another, which animates their passion for freedom and which makes them so devoted to peace, could be universalized, the world would take a long step toward the realization of the Prophetic teaching.

Yet throughout my life in America I have also felt a sense of loss. While in relationship between man and man America has risen to moral standards never before attained on so wide a scale, in the relationship of the individual to himself, my native village of Slobodka often seems to me to have had an advantage over the metropolis of New York. Despite unpleasant social organization, there was in Slobodka cheerfulness and delight in sheer living which is lacking in America. Americans have continually to seek new ways of amusement, to forget themselves and their troubles if possible. Slobodka offered its people no picnics, movies, theaters, or concerts. We did not know the meaning of "vacations." But, curiously, we did not need them. We were happy, in ourselves, in the environment which we created in the midst of physical squalor and governmental tyranny.

In the course of the years, I have often reflected that while I would consider it a catastrophe to be returned to the Slobodka of my youth, and I could hardly survive in its atmosphere of absolutism now that I have tasted democracy and freedom, much of the joy of my life in America is a heritage deriving from Slobodka. My happiness in the basic fact of existence, irrespective of circumstances and conditions, of pains, of adversity, of calamity, originated in Slobodka. My faith in man's future, my belief that we are about to enter a new stage in the world's history, my conviction that the ideals of the Prophets and the Talmud for mankind will be fulfilled in the coming generation, derive from what I have seen in America.

When I try to communicate the delights of my life in my native village to my neighbors here who have never experienced it, I am confused and inarticulate. I seem to be describing a joy, constant, profound, overwhelming, and transcendent, of which they have no inkling. They do not understand how one can be happy when one is hungry; yet I often have been. They seem to think that life in a crowded dwelling must make one miserable, but in Slobodka it did not. I have never known greater happiness than I witnessed daily in Slobodka; yet Slobodka was poorer than any settlement that I have ever seen in America.

Nessa Rapoport

"Cultural Confidence"

The following is a speech delivered by writer Nessa Rapoport on March 29, 1993, to a group of guests invited to preview the newly expanded Jewish Museum. Ms. Rapoport is the author of a novel, Preparing for Sabbath, *and of* A Woman's Book of Grieving. *Here she stresses the importance of nourishing and maintaining Jewish culture.*

Whenever I'm asked to speak about the centrality of Jewish culture to our identity and continuity, I'm tempted to announce: This lecture is being brought to you by the people who gave the world monotheism, the Bible, the Sabbath, the theory of relativity, psychoanalysis, and American feminism.

I am always puzzled, therefore, when outstanding Jewish leaders speak of culture as a frill—nice when you can get it, good to take guests to from out of town, but last on the list of essential Jewish priorities, and first to be cut in a budget crunch.

If we look back on our unique history as a people, what has enabled us to transform the world if not culture? We have never dominated by numbers; we have never had the most power, money, or citizens—and we never will. Our strength and our gift lie in imagination—words, books, symbols and images that have been, in their seeming dreaminess and impracticality, precisely the most lasting, venerable building blocks of universal civilization.

I am not speaking as an established member of the institutional Jewish community, even an institution as beloved to me as The Jewish Museum. Rather, I speak as a Jew who both makes culture, by writing, and has been the beneficiary of Jewish culture through the luck of my having been born into a family that understood what really sustains us.

I think about my grandmother, an observant Jew in Canada who, with my grandfather, raised five observant children, including my mother. My grandmother was also the first woman to receive a Ph.D. in physics from the University of Toronto. She had a broadcast program on Canada's national radio, and was sent by the network to the United Nations. Why did she devote herself to founding the first Jewish progressive day school in Toronto? How did my grandparents succeed in communicating to all nineteen of their grandchildren the beauty and primacy of our inheritance?

I think about my uncle, then deputy mayor of Toronto, sitting in City Hall late on a summer Friday afternoon, when one of his colleagues turned to him and said, "David, don't you have to go home before you turn into a pumpkin or something?"

How was my uncle able to exemplify so openly his devotion to his spiritual and his civic vocations, allowing each to enhance rather than preclude the other? How were my relatives able to preserve such an ardent commitment to Jewish tradition and yet live so deeply immersed in Canadian and American culture?

One answer is: They had Jewish cultural confidence. To paraphrase I.B. Singer, who said, "Every writer needs an address"—Every Jew needs an address. My grandparents and their children knew where they came from.

How do young Jews today acquire such confidence if they are not the beneficiaries of this optimistic, educated vision? I would argue that they learn their address

Jewish Orphanage Consecration of Girls' Wing. August 30, 1914. Jewish Historical Society of Western Canada, Manitoba Canada. *Women volunteers were a major element in the successful endeavors of Jewish social service agencies.*

from *this* address, from being able to come to a place whose art and artifacts are brought to life each day through exhibits, programs—and, above all, the greatest act of Jewish genius: interpretation. For the responsibility of a Jewish museum is not merely to display objects from an ancient time but to translate and explain what has come before us to those who will carry it on after us.

Is this a frill? This task is absolutely essential, not only for the Jews but for the world. Those of us who live in New York have seen museums such as the Met go from sleepy backwater institutions to hot tickets in merely two decades. Part of that is fashion, but the greater part is hunger: our hunger for the past, for something valuable and permanent that can be revered beyond the trend and glitz of the moment.

Well, our people are very hungry. They want not only to walk past display cases of old menorahs but to see how an ancient practice can light up their lives. Equally, they want to see the way Judaism takes its place alongside other great world traditions; or how Jewish artists who dwell in our American cities have drawn from their identities and offered a new way of looking at life to everyone, Jew and non-Jew.

It is the end of the century, always a time of stocktaking in international history. And it is the end of a millennium, a rare moment in our history on earth. What is our place, we will be asking as we celebrate this Christian date in the most open, blessed, and embracing society our ancestors could have dreamed of? Yes, many are bemoaning the attrition of the Jews, the statistics we can quote like baseball cards of the rate of intermarriage and assimilation.

I prefer to see it this way: Almost fifty years ago, a culture of nearly a thousand years was virtually obliterated. Most of us are descendants of that culture. It is important not to confuse Jewish success in America with Jewish cultural success. We have many doctors, lawyers, bankers and politicians. We have far fewer Jews who know where they come from, have access to our astonishing literary culture through our languages of Hebrew, Yiddish, Ladino, and others; or to our symbolic culture, exemplified by the collections contained within these walls.

And yet. In fewer than fifty years we have begun to build a Jewish culture in this country, which is unquestionably the address of the next great Jewish diaspora civilization. Our fortunate challenge is that of transmitting our culture in the remarkable freedom we enjoy in America, a far more preferable challenge to that of our ancestors who lived under repressive, intolerant regimes and societies.

I do not doubt that we are capable of meeting that challenge. We come from a culture that has retained its vitality over thousands of years, that neither earthly rulers nor devotion to other gods has been able to render extinct. This culture has its own power, which we can draw on fruitfully. In energetically supporting those visionaries who create, renovate and dream big dreams on behalf of our culture, every one of us is making history.

INDEX

Page numbers in *italics* refer to illustrations.

PHOTOGRAPHY CREDITS

Color Illustrations: Art Resource, NY: cpls. 18, 19, 29, 30, 38, 42, 46, 49, 56, 122, 124, 130, 132, 134, 138; Joel Berkowitz: cpl. 28; Richard Carafelli: cpl. 123; John Reed Forsman: cpls. 12, 24, 34, 43, 47, 55, 73, 87; Pedro Guerrero: cpl. 100; Robert Kisin: cpl. 119; George Lane, S. J.: cpl. 114; Richard Leeds: cpls. 97, 98, 112; Erich Lessing: cpls. 13, 14, 15, 18, 56; Marvin Rand: cpls. 17, 41, 59; Paul Rocheleau: cpl. 82; Paul Rocheleau/Light Sources: cpl. 83; Robert Rubic: cpls. 44, 68, 69, 70, 72, 74, 77, 78, 91, 92, 93, 94, 142, 143; Steve Sarno: cpl. 147; Lee Stalsworth: cpls. 116, 118, 126; Ezra Stoller/©ESTO: cpls. 99, 103, 104, 115; Malcolm Varon: cpls. 25, 95, 96, 109, 110, 111, 113; Sarah Wells: cpls. 50, 51.

Black and White Illustrations: Art Resource, NY: pp. 84, 157, 266; Edwin Connelly: p. 47; Robert Rubic: pp. 133, 272.